Preserve and Protect

Allen Drury

Preserve and Protect

Transaction Publishers

New Brunswick (U.S.A.) and London (U.K.)

Transaction Large Print Edition copyright © 2000 by Transaction Publishers, New Brunswick, New Jersey. Published in 1968 by Doubleday & Company, Inc. Copyright © Allen Drury.

This book is printed on acid-free paper that meets the American National Standard for Permanence of Paper for Printed Library Materials.

Library of Congress Catalog Number: 99-048201
ISBN: 978-1-4128-1293-1
Printed in the United States of America

Library of Congress Cataloging-in-Publication Data

Drury, Allen.
Preserve and protect / Allen Drury.
        p.   cm.
    ISBN 1-56000-471-1 (Ig. print) 1. Large type books. I. Title.

PS3554.R8 P74 1999
813'.54—dc21   99-048201
                                                      CIP

CONTENTS

MAJOR CHARACTERS IN THE NOVEL

At Andrews Air Force Base:

Harley M. Hudson, President of the United States

In Washington:

William Abbott, President of the United States
Lucille Hudson, former First Lady
Orrin Knox, Secretary of State
Beth, his wife
Hal, his son
Crystal Danta Knox, his daughter-in-law
Robert Durham Munson of Michigan, Majority Leader of the United States Senate
Dolly, his wife
Governor Edward M. Jason of California
Ceil, his wife
Patsy Jason Labaiya, his sister
Mr. Justice Thomas Buckmaster Davis of the United States Supreme Court
George Harrison Wattersill, an advocate
Robert A. Leffingwell, director of the President's Commission on Administrative Reform
Helen-Anne Carrew, a columnist
Walter Dobius, a columnist
Frankly Unctuous, a commentator
LeGage Shelby, director of Defenders of Equality for You (DEFY)
Senator Fred Van Ackerman of Wyoming, spokesman for the Committee on Making Further Offers for a Russian Truce (COMFORT)

Rufus Kleinfert, Knight Kommander of the Konference
    on Efforts to Encourage Patriotism (KEEP)
J. B. "Jawbone" Swarthman of South Carolina, chairman
    of the House Foreign Affairs Committee

At the United Nations:

Lafe Smith, Senator from Iowa
Cullee Hamilton, Representative from California
Lord Claude Maudulayne, the British Ambassador
Raoul Barre, the French Ambassador
Krishna Khaleel, the Indian Ambassador
Vasily Tashikov, the Soviet Ambassador
Prince Obifumatta, Ajkaje of Gorotoland
Felix Labaiya-Sofra of Panama

On the National Committee:

Roger P. Croy of Oregon
Esmé Harbellow Stryke of California
Asa B. Attwood of California
Pierre Boissevain of Vermont
Mary Buttner Baffleburg of Pennsylvania
Lizzie Hanson McWharter of Kansas
Anna Hooper Bigelow of New Hampshire
Lathia Talbott Jennings of South Dakota
Lyle Strathmore of Michigan
Luther W. Redfield of Washington
Ewan MacDonald MacDonald of Wyoming
Blair Hannah of Illinois

NOTE TO THE READER

Most of the characters in this novel, and the background of most of the events in it, have appeared in its predecessors, *Advise and Consent*, *A Shade of Difference* and *Capable of Honor.*

In *Advise and Consent* (1959) will be found the story of the nomination of Robert A. Leffingwell to be Secretary of State; the accession of Vice President Harley M. Hudson to the Presidency; the successful Soviet manned landing on the moon; the death of Senator Brigham Anderson of Utah; the appointment of Senator Orrin Knox of Illinois to be Secretary of State following the defeat of Bob Leffingwell by the Senate. There, also, will be found the marriage of Orrin's son Hal to Crystal Danta, the marriage of Senate Majority Leader Robert Munson of Michigan to Washington hostess Dolly Harrison, and many other episodes leading into later books.

In *A Shade of Difference* (1962) will be found the visit to South Carolina and New York of His Royal Highness Terence Wolowo Ajkaje, ruler of Gorotoland, with all its explosive effects upon the racial problem in the United States and the United Nations; the beginnings of the rebellion in Gorotoland; the early stages of Ambassador Felix Labaiya's activities in Panama; the opening moves of California's Negro Congressman, Cullee Hamilton, in his race for the Senate; the opening moves of California's Governor Edward M. Jason in his campaign for the Presidential nomination; the death of Senator Harold Fry of West Virginia and his decision to entrust his son Jimmy to Senator Lafe Smith of Iowa; and many other episodes leading into later books.

In *Capable of Honor*, (1966) will be found the bitter convention battle between President Hudson and Governor Jason; the selection of Orrin Knox for the Vice Presidential nomination; the escalation of the war in Gorotoland, the outbreak of war in Panama, and the United Nations debates that culminate in the first United States vetoes in history. There also will be found the ominous coalition of Defenders of Equality for You (DEFY), the Committee on Making Further Offers for a Russian Truce (COMFORT), and the Konference on Efforts to Encourage Patriotism (KEEP) which turns the convention into a near-battleground and paves the way for the events that surround the selection of a President and Vice President in the present novel.

Running through previous novels, through this and others to come—as it runs through our times—is the continuing argument between those who would use responsible firmness to maintain orderly social progress and oppose the Communist drive for world dominion, and those who believe that in a reluctance to be firm, in permissiveness, and in the steady erosion of the law lies the surest path to world peace and a stable society.

I

THE SPEAKER'S BOOK

1.

SOMETIMES HE READ. Sometimes he dozed. But mostly, as Air Force One moved swiftly back from San Francisco to Washington across a summer-somnolent land, the President of the United States thought.

Not particularly profound or major thoughts: the furious national convention just concluded in the lovely city by the Bay had left him too tired and too emotionally exhausted for that. Just the rather wandering, musing thoughts of a gentle man still surprised by his own capacity for deviousness, his own surrender to anger and retaliation, his own grim pursuit of the power he had once thought himself too mild and generous ever to need or want.

He had meant it a year ago when, upon his accession to the White House following the death of his brilliant predecessor, he had told a hushed and emotional Senate that he did not want another term and would not run. Now international crisis and those hostile columnists and broadcasters who had produced the savage commentaries, the hurtful news stories, the suavely damaging broadcasts and the screaming headlines about him and about the convention had changed all that.

(PRESIDENT FORCES BITTER DELEGATES TO TAKE SECRETARY OF STATE ORRIN KNOX FOR VICE PRESIDENT ON PRO-WAR TICKET, they said now. GOVERNOR EDWARD JASON OF CALIFORNIA, DEFEATED IN PRESIDENTIAL AND VICE-PRESIDENTIAL BIDS, MAY LAUNCH THIRD PARTY IN CAUSE OF WORLD PEACE.)

He had meant it when he announced a month ago that he would not attempt to dictate the choice of Vice President. Ted Jason and the cynical souls supporting him had changed all that.

He had meant it, years ago, when he thought that all he wanted from life was a loving family, a good home, a peaceful life.

The strange ways of power and politics in a strange and complex country had changed all that.

So here he was, plan-changer, word-breaker, grasper after power as avid as his fellows: Harley M. Hudson, President and candidate, learner with the rest that certain roads of power, once entered, sometimes cannot be abandoned.

Nor should they be, he told himself as the giant craft passed into Maryland, providing a man believed he could see a road that led at last, through whatever dark forest, toward some ultimate benefit for the United States. If a man saw somewhere ahead some shining upland where the puzzled, unhappy, beloved Republic might rest at last, if history had given him a chance to lead her to it, then he had a right to seek power, a right to get it if he could, a right to hold and use it as the Lord gave him strength.

Most things were justified by this . . . for Presidents in

pursuit of their fearful duty, he was finally beginning to believe, all things.

Much had been made of honor at the convention, as Ted Jason had said in his agonized speech of withdrawal, after Harley had won their savage battle for the Presidential nomination and then had thrust Ted aside to choose Orrin Knox for second place. And this was true, and each of them had been forced to come to terms with honor in his own way, as best he could.

For himself, the President had done what the imperatives of history required. So, no doubt, had all the rest, from Ted to Walter Dobius, that hostile and rather ridiculous bellwether of the press whose syndicated column in 436 newspapers gave him such enormous impact on the ideas and policies of his time.

The President was satisfied in his own conscience about the angry events of recent days: let Ted and Walter and the rest make what bargains they could with theirs.

There came a point where a man could not worry about others' peace of mind.

His own was problem enough.

He closed his eyes, his plain, pleasant face slipping into repose. He wished Lucille were with him, but the First Lady was on her way to "Maine Chance" for a week of recovery from the convention's turmoil. He wished Orrin Knox were, too, but the Secretary of State and Beth were taking their son Hal and his wife Crystal to Carmel, so that Crystal might recover from the beating by anonymous Jason supporters which had resulted in the loss of her baby.

Quite frequently, the President mused with a wry little smile, the people you needed most were far away. All you

3

had was the comfort of knowing that they were probably thinking of you. He knew Lucille and Orrin were. His face relaxed completely. For the last time on his journey home, he slept.

"There it is!" cried the New York *Times* at Andrews Air Force Base in nearby Maryland, just outside the District of Columbia. "It's a bird—it's a man—"

"It's Fearless Peerless," the Chicago *Daily News* replied, using the ironic nickname the press corps had given Harley a year ago when he faced down the Russians at Geneva, "so cut the disrespectful, irreverent, God-damned chatter."

"Shall we kneel down and touch our heads to the ground?" the Washington *Post* inquired.

"Better lie down in a line and let him use us for a rug to walk to the White House helicopter, hadn't we?" the Washington *Evening Star* suggested in wry reference to the way the President had triumphed over the opposition of a majority of press and television at the convention. "That might be more fitting, under the circumstances."

They all laughed, somewhat ruefully, but dauntless still; not noticing in the flurry and excitement and sudden bustling all about that in the jostling, police-held crowd pressed up against the fence behind them, one other, gifted by a sometimes puzzling Almighty with the gift to change the world, laughed too.

In Gorotoland in Central Africa at that moment, at the ancient city of Mbuele in the highlands, Prince Obifumatta Ajkaje and his stern-faced Communist advisers were even then rejecting, for the twenty-seventh time, the cautious peace feelers put out by Britain through the circuitous route of Ceylon, Nigeria and Guyana, in an attempt to end the steadily escalating war with the United States. And in the capital, dusty Molobangwe on the plains, his cousin Prince Terence, "Terrible Terry," head of the legitimate government, was reviewing the latest detachment of U.S. troops, whose arrival, as yet unannounced, would lift the formal American commitment to one hundred thousand men.

In Panama, Felix Labaiya, standing alone as he liked to do on the terrace of his ancestral estate, "Suerte," staring down the long valley that led from Chiriqui to the sea, was calculating what the convention's humiliation of his brother-in-law, Governor Jason, might drive that brilliant, ambitious mind to do. On the basis of what he thought he understood of Ted, who now was virtually trapped into launching a "Peace Party" in the coming election in an attempt to defeat the ticket of Harley Hudson and Orrin Knox, Felix was making his decision with a renewed determination. He would order his forces to fight on in their battle to overturn the legitimate Panamanian government, seize the Canal, and force the United States once and for all out of his fiercely loved land.

At the UN, the Soviet Union, Yugoslavia, Cuba and nine Afro-Asian nations were preparing yet another resolution demanding United States withdrawal from around the globe, agreeing that they would reintroduce it regularly each month from now on so that America, if she so desired, might keep on affronting the world with her hated and inexcusable vetoes in the Security Council.

In San Francisco, the disgruntled, the hopeful, the idealistic, the subversive, the believers in Ted Jason and

5

the Right Position on Things, the famous names and prima donnas of the world of Walter Dobius who were now more than ever determined to keep Harley and Orrin out of the White House, were beginning to drift into the ballroom of the Hilton. An hour ahead of time, cameras, lights and microphones were in place to record the organizing session that would set the time and place for the Peace Party's rump convention.

And at Andrews Air Force Base, the Mayor and City Council of Washington, the members of the Cabinet, the members of Congress, the members of the diplomatic corps, the public, the reporters, and one other, waited.

Gracefully the giant craft glided toward the runway, ten miles from the great white city on the Potomac where the hopes and dreams, the triumphs and failures, the pasts and futures of so many men and causes were centered, while all around the lovely, rolling green countryside drowsed in the peaceful beat of a soft, exhausted twilight, late in the month of July.

"Do you suppose he'll have anything to say to us?" the *Times* asked as they watched the beautiful machine coming lower and lower, nearer and nearer, skimming now scarcely a hundred feet above the ground. "Something about God and Motherhood and why it's all right for us to be fighting two wars at the same time on opposite sides of the earth?"

"Come on, now," the *Post* said. "None of this subversive humor at a time like this."

"What time is it?" the *Evening Star* asked idly, and behind him from somewhere in the crowd a voice said, "8:12" in an odd, tense tone that disturbed them a little, though they did not quite understand why. And that was how they knew, for as long as they knew.

Down it came, Air Force One, veteran of so many journeys, some happy, some tragic, all heavy with the precious burden of the Presidency. Some viewers, standing far back, were able to report later that they thought they had seen Harley Hudson looking out and indeed it was a fair presumption that by then he was awake and preparing himself for those formal little solemnities that always take place when the Executive returns to the capital. Senate Minority Leader Warren Strickland, arriving late and just emerging from the terminal on his way to the ramp, was such a one. He always refused to be quoted later, but he was quite sure his old friend was waving in response to the waves and shouts that were beginning to rise from the small but friendly crowd.

"Get her down, boy!" the *Christian Science Monitor* said with a sudden sharp intake of breath. "Why doesn't he put her down?"

"He will," the *Post* said quickly, but in spite of himself a nervous tremor came abruptly into his voice.

"My God," the *Times* said explosively, "she's landing on one wheel!"

"She's coming this way!" the *Star* shouted frantically.

"Something's wrong!" the *Monitor* cried in a horrified sing-song. "Something's wrong, something's wrong, something's wrong!"

And indeed there was, though no one ever knew exactly later, despite all the investigations by the Civil Aeronautics Board, the Air Force, the President's Special Commission, six committees of Congress, innumerable articles, television specials, broadcasts and books, what it was. Those who might have been able to say, assuming they had known, were not there to testify. Nor were many of those astute and perceptive professional observers who might otherwise have given an accurate account to the public.

For Air Force One had a date with a good many of them, as one wheel crumpled and the other failed to make contact, as she teetered and tottered to a horrible screaming of reversed engines and the beginnings of the sickening sound of metal ripping apart, as she rocked and veered and swung about, as she bumped and jumped and then in one great BOOM! landed flat on her belly, slid, exploded, and burst into a single enormous hurtling balloon of fire that raced inexorably toward the waiting crowd.

For a terrible split second the Mayor and City Council of Washington, the members of the Cabinet, the members of Congress, the members of the diplomatic corps, the public, the reporters, and one other, robbed forever of his chance for glory by an Almighty Whose capacity for irony is quite a bit greater than men are willing to concede, stood paralyzed together in the gentle twilight now filled with the awful sound of human certainties being revealed for the frail and futile things they are.

Then as the great tumbling ball of flame and debris rolled toward them, they began to scream and run.

But many of them did not run far, or, mercifully, scream for long.

2.

THUS WITH A dreadful abruptness it becomes necessary once again for the nation and the world to experience the death of an American President. It is occurring too often in this hectic age: the nation is becoming traumatic.

The world, which secretly or openly always enjoys the discomfitures of its most powerful, most patient and most confused member, responds as might be expected.

In London ("We Have Lost a Good Friend"), in Paris ("A Curious Figure Passes from the Scene") and in Moscow ("H. Hudson, American Politician, Dies") the reactions are at least reasonably respectful. But in Asia, Africa and some parts of Latin America, the chorus of jubilation mounts. From India's "President Hudson Dies in Midst of Questionable Overseas Adventures" to Dar-es-Salam's "Invader of Africa Cut Down," to Cairo's "American Assassin Gets Deserts," to Cuba's "World Breathes Thanks as U.S. Criminal Killed," the note of naked satisfaction sounds throughout. In these first hours in which the fantastic news races the globe, the response is one of immediate emotion, for the moment only. It will be a while before the ultimate implications sink in.

Not so, of course, in Harley Hudson's native land, where a President need do no more than suffer a slight head cold to start the speculations whirling. Confronted by actual death in the White House, those whose profession it is to assess implications and consequences go at once to work. Everyone who has access to newsprint, editorial, magazine or television tube is instantly a-cackle. This time the implications and consequences are not only enormous: they are without precedent. Never before has a Presidential candidate died before an election. The fact that Harley is actually gone, as Senate Majority Leader Bob Munson of Michigan remarks bitterly to his wife Dolly when he calls her at "Maine Chance" immediately after hearing the news, is almost forgotten in the rush of conjecture about What Will Happen Now.

Some are like Helen-Anne Carrew, that astute observer of society and politics for the Washington *Evening Star,* whose instinctive, startled reaction in the San Francisco Hilton's press room—"If Orrin Knox doesn't have all the luck!"—is immediately succeeded by a shame-faced, sad and genuine, "Poor Harley, poor Harley!" There are others, like her ex-husband Walter Dobius, who waste no time on such sentimental maunderings but plunge at once into the analysis, and creation, of the news.

"The place of Harley M. Hudson in the sometimes sorry story of America in these troubled times," Walter types swiftly now in his hotel room (he has avoided the press room since he and Helen-Anne had their savagely bitter and by now quite historic shouting match there, forty-eight hours ago) will have to remain for history to decide.

"As the man who, in the weeks just past, deliberately and some think quite irresponsibly plunged the United States into simultaneous wars in Gorotoland and Panama—as the man who in pursuit of those irresponsible purposes ordered the first American vetoes in the United Nations—he may have much to answer for.

"Personally, he was a likable and rather inoffensive individual, tossed to the top by one of those strange quirks that all too often decide the course of American government.

"Politically he was, in the opinion of many, a disaster.

"But he is gone now, and even before he is decently buried, the clamor begins: What will happen now? Will some back-door deal be worked out by which Secretary of State Orrin Knox, the man who bears equal responsibility with the late President for America's recent disastrous course in world affairs, automatically succeed to the position at the head of the ticket for which many believe him neither qualified nor entitled?

"Or will the great convention which is just dispersing here in San Francisco be immediately reassembled—such recall is in the power of the National Committee—to choose a new nominee for President? And will California's Governor Edward M. Jason, humiliated and put down by President Hudson and Secretary Knox—yet still the undoubted favorite of a majority of the delegates had they been free to select him—have the second chance which in all justice and by all standards of common fairness is rightly his?"

This, quite obviously, is what Walter and Walter's world most desperately desire, and already from the small but powerful group of columnists, commentators and publications who see things as he does, the suave suggestions are coming forth in these first stunned hours:

The convention must be reassembled.

Ted Jason must have another chance.

There is no other way things can possibly happen.

It is inevitable.

But, as is so often the case with these deliberate attempts to convince the public which are so persistently launched by the tight-knit little consortium of top-flight talents whose opinions Walter sometimes forms and sometimes acts as spokesman for, the insistence that it is "inevitable" is of course quite untrue. It is what Walter's world would like to rush the country into believing before anyone has time to think of an alternative, so that there will be a solid weight of press-created national opinion upon those who must make the decision. But this does not make it true, nor does it, in this case, make it inevitable.

Governor Jason's supporters are aided powerfully now, as they have been throughout the convention and pre-convention period, by many of the nation's major commentators and publications. But whether they will triumph depends upon a number of astute and thoughtful individuals.

Some of them are extraordinarily tough.

Several, having weathered many storms and survived many battles, are quite immune to pressure.

And some have nothing any more to lose.

The widowed First Lady, for instance, who has just made the human mistake of breaking down in public and has thereby shadowed forever her place in legend, is such a one. Lucille Hudson is devastated by grief right now, but after the ceremonies and the pomp and circumstance are over, the shrewd brain that functions behind that fluffy pink-and-whiteness will begin to operate again: its conclusions will not be of assistance to Governor Jason.

Senate Majority Leader Munson is another who has things to do and people to see, and will not be deflected by press campaigns or any other pressures that may be brought against him. At this moment he is acutely aware that no one knows what will happen: the game can go in any direction.

Acting alone, the fifty-three men and fifty-three women of the National Committee (representing the fifty states, District of Columbia, Puerto Rico and the Virgin Islands) can select new nominees for President and Vice President. Or they can reconvene the convention and let the matter be fought out there. Whatever the procedure, there is the not-improbable chance that the new nominees, under these difficult conditions of strain and confusion, will not carry sufficient electoral votes in November to win a clear-cut victory. In which case, the matter will return to Capitol Hill to be decided by the House of Representatives, with no one knows what further strains and stresses on the fabric of American government and the strength and stability of America's policies foreign and domestic.

So there is much for Bob Munson to do, and already he is doing it, telephoning many important people around the country from the *California Zephyr* as it climbs slowly through the Rockies on its way to Denver. And he is doing it without reference to the forces of public opinion already being massed against the outcome he would like to see; although, being an old and very experienced hand at the game of national politics, he knows these forces cannot be ignored. They must be met head on and conquered.

For Orrin and Beth Knox in Carmel, California, this knowledge also is so immediate as to be virtually instinctive. Three times the Secretary of State has sought the Presidential nomination, and on this third try, after saying he would not accept second place—as so many people high in American politics say they won't do things, and then do—he has agreed to run with Harley in order to strengthen the policy of firmness toward Communist imperialism that they have believed best for the security of the republic and the peace of the world. Now, instantly, fantastically, unbelievably—except as one has to believe these things in a nation's life, for there they are—Harley is gone and Orrin is left alone to stand for the cause they both believed in.

For the first half hour or so, while Beth calls Lucille at "Maine Chance" and they weep together, he sits in Carmel and stares down at the rolling sea from the beautiful cliffside home on Spindrift Drive that Esmé Harbellow Stryke, National Committeewoman from California, has given them to use for as long as they wish. Esmé is an odd one, he thinks now, fighting him as bitterly as she did at the convention and then turning around and giving him the use of her summer home. He hadn't known she had a conscience, but apparently she has: in her strained, embarrassed voice when she called the St. Francis Hotel and made the offer, he thought he detected an apologetic guilt for the terrible episode in which his daughter-in-law, Crystal Danta Knox, lost her baby after being pummeled in the fog outside the Cow Palace by ferocious black-uniformed bullyboys backing Governor Jason. It wasn't Esmé's fault, but she was nice enough to try to make amends.

And now, he thinks with an ironic amusement, she is stuck with it, because as surely as that wave just smashing on the rocks will be succeeded by the next, Esmé is going to be back fighting him the moment it becomes clear when and where the battle is to be joined. He is as certain of that as he is certain that he is going to have to meet Ted again for the Presidential nomination. Now that Harley is gone there is no question whatsoever in his mind that he must step up and take the nomination; and he knows that Ted, for all his fiddling with a "Peace Party" is going to have exactly the same idea.

"Peace Party!" . . . Orrin is willing to bet, with a grim little smile, that at this moment the "Peace Party" meeting at the Hilton is being dismantled as swiftly as it was put together.

In this he is entirely right, but the curious thing about it is that it is being done without any real communication between the "Peace Party's" organizers and their assumptive candidate. The Governor of California is still incommunicado. No one has been able to reach him, and aside from the correct and formal statement which he has issued through his press secretary on hearing of the President's death, he might as well not exist.

Who really knows, at this frightful moment when the gagging crews at Andrews Air Force Base are still cleaning up what remains of Air Force One and trying to rake together enough human scraps to fill a Presidential coffin—at this moment when the nation is still stunned by the enormity of the catastrophe that has taken not only Harley Hudson but three Cabinet members, four members of Congress, three members of the diplomatic corps, six of the press corps' ablest reporters and—thirteen members of the general public—who knows what Governor Jason will do?

His wife Ceil has left him, at least for the time being, apparently because of his tacit approval of the violent methods of some of his supporters at the convention. His ex-campaign manager, Robert A. Leffingwell, who still carries great influence with many of the nation's liberals despite his recent defections from their cause, has gone over to the Hudson camp. The ruthlessness with which he has pursued the Presidential office has created an uneasy, insistent questioning in the minds of many of his countrymen.

What will he do? Many would like to know, but none has the word. Like Orrin Knox in Carmel, Ted is sitting in his Mark Hopkins Hotel room, thinking. Presently he picks up the telephone and calls the man whom Orrin has already tried to reach. But there is no answer for anyone in the room of Robert A. Leffingwell, and no one knows what he will do, either. True, he left Ted Jason to place Harley Hudson in nomination. But he has not said yet how he feels about Orrin Knox, who as Senator from Illinois led the successful Senate fight to defeat Bob Leffingwell for Secretary of State a year ago. Bob's loyalties yesterday lay with Harley, the man who rescued him from political oblivion after that defeat. Where do they lie now? Two or three times again, from Carmel and from Sacramento the phone rings in Bob Leffingwell's room. But the switchboard says he is accepting no calls, and the question remains: what will he do?

What will they all do, for that matter, all those whose hopes and ambitions, dreams and desires, went into the making of the wild, chaotic convention just concluded? Cullee Hamilton, Negro Congressman from California, candidate for Senator from California, steady and decent and no friend to Ted Jason . . . Roger P. Croy, former governor and now National Committeeman from Oregon, no friend to Orrin Knox . . . Patsy Jason Labaiya, sister of Ted, estranged wife of Felix . . . Senator Lafe Smith of Iowa, close friend of Orrin, Harley and Bob Mun-

16

son . . . Rep. J. B. "Jawbone" Swarthman, chairman of the House Foreign Affairs Committee, friend or not-friend of the Hudson policies, as it has suited him . . . Supreme Court Justice Thomas Buckmaster Davis, sometime friend of Bob Leffingwell, all-time enemy of Orrin Knox . . . Senator Fred Van Ackerman of Wyoming, bitter enemy of Harley and Orrin, spokesman for the Committee on Making Further Offers for a Russian Truce (COMFORT) . . . LeGage Shelby, old friend and present enemy of Cullee Hamilton, national chairman of Defenders of Equality for You (DEFY) . . . Rufus Kleinfert, Knight Kommander of the Konference on Efforts to Encourage Patriotism (KEEP) . . . and all those in the world beyond, whose nations and peoples are so deeply affected by the occupant of the American Presidency, such men as the Secretary-General of the United Nations . . . Krishna Khaleel, Ambassador of India . . . Lord Claude Maudulayne, Ambassador of the United Kingdom . . . Raoul Barre, Ambassador of France . . . Vasily Tashikov, Ambassador of the U.S.S.R. . . . Prince Obi . . . Terrible Terry . . . Felix Labaiya . . . and all the others who have so profound and basic a stake in the outcome.

But most important of all, what will the President of the United States do? Because there is one, of course, product of that American capability, built in by her founders and so annoying to those who would like to see her toppled, to maintain her national continuity even under so heavy a blow.

Even now, at his sister's vacation cabin at Lake Tahoe, the pragmatic old veteran who has been Speaker of the House for the past twenty years is being sworn in by a trembling young Forest Service ranger whom he has pressed into service for the occasion. "Mr. Speaker" at this moment is in process of becoming "Mr. President," just as the Constitution says he must in the absence of a Vice President. Harley didn't have one, though he had the authority under the twenty-fourth Amendment to fill the vacancy created by his own accession to the White House. He had told the Speaker once that he was going to step down in a year anyway, and meanwhile he didn't want to create all sorts of political hostilities in Congress by choosing one of them over another. This had disturbed the Speaker and caused much national concern, but Harley was the President and the option was his. He didn't choose to exercise it, and so here is history being made at Lake Tahoe: Mr. Speaker is becoming Mr. President.

"If you will repeat after me, sir—" the young ranger says. The Speaker interrupts with a wave of the hand that starts out to be impatient but thinks better of it.

"I've attended a few, son," he says, not unkindly. "I know how it's done."

"Yes, sir," the boy says, blushing, and begins, stammering slightly in his excitement, "I, William Abbott—"

"I, William Abbott," the Speaker repeats gravely, and everything is silent save for the click and whirr of cameras and the nearby battle of a pair of blue jays in the pines whose argument will go down in history on the tapes and films of this historic event.

"—do solemnly swear," the young ranger goes on, and the Speaker's voice grows a little stronger, though on his sister's worn Bible his right hand trembles ever so slightly—

"—do solemnly swear—"

"—that I will faithfully execute the office of President of the United States—"

"—that I will faithfully execute the office of Preside[...] of the United States—"

"—and will to the best of my ability—"

"—and will to the best of my ability—"

"—preserve, protect and defend the Constitution of the United States."

"Preserve," the Speaker says, his voice falling suddenly to a soft, grave, deeply determined note, "protect and defend the Constitution of the United States."

"Mr. President!" a cameraman shouts, and with a little smile he turns and faces the clicking, whirring, omnivorous machines, his sister and brother-in-law at his side. Their weathered faces blink into the lights a little uncertainly, plain, simple, unaffected, as if, for a second, beseeching the support and understanding of the world.

Behind and below them, over the porch railing, the beautiful lake can be seen, stretching far away in the gathering darkness to the distant lights against the distant mountains on the farther shore. Quite by accident, by no one's design but simply because the Speaker happens to have been there when he got the news, a curiously bucolic air is lent the occasion. For just a second something subconscious, almost visceral, touches the hearts of his watching countrymen—something harking far back into the innocence of an earlier America, this swearing-in of the new President of the United States in a simple log cabin, in a forest, by a lake.

As if the actual ceremony has released them all, within the hour a few answers begin to be given to some of the questions of what-will-they-do.

The first headlines read:

T SWORN IN, RETAINS CABINET. NAMES
SION TO PROBE HUDSON CRASH. MAY
ᴺ NATIONAL COMMITTEE IMMEDI-
AFTER FUNERAL TO CHOOSE NEW
ᴺOMINEES.

They are followed quickly by:

PRESSURE MOUNTS FOR RECALL OF CON-
VENTION.

And shortly thereafter:

SECRETARY KNOX ANNOUNCES, "I EXPECT
TO HEAD THE TICKET."

And moments later:

GOVERNOR JASON REPUDIATES THIRD PARTY,
PLEDGES FIGHT FOR TOP SPOT.

It appears that the tale as before is about to be retold.

But there will be differences.

3.

SO THE POWER had come to him, the President thought
as the last cameraman gathered his gear and departed,
as the last gaping tourist, privileged by sheer happen-
stance to have been in the vicinity, gathered his gaping
wife and drowsy kids and drove away.

The power had come to him: the ultimate power of
America, which he had never sought and never wanted,
being one of those who find in Washington their proper
place and fill it to the full, knowing that this is right for them
and that no amount of striving will make it any better or produce from it satisfactions greater than it already provides.

20

There were not many such, he reflected with a grim little amusement. Not many such. Mr. Speaker had been a rarity because he had always known exactly the power he wanted, had gone after it, won it, and settled in without another ambition forever after.

Until now.

Until now . . .

He sighed, a small unconscious sound that went unnoticed in the velvet night with its enormous stars shining over Tahoe, its little cool wind rustling in the pines, its distant sounds of laughter and music from somewhere down the shore.

He was alone on the porch for the first time in five hours. Inside, his sister and brother-in-law were getting ready for bed. In the two neighboring cabins, commandeered for press and Secret Service, the final poker game had ended, the last hectic political argument was over, the lights were going out.

He would have liked to have known what they had said about him this evening, that shrewd, experienced crew whom he had known so long and so well in Washington. He was pretty sure they had always respected Mr. Speaker, for he had conducted himself with a dignity and forcefulness that had guaranteed they should. But in this past week at the wild convention, things had not been the same. For the first time his power had slipped, his commands had been flouted. His influence had been mocked and made the target of bitter attack. He had lost ground—too much ground. Senator Fred Van Ackerman had shrieked "Old man!" at him in their bitter confrontation on the podium while the delegates listened in tense silence below: "An old, used-up man who has been around too long!" And toward the end, though this was the fifth national convention he had chaired—or perhaps precisely because it was the fifth—he had almost lost control of the delegates, almost been exposed to the final humiliation of an open and successful revolt.

In his own mind he had left San Francisco a defeated man, and he had not known whether he could recover from it. He had, in fact been giving serious consideration to the idea of putting the matter up to the party caucus in the House when Congress reconvened: should he step down as Speaker? Of course he had known there was not the slightest chance they would accept it, but he had really not been thinking of it as a grandstand play. He had really almost come to the point where he had honestly meant to do it, so disturbed and depressed did he feel when he left San Francisco.

And then suddenly—this. You never knew, in public life. You just never knew. The most fantastic thing you could dream could always be topped by the Lord's reality. The Lord, the President had found over the years, had quite a sense of humor. He was often just full of tricks.

Not, of course, that this particular example had been entirely unexpected. The method of it was certainly unexpected, so much so that the President, like every other American awake as midnight neared, was still almost totally unable to believe it. His first official act—after expressing condolences to Lucille Hudson and the families of the other victims—had been to appoint a commission. Already the retired dean of the Harvard Law School whom he had named to head it had called with the first of the sabotage rumors that had come to him; and of course there would be many, many more as the months and years drew on.

But whatever the commission concluded, it could never quite restore men to where they had been before the event. Some necessary self-confidence in everyone had been fundamentally shaken. Such events were so appalling, basically, because for just a moment they cut the ground right out from under life, revealed it for what it was, so frail and flimsy a thing; made of men's institutions and their hopes so helpless and feeble a mockery; shattered all certainties, destroyed all pretensions, showed men what they really were in the scheme of things: nothing. That was the Lord's real humor. He said to men, "You think you're pretty good, don't you? Well, watch for a minute."

But though the method was unexpected and unbelievable, the possibility had never been entirely absent from the mind of the man who would have to bear the burden if it came. Ever since Harley had decided to leave the Vice Presidential office vacant the possibility was always there. The Speaker had hoped it would not come to him in his mid-sixties, for many reasons: one of the main ones, emphasized harshly by his opponents at the convention, being the fact that he was in his mid-sixties.

But the event happened. The burden came. The Lord and history combined forces and said: Don't look over your shoulder for anyone else, friend. Nobody's here. It's you, all by your little self. So hop to it.

And so you did, the President reflected, and again the little unconscious sigh escaped him. With a few exceptions, life had gone so much to order for William Abbott since he entered the House from Colorado forty years ago that it hardly seemed right now that in his closing years such a violent shift in plans should have come about.

Fortunately he wasn't a worrying man, nor did he have any doubts about his ability to handle it. It was just that, as in that story Alben Barkley sometimes told when— the Speaker then a young and willing protégé of Sam Rayburn—they used to sit around in Mr. Sam's office replenishing body and spirit after a particularly tough session: "It's the unexpectedness of it."

Unexpectedness, all things considered, had not been a feature of his life or his career since the day, at some point in the sixth grade in tiny Leadville, high in its cold, bright niche of the Rockies, when he made up his mind that he would be a member of the Congress of the United States. The figure who had inspired this decision at the age of twelve, he often reflected later with some amusement, had hardly been the type usually found in inspirational literature. He had, in fact, been a drunkard, a womanizer and, in the belief of many of his hard-bitten associates in the mining industry, a peculator as well. He was, in short, a typical inspirational figure of a society in which men are free to be as noble or as base, or as much of both, as they can manage. But to little Billy Abbott in the sixth grade, hearing him roll out the ancient, well-tried clarion calls of democracy against a background of great snow-covered peaks stabbing jaggedly into a sky so deeply blue and clear as to be unbelievable, he was inspiration enough.

The Speaker-to-be had come home from the special school assembly at which the rather raffish keeper of democracy's Grail had spoken to tell his mother that he was going to run for Congress. "When?" she had inquired, not looking up from the stove where she was preparing lunch. "Next year," he said firmly. "I'll be there," she promised, and when he announced his candidacy ten years later, she was, accompanying him on his strenuous travels by auto, jeep and horseback around the still almost frontier district; entertaining for him at the "Breakfasts with Bill" that did so much to persuade his women constituents to vote for their handsome young bachelor; giving him shrewd and sensible advice with all the calm pragmatism of her Scandinavian nature.

So, also, did his father, though he did not participate very actively in the campaign. He didn't have to: everybody knew Dr. Abbott, who had come West from Vermont as a young man to cure his tuberculosis and had somehow found his way to Leadville. There his reputation as an excellent doctor and a man of sound wisdom soon traveled far along the high, lovely meadows, up the tumbling river valleys and into the mines where hardy, pragmatic men wrestled with the earth to seize her treasure. "Doc" Abbott in his own quiet way was the greatest asset his son could have: a natural advance-man who had been preparing the way with diligence and rectitude for thirty years and more. He too was capable of shrewd advice, always uttered in a terse, monosyllabic way. Between them, he and his wife gave their son all the support and guidance he could possibly need, having provided him initially with a strength of character and toughness of will that were to be his surest reliances in the years ahead.

"I'm half-Yank and half-Swede," he used to tell his audiences in the early days, "and that's a tough combination to beat."

25

They always laughed and applauded and agreed delightedly with one another that that sure was right, all right.

His first campaign, against the same gallant knight who had first inspired him, now ten years older, drunker, shabbier and shadier, had not been a success in spite of what everyone in the district knew about the two of them. There was still a reluctance to kick out the old man; after all, people were human, and he was one of the most human. In a hard way of life that nature at her harshest had made even harder, the incumbent was not the only man who drank, womanized, didn't pay too much attention to the finer items of dress, and now and again dipped too far into the till. And they knew him; and they were tolerant; and underneath the harshness, they were kind. So they gave him one last term, meanwhile sending some of their shrewdest men to tell him maybe he'd better quit and take that judgeship Harry Truman was offering in the East. And within a year, having thought it all over and being no fool, he thanked them for their kindness and announced his retirement. The field was open to young Bill Abbott. The following year he went to Washington.

He took with him the love of his parents and only sister, the faith of his constituents, and an education which had thrust him early, as it does so many who ultimately find their way to Capitol Hill, into the lively world of campus politics. He had decided he would educate himself to be a teacher, since common sense indicated that sixth-grade ambitions are not always achieved and one might conceivably, however worthy, have to live one's life outside Congress. But the area he decided to teach in, of course, was political science and government, and it would have been surprising if he had gone through four years of it without seeking student office.

He ran twice at the University, for president of the freshman class, which he lost, and for president of the senior class, which he won. The years between were devoted to managing the campaigns of others—"all part of my education," he told his closest friend. "But I thought you were going to be a teacher," his friend remarked with a smile. "Oh, I'm going to teach people things," he responded cheerfully. "Maybe not in classrooms, but I'll teach 'em."

If there was any one lesson that loomed above the others at that early stage, it seemed to be: steady does it. There were no extremes in Bill Abbott's nature, and if this made him at times a somewhat dull, one-track type of companion, this was more than compensated for by the absolute reliability and trustworthiness that soon came to be attached to his name. These, in fact, were the two traits that his associates had always considered characteristic. "Billy's a rock," they said on campus. "Bill Abbott's a rock," they said in his first twenty years in the House. "The Speaker's a rock," they said in his second twenty.

And the President would have to be a rock now, he told himself as the noise down the shore began to diminish, the few lights he could see from other cabins along and across the lake began to go out, and the night took full possession. Yes, sir, the President would have to be a rock now.

Perhaps it was the rocklike, one-track quality that had kept him from ever achieving what so many other men had, a wife and family. "You're so damned reliable, some girl should have snapped you up long ago," one of his colleagues remarked jokingly when he was thirty and some bored reporter, with nothing else to write, had dreamed up a list of "Washington's ten most eligible bachelors" and put him at the top of it. "In Leadville," he replied, "we learn to move fast or get our tails frozen off. Guess I just outrace 'em." And there, even in his own mind, he left it, as the years drew on, his routine became more settled, and other bored reporters kept the legend of his eligibility alive.

Whether he actually was eligible, he never really paused to analyze. Certainly it was easy enough to plunge into the work of Congress so deeply that he could sooner or later forget the few hurtful things that happened along the way. He had tried to establish something lasting, now and then: it didn't succeed, for some reason he never quite understood. The antidote was work, and by the time another decade had passed, "Old Bill's really married to this House," was the way they put it on the Hill. "What do you suppose he *does?*" they asked now and then when they were musing in the cloakroom. But nobody ever knew, and by that time he had already gathered about him such a mantle of calm, pragmatic dignity that nobody ever dared inquire too openly. Whatever he did, he reflected with a harsh amusement one time when he overheard such a conversation as he walked through the corridors, no real gossip about it ever got around in that gossipy place.

So he stayed unmarried and wedded to the House, and as with some other famous bachelors in Congressional history, fidelity paid off with an ever-growing astuteness in legislative matters and an ever-greater dependence by his colleagues upon his sound common sense, good judgment and unfailing stability. No one ever saw Bill Abbott really upset except his secretary; and she, bless her funny widowed old heart, had hovered over him with a fierce protectiveness for thirty years and never said one word to her children or anyone else about the few times when she had come into the office and surprised him staring out the window with a sad, desolate set to his face and tears in his eyes. Such occasions always made her retire hastily and cry too, but within the hour the buzzer would sound and there he would be again, calm and efficient and so dignified that even she never dared mention it to him.

The years passed and he worked hard and well at his committees, Appropriations and Foreign Affairs, and gradually, because he was such a rock and because other potential rivals one by one fell away as they moved through the decades together in the House, he became the almost inevitable heir apparent for the one office he really wanted, the Speakership. It was an office that had undergone its mutations through the years, from time to time being restricted by widely publicized revolts among the membership, but always, sooner or later, its powers were gradually restored until it became again what it basically always is, one of the four or five most powerful offices in the government.

Its strength, he perceived after serving under Mr. Sam and his successors, depends in large measure upon the character of the occupant. "Revolts" are usually against the Speaker's personality and methods, not so much against the inherent powers of his office. Any whittling-away that is done can be smoothly and painlessly restored by the next man who comes along, if he is strong enough. Bill Abbott, watching them come and go, had no doubts about his own abilities to make of it just about what he wanted.

When the time came, following the death of an old and generally incompetent Speaker who had let many of his prerogatives slip from his humbling hands, Bill Abbott had little to do but express his desire and the battle was over. There was some opposition at the White House, because, while Bill had usually gone along with the Administration, he was recognized as a stolidly independent character who, at some crucial point, might not. A Speaker more pliable had been the wish of the then occupant of 1600 Pennsylvania Avenue, a man who liked to have obedient men around him. But the will of the House was so obvious that the President, after a little grumbling, made the best of it by writing a letter in the Franklin Roosevelt style to an obscure freshman Congressman from New Hampshire—"Dear Johnny: You are kind enough to ask my advice on your choice for Speaker. If I were a member of the House, I think I would vote for—" and Bill was in. The lesson of who had come around to whom was not lost on the House or anyone else.

Perhaps because of this initial victory, he could reflect now, as the full impact of today's events began to hit him and a creeping tiredness started to flood his mind and body, that he had managed to get along well with all the Presidents he had served in the twenty years of his Speakership. There had been frictions from time to time, and occasionally a pitched battle, and some of these he had won and some he had not. But he had supported most domestic legislation, and certainly he had given full endorsement to basic foreign policies. He had even approved, although somewhat reluctantly because he was aware of the great uneasiness on the Hill, Harley's tandem decisions to go into Gorotoland, fight in Panama, and use the veto in the United Nations. The issues had been difficult and complex. Yet the facts that had brought them to climax had seemed sufficiently clear to Harley, and they seemed sufficiently clear to him.

In Gorotoland, Prince Obifumatta and his Communist advisers—masquerading as the "People's Free Republic of Gorotoland"—had launched an attempt to overturn the legitimate government of his cousin, Prince Terry, as soon as Terry had successfully persuaded the UN to help him oust the British from their last remaining foothold in Central Africa. At first, President Hudson had kept the United States aloof from the struggle, but when Prince Obi's forces had threatened an American missionary hospital and a Standard Oil installation, he had issued a stern hands-off warning. Obi and his friends, in common with the rest of the world, which had been conditioned by many American threats and little American action, did not believe him: forty-four missionaries had been tortured and killed, the Standard Oil installation had been blown up. Harley had ordered intervention, and immediately an enormous howl against "American aggression" and "oil imperialism" had risen around the globe. Many of the loudest screams came from America itself, where the group of influential columnists, publications, educators, churchmen, idealists and zanies, whom such as Walter Dobius spoke for, immediately attacked their own country with every vial of vitriol at their command.

In Panama, simultaneously, Patsy's estranged husband, the Panamanian Ambassador Felix Labaiya-Sofra, finding the United States committed on the other side of the sea, had finally put into operation his long-brewing plans to seize the Canal and drive the United States forever out of Panama. He, too, had Communist advisers and they, too, had the usual shining labels to cover the usual grimy deeds. Basically the coup was the result of Felix's longtime ambition to rule his country and the Communists' longtime ambition to capture the Canal; but they called it "The Government of the Panamanian People's Liberation Movement."

Again Harley ordered intervention and again the world howled, if possible more loudly than before. The UN in a series of hectic special sessions had passed resolutions condemning American aggression and calling for American withdrawal. Harley Hudson had astounded the world and pushed his critics to the point of near-catalepsy by ordering the first American vetoes in history.

The consequence had been to throw the country, and the Presidential convention which shortly followed, into turmoil. But over and beyond the standard shrieks that had greeted every American move to oppose Communism since the Korean War, a genuine uneasiness and dismay had been created, and nowhere had it been more loudly or accurately reflected than it had been on Capitol Hill. There such men as Arkansas' Senator Arly Richardson and Rep. J. B. "Jawbone" Swarthman, chairman of the House Foreign Affairs Committee, had joined in bitter denunciations of the President's actions. Resolutions supporting him had passed by only the narrowest of margins in both the Senate and the House.

Against this background, the Speaker had laid his enormous prestige and influence on the line for Harley, and in consequence his prestige and influence after the convention were not what they had been before. But all that was academic now, because now he had power greater than that could ever be, and could do as he pleased.

And what would he do? Well, he imagined, just about what Harley would have done if Air Force One had behaved. The United States was in Gorotoland and Panama and Harley had told him privately a couple of days ago, "If I have anything to say about it, we're in there to win as fast as we can." It seemed a sensible policy to Old Rock Abbott then, he told himself with a wry self-mockery, and it seemed sensible now. Old Rock would keep it moving right along. Harley, God rest him wherever he was, could count on that.

But first, of course, the funeral and all it would demand of its participants; and then the necessary briefings so that he would know what he was talking about behind that big desk downtown, as no one on the Hill or anywhere else could really know except the one man in the world who sat behind it; and then something decisive and direct, whatever the risk, because the risk of letting things drag, he felt, was greater than any other risk might be.

And here as he started to stand up and then sat slowly down again, one hand on the railing, his eyes wide in the night as he stared at the dark shore across, he came up against what was of course the most pressing problem of all. What of the election? What of a campaign without a candidate? What was he going to do about the national ticket that now was only half a ticket, and that half named Orrin Knox?

The thought of that volatile, goodhearted, impatient, idealistic, prickly, difficult, ineffable character brought a half-smile, amused, affectionate, almost tender, to his lips for a moment.

Dear old Orrin! What on earth was going to happen to him now?

A year ago, at the height of the Senate battle over the nomination of Bob Leffingwell to be Secretary of State, when the Speaker and Orrin had met on the House steps in the terrible hours after Senator Brigham Anderson's suicide, he had told Orrin he would back him for the Presidency. True to his word once given, which was one of his major characteristics and strengths, he had done as much as he could in the convention just past. They had both of necessity deferred to Harley when he changed his mind and decided to run, but as soon as the Speaker understood that Orrin would defer still further and accept second place, he had done all he could to assist him there, too.

He still thought Orrin Knox the best-qualified man in the country to be in the White House.

Except for one thing.

Now *he* was in the White House.

He had only held the office five hours, but the Presidency, as always, was imposing its own perspective.

The Hudson-Knox ticket had carried the convention, but at an enormous cost in bitterness and division within the party. The President's instinct now, as it had been

34

during his years as Speaker, was to deplore party division and do everything he could to heal it over. Yet he was not fool enough to think it could be done under present circumstances, inflamed as they were by the forces supporting the candidacy—now obviously the revived candidacy—of Governor Edward M. Jason of California.

Ted Jason, too, had been given a new position in the world by the crash of Air Force One. Five hours ago he had been so bemused and so bewildered by the destruction of his hopes at the convention that he was letting his supporters force him down the blind alley of a third party. All those powerful elements in the press, the intellectual community, the universities and the churches who were so bitterly opposed to American attempts to stop Communist aggression in Gorotoland and Panama had been about to push Ted to a political destruction he seemed powerless to resist.

Not all their editorials, columns, broadcasts, headlines, one-sided photographs and news stories, statements, marches, protests, full-page ads in the New York *Times* and pious, pompous petitions to the White House had been able to force the convention to take the Governor. So they had been about to make him their sacrificial lamb to head a phony "Peace Party" which would, they obviously hoped, throw the election into chaos and paralyze the nation's foreign policy during many crucial months.

And Ted had apparently been about to let them do it. The organizing session of the rump convention was gathering at the San Francisco Hilton as the news flash came. The Governor of California was about to slip into the vortex, carried by ambition beyond the point that any sensible, responsible politician in his right mind would let himself go.

Had he really wanted to create chaos in the country? Had his ambition really been so great that it could contemplate rule or ruin?

The President—who was, as the House had long ago found out, a most charitable man at heart—could only conclude so. Certainly he had to conclude so on the basis of the latest headlines from Ted: GOVERNOR JASON REPUDIATES THIRD PARTY, PLEDGES FIGHT FOR TOP SPOT. Ambition apparently was still the driving force. It had now turned Ted right around 180 degrees and set him back on the road. The President took a little comfort from the fact that at least it was the right road: it was within the party again, through regular channels that would restore the contest to some ground of responsible politics. But it certainly would do nothing to restore harmony to the party or unity to the country. It would instead keep alive and further aggravate the already deep divisions concerning America's course in world affairs.

Why couldn't Ted have been a big enough man to get behind Orrin, who was Harley's logical and rightful heir, and who deserved it if anybody did? Why did he have to continue to be ambitious and obstructionist?

Of course, the President recognized with a sardonic shrug in the forest night, not everyone considered Ted ambitious and obstructionist. Millions thought him the greatest patriot in America. The conviction had been strengthened over the past couple of months, and was being strengthened now, by the powerful personalities and publications that did so much to influence public opinion in America. Somebody had brought him Walter Dobius' column and the initial expression of editorial opinion by The Greatest Publication That Absolutely Ever Was. He had also seen the late news round-up chaired by Frankly Unctuous, that suavely destructive hero of the tyrannical tube. The same format had distinguished them all: a little politely dutiful earth quickly tossed over Harley—a hasty reference to his own almost incidental accession (the New York *Times* had already produced the attack phrase for the pack to use: "The Caretaker President," it called him)—and then a long, earnest discussion of why the party must now turn to the only logical candidate to lead the nation out of the disastrous situation created by the late slightly lamented and his awful Secretary of State, Orrin Knox.

Well, the President thought with a grim line to his jaw that members of the House would have recognized, "Caretaker," was he? Very well, he'd take care. Of the country, and of Orrin, and of Ted Jason and the lot of them, if it came to that.

Half-Yank and half-Swede, and that's a pretty tough combination, all right, all right. Maybe they thought they could stampede him with such phony items as PRESSURE MOUNTS FOR RECALL OF CONVENTION. It had been datelined Washington, and had begun: "Powerful political forces here who cannot presently be named called tonight for a reconvening of the national convention to select successor candidates to the late President Harley M. Hudson and Vice Presidential Nominee Orrin Knox."

Powerful political sources here who cannot presently be named!

The President snorted.

He knew those sources from long, long experience in Washington:

Remington, Olivetti, Smith-Corona, Underwood and L. C. Smith. And most of them working overtime for Ted Jason.

He snorted again.

"Caretaker President" and the bland assumption—spurred on, of course, by the carefully concealed fear that he might just decide to "do a Harley" and run himself—that he would obediently get out of the White House as soon as possible.

"Caretaker President" and the bland assumption that they could force him to reconvene the national convention.

"The new President occupies a unique position in the party hierarchy in that he was, as Speaker, chairman of the National Committee," the *Times* had written. "Presumably he retains this office, in the absence of any word from him—" That's right, the President thought grimly—"and so has it in his power to call the Committee at once and instruct it to reconvene the national convention—"

Or not instruct it, he told them dryly. Or not even call it, for a week or two, until poor Harley had a chance to get a little decent rest and honorable men could again begin to take up political matters.

Except that of course he knew better than that. Honorable men and dishonorable men were all busy on politics this minute, and had been from the moment they heard the news. It was the nature of the system, and no point in being pious about that.

But there were fictions that could be used, and like

everyone in politics, he had used them on many occasions. The fiction that a great quietus lay on politics until a leader was decently buried was one of them. He could use it now as he had before and outwardly keep up the pretense of respectful inaction, though he knew he would be bombarded—and might do a little bombarding himself—on all sides in the next few days.

One thing nobody could do: nobody could make him move faster than he wanted to. Walter could write, Frankly could fulminate, The Greatest Publication and its colleagues could assault the world with new indignations each morning, Orrin and Ted could stand in line and pound on his door, and still nobody could make him move.

He had learned the value, in the House, of taking some time to think, and now he was going to stand firm for a while and have it.

Nobody had ever pushed the Speaker around much.

Nobody was going to push the President around, either.

He realized with a start that it must be almost one A.M.

"My God, I'm tired," he remarked quietly to the little predawn wind that was beginning to probe through the pines. He stood up abruptly and went in to bed, where he fell asleep without delay and without dreams.

4.

"SWEETIE," Patsy Jason Labaiya said from her enormous redwood desk in Dumbarton Oaks next morning, "you simply must talk to him. You simply MUST. He won't listen to me, I KNOW that. It's got to be someone he respects, like you."

For a moment she thought her sister-in-law was going to hang up, for there was no sound from the other end of the line at "Vistazo," the enormous Jason ranch in the burnt-umber hills above Santa Barbara. But presently Ceil Jason responded in a tone that was, for her, surprisingly impatient.

"Oh, Patsy, why won't you stop meddling? Things have gone to a point now where I don't think anyone—"

"But they haven't gone to that point at all, sweetie!" Patsy interrupted indignantly. "Not at ALL. Now that Ted's repudiated that STUPID third party, everything's just the way it was. He can run for President again, now that that old fool—"

"Patsy!" Ceil exclaimed, genuinely shocked.

"Well, I'm sorry he got killed," Patsy conceded defiantly, "but I'm not sorry he's out of Ted's way. He never should have done and said the things he did."

"And Ted should have said and done what he did?"

"He only did what he felt he had to do to win the nomination," Patsy said.

"But he didn't win it, did he?"

"No," his sister said with a sudden waspish note in her voice, "because that—that—*gang*—of old reactionaries led by Harley and Orrin blocked him from doing it. That doesn't mean the convention didn't want him, and doesn't

40

want him still. Now, you KNOW that, Ceil, so why keep pretending?"

There was a sigh, half-exasperated, half-amused, from "Vistazo."

"Patsy, you wear me out. What makes you so sure the convention still wants him? Anyway, who says the convention's going to have a chance? The President doesn't have to reconvene the convention—"

"No, but sooner or later he's got to call the National Committee, and *they* can reconvene the convention. That's why you've got to call Bob Leffingwell immediately and get him to help us persuade the Committee members—"

"Patsy!" Ceil protested, overwhelmed, and not for the first time, by the Jasons' ability to ignore all obstacles and ride roughshod toward what they wanted. "That's exactly what I mean about things having gone too far. You heard Bob's nominating speech for Harley and the attack he made on Ted. 'Devious' and 'playing fast and loose with principle' and all the rest of it. How on earth can you ask him to work for you now?"

"Oh, poof! Poof, POOF! That was an entirely different set of circumstances. Bob didn't nominate Orrin, did he?"

"No, Harley did."

"Well, then: why assume Bob's for Orrin now? He owed Harley a debt for salvaging his career after he was defeated for Secretary of State, but who defeated him? Orrin Knox! Maybe that wasn't 'going so far nothing can be done about it' I ask you!"

"Even so, I don't think there's any reason at all to believe that Bob Leffingwell is going to come back to Ted just because he may not like Orrin. And I don't think he's all that influential, either, especially after all the things that were said about him at the convention."

Patsy sniffed.

"Everybody said a lot of things about everybody at the convention. That's what conventions are for. People's emotions don't change basic political realities. The reality is that Ted is going to win that nomination now, and that Bob will have to back him against Orrin. And Bob is influential, Ceil. He's lost a little ground, maybe, but the minute he announces for Ted, Walter Dobius and everybody else in the press will start praising him again. He hasn't lost them permanently. They'd love to come back if he'll give them the chance. The professional liberals," she said with a dry savagery that startled her sister-in-law, who had thought she was one of them, "never really like to abandon a hero in whom they've invested their time and reputations. They'll take him back if he gives the slightest sign that he's willing to behave from now on."

"Bob isn't a member of the National Committee—"

"We're going to organize this just like the convention," Patsy said. "We're opening a headquarters here in Washington tomorrow morning and we're going to issue releases and hold press conferences, and all the rest of it. Bob can head it up again if he wants to. It would be a great help to us. We're already getting marvelous support from the press and the networks. You've probably seen Walter's column and some of the editorials. CBS wants to do a half-hour interview with Ted from here after the funeral on Wednesday, and NBC is planning to do one, too, I believe. They're going to call it 'Party Without a President.'"

"That should please President Abbott," Ceil remarked. "That should please him very much. Don't you think he's the man you should be working on, not Bob Leffingwell and the Committee members?"

"He's only ONE," Patsy said tartly.

"But look where he lives now. A rather big ONE, I'd say."

"He can't control what the Committee does! All he can do is try to influence it for Orrin, I suppose. And we're going to influence it for Ted. So our chance is as good as his. Better, because the convention still wants Ted. Can't you see," she demanded, "what a perfect COUP it would be if he and Bob are reconciled? Right now Bob still has a lot of his old liberal support, and by nominating Harley he's picked up a lot of conservatives, too. He's a symbol of the honest man who genuinely stands in the middle, now. He genuinely does. They'll listen to what he says. But, sweetie, *he* won't listen to *me*, because he doesn't like me right now. He does like and respect you, I believe. So you've got to call him for us. He's apparently trying to avoid Ted."

"Why should he like me?" Ceil inquired. "I'm Ted's wife." She uttered the sudden little sardonic chuckle that sometimes upset her in-laws. "In a manner of speaking."

"That's exactly why, dear," Patsy said smoothly. "You are—but there's a little doubt about it at the moment, because you've been so dramatic, leaving him at the crucial moment of the convention and sneaking away down there—"

"I didn't sneak," Ceil said mildly. "I told him where I was going."

"Well, anyway, you LEFT. That's the main thing. And

yet you're still his wife, of course, and I suppose will remain so—you will, won't you?" she asked in abrupt alarm. "You aren't really thinking about doing anything foolish—"

"Oh, no," Ceil said in a tired tone. "I just wanted to think things out by myself. If a simple desire for reflection is something the Jason family can understand."

"Then that makes you the perfect one to call Bob," Patsy said triumphantly. "You're—*with* Ted, but you're not actually too—*close*—at the moment. It gives YOU a nice independent status, too. Have you talked to Ted?"

"Not lately."

"Well. I'm sure this is EXACTLY what he would want you to do."

'No doubt."

"Well. You will, then."

"I'm not making any promises."

"Well, at least you'll think about it—" Patsy began in a concerned tone.

"I'm thinking about a lot of things," Ceil told her. "Goodbye, Patsy. Thanks for calling."

"But, Ceil—"

There was a firm click! from California, and the line went dead. Damn her, anyway, Patsy thought angrily. Ceil had always been an uncertain element in the Jason campaign to put Ted in the White House. Sometimes Patsy thought that all Ceil ever wanted to do was be beautiful and ride on Ted's name to wherever it might take her. She had never really *believed* in him the way his sister did.

She looked out through the vines that shaded the big windows of her study, to the tennis court and the pool beyond. It was close to noon. Nothing stirred. Washington's suffocating summer heat had the world flat on its back.

"Thank God for air-conditioning," she said aloud. She put her finger tips together and narrowed her eyes.

"Well!" she said. "What shall I do next?"

But as always with Patsy, the question was rhetorical. She already had an idea, and pulling the telephone once more toward her, she dialed a number and began to set it in motion.

At the same moment, at the airport, Senator Munson, who had left the *Zephyr* in Denver to meet his wife Dolly and the widowed First Lady and her two Secret Service escorts, was facing half a dozen reporters after a swift and uneventful flight in the special Air Force plane provided by the President. They wanted to know a lot of details that he wasn't about to tell them: Had Lucille Hudson balked at taking an airplane back to Washington? Had she been worried because it was an Air Force plane? Was she in reasonably good spirits? Had she been crying? Who did he think the party's new standard bearers would be? Would Orrin Knox get the nomination now?

All of these he had refused to answer, with a curt impatience that prompted the New York *Times* to murmur to The Greatest Publication That Absolutely Ever Was, "Our Robert seems awfully tense about something. You don't suppose Abbott's putting the hex on Orrin, do you?" To which the G.P. murmured back, "It might be worth a little analyzing, I should think."

They were about to press him further and see if they couldn't make him mad enough to say something interesting, when the cabin door opened again and the First

Lady, heavily veiled, came slowly out on Dolly Munson's arm and started down the steps. In the ensuing hubbub the photographers got some wonderful pictures, even if the reporters didn't get quite the factual story from Senator Munson that they wanted. But they were old hands at interpreting the moods of the great, and a few minutes later The Greatest Publication's man was back in his office in the National Press Building tapping out the think-piece that he would send to New York to run alongside his colorful and moving account of Lucille Hudson's return to a black-draped White House.

"An obviously troubled Senate Majority Leader Munson," it began, "apparently concerned that the death of President Harley M. Hudson may blast the Presidential hopes of his longtime friend, Secretary of State Orrin Knox—"

WHITE HOUSE MAY DUMP KNOX IN NEW BALLOTING, MUNSON FEARS, the headline said.

An hour later at "Salubria," his lovely old home in Leesburg, forty miles out from the capital in the slumbering Virginia countryside, Walter Dobius, just back from San Francisco, read the item on his news-agency ticker ("Can you match Greatest Wh Hu Knox dump?" the New York office had queried the Washington bureau, and the Washington bureau had speedily obliged). Then he put a sheet of paper in his typewriter to start tomorrow's column.

"It is apparent already," he wrote swiftly, "that the arrogance with which Secretary of State Knox has claimed the Presidential nomination following the death of President Hudson may be somewhat premature. If the attitude of Senate Majority Leader Robert M. Munson of

46

Michigan is to be believed—and most observers here consider the Majority Leader to be one of the nation's shrewdest political weather vanes—there appears to be what might justly be termed a growing disenchantment with the Secretary's ambitions on the part of the new President, William Abbott. . . . "

Within two hours after that, the correspondents of the London *Times,* the London *Observer* and the *Guardian,* the little man from Tass, the correspondents of the French, German and Italian news agencies, the man from the *Times* of India, the lady who wrote for the Swedish newspapers, and the correspondent of *News-Arabia,* had all cabled stories to the general effect that the new President was rapidly cooling toward Secretary Knox and would probably toss him off the ticket. And by the time he presented his special six P.M. Sunday news broadcast "The Course of the Week," Frankly Unctuous was able to fix the camera with a forthright, candid and earnest eye and tell his countrymen in his customary suave, plum-pudding tones:

"It is already apparent here in this capital still rocking from the terrible tragedy that has brought a new man into the White House, that the new man may not be so wedded to the Presidential hopes of Secretary of State Orrin Knox as the Secretary would obviously like to believe.

"The tip-off may have come shortly after noon today when Senate Majority Leader Munson, arriving from the West with the widowed First Lady, appeared to be worried and reluctant to discuss Mr. Knox's prospects with reporters.

"It is being generally assumed here that Senator Munson, who worked in the closest relationship with

47

President Abbott during the latter's long tenure as Speaker of the House, may possibly know something that Secretary Knox does not know. If this growing conviction among those who study politics day by day should prove to be correct, it may well be that the Secretary's claim upon the nomination—which he volunteered yesterday scarcely three hours after President Hudson's tragic death—will turn out to be premature. Add to this growing uncertainty about Mr. Knox's prospects the equally lively conviction that Governor Edward M. Jason of California now has once again become the major contender for the nomination, and it is easy to see—"

"It's easy to see, you twisting son of a bitch," the Majority Leader said quietly in the comfortable home of Orrin and Beth Knox in Spring Valley, "that all you bastards are now out to get poor old Mr. Knox again. Why don't we just turn you off and enjoy a little silence for a change?"

And reaching forward to the set, he did so and then sat back with a sympathetic look at his host.

"Orrin," he said, "I'm afraid you've got another fight on your hands.

"When did I not have?" the Secretary of State inquired. "I no longer care, Bob. I've got to go ahead living, I can't afford to let myself be handicapped by that sort of thing. And maybe by now the techniques are so obvious that the public is beginning to be on guard a little. This performance Frankly and Walter and the rest are putting on is typical. You arrived at the airport and refused to talk—"

"I was really worried about getting Lucille back to the mansion before she broke down again," Bob Munson said mildly. "I also resented all those political questions at a time like that. I haven't talked to Bill about you."

"Oh, I know you haven't. Your crime, you see, was that you didn't want to answer. So the door was wide open for the broadest possible latitude in interpreting your non-cooperation. This tied in neatly with the general urge to cut me down before I can get started, so the standard techniques went right to work. You heard Frankly:

"The President *'may not be so wedded'* to my 'hopes' as I *'would obviously like to believe.'* You gave the *'tip-off'* because you *'appeared'* to be *'worried and reluctant'* to discuss my future. Nobody says you actually were worried and reluctant, of course, you just *'appeared'* to be. Because you have had *'the closest relationship'* with the Speaker, you *'may possibly'*—not for sure, but *'may possibly'*—know *'something'* that I don't know.

"If this *'conviction,'* which naturally is *'growing'* among *'those who study politics day by day'* should *'prove to be correct,'* it may be that my claim on the nomination— which I *'volunteered scarcely three hours'* after Harley's death, heartless bastard that I am—will turn out to be *'premature.'*

"These same carefully anonymous students of *'politics day by day'* share the *'equally lively conviction'* that Ted has *'once again become the major contender for the nomination'* and so *'it is easy to see'*—just what is it easy to see, Bob?"

"It's easy to see that the English language in certain hands these days has become so smooth as to be practically subliminal," the Majority Leader said dryly. "It's easy to see that this is the sort of thing that comes out of Washington day in and day out about any person or cause that the major commentators and publications don't like. All the public has to do is read and listen with an ounce of attention and there they are almost every time you pick up a paper or turn a dial—the little knife-words and knife-phrases that cut a man down. The few earnest but unfashionable correspondents, broadcasters and publications who don't love Ted Jason aren't going to be able to do much to stem the tide. . . . Except, of course," he said more soberly, "that it's got to be stemmed."

"Why does it?" Orrin inquired in an oddly distant, off-hand manner. "We've got a President in the White House. He's committed to the policies we believe in. Why should we worry? They'll have a tough time getting him out if he decides to run."

"I don't think he will run," Senator Munson said slowly. His host gave him a sudden sharp look.

"But you don't know."

He shrugged.

"No, I don't know. But from what I know of Bill, in my long, close relationship, I would find it a little hard to believe."

"But not impossible," the Secretary said. "Not impossible. And maybe it would be best, Bob. Maybe all this will work out all right. Maybe I should be the sacrificial lamb, so they can all concentrate on me while Bill goes about lining up the National Committee to give him the nomination. Shall we work for that?"

The Majority Leader studied him for a moment. Then he smiled. "Who is this noble soul I'm talking to? Is this the Orrin Knox I know from yesteryear, The Man Who Would Be President? Say not so!"

"You can laugh if you like," Orrin said calmly, "but that's the way I feel now. That convention wasn't easy for me, either, Bob. Nor has it been easy to try three times for the Presidential nomination, and lose. I've about had it, with politics. I'll take it if I can get it, certainly, but I don't think any more that the end of the world is going to come if I don't. I used to, but I think I've been cured. I'm perfectly willing to leave it to Bill, if that's what he wants. He's a good man."

"One of the best," Senator Munson said. "But I don't think he's going to let you get out that easily."

"What does he want me to do, then, stay where I am and run for Vice President? I'm perfectly willing to do that, too, if that's what he wants."

"Now, just how does that jibe," Senator Munson inquired thoughtfully, "with your 'volunteering' for the nomination? What were those headlines I saw last night? SECRETARY KNOX SAYS, 'I EXPECT TO HEAD THE TICKET'—"

Orrin shrugged.

"I was just establishing my territory. To hold for me, or hold for him, if he wants it. I didn't think it should go by default."

"I must say you're in a funny mood," Bob Munson told him. "Is it because Beth and Hal and Crystal are still in Carmel, or—"

The Secretary's face became uncharacteristically somber for a moment.

"I think it's because of Harley, basically."

Senator Munson nodded.

"What a hell of a thing," he said slowly. "Poor Harley. What a hell of a thing!"

"It makes all ambitions seem a little pointless, you know?" Orrin said. "To say nothing of all those other poor devils who died with him. It really was *frightful*, and yet here we sit—"

Senator Munson smiled wryly. "Discussing ambitions."

"Yes," the Secretary said somberly. "Yes . . . But"—and he too smiled for a moment—"he would have understood, bless his heart. You can't keep politics from going right along, particularly under circumstances like these."

"For which there are no precedents," Senator Munson said with a certain grimness, "so I think we'd damned well better make some. Now: you've got to proceed on the assumption that the Speaker—the President—isn't going to run. So get out of this noble mood or whatever it is, and get busy. And don't you show any signs of weakening, to anybody."

"Oh, I'm not going to," Orrin said. "I'm not taking any press calls, so how can I disclose to them how trembling and uncertain I am? Only you, old friend, have The Tip-Off—being one of those who study politics day by day."

"And don't get too flippant, either," Bob Munson said. "This is no picnic. The Jasons are out to win this time. Patsy's opening an office at 1001 Connecticut Avenue tomorrow morning and the game will be on."

"You know," Orrin said in the tone of voice that so many in Washington, even the most friendly, used when discussing the Jasons, "sometimes I simply get speechless at the bad taste of that family. It's all very well to talk politics, everybody is, right now, but to actually go ahead and open an office and start campaigning before the President is even laid in his grave—only the Jasons would have the gall and the boorishness to do it."

"They're quite a crew," the Majority Leader agreed, thinking of Ted in his big dark-paneled, green-carpeted office in Sacramento; of his aunt, Selena Jason Castleberry, giving her wild parties for wild causes in New York; her sister, Valuela, painting a little, loving a lot, in Portofino; their brother Herbert, Nobel Prize-winning scientist and leader of demonstrations, always ready to march in the name of world peace and the damnation of his own country; Patsy, whirling about in Washington, getting her long-distance divorce from Felix Labaiya down in Panama, devoting her time and noisy concentration to the Presidential ambitions of her brother. Quite a crew, sitting atop their millions that dated back to the Spanish occupation of California: quite a crew, who bought what they wanted if it could possibly be bought, and sometimes bought it anyway. Now, having failed to put Ted over at the convention, they were about to throw their enormous millions once more into the opportunity presented by the catastrophic behavior of Air Force One.

Bob Munson sighed.

"What's the matter?" Orrin asked.

"Just agreeing with you about the Jasons. But, that means you've got to come on strong and stay ahead of them, if you can. What do you plan to do?"

"I thought you'd advise me," the Secretary said with a smile. Then he became serious. "What I've got to do, as I see it, is to continue exactly as I am. I'm going to issue a statement this evening, which I think will push Ted down the front page a little, I hope, to the effect that the United States will continue to fight for freedom and stability in Gorotoland and Panama with all the vigor and power at our command."

"That sounds quite Presidential," the Majority Leader said. "Have you cleared this with Bill?"

"Certainly."

"Oh, you have been in touch with him, then."

"He called a little while ago."

"But he didn't mention the nomination."

"No. Why should he?"

"There you go again," Bob Munson remarked, "being whimsical. So all right, you've talked to him. How did he sound?"

"Rather Presidential himself. And a little disturbed by the first findings of the commission on the accident. They've already discovered, you know, that two of those crew members were in some sort of Communist operation with headquarters in Annapolis. And they found one corpse carrying a loaded pistol with the safety catch off, who also had in his pocket a picture of Ted and a copy of Walter Dobius' last column on the convention—in which, you may recall, he virtually urged armed rebellion because Harley and I had won. So, who knows?" He shrugged. "I don't."

"I doubt very much," Senator Munson said dryly, "that the last little item—the gentleman with the gun, the picture and the column—will ever see the light of day on the newsstands. It's the sort of thing that somehow just gets lost somewhere between the copy desk and the street in most publications of the pro-Ted type. Now, if the poor crazy fool had been carrying *your* picture—my *God*, what a sensation."

"I'm afraid you're very cynical," Orrin said. "I'm sure the man will be mentioned in a footnote on Page 3001 of the commission report. Any citizen who wants to read that far will be able to find it. Anyway, Bill sounded as though he had slipped into harness without a hitch. But then, when hasn't he measured up to the jobs he has had to do? Do you realize how much of the government has depended upon Mr. Speaker in the last twenty years?"

"I do," Bob Munson said, "but it isn't an office the public knows too much about. I want to talk to him myself. When's he coming back?"

The Secretary smiled.

"He said he liked it at Tahoe—the cabin's on a little point and they can hold it like a fortress against the press. 'Except my water side,' he said. 'My water side's a little vulnerable, but after I've been here a month or two I'll probably have it fortified.' I expect he'll stay out until the funeral. He doesn't want to be too accessible, and he also wants to let Lucille have the house until she's ready to go."

"It won't be long," Bob Munson said. "Dolly's over there right now helping her pack. I expect she'll be out Wednesday afternoon right after she gets back from Arlington. She told me she didn't want to spend the night there alone after he left it."

"And then back to Grand Rapids?"

"I don't know," Bob Munson said slowly. "I think perhaps she might want to get involved in the campaign. I'm not sure, of course, but perhaps if you—"

"Oh, I couldn't ask her," Orrin said, looking shocked. "Although," he added honestly, "it would be nice if she did." He looked around the comfortable room, cool and dark in contrast to the heavy heat outside. "Are you sure you don't want anything to drink?"

"No, thanks. I really must be running along in a minute. I've got to get back to the White House to plan the funeral, as she asked me to. And I've also got to do some more telephoning about the National Committee meeting."

"What's your guess on when it will be?"

"You mean Bill didn't tell you?" Bob Munson inquired in mock surprise. The Secretary shook his head.

"And I didn't ask. I don't see how he can wait much beyond the funeral, though. Walter Dobius and Company and I agree on that."

Bob Munson nodded.

"Right, there's got to be action, and fast. If I know Bill, he's doing a lot of thinking about how to approach it. What are you going to do for a campaign manager, by the way? Is Stanley going to help you again?"

Thinking of the Senate Majority Whip, Stanley Danta of Connecticut, still shattered by the brutal attack on his daughter Crystal at the Cow Palace, the Secretary sighed.

"I don't know that Stanley has much heart for it. I think I may have to find someone else."

"That was my feeling when we started east on the *Zephyr* together," Bob Munson said. "He hated to leave the kids, but felt he had to get back here to tend to some things on the Hill. The minute the news came about Harley, he seized the excuse of releasing you and flew back to Carmel."

Orrin nodded.

"Yes, that's really why I decided to leave them there and come on back. I wouldn't have left until Tuesday if he hadn't been there to keep them company." He frowned. "I wish Beth would hurry up and arrive. She ought to be here with Dolly, helping Lucille."

"And helping you," Bob Munson said. Orrin smiled.

"And helping me. She'll be arriving this evening, I believe, and then I'll be in better shape for whatever comes. . . . About a campaign manager, I . . . have an idea."

Senator Munson nodded.

"Yes, so do I. But will he do it, and is he all that valuable to you?"

The Secretary frowned again.

"I don't really know, exactly. Robert A. Leffingwell is a puzzle, to me. I still haven't got him quite figured out. I can understand his supporting Harley, but whether he would have gone farther had Harley lived, whether he would have actively supported a ticket with me on it too, I don't know. And," he added thoughtfully, "I don't really know exactly what his value is; whether he really is that important in the scheme of things; whether the beating he's taken from the press since he left Ted to back Harley may not have hurt him so much with the public that he'd be more handicap than help. I've tried to reach him several times, because I do want to talk to him and find out what I think about him after I've done so. . . . It's an idea. I'm not closing it out. It could be he'd be very helpful. It's a possibility."

"I think you should have a real talk with him," Bob Munson said. "And go into it with an open mind and a friendly manner. That's the only way to find out."

"I will as soon as I can find him," the Secretary said with some annoyance. "But where is he? Talking to Ted, I suppose. That would be just my luck."

But in this instance, though he did not know it, his luck was holding all right, because Bob Leffingwell was not talking to Ted at the moment. Nor was anyone else. The Governor of California, in fact was sitting all alone in his office in Sacramento, staring out over the beautifully kept lawns that looked so cool and shaded under their enormous trees despite the fact that right now the capital of California was even hotter and more humid than the capital of the country.

Inside the east wing of the Capitol building, however, it was genuinely cool, hushed and quiet on this Sunday morning. A couple of state troopers were on duty, a few tourists wandered even on so sweltering a day, a janitor or two shuffled along the gleaming halls. Otherwise he had his domain to himself, and that was the way he liked it, at this moment when so many things were crowding in upon him, clamoring for decision.

The most important of all, of course, was already decided: immediately after the news of Harley's death had flashed upon the screen in his room at the Mark Hopkins Hotel, he had cut himself loose, with an instinctive, almost animal, repugnance, from the tatterdemalion ragtag-and-bobtail of the foredoomed "Peace Party." Within five minutes he had framed his statement repudiating the third-party movement and affirming his renewed determination to seek the Presidential nomination. He had spent the next hour rewriting it until it was as succinct and powerful as he felt it should be. As soon as the Speaker's swearing-in had been completed at Tahoe, Ted was on the telephone dictating it to his secretary in Sacramento. Fifteen minutes later she had called the wire services, and within the hour it was top news across the nation.

Not, inevitably, the only top news: right along with it had come Orrin Knox's confident statement that he expected to head the ticket. Ted Jason did not know how confident his opponent was in reality, but of necessity he had to sound confident, and he had managed it very well.

"The United States has lost a great President and a great leader in the cause of world peace," Orrin had said. "He was my friend and my commander in the battle against the forces of aggression that everywhere threaten free men. I honor his memory as I valued his friendship.

"The task he began must be completed. American foreign policy must have the continuity and firmness that alone can guarantee the survival of this nation and of freedom everywhere.

"A leader is fallen but the battle goes on.

"An election must be fought and won.

"I expect to head the ticket.

"I expect to finish the great work he began.

"I call upon all of you who believe in an America firm in strength and firm in justice to give me your help and support in the task we must all carry forward together."

Ted had been no less confident, forceful and uncompromising:

"America has lost a distinguished and able leader, who led her, as he sincerely believed best, through perilous times. Those of us who disagreed with some aspects of his policies were ever aware that his ideals were admirable, his purposes sincere, his integrity unimpeachable. No one could have asked for a more dedicated and honorable man to lead this nation.

"His tragic death reopens many issues that appeared to have been settled by his nomination at the convention just concluded. Because of this, those of us who disagreed with certain policies are now freed of political commitments. Many things must now be reapproached and reappraised. The way is open to reconsider decisions that only yesterday seemed settled for the duration of the present campaign.

"For myself, let me make it clear that I repudiate, once and for all and absolutely, any attempt to divide America by the creation of a so-called 'peace party.' The formation of such a third party was proposed, as you know, by those claiming to be my supporters. This was done without my instigation and without my approval. Now, any such political adventuring is even more inexcusable and pointless than it was before.

"What happens now must occur through the regular channels of the party. A nominee for President and, presumably, a nominee for Vice President, must be selected. And our great party must decide once and for all what it stands for.

"I was a candidate for President before. I am a candidate now. Whether by selection of the National Committee or through a reconvened convention, the party must choose.

"Either this great nation follows the course of further international adventuring, ever-spreading foreign commitments, ever more entangling military involvements— or it follows the course of prudence, decency and peace.

"I offer myself again, as I did before, as one who believes our best course to lie in negotiation, reasonable compromise, and an end to jingoism and bullying belligerence.

"I speak now, as I did before, for peace. I call upon all of you who believe America can best be served by sanity and prudence to join me in the renewed battle.

"We must not fail."

Rereading the two statements as they lay before him on the front page of the Sacramento *Bee*, the Governor reflected that his own accomplished several things. It paid graceful tribute to the man who had so brutally shouldered him aside at the convention, thereby displaying a forgiveness he could never have shown had Harley lived—an absolutely necessary forgiveness if the votes of many goodhearted citizens were to come his way. It cleared his mind of the heavy burden of self-contempt that had dragged it down since the bleak post-convention moment when Senator Fred Van Ackerman, that savagely unprincipled demagogue of the irresponsible left, had telephoned and virtually forced him to accept the third-party idea. And it established him again as the champion of all those forces that were so bitterly and vociferously opposed to American involvement in the twin conflicts of Gorotoland and Panama.

Thus he had freed himself of the fatal incubus of the hodge-podge "Peace Party," something he would never have agreed to at all had he not been so absolutely stunned by the convention's repudiation and President Hudson's bitter speech attacking him. At the same moment he had skillfully re-established his claim upon the position favored by those who had supported him but could not follow him down so blind an alley. The Greatest Publication was such a one: it had warned him against the third party even though its editorial board was unanimously for him and had given him every possible break in friendly news-coverage, flattering photographs, and editorial endorsement during and before the convention. Some of the major columnists and commentators were equally hesitant, aware that American history gave little encouragement to third parties.

Of the small but enormously powerful group who influenced and in large measure dominated public opinion, only Walter Dobius, carried forward furiously on the wave of his angry hatred for Harley Hudson and Orrin Knox, had openly endorsed and encouraged the third party idea. Even he, Ted Jason was willing to wager with some irony, was greatly relieved that Harley's death made it no longer necessary to carry through on a cause so devoid of practical hope.

For Walter, for The Greatest Publication, and for all their friends and fellow-believers of press, television, church, drama, campus and periodical, everything was now all right again: Despised Harley was dead, Orrin stood exposed alone to the attacks of those who could once more reunite against him with a good conscience and a strengthened will, and the Governor of California was in the clear. Once again he was the hero of all those who, either sincerely or for purposes not so sincere, devoted their time and energies to opposing, hindering, demeaning and generally weakening their own country as it sought, with an uncertain success, to stand firm against its enemies and the enemies of freedom everywhere.

Respectability and the support of many of the nation's most powerful institutions and individuals were his again, and it was with some confidence that he looked forward to the next few weeks: confidence and, much more important, the renewed self-respect which, coming out of the angry morass of the convention, seemed almost a miracle to him now.

Miracle, because it had followed upon things that could have destroyed a weaker man and had almost destroyed him: the increasing, politically motivated violence in the convention which, he was sufficiently confident to admit to himself now, he had tacitly if not openly condoned—the appearance of the black-uniformed bullyboys produced by COMFORT, DEFY and KEEP, those strange ideological bedfellows, culminating in the attack on Crystal Danta Knox which was probably, he could see now, the decisive turning point of the convention and the beginning of the end of his own chances—followed by his humiliating defeat for the Presidential nomination—the President's crushing denial of his right to the Vice Presidential nomination—his own deep despair and the dreadful dazed, helpless, almost comatose condition in which he had submitted to Fred Van Ackerman's bullying and agreed to appear at the third party meeting. He had been as near nadir as he had ever come in all his life, probably as near as any Jason had ever come in all the long years since the family first began its climb to fortune in Spanish California. He literally did not know what would have become of him had the President not been killed.

He drew a sudden long, shivering breath. How awful the prospects had been for the golden hero of the Golden State; how miraculous his salvation. Surely there must be a purpose in it somewhere!

As quickly as it came, the mood passed. Governor Jason was not one to brood overlong on might-have-beens. If there was purpose, it was up to him to implement it. By some strange kindness or irony, the Lord had given him another chance. This time he would not destroy it but would see it through with vigor, integrity and all the determination of a clever mind, to which family character and great wealth had long ago given the habit of decisive command. Three days after his descent into the abyss of abandoned hope, he was on the way back; and with only a very little extra luck, he would not only regain his former position but go on from it to the goal he had been within sight of when the convention roared out of his control.

"In January," he said with a quiet certainty to the silent office, "Edward Montoya Jason will be President of the United States."

As if in response, the telephone rang; and lifting it to listen while the switchboard carried out his instructions to take the message but deflect the caller, he heard a voice he had not expected to hear unless he initiated the call. He felt a sudden surge of happiness. That she had called first seemed somehow to put the seal on all his certainties.

"I'll take this, Operator," he broke in; and then, his voice, despite his best efforts, trembling a little, "Good morning. Where are you?"

"I'm still at the ranch," Ceil said. "Have you been home?"

"No," he said. "I just came up from San Francisco this morning. I came directly here."

"Have you had breakfast?"

"A little."

"Well, you ought to have a good one. These are challenging times."

"Yes, I know," he said, absurdly relieved that she should use her usual bantering tone. "I'm not being too active at the moment, though—just sitting here thinking."

"Is anyone with you?"

"No," he said; and ventured, "Not even my wife."

"Whose fault is that?"

"I don't know," he said, trying to keep it light though his voice trembled a little again. "I came back to the

Mark and found a note that you had gone to 'Vistazo.' I didn't think I had kicked you out."

"I suppose it was a little abrupt," she conceded. "But I suddenly had just had it."

"I thought I had too," he said quietly.

"It wasn't very obvious at the time," she said thoughtfully. "You didn't give that impression."

"I have some pride, after all."

"Yes, I know. . . . What are you doing now?"

"Just thinking."

"The Capitol on Sunday's a good place for it, I guess. I saw your statement, of course."

"Did you like it?"

"I thought it was very good from your standpoint."

"That isn't what I asked," he said, attempting jocularity.

"Well, I don't know how else to state it," she said slowly, and he could visualize the characteristic little frown of concentration. "It wasn't so good from mine."

"Why not?" he asked, and because he was afraid of sounding plaintive, sounded sharp. "I'm sorry," he said instantly. "I didn't mean to sound impatient. I'm—still under a lot of strain, I guess."

"That's all right, I understand. I meant that it seemed a little—self-serving, maybe. But then, I suppose any such statement has to, of course."

"Didn't Orrin's?" he asked, again sharp; and this time he did not apologize.

"Oh, yes," she agreed. "I'm not arguing that."

"What would you have me do?" he demanded. "Not run?"

"I don't think you have a choice in the world."

"All right, then."

"Either from a political standpoint or a family one."

65

"What do you mean by that?" he inquired, making it lighter. "My fatal Jason blood?"

"Your fatal Jason compulsion to take top prize if you possibly can."

"Do you think it's just for the prize?" And again, to his annoyance, his voice trembled a little. He didn't want to sound supplicant, but he knew he was. "Don't you think I have any ideals and principles about it?"

But at this there was dead silence from "Vistazo" and he knew exactly what she was saying to him: *Ideals and principles after the things you did and condoned at the convention?* And suddenly he was overwhelmed by this himself, and for several seconds was silent also, buffeted by a hundred unhappy thoughts. Finally, because he must, he spoke.

"Ceil—" he said tentatively. "Do you think I'm really as—as awful—as—as I have seemed to be?"

"Do you want an honest answer?"

"I know I always get one from you," he said, attempting a little laugh that didn't really come off.

"Yes," she said, and sighed. "I suppose you do. That's probably the trouble."

"No trouble. I just want to know if I am."

"Well—" she sighed again. "What am I supposed to say to that? I think you did things you shouldn't have done. I think you permitted things to be done in your name that shouldn't have been done. I didn't approve of them. So I left. I haven't changed my mind about them. They still disturb me, very much. I think what you ought to do now is stay out of it. Orrin has a right to it. The convention decided for the President and Orrin, let Orrin have it. He's the logical choice of the opinion that really,

I think, represents a majority of the country. Why should you revive all the bitterness and hatred now? Haven't we had enough of it in the last couple of months? Aren't you satisfied?"

He was silent for a moment while all sorts of angrily defensive things came to mind and were rejected. Finally he spoke, more quietly than he had thought he could.

"That isn't really very fair. I haven't been 'satisfied' with the bitterness. It's been an inevitable accompaniment of the kind of commitment Harley and Orrin made for us overseas. These adventures aren't popular, you know. People *are* bitter about Panama and Gorotoland. It seems to them to be the Korea-Vietnam pattern all over again. Inevitably it gets into politics. I can't help it if those who are bitter want me in the White House. They have to have some hope that things will improve. I can't turn my back on them when they believe in me."

"It's marvelous," she said in a musing tone that robbed it somewhat of hurt, "how the Jasons can always rationalize what they want to do. As I see it, the convention reached a decision. The bitter people have lost. Why don't you encourage them to accept it and join ranks with the rest? Why keep trying to split the country apart? Who does it help, except those who hate America?"

"Ceil," he said quietly, "now you're not being rational. I'm not 'trying to split the country apart.' It is split apart. I'm trying to heal it again."

Once more there was silence from "Vistazo." When she spoke it was in a tired and dismissive tone that re-awoke all the uncertain terrors that had surrounded him when she fled the convention.

"Well . . . I'm sorry I called. Obviously it's too late for you to back out now, and obviously you don't want to.

So there's nothing I can do. Is President Abbott going to support you?"

"I would consider it unlikely," he said, diverted for a second back to politics; and then, the terrors breaking through in a way that quite surprised him, self-assured Jason that he was, "Ceil, Ceil! I wish you were here!"

"So do I," she said quietly. "But I can't, for now."

"What will you do?" he asked, and his voice was trembling again, though he fought desperately to control it. "Stay down there, or"—suddenly he sounded desperately unsure—"You aren't going to really leave me, are you?"

"I expect not," she said, after a moment. "After all, you're my husband and I love you."

"You do?" he asked humbly. "I'm not—very sure, right now."

"Let me think a little. I need the quiet. I'm going to take Trumpet and go riding over the hills this afternoon. Then I may go to the beach for a while with the Macombers. They're going to be next door all week, so tomorrow I may go again. I'll read some and rest some. Don't worry about me. The staff is taking good care of me and the press doesn't know I'm here, so I'm not being bothered with that. We can just rock along for a while the way we are. It will probably be good for both of us."

"Not for me," he said, but her response was back to bantering.

"Oh, yes. The candidate may suffer but the man may profit. And I too. Goodbye, my darling. Have a good lunch to make up for the skimpy breakfast."

"Ceil," he said, hating himself for asking, but knowing he must, "will you refuse my calls if I try to reach you?"

"Oh, no," she said quietly. "Never. Call whenever you want to. I'll be here."

After that, he was not too prepared for his sister when she called five minutes later, bright and ebullient, from Washington. But he decided to talk to her because it would keep him from succumbing to the black melancholy into which Ceil's call was threatening to plunge him.

This was a new thing for him. Ceil's striking blonde beauty and honest personality had meant many things to him over the years, but she had never had this effect on him before. He had always felt that in the last analysis she needed him rather more than he needed her. Suddenly this was no longer true. It was odd and unsettling.

For this mood Patsy, if not an absolute antidote, was at least a jolt. She was obviously off and running about something.

"DARLING," she said, "you'll never GUESS what I'm going to do."

"I don't dare."

"No, seriously, now, it's going to be such a help to you. You MUST listen seriously."

"I will," he said, "but I won't promise anything."

But after he heard what she had in mind, he thought for several moments and then told her to go ahead; an indication, perhaps, that he still was not functioning quite normally, in the aftermath of the strange convention.

Left to himself again, he contemplated the cool, dark lawns and the stately trees for a while longer and then tried once more to call Bob Leffingwell, now, presumably, returned to his home in Arlington, Virginia, across the Potomac from Washington. He did so fully aware of the probable mood of the director of the President's Commission on Administrative Reform, whom he had last seen three days ago when they had parted in mutual bitterness and dislike. Bob Leffingwell had served him faithfully as campaign manager up to the point when violence got out of hand at the Cow Palace. Then he had resigned without any pretense of concealing his horror and contempt. His next appearance had been on the podium when he had started the convention stampede by nominating President Hudson and taking nearly half the New York delegation with him.

This had brought him the automatic condemnation of that professionally liberal world which had endorsed him so vigorously when he and Orrin Knox were having their historic battle over his nomination to be Secretary of State. But it had brought him a strange sort of regeneration in the minds of all those good citizens who felt that his action somehow canceled out his childish and dreadful mistake when he had lied to the Senate Foreign Relations Committee about his foolish youthful connections with Communism. Now he was being subjected to a steady stream of withering scorn from such as Walter Dobius, The Greatest Publication, *Newsweek,* the *Post,* the *In-Group Quarterly,* the *Saturday Review* and all their gallant band of brothers. But this was counterbalanced and perhaps outweighed by the sober and generally respectful reappraisals that were coming from less partisan and more responsible sources.

Bob Leffingwell at the moment, Governor Jason realized, was riding rather high again. He was once more respectable with that great group of independent voters in the center who decide most elections. The man who could persuade him to come over to his side would have gained a powerful asset. Particularly if he were the same man whom Bob Leffingwell had so dramatically repudiated only seventy-six hours ago.

At first blush, Ted knew, this would seem to many a strange flip-flop for Bob. But all it required to make it easy, in the sometimes rather fantastic atmosphere of American politics, was the right tone and the right style. Bob could say—Ted already had his statement blocked out for him—that now that President Hudson had been so tragically taken from the scene, he could not in all honesty support Secretary Knox for the Presidential nomination. He could say that his support of President Hudson had been essentially personal; that he had been further persuaded to support the President by the unfortunate trend to violence that the Jason campaign had seemed to be taking; that he now had the personal assurance of Governor Jason that this trend had developed without the Governor's knowledge or approval and would not occur again; and that he accordingly could now with a clear conscience return to support of the Governor, whose policies of sober negotiation and peaceful compromise in foreign affairs were, and always had been, much more satisfactory than the dangerous and ill-advised military adventures of Secretary Knox.

It could be done, and easily, and out of it Bob Leffingwell could hold his new-found conservative support and at the same time regain the support of his temporarily hostile friends of the professionally liberal persuasion. He could appear to be an honestly troubled man who was now confronted with the opportunity to reassess his position.

Hopefully, this would be an accurate description of his present state of mind. A humble and apologetic call from the Governor might be just what was needed to bring him over. Somehow Ted had to find him. When the phone rang ten times without answer in Arlington, he hung up; but five minutes later he called the switchboard and gave instructions that the number was to be tried every half hour until he said to stop.

I am probably, Bob Leffingwell thought, one of the few people in the Potomac basin at this moment who are foolish enough to sit outside; but his lawn, too, was green and shaded, and the tulip trees and dogwood gave it an illusion of coolness. At least it was cooler than the city across the river that shimmered and danced before him, seeming to expand and contract and expand again, as he sat staring at it thoughtfully from a chaise lounge by the pool. Washington almost seemed to float suspended in the haze, evanescent, mysterious, perhaps an illusion, perhaps not even there save in the harried minds of those whose lives revolved around it.

For a moment he was amused by the conceit, but then it seemed to him that it was almost no conceit at all but the reality. What a mirage it was, that city, and how feverishly it could be conquered or changed or shattered or rebuilt in the hectic imaginings of those who sought in it their fame and fortune. Was it really that all-dominating, really that all-important? Wasn't it perhaps something that was created at embassy receptions, in parties at Dolly Munson's, in Press Club gossip, in the endless arguments of Capitol Hill that changed but never changed, in the endless jockeying for position, political or social or financial, that occupied the waking energies, the dreams, the hopes and the substance of many fiercely brilliant and ambitious people? Where did illusion end and reality begin in the Washington he knew—not the

Washington of the dark streets and the steadily rising crime rate and the poverty and the drudgery and the ugliness and the filth, but the dream-city, beautiful and stately, that still guarded and gave form to the shining ideals and worried hopes of a confused, uncertain, basically decent and still goodhearted people?

Was it reality now, that his telephone should be ringing, and that he should have a pretty good idea of who was trying to reach him? Was that the sort of reality that mattered to the black families on the dirty streets tucked away behind the magnificent avenues, was that what the knifer or the robber or the rapist thought about as he moved through Rock Creek Park or Capitol Hill or along the Tidal Basin in search of the unwary and the unattended, was that the kind of reality they were concerned about in Lafayette Park? Or was it just a reality that existed in some precious, fragile world somewhere on some special Cloud 9, kept up there by an exercise in mass illusion on the part of all the people who knew their dream-city had to be kept suspended in the air because they would all fall with it if it were not?

He sighed and an expression almost of distaste crossed his face. The two cities were one. The Cabinet member who dined at Dolly's tonight could be called away by a telephone call concerning the latest racial riot, the shadows that drifted through the parks could be rescued or driven into the ground by what they might decide in Congress, the lovely homes in Georgetown and other gracious places would stand solid on their foundations only as long as those who lived in the dirty streets and alleys could be convinced that someone was actively trying to help them. The illusionists could keep their shining city aloft only as long as the realists found their ugly one getting better. And salvation in the ugly city depended, whether its residents knew it or not, upon the decisions of those who walked the shining streets. They were locked in dreadful embrace and neither could be free of the other.

Of course it mattered to all of them who were calling Bob Leffingwell on the telephone. It might very well be the next President of the United States, and in a thousand ways subtle and not so subtle they would all be affected to the end of their days by who he was and what he did.

But for all that, Bob Leffingwell had no intention at the moment of answering the persistent ringing that came at regular intervals faintly from the house. Whether it be Governor Jason or Secretary Knox or the shrewd old Congressional veteran who now had the power, he just didn't have much stomach for a long, exhausting conversation with any of them. He was aware of his own advantages at the moment, and the longer he kept himself secluded and aloof, the stronger they would become. There was no reason to get involved sooner than he had to.

In a sense there was no reason to get involved at all. Direct participation in politics had not been Robert A. Leffingwell's habit. At least, he reflected with a cynicism to match theirs, that was the reputation carefully built up for him over two decades by all his powerful friends of the communications world who had done so much for his career up to three days ago, and now were turned against him so implacably. How savagely they were howling for his scalp! Or rather, how smoothly and suavely, not howling, not raising their voices, just turning the knife and using the nasty phrase, were they scientifically trying to destroy him.

Just today, for instance, he had seen *Newsweek's* final convention issue. It had contained a boxed insert, "The Strange Case of Robert A. Leffingwell," which was a classic of its kind. Puzzled, concerned, wistfully sad and determinedly damaging, it had said in part:

"Minor highlight (Minor? Bob Leffingwell thought dryly. When I was the one who started the real stampede to Harley?) of an already chaotic convention came when Leffingwell, up to that moment apparently an enthusiastic supporter of Ted Jason, abruptly abandoned him to lead nearly half the New York delegation into the Hudson camp. Explanation for the strange switch by Bob Leffingwell—who lost the Secretaryship of State a year ago because his veracity about a youthful Communist fling proved unequal to the task of testifying before the Senate Foreign Relations Committee—was perhaps best summed up by one disillusioned liberal delegate. ('*Unidentified*,' Bob Leffingwell remarked aloud. 'Description supplied by me.') This observer, who had watched the Leffingwell career with undisguised admiration for twenty years, was heard to remark glumly: 'Apparently the White House can out-promise anybody.' Best guess on the new Leffingwell job: director of foreign aid, not too far from the State Department he could have had if it hadn't been for those little red lies."

One week before, when he had been managing the campaign of Ted Jason, who represented an anti-war position harshly critical of the United States Government, the story had been different:

"One of the major elements in the Jason convention drive this week was the brilliant leadership provided by Robert A. Leffingwell, long an unimpeachable liberal of the finest type. Aided by a staff as dedicated and selfless as himself, Bob Leffingwell's skill and integrity appeared to be pushing the Governor into a well-nigh insurmountable lead. . . . "

How transparent they all were in a certain segment of the media, he thought with a genuine contempt. How obvious to everyone but themselves, in their ideological enthusiasms, their switches, their twitches, their self-centered, self-interested hating and loving that colored everything they wrote and broadcast. How pathetic, really: for they were heirs of a great tradition who did not have the integrity to keep it pure.

Whether they were really hurting him, he could not assess accurately at the moment. He rather thought not, because aside from that small but powerful clique, a different tone was beginning to come into the press.

What he had done a year ago was at last being put into perspective. He was being, finally, forgiven.

Not that he could ever forgive himself, of course, for lying to the Foreign Relations Committee; and not that any perspective could ever erase from his mind and heart the wound he had given himself when he let desire for the office of Secretary of State override his natural decencies. But at least, he told himself, the public image was improving; and after all, in this age of mirrors, wasn't that all that mattered?

After a moment he told himself with a little smile that this was too cynical. His desire to become Secretary of State, after all, had included a purpose. It was far more than ambition for office. He honestly did believe that he could negotiate with the Communists in such a way as to encourage peace—or whatever that uneasy state of non-fighting accommodation might be that the world could accept as peace in this unhappy century. He honestly did feel that he could help to save America from disasters he believed a more belligerent policy would bring about.

Like so many who meet head-on in the never-ending struggle to determine who will control the great republic's destinies, he was as convinced of his righteousness and idealism as his opponents were of theirs.

And yet he had nominated Harley Hudson, the man who had met Communist imperialism as staunchly as a Truman by sending troops into Gorotoland and Panama the moment the Communists moved. He had flown in the face of the great agonized howl that had ascended and was still wailing up from campuses, churches, ad-takers in the New York *Times*, marchers, demonstrators, emergency committees, professional peace-lovers and the world of Walter Dobius, and had supported the man they so violently and viciously opposed. He had deliberately invited their violence and viciousness upon himself. Why?

Granting that motives were mixed and many, and in Washington triply so, he supposed that basically it must have been because he was grateful to Harley Hudson for saving him from the depths of his defeat by the Senate for Secretary of State. Harley had created the President's Commission on Administrative Reform and put him at the head of it, and the process of recovery had begun. In return he had given good service in the past year, recommending many reforms in the Executive Branch and being fortunate enough to see one or two of them adopted by Congress. Cautiously he had begun to venture out again in the world of ideas, writing a few articles, accepting a few speaking engagements. Eagerly his friends in the news media had come to his support, rapidly they had begun to rebuild his shattered reputation. While deploring his judgment in lying to the Senate, they had nonetheless stoutly defended his basic good character and his long liberal record. And then, in their grossly slanted and bitterly unfair coverage of the wars in Gorotoland and Panama, they had set out to destroy the man who had saved him. This more than anything, he felt now, had probably inspired his backing of President Hudson.

That, and perhaps dislike of Governor Jason. He had accepted the chairmanship of Ted's campaign with serious misgivings, and only because Harley up to the last moment had maintained that he would not run. In a series of moves, all shrewdly conceived and cleverly timed, Ted had laid claim upon the liberal position. It had been an easy game, the kind a man who has no responsibility and great ambition can always play with a busy and preoccupied President who has the world on his shoulders. He had flitted around a harassed and harried Executive like an angry wasp, stinging at will.

Did Harley take a position on some major issue? Ted could always make a speech taking one a little more extreme. Did Harley act honestly on the basis of the facts as he knew them? Ted could always rise with a high moral indignation to demand that he do something else. Did Harley have to balance every word and move against all his national and global responsibilities? Ted only had to go on "Meet the Press" and make fine, free-swinging generalizations that hinted ominous things about the President and glorious things about himself.

It was all very easy for a man unscrupulous enough and rich enough and irresponsible enough; and Ted had turned out to be all three. As a result, powerful publications and commentators had flocked to his side and dutifully given him the Big Build-up they always give any Presidential candidate they have decided to support. Bob Leffingwell had soon found what he had suspected all along, that behind the smiling candidate there lay a ruthless ego and a driving ambition that did not know when to put on the brakes. "The Shame of The Convention," the *Wall Street Journal* had called the political violence that had broken out among the Jason forces; and Bob had seen Ted allow the violence to begin and then to grow to the point where it became a monster almost uncontrollable. At that point he had left. And so the deluge of vituperation pouring on Harley had inundated him.

On one point, however, he felt that he was unassailably consistent; he had not endorsed Orrin Knox for Vice President, and indeed had withheld his vote in the final, halfhearted ballot that had confirmed Orrin's nomination. His loyalty had been to Harley only, and he had left San Francisco not knowing whether he would be able to actively support the ticket. No man had been more responsible than Orrin, then senior Senator from Illinois, in rallying the Senate to defeat the Leffingwell nomination. He had long ago conceded Orrin's sincerity in the matter, but that did not make it any easier to forgive him. That, he suspected, he would probably never do.

So now, he told himself quizzically as he stood up with

a restive air and walked to the edge of the pool, he had a problem. He took a deep breath and dived in; swam the length of the pool underwater; came up, took another deep breath, plunged under and swam back. He surfaced, puffing and blowing, and climbed out. Helen-Anne Carrew stared at him blandly from the chaise lounge.

"Oh, hi," he said, drawing up another from under the trees. "I didn't hear you arrive. How about a drink?"

"Gin and tonic will do," she said, and looked pointedly at the house. "Nobody home?"

"Just us squirrels and cardinals," he said pleasantly. "And don't be so subtle. I'll be right back. . . . Now," he said, stretching out comfortably and giving her an appraising glance, "what's on your mind?"

"Sweetie," she said cheerfully, "an old harridan like me has nothing on her mind but news, news, news. I must say you do mix a good drink. What are you going to do about it?"

"Nobody can ruin gin and tonic," he said comfortably; and then grinned at her expectant expression. "Which 'it' of the many one must do something about are you referring to?"

"Well," she said, "there is, A, an empty house, and, B, a Presidential nomination—"

"Oh, those," he said with an elaborate yawn. I thought you meant something really important, such as your distinguished ex-husband's column this morning."

"Walter Dobius," she said firmly, "is out of his mind. Ignore him."

"How can we?" he asked, making a sweeping, ironic gesture with his glass toward shimmering Washington. "Everybody but *everybody* listens to Walter."

"Trying to ease you back into the Jason camp, isn't he?"

He shrugged.

"I'm here to find out if you're going to go," she said. "Three people I thought I'd check on today. One is Ceil and one is Lucille Hudson and the third is you. If I can pin you all down I'll have a hell of a column for the dear old Washington *Star*."

He smiled.

"Any luck?"

"Ceil is charming and evasive. She did talk to me, because she said I was the only reporter with brains enough to figure out where she was, but that's about all she said. I don't know what the situation is in that household. Any more," she added blandly, "than I know what it is in this one."

"Louise is in New Hampshire at Lake Chocorua," he said with an equal blandness. "I thought you knew."

"Mmmm-hmmm."

"And of course you can't reach Lucille."

She shook her head.

"Of course not. The White House is tighter than a drum, naturally." A sad expression touched her face. "You know, this thing is really awful. Really *awful*. Poor Harley, and all those innocent people—"

He frowned.

"Were they? All?"

"I don't know," she said, frowning too. "Lots of rumors going around, of course."

He nodded with some distaste.

"I can smell them clear across the river."

"Me, too. There was something fishy. That plane has

made ten thousand trips and never had any trouble. Why did it go down with Harley, and just at this particular time?"

"Unanswered questions," he said, "to echo down the centuries along with the others. The Presidential Mysteries. . . . Well, if Ceil won't talk and you can't reach the First Lady, what are you going to do?"

"Lover," she said with her ribald chuckle, "I'm going to hold you under water until you tell Helen-Anne everything. First of all, about your wife—"

"Louise is very doctrinaire," he said calmly. "She always has been. She was an intense little girl when I married her and she's intense still. You have to see that sort growing up, from campus to committee to cause, to know what I mean, but there is a certain absolutely humorless type. She's it. It goes with rimless glasses, no make-up, and the hair in a very tight bun. She's gone away because she was bitterly opposed to Harley Hudson and everything he stood for, and I nominated him. She called me Tuesday night in San Francisco and threatened to leave if I did. I did, and she has. That's all there is to that, and I'll trust you not to print a word of it, thank you very much."

"No," she said slowly, "I suppose I'd better not. Good luck with it. If that's what you want."

"I don't know what I want," he said. "At the moment, it doesn't mean anything to me. I couldn't care less. She's gone, so what. That's about the way I feel right now."

"Will she file for divorce?"

He shrugged.

"I don't know. I doubt it, at least not until the season's over at Chocorua. She enjoys that cabin."

"That's a bitter thing to say," Helen-Anne told him.

He shrugged again. "Absolutely dispassionate, I assure you. Now, about the Presidential nomination—"

"Yes," she said, "do let's get back to the Presidential nomination. First, let me mix you a drink, this time."

"OK," he said, handing her his glass. "This will be the final, for now."

"Me, too, I've got to get back and write my column after I leave here. Is everything where I can find it?"

"It's all beside the sink," he said, yawning and rubbing the back of his neck. Two cardinals flew by, busy; a squirrel pranced; the world drowsed.

"God," Helen-Anne said, handing him his drink, "am I sick to death of *Jasons!* Except Ceil, of course. She's a great lady."

"She's wonderful," he agreed. She gave him a shrewd look.

"So are you going to support her husband for President?"

"Helen-Anne," he said soberly, "to tell you the truth, I really don't know."

"Orrin's the better man."

"Yes," he said with a smile. "We all know how you feel about Orrin. Anyway, who cares what I do? I thought," he said, his eyes narrowing with pain as he remembered the violent cries of "Liar!" that had been hurled at him by the National Committeewoman from Pennsylvania, "that Mary Buttner Baffleburg pretty well took care of me at the convention."

"Mary Baffleburg is an overstuffed Pennsylvania Dutch sausage."

"But she's going to have a vote for President when the Committee meets, isn't she?"

"Perhaps. We don't know yet how the Speaker—the

President—is going to handle it. Anyway, don't downgrade yourself. You're in a good spot. They'd both love to have you on their side. You'd take the conservatives to Ted and the genuine liberals to Orrin."

"What a political hermaphrodite! Not many heterosexuals can make this claim."

"OK, joke," she said, "but I'm telling you the situation. Haven't they been trying to reach you?"

"The phone's been ringing, off and on. I haven't been answering."

"My," she remarked, "aren't we high and mighty, for a—"

"What?" he said quickly. "Liar?"

"Bob Leffingwell," she said sharply, "will you stop beating yourself over the head with that? It's *all over.* The situation has changed. You've been forgiven, to a considerable extent, so stop dramatizing yourself. Life's moving on. Get with it. . . . What I started to say," she added, more mildly, "was that you were rather high and mighty for a political has-been—and then I was going to say that really you *aren't* a political has-been—and *then* I was going to say—oh, the hell with it. If you want to sit here by your pool and feel sorry for yourself, God bless you. I've got better things to do."

And picking up her enormous handbag, from which a conglomeration of note paper, press releases and several sections of the Sunday New York *Times* threatened to spill, she stood up abruptly.

But he waved her down again.

"Helen-Anne," he said, "you stop dramatizing, too. You're about the only person I know in this town at the moment who is capable of giving me honest advice. What do you think I ought to do?"

"Well," she said, subsiding with some reluctance, "I do have better things to do than nurse wounded egos, I can tell you that. Helen-Anne is a busy girl, right now. What *I* think you should do is go and talk to Orrin Knox, if you want my frank opinion. God knows you've talked to Ted enough, but I'll bet you never have talked to Orrin—really talked to him, I mean."

"Our relations, over the years," he said with a certain wryness, "have hardly been such as to induce any boyish confidences. Before I was"—and even now, a year later, he hesitated painfully over the word—"nominated, I didn't have much occasion to see him, except at a few cocktail parties around town. And then after I was nominated, we really didn't have much opportunity for a cozy chat. And since then . . . No," he agreed thoughtfully, his eyes far away as he stared at the distant dome of the Capitol, riding like a galleon through the gentle haze, "I never have really talked to Orrin Knox."

"My advice to you is, do it," she said bluntly. "Unless, of course, you're going to go crawling back to Ted."

"No," he said with a sudden sharp annoyance that made her think perhaps she had gone too far, "I'm not going to go crawling back to Ted. He's doing the crawling, if anybody is. They can all come crawling, as far as I'm concerned!"

"Now you are getting too high and mighty," she told him soberly, once more gathering up her gear, yanking a comb through her tangled silver-gray hair, rising to her rather dumpy, ungainly stance. "I think you'd better have another drink Bob, and then I think you'd better start answering the telephone, and then I think you'd better give some serious thought to going to see a few people.

And not in the mood you expressed just now, but with a reasonable degree of humility. Pride and arrogance ruin more people and thwart more plans in this town than anything else, I've always thought, and you may think you're humble but you sure as hell don't sound it. I think you'd better be, if you really want to contribute anything to getting this God-awful situation straightened out." She gave him a quick, shrewd look. "I don't think you've really learned anything. You just think you have."

For a long moment, staring at her with those handsome gray eyes that always contributed so much to the picture of the very parfit gentil knight of government that his admirers liked to think he was, he said nothing. Then he stood up, smiled, and held out his hand.

"Helen-Anne—" he said. "Old friend—old buddy—aide and adviser through thick and thin—"

"Oh, go to hell," she said, batting aside his hand but beginning to smile in spite of herself.

"—I think you have a point. I really do. I shall treasure it. I shall sit for a while and think—no more drinking, though, that might defeat the whole purpose—and then I shall go humbly to the telephone and humbly on my rounds, and we shall see what happens. . . . And you," he added, again offering his hand, which she took this time with a firm pressure, "don't write one single solitary thing about what I may or may not do, OK?"

"Damn!" she said. "The stories I've killed for my country."

"I know it," he said, quite seriously. "As one American, I appreciate it."

"Now you're getting maudlin." But she looked pleased. "I can't avoid speculating some, sweetie, everybody is. Tell me what the facts are when you can, OK?"

"I will," he said, taking her arm and walking her around the house to her car. "I'm sorry I haven't been able to give you more today."

"You've given me quite a bit. I hope it's been mutual."

"Oh, it has," he said, lightly but with a serious note underneath. "It has. I hope you find something for that column."

"It doesn't have to be done until tomorrow, but I want to get it out of the way today because there's a lot of funeral coverage I'm going to have to help with, starting tomorrow morning."

"I know," he said, suddenly somber.

"Maybe—" she said, deliberately breaking the mood before it could depress them too much, "Maybe I'll call Patsy. She's always good for a horselaugh when I haven't anything else to write about."

But a few minutes later, when she was back over the river and out southeast in the deserted city room of the Star, she found Patsy singularly uncooperative. "I think you're working on something, girl," she told her. Patsy only laughed in a deliberately annoying way and refused to be drawn out, beyond saying in a dreamy voice, "Oh, I might just think of something to liven things up a bit." But Helen-Anne was not an old hand at the game for nothing.

Like any experienced Washington correspondent, she could make bricks without straw when she had to.

"In a Washington hushed and saddened by the tragic death of Harley M. Hudson," she typed swiftly, "politics, as always, takes no holiday. Even as the President's body was being prepared for formal lying-in-state at the White House Tuesday, and at the Capitol Wednesday morning, speculation was already rife today that Robert A. Leffingwell, key figure in the convention just concluded, may be even more of a key figure in the Presidential nominating yet to come.

"Governor Edward M. Jason of California was believed to be trying desperately to reach this glamorous figure, who only three days ago—"

But when Bob Leffingwell, after another dip in the pool and a few more minutes of somber contemplation of the great white city sprawled along the Potomac, went finally to answer the insistent telephone, it was not the Jason he expected who was on the line.

"This is Ceil," she said quietly from California. "I want to give you some advice."

"Lots of people do," he said, carefully refraining from surprise. "I value yours more than most. Fire away."

"This is Walter," he said bluntly from "Salubria." "I want to give you some advice."

"I'm not in the market," Governor Jason said coldly from his office in Sacramento. "Why don't you call me after the funeral?"

"Now, see here," Walter Dobius said with a sudden surge of anger. "This is important."

"Everything you say is important, Walter. It's the one thing we're all agreed on."

"I think you should call Bob Leffingwell," Walter said, trying to control his irritation and managing with some difficulty. "I think he may be able to help you."

"It never would have occurred to me," Ted said in a startled voice. "How's the third party coming, Walter?"

There was a silence in Leesburg. Finally "America's greatest philosopher-statesman of the press" (as the New

York *Times* had called him on the twenty-fifth anniversary of his column a couple of months ago) spoke in a tightly controlled, level voice.

"I would not want you to think," he said carefully, "that my support or that of any of my colleagues is automatic, Ted. It can always be changed."

The Governor snorted.

"To Orrin Knox? Now tell me another."

"Ted—" Walter Dobius began with a rising inflection, but the Governor cut him short and it was quite apparent that they now had to deal with a Jason who had recovered and never intended to lose control again.

"You have nowhere else to go, Walter, and all of you from Manhattan to the Golden Gate are perfectly aware of it. You aren't going to support Orrin. You are going to support me. And on my terms. That's the fact of it. Right, Walter?"

Again there was silence, broken, the Governor noted with a grim satisfaction, by a little heavy breathing from "Salubria." At last Walter Dobius spoke in tones even heavier and more pompous than he usually used.

"You are insufferable. Absolutely insufferable."

"But the great hope of America and world peace, Walter," Ted Jason said with a savage irony. "Never forget that."

And hung up, which, in the rarified world he inhabited, of columns that told his country what to do, public speeches that influenced large segments of press and public, and sagely given private advice to kings and potentates who looked to him as perhaps America's major editorial voice, did not often happen to the man whom Lyndon Johnson had long ago nicknamed "Walter Wonderful."

The conversation only demonstrated, he told himself

after his anger had subsided somewhat and he could sit back reflectively once more at the desk from which so many significant words had gone forth to influence the world, what could be expected from a man of the Governor's devious and unreliable character. Ted had always been too independent. Walter had known in his heart that it was a chancy game to rely upon him, but there had been no alternative to the insanely dangerous war policies of the President and Orrin Knox.

At least Governor Jason represented a policy of negotiation and peace; at least he genuinely did believe in a "new spirit toward the Soviets," a "détente between East and West," a "thaw in relations between the Communist and capitalist worlds," and all those other phrases, comforting to the timid, however unfounded in fact, which were so beloved of Walter's world from New York to San Francisco.

He was also Governor of the largest state in the Union, which was a rather important factor, too.

It was important enough, in fact, so that even Walter and his friends could not very well do anything about it. Like Ted Jason or despise him—and some, including Walter, now inclined strongly to the latter—there he was. A political reality of the highest magnitude, once more in command of himself and the situation which confronted him.

To that situation, Walter reflected after a few more moments of calming down, he, Walter, must now apply himself with all the skill and influence he possessed. That this was great and far-reaching, he knew. That it really "controlled" the press, only his more naïve countrymen claimed.

There were those who, reading some criticism of

Walter in some unfashionable publication or book, would say, "I just don't believe that one man could have that much control over the press." But no intelligent critic, of course, ever claimed that Walter did. Walter was influential because he was a member in high standing of that small group of columnists, commentators, newspapers, magazines and television programs that largely influence and affect the general thinking of the American nation. He did not "control" his peers any more than they controlled him. What he did do, and with great effectiveness, was sometimes to originate, and sometimes to clarify and synthesize, the major ideas and emotions they held in common.

Thus a few weeks ago he had called together The Greatest Publication That Ever Was, the *Times*, the *Post*, *Newsweek*, *Look*, CBS, NBC and a few others, for one of those exchanges of ideas that quite often precede the selection of the Presidential candidate they will all support. In some previous elections this consensus had been reached, not at any formal gathering, but rather in a series of informal dinners, cocktail party meetings, transcontinental telephone calls, even casual meetings at golf courses, clubs, public events, at which the general desire had gradually been formed and articulated. Walter's little meeting had probably not been necessary, so deeply committed had they already become to Governor Jason. But he had a sense of neatness that required it; and, as the general director of the *Post* remarked dryly afterward to his crony, Associate Supreme Court justice Thomas Buckmaster Davis, "Walter's ego needed it, too."

But, as always, he had not "controlled" them. He had simply stated, in the clearest, most powerful and most widely syndicated form, the thoughts and purposes toward which the policy makers were moving within those citadels of journalistic power from which so many decrees and decisions affecting America's ultimate destiny were handed down to a public apathetic because it was simply so overwhelmed by the furious onward rush of national and world events.

"It's too much for me," people said. *"I just can't understand it any more. I just try not to think about it."*

So the public, for the most part, accepted what Walter and his world had to tell them, without question and without the native skepticism that in earlier days had been one of the saving strengths of America. Now it was no longer, "Show me!" and, "Says who?" Now, Walter sometimes told himself with a superior contempt, it was a blank look, a dull shake of the head, and a Mortimer Snerd-like, "Ddhhhuuuhhh? Izzatt *so?*" which greeted the pronouncements of himself and his friends. It was not surprising if they often had a field day.

But this, he knew as he stared out thoughtfully upon the suffocating afternoon, rested upon a flimsy basis. You could never, even at this late stage in many decades of conditioning, quite count upon the American majority to be supine and placid. There still were unruly skepticisms that popped up now and then, there could still be a sudden disconcerting tendency to demand real answers, there still could be an almost atavistic, instinctive throwback to the days of, "Says who?" And when that happened, Walter and his world were in trouble. Voters didn't vote the way they were supposed to, the country didn't respond as dutifully as it should to carefully calculated words, photographs, headlines, broadcasts.

An old independence could come abruptly and disconcertingly back.

So you had to be clever and shrewd and persistent and never, ever, lose sight of the main objective, which was to persuade the country to think and behave the way you, as superior and intelligent beings, knew that it should and must if America was to be saved from her follies and peace was to be secured for the world.

How to do this through the medium of Ted Jason was now, once more, the problem. The convention, dominated by Harley Hudson and Orrin Knox, had perhaps been hopeless from the start (Walter could never admit to himself, though certain of his disgusted colleagues were admitting it to themselves, that he and they had perhaps been responsible for the growing tension that had finally brought revulsion and cost Ted the nomination). But now the crash of Air Force One had given them all a new chance.

There must be no slip-ups this time. For all his repulsive independence and disrespect, Ted should and must be the candidate. It must be handled with the greatest astuteness and skill.

He could almost have groaned with annoyance and dismay—an uncharacteristic "God damn it!" did surprisingly break the muffled silence of the cool, dark study—when he saw a car come up the curving drive and stop under the classic white portico. Out of it came the last people on earth he would expect to show astuteness and skill about anything. His first impulse was to call Roosevelt and Arbella on the intercom and tell them to say he wasn't home. But then the longtime Washington reporter's practicality returned. Whatever he thought of them, and however dangerous he thought them to be to the kind of political operation needed now, there was no doubt that in Senator Fred Van Ackerman of the Committee on Making Further Offers for a Russian Truce (COMFORT); LeGage Shelby, director of Defenders of Equality for You (DEFY); and Rufus Kleinfert, Knight Kommander of the Konference on Efforts to Encourage Patriotism (KEEP), there were represented the three main elements in the country whose strange political bedfellowship provided the principal foundation of the Jason campaign.

He sighed, braced himself and went slowly down the stairs with a stolid, unhurried dignity and a certain trepidation he would not have cared to admit, to answer Fred Van Ackerman's imperious knocking.

Sometimes she read. Sometimes she dozed. But mostly, as the great house lay silent around her, the former First Lady of the United States thought.

Earlier, the White House physician and his soft-spoken young assistant had tried to give her sedatives, but she had refused them, aside from one tranquilizer which had seemed to stop her tendency to burst into tears when she didn't expect it. She had thought she would be cried out by now, so bitterly had she wept most of last night, but all the way across the continent this morning it had welled up again every few minutes. Despite the worried sympathy of Bob and Dolly Munson, she had not been able to stop until just before they landed in Washington to face the barrage of cameras and newsmen. Then the inner iron that lay beneath the pink-cheeked, roly-poly fluffiness had come to her aid and she had managed to get down the steps and into the waiting limousine, with its little fender flags at half-mast, without breaking down again.

After that she had been engulfed in a curious, glacial mood that had continued, with one exception, all afternoon. For the most part she had remained in bed in the family quarters on the second floor. But once she had felt an irrational desire to find some old scrapbook, stored, she thought, in a closet on the far side of the mansion. She had slipped out, aided by Dolly, who had taken up vigil in the library, and had gone looking. But she had not remained long enough to find it. No sooner had they reached the east wing than they had heard a muffled hammering below.

"Oh, of course," she had said in a distant voice. "We're over the East Room. They must be setting up the catafalque." Dolly had caught her just as she started to faint, and when she came to, she was back in bed. That time she had cried again for quite a long time. Finally she had stopped. Now, in a curious in-between world in which she realized but could not realize that her husband was dead, she looked out over the lawns and trees to the Ellipse, the Washington Monument, the slow, lazy river and the gentle rise of Virginia beyond.

How many times had she paused to enjoy that view in the year and three months—was it really only a year and three months?—of her husband's Presidency. (She was not yet able to think of him by name. It was "my husband" or "the President" or "he." To think or say, "Harley," would have opened some final chasm of desolation and bereavement she was not yet strong enough to face.) She could remember their first meal in this house, shortly after seven o'clock on the evening after he had been sworn in, and how tense they were as the full awareness of his awesome new responsibilities had overwhelmed them. But after they had finished and were standing for the first time on the balcony looking out upon this same scene, he had put an arm around her shoulders and given her a sudden squeeze.

"Well, Mother," he had said with a slow smile, "I guess were going to find out if a simple, homespun, all-American boy from Grand Rapids can do it, aren't we?"

And abruptly the burden had lifted and she had said, "You know perfectly well he can. I've never doubted it for a minute."

"There are some who have," he said, the smile broadening. "Including, I must confess, me."

"Well, I haven't," she said firmly, and he squeezed her again

"I know. That's why I don't feel half as scared right now as I probably ought to."

"You won't have time to feel scared at all," she said. "You'll be too busy."

And so it had come about, for he had been whirled immediately into the Geneva conference with the Russians that his predecessor had agreed to just before his death. And after that crisis there had been a thousand others, major and minor, foreign and domestic, culminating in the crises in Panama and Gorotoland which he had met with unhesitating firmness despite all the voices of anguish, anger and alarm that had welled up against him.

Press attacks, television attacks, riots, demonstrations, flag-burnings, draft-dodgings, Congressional hearings, statements, speeches, petitions, full-page ads in the New

York *Times,* and the savage, relentless tide of Washington gossip that always attempts to destroy any President who dares do anything counter to what the nation's self-appointed guardians in their self-righteous wisdom deem best—all of these had descended in full measure upon her husband and his Secretary of State. He had worried about it a lot she knew that; he had studied and pondered and even, on a good many occasions, prayed. But when his basic decisions were taken, he did not look back. By so much had he grown, in this tragic house that held so much of history; this unique, mysterious, unknowable domicile that took the men who came to it and transformed them irrevocably into beings far different from what they had been when they entered its doors for the first time as master.

Master? No man was ever really master of this house for long. Too many echoes were in the air, too many predecessors looked over his shoulder, too many past decisions kept him company as he faced his dreadful responsibilities. Now and again he might assert himself, use the fearful power that was his to change or initiate events. But before long events regained control and he found he was merely their instrument. He found he must start over, or change course, or do something else than he had at first believed he should—and could.

Her husband's predecessor had set in motion certain things: who knew how he would have finished them? Her husband had to decide, bound by what his predecessor had already done. Her husband had set in motion certain things: who knew how he would have finished them? His successor would have to decide, bound by what her husband had already done. Certain long-range tendencies appeared in the lives of nations, came to fruition, ran their course, subsided. It did not matter a great deal who attempted to change them along the way: they began, had their time, passed. Presidents, potentates, chairmen of "peoples' republics," possessed only the option to decide a few details; and while details sometimes could be fearfully important, the basic river of history flowed on between the banks predestined by the shortcomings of human nature, and would not be deflected.

Thus, no matter who had been in the White House, America would have opposed the imperialistic aggressions of Communism—the sheer instinct of national survival, as long as it lasted, would have determined that. It might have been done with more skill in this instance, less grace in that, but it would have been done, and with just about the same blundering, dogged determination. Even Governor Jason, had he ever the chance, would proceed along basically the same lines. Even Governor Jason, the hated and despised, whom she now, in some blind, irrational way that had no foundation in fact so far as she knew, considered responsible for her husband's death.

Ted Jason and all his ambitious, ruthless schemes . . . her husband had been right to keep him off the ticket, right to thwart his ambitions, right to shut him out of government. He was a bad, bad man and he had helped to kill Harley.

He had helped to kill Harley.

And suddenly she began to cry as she had not cried before, silent, wracking, terrible; knowing, in some dimly grasped way that she had hardly time or ability to understand, in the depths of grief to which she now de-

98

scended, that when it was over she would do what she could to assure that everything would be the way Harley wanted it.

Harley Hudson might be gone but Lucille Hudson was still here; and even as silent weeping gave way to strangled, grotesque, horrible sounds and she bit at a pillow to try to keep them muffled, she understood that she was not going back to Grand Rapids. She was going to stay right here and continue to be a part of Washington for his sake, in any way she could.

"Secretary Knox!" the photographers cried. "Secretary and Mrs. Knox—Senator—could we have you over here, please? Would you just come over this way a little, please? Please, Mr. Secretary!"

"Do you mind?" he murmured, looking down at Beth: comfortable, solid, unpretentious, somewhat windblown, obviously tired, but with her keen eyes amused as they so often were by the imperatives of prominence.

"Have I ever?" she inquired with a smile, and suddenly he knew, as he always did when she was with him, that everything was going to be all right.

"No," he said with an answering smile that the *Post's* photographer captured, but which was not used. ("It makes the bastard look too likable!" the general director protested with a wry chuckle, tossing it into the discard basket and substituting one that made him look worried, disheveled and tense.)

"Very well," she said. "Strike a pose, Senator."

And so they did, and were photographed standing near the terminal entrance. CANDIDATE AND WIFE, said *Life* in its next issue. THE EVER-HOPEFULS, said *Look*.

In the State Department limousine, as the driver knifed it skillfully through the home-going Sunday traffic in the softly dying twilight, they were recognized twice and each time the neighboring car almost went off the road. After that they sat back as far as they could and at first were silent. But when they went over the bridge and entered the city, she gave him a thoughtful look and asked with a smile,

"How are you bearing up, Mr. Secretary? All right?"

"I'm managing," he said. She squeezed his hand.

"That's good. I'd hate to think you were being bothered by anything."

"It *is* damned annoying—" he began with an explosive emphasis and then stopped with a sudden wry grin. "Hank," he said, employing the nickname he had first begun to use years ago at the University of Illinois when she was Elizabeth Henry, "this is going to build up into the damnedest foofooraw you ever saw."

"Considering the number of foofooraws you've been in," she said, "I find it hard to believe that this is going to be the damnedest. However, what can I do to help liven it up?"

"Just stand by me," he said, the grin fading. "I expect I'm going to need it now more than I ever have."

"There's great doubt as to whether I will," she said solemnly. "But perhaps if you promise me a job in your new Administration—"

"All right, all right," he said relaxing into his first moment of genuine amusement since Senator Warren Strickland had called him in Carmel with the news of Harley's death. "So I'm sounding stuffy and pompous. Maybe it won't be as bad as that. But it's going to be a

100

hell of a fight. And, Hank"—and again a somber expression touched his face—"I'm getting a little tired of fighting."

"Well, I'm not," she said. "Four days at Esmé's place were just what I needed. Particularly since she called this morning and wished you luck."

"She did?" he asked in genuine surprise. "That I don't believe."

She chuckled.

"Neither did I. But it was a nice gesture. She was very vague about Ted when I asked her. I gathered she hadn't been able to reach him. Nor has anyone else."

"He seems to be in touch with the press," Orrin said dryly. "How are the kids?"

"Feeling better. Crystal's coming along fine and I think Hal has decided to remain with the human race, after all. The doctors say there can be another baby—"

"No, really?" he asked delightedly.

She nodded and squeezed his hand again.

"I thought that might put a spark back in you, Grandpa. Yes, it's apparently going to be all right, so everybody's feeling much better. Including Stanley, whom I left in charge. *He* really *doesn't* want to fight any more.

He nodded.

"I can't blame him."

"So now you need a new campaign manager."

"Any ideas?"

She gave him a quick glance.

"The same one you have, I expect."

I'm not sure I want him," he said slowly. "I'm not sure it's going to be conducted in quite the sort of atmosphere in which—"

But even as he spoke the limousine turned and moved into Pennsylvania Avenue toward the White House, and at once they became aware of police, strobe lights, television cameras, shouts and cries, a mass of shifting, surging people. As they came closer they could see that its focus was a long line of picketers, young, old, white, black, male, female, bearded, non-bearded, clean, filthy, happily intermingled and swaying in a stomping conga formation along the iron railings in front of the mansion.

Its members carried torches and banners which they displayed eagerly for the encouraging cameras— "GOODBYE, HARLEY, NO MORE WAR! . . . COMFORT SAYS: NOW'S THE TIME TO STOP THE CRIME . . . KEEP DEMANDS AN IMMEDIATE END TO OVERSEAS ENTANGLEMENTS! . . . END THE WHITE MAN'S WAR!—DEFY. . . . YOU'RE NEXT, ORRIN—ONE DOWN, ONE TO GO!"

And in measured cadence there came clearly through the soft night air the mocking, triumphant chant:

> *Air Force One,*
> *What have you done?*
> *Set us free,*
> *Tee hee hee!*

"My *God*," he said with a disgust so deep he had not known it was still there after all these years of shabby guttersnipe outburst in America, "is there no decency left in this land? *Driver!* Take us into the White House!"

"Mr. *Secretary*—" the driver began in alarm, and Beth said, "*Orrin!*"

But his face set in an implacable mask and he repeated angrily, "Take us on in. Run them down if they don't give way!"

But fortunately for all concerned, the White House police had seen them coming, recognized the car, and were already deployed in a flying wedge that opened a path to the West Gate. Through this the limousine moved swiftly, but not before others recognized them too. Stones, eggs, torches slammed against the car, an angry animal howl followed them up the drive. As they stopped beneath the portico, the chanting line converged into a mass that shoved and pushed against the railings. Wild obscenities shattered the placid evening of Pennsylvania Avenue; not for the first time nor the last, but probably never before in such a context.

As they looked back from the top of the steps they could see police deployed along the inside of the fence; see the first clouds of riot gas begin to boil; hear a single, shattering gunshot, the start and finish of a scream.

Dolly Munson met them at the door, her eyes wide with trouble and concern.

"Get inside," she said, pulling them in. "For God's sake, get inside!" The dream-city and the real city had come together, and the deceptively peaceful mood, which in Washington is never really very peaceful underneath, was peaceful no more.

5.

TWO HOURS LATER in Spring Valley—SECRETARY KNOX BESIEGED IN WHITE HOUSE, ESCAPES THROUGH UNDERGROUND PASSAGE TO EXECUTIVE OF-

FICE BUILDING, the early editions said. NEGRO DEMONSTRATOR KILLED IN ANTIWAR PROTEST—his first act was to mix himself a strong Scotch and soda and take it into the den. He had left Beth at the mansion, helping Dolly and the White House physician calm a Lucille Hudson driven almost hysterical by the noise outside. Six State Department security men had come with him and were now staked out discreetly among the trees and bushes. The neighborhood was silent and apparently deserted as midnight neared, but for all practical purposes he was besieged in his own home, too.

He took a deep breath and a deep swallow and put his head back against the well-worn top of the rocker. There he sat for what seemed to him a long time, hardly moving, hardly thinking—at least, not coherently, though a thousand things raced back and forth inside his head. None seemed to make much sense, except that if there had ever been any doubt that he would continue to seek the nomination, the riot had ended it forever. Those who had conceived the insane idea that such tactics might intimidate Orrin Knox did not know Orrin Knox. Yet why did anyone not know Orrin Knox? He had been around long enough.

It was apparent, however, that this would be a dangerous and possibly bloody business. The violence that had disgraced the convention had not died after all: it had only been sleeping for the past four days.

The employment of violence as a political weapon had never been fashionable in America, but increasingly in these last few hectic years the alien idea had been imported that the way to conduct the American democracy was with guns, riots, destruction, assassination. Rioting was no longer the happy, haphazard, idiot-child pastime of looting and burning that had characterized the middle stages of the civil rights campaign. Now it was cold-blooded, deliberate, engaged in by whites and blacks integrated at last in sickness and hatred, organized to capture the mastery of public opinion and the intimidation and downfall of government. Riots now were scientific, purposeful, political—and to the decent and the stable they were terrifying, because they harnessed the animal that crawls from the gutter to the animal that conspires in clandestine rooms.

Of course the pretended purposes were still all noble. But the only real purpose was to destroy the Republic, and finally America's enemies had devised a technique that could really, conceivably, do it. The idea had never succeeded before because those who spawned it had always been alien. Now they had persuaded native-born to do it for them.

The two cities were one and might never be separate again.

He thought of Lucille Hudson, widowed at the White House in an accident whose true causes nobody yet knew or would probably ever know; he thought of Beth, who could be widowed too; of Crystal and Hal, who had already suffered from the beast let loose; of all the decent ordinary citizens, unprepared for such tactics of internal self-destruction and too basically fair and tolerant to respond in kind. And he wondered what would happen to America, and to him, and to all he treasured and had worked so long and hard to maintain. And once again there came into his mind the thought that had struck him a year ago on the night he had been going through such mental tortures over the offer of Harley's predecessor to back him for President if he would only abandon his opposition to Bob Leffingwell's nomination to be Secretary of State.

He had been wandering beneath the Capitol, on the sloping lawn that leads down from the west front to the Mall, the city, and the White House beyond that he had wanted so much—still wanted so much.

He had turned and faced the magnificent old jumble.

The great dome had loomed above him against the deepening sky, shimmering, perfect, white and pure, over the city, over the nation, over the world. On the Senate side the flag slapped lazily in the gentle breeze. Utter peace, utter serenity, lay upon the Hill.

Surprising and sudden, tears came into his eyes.

O America, he thought, and it was like a crying in his heart: *O America!* Why do you suffer us your people, who are such fools, and what have we done to deserve you?

Then he had shaken his head with a quick, impatient movement and gone back up the long flight of steps to defeat Robert A. Leffingwell. . . .

And *O America!* he thought now, and again it was a crying in his heart: *O my country!* What will become of you in these days when your children hate one another and turn without tolerance and without compassion to rend themselves and you in their insane stupidity and spite?

He realized that tears were in his eyes on this occasion too, even as he realized that one of the security men outside was rapping on the kitchen door with the agreed three knocks. He rose somewhat unsteadily and went to answer. For several moments he found it difficult to focus on the visitor who stepped forward, closing the door quickly behind him.

"Oh," he said finally. "It's you. How ironic. I was just thinking of that night—I was just thinking of the night I stood on the lawn below the west front—and looked at the Capitol—and thought about America—and went back in the chamber—and beat you."

"That was quite a night," Bob Leffingwell said softly; and held out his hand. "How are you, Orrin?"

"A little shaky, I'm afraid," the Secretary said, with a laugh that indicated as much; and then returned his visitor's firm grip. "I'm glad to see you, Bob. I've been hoping we could meet soon. Come on in the library. I think"—and again he uttered a rather unsteady little laugh—"I think we're relatively safe here. Can I get you something to drink?"

"What are you having?" Bob Leffingwell asked. "Scotch? I'll join you."

"Good," Orrin said. "Sit down, I'll be back in a minute."

Left alone in a house to which he had never been invited as guest in all the years of their frequent contention, Bob Leffingwell studied it thoughtfully. It looked as he had known it would: solid, erudite, lived-in, comfortable—safe. But nothing was safe on this night, or perhaps ever again in America. He shivered and for a moment he, too, was lost in thought, called back abruptly by his host's return.

Orrin handed him a glass, picked up his own, sat again in the rocker by the empty fireplace.

"Did you come by the White House?"

'Yes, it's quiet, now. Some debris in the gutters, all the floodlights on, eight or ten cops still on duty along the fence, but otherwise calm. The Avenue's quiet, nobody on the Lafayette Park side. I guess they've had their fun for the night."

A wry expression touched the Secretary's face.

"Oh, the fun's just beginning. It isn't every day you run to ground a Secretary of State and a candidate for President. I'm sure we'll be hearing for the rest of the campaign how I scuttled out with my tail between my legs. But of course it would have been foolhardy to go out the front way."

"Foolhardy to go in," Bob Leffingwell suggested with a smile. "But typical."

"I suddenly got awfully fed up. . . . Your health."

"Yours too," Bob Leffingwell said, and found somewhat to his surprise that he really meant it.

For a moment they drank in silence. The Secretary broke it in a thoughtful tone.

"I've just been sitting here wondering where this country's going."

"Yes," Bob said, his face suddenly grim. "You're not the only one."

"We've managed to survive an awful lot of this mindless irresponsibility in recent years, but there's an extra viciousness to it now. For the first time in all my years in public life, I feel our enemies may really have us by the throat. And I've been thinking whether maybe I'm to blame, and whether I ought not to get out."

"You weren't to blame at the convention," Bob Leffingwell said. "You weren't to blame tonight. And you won't get out."

"No," Orrin said slowly, "I won't. But I really wonder how much blame I bear for this. Maybe I haven't tried hard enough to see the other point of view. Maybe I've become as rigid and arbitrary as the professional liberals are. It's an easy, smug, intolerant state of mind to fall into. Maybe they've driven me to it in self-defense . . . or maybe I'm just rationalizing."

His visitor looked thoughtful.

"No, I don't think so. They've driven me into some unfortunate exaggerations over the years, too. It cuts both ways."

The Secretary gave him a quizzical glance, half-amused, half-disbelieving.

"I never thought I'd hear you admit it."

"You probably never thought I'd be honest enough or perceptive enough to even think it," Bob Leffingwell said dryly. "I got a pretty clear picture of what you think of me during the State Department nomination."

"Well," Orrin said, "I believed it to be the correct one at the time. I don't apologize for it. But people change— opinions change—certainties change. You've changed." He frowned. "I like to think maybe I have, too, I don't know." The frown gave way to a wry amusement. "The mellow, aged-in-the-wood Orrin is not visible to a good many of my more violent critics, but he may be there, underneath it all."

"Oh, yes," Bob agreed. "You've changed."

"Enough to support for President?" the Secretary asked quickly, and for several moments his visitor looked at him with a thorough, analytical gaze.

"I don't know yet," he said slowly. "I really don't know. Have I changed enough so that you want me to support you?"

"You have politically," Orrin said promptly, and Bob Leffingwell laughed.

"Blunt, candid, I'll-be-honest-if-it-kills-me Orrin Knox! How else have I changed—if at all?"

It was the Secretary's turn for an analytical gaze.

"For one thing," he said slowly, "we're both a year and three months older, which should have some effect on a man even at our advanced ages. And for another, I think you have had occasion in the past few months to perceive the nature of some of your journalistic and academic supporters. And for a third, you had the guts to go all out for Harley, and that, in the context of your past life and record and in the context of those who helped to create your reputation, was a hell of a courageous thing to do. I admire you for it very much."

"I got your note at the hotel. I appreciated it—"

"Even though you did think it was all politics."

"I thought there might be a little in it," Bob Leffingwell confessed wryly, "but even so, I appreciated it. After all, you did put it in writing. Yes, I nominated Harley, bless his heart. Just out of sheer kindness, he did everything he could to salvage my career—"

"And I did everything to destroy it," Orrin said with calculated bluntness, since he thought he might as well test this new Leffingwell right now. His visitor did not take offense.

"No," he said mildly. "Most of that I did myself, when I lied to the Foreign Relations Committee."

There was a silence in which they could hear a car come along the street; a sharp challenge from one of the security officers; a muffled conversation; the sound of the engine dwindling away. At last the Secretary spoke quietly.

"A hard word to use about oneself. And a very honorable admission. I respect you for it."

"I don't say it to everyone," Bob Leffingwell said with a certain bleakness. "But some people have a right to hear it. You, perhaps, most of all." He sighed deeply and stared down at his hands. When he spoke again his voice was very low. "You were right to defeat me . . . and that, too, you have a right to hear."

Again there was a silence, which his host took a long time to terminate.

"I think I should be very lucky to have you support me," he said at last. "And very honored, too. And that I would say, I think you can believe me, had you no political influence in the present situation at all. "

"Thank you," Bob Leffingwell said quietly. "I do believe you. Suppose you wonder why I really came here tonight."

Orrin smiled and the tension eased a little.

"I'll admit I'm a little curious."

"Well, basically," Bob said in a lighter tone, "I wanted to. But in addition to that, two ladies told me to."

"Oh?"

"One was Helen-Anne—"

"She would," Orrin said, and they smiled at one another, probably the first genuine smile they had exchanged in several years.

"And the other was Ceil Jason."

"*Oh?*" Orrin said softly. "Well, I'm damned."

"Yes," Bob Leffingwell agreed. "So was I"

"Surely she didn't tell you to support me—"

"She told me to make up my own mind and have the courage to stick to it. Which, I suppose, amounted to the same thing."

"You know," Orrin said, still in the same musing tone, "I think Ted is a luckier man than he may know. I think she must love him very much."

"Yes," Bob Leffingwell agreed, "I think she must, though I'm sure he wouldn't see it that way. He'd probably think she was betraying him by trying to get him out of this." An expression of distaste crossed his face. "More fool, he."

Orrin looked amused.

"You don't think too much of our great governor, do you?"

"He's an odd duck," Bob said thoughtfully. "In some ways, a very brilliant man—mentally, and in his grasp of detail, and his decisiveness, and his general approach to things. I don't think he has much heart, to use a tired cliché—there's too much that's cold and calculating underneath."

"But Ceil loves him."

"Apparently."

"So he must have something."

"Oh, he has. I'm not saying he hasn't. He's a most competent gentleman—and a most formidable opponent, I think, even now, even with the last five sorry days, even with his insane flirting with violence which drove me away, and has lost him a lot."

"He'll regain it," Orrin said tartly. "He's regained it already. The public's attention span is about ten minutes. They're already forgetting the shabby side of it. Harley's death has wiped out many things. Ted's on the upswing again—formidable, as you say. So, are you going to support him, then, if you won't support me? After all, he stands for negotiation and short-of-war and let's-don't-be-beastly-to-the-Reds. You like that, I take it."

For a moment Bob Leffingwell looked at him with a real hostility reviving in his eyes. Then he shrugged.

"The Knox technique, I know it well—I ought to know it well. Challenge a man, throw ideas at him, knock him off balance, even insult him a little, see how he reacts, move from there." He smiled, a trifle grimly. "You can't do it to me any more, Orrin: I've recovered. I recovered a little while ago, when I told you you were right to defeat me. From here on, I'm on the upswing too. Now, first of all, who said I wasn't going to support you?"

The Secretary gave him a shrewd look and chuckled.

"You didn't say you were."

"That's right. And I won't say it, either, at least not tonight. I may never say it. Then what?"

"Then I should be quite disappointed. Because as I told you—after you started your upswing—I should be honored to have you. I can, however, get along without you."

"It's mutual," Bob Leffingwell said, and the hostility returned and for a moment they were enemies again until Orrin broke it with a smile.

"Sure. It is. You couldn't be more right. So starting from that, how do we proceed? Together?"

"I don't know yet," Bob said slowly. "I honestly don't. About my views, however—they can change too, you know. They're no longer what you're trying to say they are; and they aren't with yours, either. There's an in-between, you know. Everything doesn't always have to be absolute."

"Granted," the Secretary said. "Granted. It doesn't have to be absolute until the moment comes when it's fight or go under. Then it becomes absolute. And all this fuss—aside from those, and of course they do exist, who oppose all policy simply because they actually, cold-bloodedly wish to destroy the country—all this fuss is simply a debate over when the absolute moment comes. Harley and I say—said—that it was at Point A, and you and Ted and others said it was at Point B. Ours was earlier than yours, and thereby hangs the argument."

"I'm not so sure that the genuine wreckers haven't taken the argument over," Bob Leffingwell said soberly. "They did at the convention, the way it ended was only a false lull, apparently—they did it tonight at the White House—who knows where and when they'll attempt it again? Apparently it could be right here in Spring Valley. Who's safe now, and where?"

"Then our battle really is cut out for us, isn't it?"

Bob Leffingwell looked grave.

"I think so."

"Then join me and help me fight it."

"Not yet."

"Then why did you come here?"

"To begin thinking," Bob said. He smiled, though this time it cost him an obvious effort. "And to find out if I could bear to talk to you."

The Secretary gave him a level glance.

"You have."

"It hasn't been a wasted evening," his visitor said, rising. "I'll be in touch."

"May I count on that?" Orrin asked, extending his hand.

"You may count on that," Bob Leffingwell said; responded with his quick, firm grip; turned to the door and was gone into the ominous night, escorted by a security man to his car, which started up quietly and rolled almost apologetically away into the silence of the sleeping neighborhood.

"What did he say?" Beth inquired a few moments later when she called from the White House to say she thought she and Dolly would stay with Lucille, who was finally sleeping.

"He said he thought the wreckers were taking over the country. He said he thought the ending of the convention was a false lull."

"I agree. Is he going to help you?"

"He won't say yet. I think so."

"I hope so," she said. "Good night, my friend. Keep safe."

"Oh, I will," he said. "They've got me under wraps tonight all right. No wreckers here!"

"And don't make fun of them," she said quietly. "They are genuinely terrifying people."

And so the master of "Salubria," too, was beginning to regard them, as he reflected upon their heated conference earlier in the day, and its immediate result at the White House this evening.

It had been the fashion of Walter's world to regard Fred Van Ackerman as a boorish but occasionally useful demagogue of the irresponsible left; LeGage Shelby as a clever, ruthless Negro leader who might be teetering on the edge of fanaticism but could be trusted to have enough brains not to fall over; and Rufus Kleinfert as a clod. It had been comfortable and convenient for Walter and his friends to regard these three and their respective organizations—the so-called peace movement represented by Senator Van Ackerman's Committee on Making Further Offers for a Russian Truce, the so-called civil rights movement represented by 'Gage Shelby's Defenders of Equality for You, and the so-called superpatriotic movement represented by Rufus Kleinfert's Kouncil on Efforts to Encourage Patriotism—as rather absurd but politically convenient manifestations that could be easily manipulated in the interests of certain candidates and certain causes.

The members of Walter's world, in short, had patronized COMFORT, DEFY and KEEP in exactly the fashion they patronized everybody else.

They had patronized them thus, in fact, until the three organizations, having coalesced behind Governor Jason (which was all right), suddenly joined in the move to throw the convention into tension and turmoil (which was not all right). Then it finally dawned on Walter and his friends that COMFORT, DEFY and KEEP, like many another package of human dynamite they had played with loosely over the years, really did have a fuse and really could explode in sudden, mindless and terrifyingly uncontrollable ways.

In the opening hours of the convention there had been many comfortable, self-satisfied broadcasts and analyses explaining to the public how it was that the idealists, fools, appeasers and Communists of COMFORT, the sick black racists of DEFY and the blind antediluvian isolationists of KEEP could logically unite behind the candidacy of the man Walter's world wanted to see in the White House. But that had been when Walter's world was still assuming that the three organizations and all who supported them throughout the country would be well-mannered and well-behaved—that they would throw the

116

fear of God into Harley Hudson and Orrin Knox and the stupid conservatives who supported their stupid stand-firm policies—that they would not do anything to affront the vast middle reaches of the electorate upon whom the results of Presidential contests depend. It was assumed that they would threaten violence, disruption and chaos, but that they would not take themselves any more seriously than Walter and his friends did. It was assumed that they would not do anything which would really endanger the stability and security of the republic.

Suddenly none of this was true any more. Out of the convention political, nihilistic terror-for-terror's sake had sprung to life. And suddenly, a little late—too late, perhaps—Walter's world had become worried and to a considerable extent frightened of the monster whose parturition they had attended and encouraged with their bland editorials and commentaries, their smooth rationalizations, their suavely irresponsible justifications. They had presided step-by-step at the birth of terror—until suddenly terror was delivered full-grown and out of control.

So now Walter's world was uneasy and afraid, and so was Walter himself. Yet he had gone down to let Fred and 'Gage and Rufus into his house with some of the patronizing mood still lingering. However concerned some of his colleagues seemed to be, Walter felt that he could still handle it, and he felt that his columns were sufficiently strong and influential so that he still had some bargaining power.

It had not taken long to disabuse him of that.

"Well, Walter buddy," Senator Van Ackerman had said with that fleering, unctuous familiarity he liked to use when he was driving someone to the wall, "I guess it's about time for you to lay it on the line for the greatest governor any state ever had, isn't it? Time to get in there and pitch, Walter boy."

"If you will come in and sit down," Walter said, turning away with dignity, "perhaps we can discuss it." And when they were in the living room, with a pointed courtesy, "Would you like a drink, Mr. Shelby? Mr. Kleinfert?"

"I neffer drink," Rufus Kleinfert said with a disapproving stare, his trace of accent at its stiffest and most pronounced. LeGage simply looked ominously impassive and shook his head without the courtesy of speech.

"Guess that leaves me, Walter," Fred Van Ackerman said, enjoying it. "I'll have a vodka gimlet, thank you very much."

"I haven't got any vodka," Walter said, and took some small satisfaction from that though he suspected the satisfaction was rather pathetic and despised himself for it. "I can give you a gin and tonic."

"Period," Fred said, with a cheerfully unpleasant smile, sitting down with the unerring instinct of a cat in Walter's favorite chair.

"Which I intend to have myself," Walter said; rang for Roosevelt, gave the order and then took a seat somewhat uncomfortably on the sofa. "Now," he said, spreading his hands on his knees in his characteristic gesture, "why are you here and what do you want?"

"We're here," 'Gage Shelby said coldly, "because we're going all out to get that nomination for Jason and we expect your help."

"Yess," Rufus Kleinfert said softly. "We expekt it."

"What makes you think," Walter asked with a coldness

to match LeGage, a softness to match Rufus, "that my help will be withheld from the candidacy I deem best for the country? Who launched that candidacy in the first place? I did, with my speech in Washington three months ago. What makes you think it is necessary for you three to come to me like a delegation from the Mafia and try to put pressure on me? Who do you think," he said, even more coldly and softly, "you are?"

"Temper, Walter buddy, temper!" Fred Van Ackerman said with his relishing, insincere humor, but neither of his companions looked at all amused.

"Unless that man is nominated," LeGage Shelby said somberly, "there's going to be blood in this God-damned worthless country. I'm telling you that for a fact. There's going to be blood."

"There already has been blood," Walter snapped. "Crystal Knox's blood, at the convention, and it cost him the nomination then, you and your damned vicious interlopers! You destroyed his chances once, what are you going to do, destroy them again?"

"Now, that's exactly—" 'Gage Shelby began, leaping up in some obscure, inarticulate excitement of rage, "that's exactly what—what—that's exactly what you white bastards always try to do, you always try to shut us off, you always try to keep us quiet, you always—you always—"

"Sit down," Walter said in an icy tone, "and be quiet! I am not trying to do anything but inject a little sanity into your heads. Violence doesn't work in America—"

"And don't give me any of your pious, pompous lectures about violence!" 'Gage shouted, while Fred studied him with a placid interest and Rufus Kleinfert sat, as always, like a large wax lump. "Don't try to tell me, white man! Your days are numbered in this God-damned worthless country—"

"As worthless as you make it," Walter snapped, trembling with rage himself but trying hard to hide it and succeeding fairly well. "Now, sit *down* or get out of my house."

For a long moment LeGage stared at him like some quivering panther. Before the moment could explode into some further outrage whose nature no one could foresee, Senator Van Ackerman spoke.

"Sit down, boy," be said with a lazy, deliberate brutality. "Just sit down and stop spilling those grits and chitterlings all over the place."

"*You!*" 'Gage cried, diverted and if possible even more infuriated. "*You*, you empty bastard! I told you never to 'boy' me again! You hear?" he demanded, so angry he was almost crying. "You hear, you *hear?*"

Yes, I *hear*," Fred said with a contemptuous calm. "So, Walter buddy," he said, turning back to their host with a dismissal so abrupt and complete that it was, in its way, as terrifying as 'Gage's violent rage, "you're going to write some more of those swinging columns and help put Ted over the top at the National Committee meeting, right?"

"I am going to do whatever I believe best to assist his candidacy," Walter said, breathing hard but managing to speak in a reasonably level voice, though it shook a little. "I do not believe that any purpose will be served either with the country or the Committee—certainly not with the Committee—by threats or acts of violence. I don't need you to come here and instruct me—*me*," he repeated, with a rage of his own, "who have been a power

120

in the affairs of this nation for more than twenty-five years—on how to conduct myself in this matter."

"No more do we need you to instruct us, Walter boy," Senator Van Ackerman said swiftly. "So that puts us all on a level, doesn't it?"

There was a silence during which LeGage stared out the window at the innocent Blue Ridge with a fearful scowl; Fred examined their host with a bland innocence; and Rufus sat like a large wax lump. Finally Walter fell back, with as much dignity as he could manage at the moment, upon the inquisitive protections of the reporter.

"What do you intend to do?" he asked in a tone he tried to make deliberately impersonal. "What can I write about your plans?"

"Oh, no, you don't—" 'Gage began with a reviving vehemence but he was stopped by an unexpected comment.

"Ve haff," said Rufus Kleinfert heavily, "our methods."

"That's right, Walter," Fred Van Ackerman said. "Ve haff, indeed. And ve don't vant to tip our hands, either, do we, Rufe, old boy?"

"You are not funny," Rufus said with a ponderous disapproval. "I regret KEEP must work with you."

"But you must, mustn't you?" Senator Van Ackerman asked with his cruel pleasantness.

"If it vere not for varrss and more varrss," Rufus Kleinfert said, "these damnable varrss, ve vould go our own vay. As it iss, ve haff—Governor Jason seems to us the best candidate to remove us from these foreign entanglements and restore us to traditional Americanism and non-intervention in other people's quarrels."

"We're with you there, Rufe, boy," Fred Van Ackerman

said heartily. "That's what we want every time, traditional Americanism and non-intervention in other people's varrss. Particularly in Gorotoland and Panama."

"Anywhere," Rufus Kleinfert said heavily. "Anywhere."

"But particularly Gorotoland and Panama," Senator Van Ackerman said.

"That iss where it iss right now," Rufus Kleinfert said with a shrug. "That iss where ve make our protest."

"And what will this protest be?" Walter Dobius demanded, suddenly fed up with this by-play among the psychotic. "Another pack of cutthroats like your friends at the convention? An attempt to assassinate Orrin Knox? Tell me," he said with heavy sarcasm. "I may want to write a column."

But these hostile witticisms were not what his guests appreciated, apparently, for all three gave him sudden ominous looks, so uniform in their staring, almost childish savagery, that under any other circumstances he would have laughed. Now, for some reason, he did not.

"Don't get too funny, Walter buddy," Senator Van Ackerman said at last in a softly threatening tone. "Things are going to happen in America that you just don't dream of in your nice liberal circles. You just think it's all a nice, sweet little intellectual game, don't you? You always have, you and your sweet-smelling friends, playing fast and loose with America just so you could make points at Washington cocktail parties and tell one another in New York how mincy-pincy"—his mouth curled in a savagely sarcastic and unpleasant fashion—"just how rootsy-tootsy, smart-ass brilliant you all are. Well, let me tell you, Walter boy"—his voice dropped to a menacing quietness—"let me tell you, things are getting into the hands of the people who *really* know what's best for America, now. You and your crowd have served your purpose, you've paved the way, you've conned the boobs and conditioned them to accept any lie if it's smooth enough, you've told them what to believe and made them so confused they don't know which way is up. You've done your job, Walter boy: you've paved the way for *us*. And now," he concluded softly, "here—we—are."

"I think," Walter Dobius said presently, "that you are all mad—literally, certifiably insane."

But again he had apparently said the wrong thing, for suddenly LeGage had his arm in a grip so tight that it brought tears to his eyes, and he realized that he—he, Walter Dobius, America's greatest philosopher-statesman of the press—was being shaken like a rag doll by the angry young Negro who towered over him.

"You just write your columns, white man," 'Gage said with a terrifying gentleness, "and don't worry about us, OK? Just don't worry about us, if you know what's good for you."

"Yess," Rufus Kleinfert agreed with an impassive stare. "That vould be best."

"Because you see, white man," LeGage said, and suddenly a cigarette lighter had appeared in his free hand, he had snapped it aflame and was holding it an inch from the beautiful colonial-style drapes that framed the innocent Blue Ridge, "it isn't just slums that burn down and dirty black people who get killed. Nice homes can burn too, and nice, clean white people can get killed. So you just do your job like we say and we'll do ours, OK?"

"If you don't put that lighter out at once," Walter said, his voice a strange combination of fury and fright, "I shall call the police and have you committed."

"Why, sure," LeGage said, extinguishing the mechanism and dropping it in his pocket, at the same time releasing Walter with a shove. "But you can't stay around and guard the place all the time, can you?"

There was a long silence during which none of them said anything, Senator Van Ackerman staring at him with a brightly interested look, LeGage studying the richly comfortable room with a coolly impersonal thoroughness, Rufus sitting like a large wax lump. Finally Walter spoke, with whatever shreds of self-respect fortified by ego remained to him.

"I shall do as I think best about this nomination," he said, breathing heavily but sounding more like himself again. "It is inevitable, of course, that I shall support Governor Jason. But I shall not do so under threat, and I shall do so in my own time and my own way. And I warn you that if you continue on the path of violence that you started at the convention, you will destroy him and everything you want to achieve, because the heart of America is still strong and decent and a majority of her people will ultimately turn upon and destroy you, if destruction is your aim."

"My, my," Fred Van Ackerman said with a cheerful grin, "if you don't sound just like Orrin Knox. Come on, fellows, on that note I think we'd better leave. 'Semper Fidelis' is getting so loud I can't hear myself think."

And he got up and started for the door without a glance at his host.

"Don't come back," Walter said coldly as the others did the same.

"Only to start a fire, baby," LeGage said over his shoulder. "If you convince us it's necessary."

"Yess," said Rufus Kleinfert.

For a good many minutes after Fred had gunned the car down the curving drive and the last traces of its angry sound had died upon the heavy afternoon air, America's leading philosopher-statesman of the press remained where he was, one hand upon the drapes, staring without really seeing at the lovely rolling countryside that he had so often gazed upon as restorative for a soul made weary by the burdens of guiding his country on her wayward course. Everything in Walter Dobius had been affronted in the conversation just closed, his pride, his ego, his intelligence, his wisdom, the integrity of his writing and his work, the love he had—perhaps his only conscious love—for his beautiful old home.

The men who had come to that home this afternoon meant exactly what they said, of that he had no doubt. They were not afraid of violence, they wanted violence, and if he opposed them, they would use violence upon him. A sudden vision of smoke rising from the toppled pillars of "Salubria" made him half cry out in anguish and rage. A moment later—for Walter in his own odd way loved his country too—a wider emotion entered his heart, an even more rending concern.

O America! he thought, ironically echoing, though he would never know it, the man he most feared and mistrusted in American politics—What is going to happen to you? What are they going to do to you, these dreadful worthless beings?

Now, hours later, after dinner and, for the first time in many years, after a difficult and futile attempt to start a column, he was sitting at his desk coming finally and irrevocably to the conclusion that something more overriding than immediate political concerns must be attended to. He had seen the White House riot on television and it had appalled him. There was no question in his mind that his visitors had gone immediately from "Salubria" to organize it.

In quick succession he made two calls to California. The first produced only the bantering disbelief of a candidate obviously unshakable in his conviction that he was once again master of everything, threatened by nothing. Walter did not stay with it long.

"You are foolish," he told Ted Jason bluntly after five minutes of pointless fencing, "and you will know it before long."

"Don't let it get you down, Walter," Ted advised, unimpressed. "Mad Freddie called me a little while ago and I told him to cool it. I said I didn't want their support and would repudiate it outright if there was any more violence such as occurred at the White House."

"'Any more?'" Walter demanded. "Why do you need any more?"

But the Governor apparently didn't hear that, remarking with some satisfaction, "I made it very clear to him, I think."

"Was he impressed?" Walter asked dryly. Ted gave a confident little laugh.

"He sounded quite well-behaved."

"Guard yourself," Walter said solemnly. "Guard all of us."

"My, how scary you sound," Ted told him in a jocular tone. "Maybe you'd better write a column. Isn't that how you usually work out your fears and frustrations?"

"You are foolish," Walter repeated, "and you will know it before long."

But of course this produced nothing more than one or two more lighthearted, self-confident japes, and without bothering to be courteous about it, because why should he, Ted didn't deserve it, he hung up.

Immediately after, he had placed his second call. It had not come through yet, but he was waiting. He thought the chances were reasonably good that it might, though he and the recipient had never been more than arms-length acquaintances, for all that they had spent so many years in Washington running the country together.

Down the lake someone was laughing again in the crisp, high air. A late boat or two, port and starboard lights aglow, skimmed the black waters with a muted nighttime roar. There were sounds of distant music, and the babble of parties. Television and radio sets had finally been silenced. Most of Tahoe's visitors had suffered a surfeit of solemn voices, solemn scenes, funereal music and the long, sad pomp of Presidential mourning. One could absorb only so much of that and then it was time to live again. The pre-interment rites were, as always, oppressive, and overdone.

This would not, he suspected now as he sat once more alone in the glider on the porch, have been the wish of Harley Hudson, who had always been the simplest and most unpretentious of men. But it was the self-conscious and perhaps somewhat guilty tribute some of the networks felt they had to pay to a man whom, living, they had more often than not opposed, attacked and generally demeaned with every electronic, photographic and verbal weapon at their command. That their ostentatious solemnities at heart really represented relief rather than regret the President was ironically aware, and he was sure

Harley would have been aware of it too. They could have had a good laugh about it, if Harley were here.

But of course if he were here, the President would not be, and wouldn't that be a happy, desirable thing? He was already looking back wistfully to the day before yesterday as though it were a million years ago. He had managed, by the sheer immovable determination that had always made Mr. Speaker so formidable a figure, to maintain his situation out here and give himself an amazing degree of privacy in which to think and plan; but it was a fragile refuge and he knew it would last very little longer. He must go back, and speedily. Events of recent hours had decided that.

Like many responsible men on this deeply disturbing night, he wondered what would happen to his country, and wondered with an extra gravity that no other man could have since his was the power and responsibility to meet whatever came. William Abbott was not a man to be stampeded by events, but it was very clear that there would be demanded of him, in many areas, much more than the Administration's opponents sought to restrict him to when they used the patronizing and detractive term, "the Caretaker President." The phrase was a deliberate attempt to hedge him about psychologically in the minds of his countrymen and sharply narrow his range of action. It would take more than that to do it, he thought grimly now. Even if he had wanted to hide from his responsibilities, which he most certainly did not, events had already proved they would not permit it.

Shortly after talking to Lucille, which he had done as soon as she had been sufficiently calmed after the riot, he had decided to fly from Reno at eight A.M. tomorrow.

His first impulse had been to switch on the intercom to the press cabin and make the announcement himself, for whatever drama it might give the weary crew who were trying so desperately to extract the last ounce of news from their Tahoe vigil. Then a sudden self-protective caution, such as he had never known before but which was to accompany him now wherever he went, stopped his hand.

Ten minutes later the Press Secretary was announcing to the poker players, the late story writers and the casually drinking gossipers, that they could look forward to a departure from Tahoe at nine A.M. They would fly from Sacramento at noon, the secretary said, shaking his head with a blandly significant leer when besieged with the excited assumption that the President would stop to confer with the Governor of California. Meanwhile the President was arranging with the Secret Service and the Secretary of Defense to be taken by casually disguised motor launch to the north shore, and from there to Reno, where he would depart at eight A.M. "Me and Abe Lincoln," he remarked with a wry distaste to the Secretary as their conversation concluded. "We have to sneak into Washington by the back door."

But that, at the moment, was the more sensible part of valor; and while he had always been a brave man, with that pragmatic acceptance of risk that goes with public life under the best of conditions, there was no point in being a fool right now. Fools of a more sinister kind were abroad in the land, and there was no predicting what new insanity they might produce if given the opportunity. There were necessary risks and needless risks, and perhaps at this particular moment announcing his routes and times too explicitly was one of the latter. He did not like the deception, but it made sense until the country had a chance to calm down a little.

When this would be, he had no idea. From the detailed reports of the riot which he had received an hour ago, it was quite apparent that an organized attempt was under way to intimidate and frighten those who carried the burden of the wars in Panama and Gorotoland. If it followed the growing pattern of political violence in America, there would be well-coordinated flare-ups all over the country, in major cities, at national monuments, wherever leading members of the Administration appeared, wherever there was a public event that carried with it sufficient press and television coverage to make a demonstration worthwhile. And if there was no excuse for a riot, well-trained and well-organized anarchists would create one: those who wished to destroy America were adept at it. The White House tonight was only a beginning. The next few weeks would be full of it, and along with it would go an increasingly ugly note of personal threat to every individual and every institution in any way associated with support for the Administration's policies.

For the moment, attacking the Administration's policies was the surest way to attack America.

He was struck again, as he had been so often in recent decades, with the sheer mindless virulence of the destructive forces of the world. Never once in all his memory had the Communists and their errand boys made a genuine effort to better the conditions of mankind. If the world had a wound, they opened it further; if the world had an evil, they made it more evil; if the world faced a potential explosion, they ran toward it, screaming, with dynamite and matches. In their mad dream of empire that could not succeed even if they achieved it—for their own actions guaranteed that it would have to rest upon a self-destroying foundation of treachery, terror, hatred and deceit—they plunged blindly down the corridors of the twentieth century like idiots loose from the keeper.

How utterly evil they were—how utterly worthless, how utterly pathetic. And how utterly dangerous.

And how utterly to blame were those, like Walter Dobius and his friends and followers, who had for so many years blandly dismissed the dangers, suavely rationalized the evil, earnestly and smoothly explained away the evidence of unrelieved viciousness that filled the record of history since 1917. And how willfully, when not self-interestedly or traitorously, had they rewritten that history to suit their own naïve misconceptions.

And how violently and tragically was history at last disabusing them of their determined and pathetic folly.

Walter had telephoned him a little while ago, and even before the President had decided grudgingly to accept the call, he had known that he was going to be talking to a worried man. Walter had tried to sound unmoved, but it had taken only a moment to detect in that pompous voice a concern much more agitated than the President had ever heard him express.

"Mr. President," he began, "I appreciate your talking to me at this difficult juncture—"

"Always glad to talk to a friend of Harley's," the President interrupted. "What's on your mind?"

"I am not concerned at present with the late President—" Walter began stiffly, but again the President cut him off.

"Perhaps if you'd shown a more decent concern when he was alive, he wouldn't be so late. Now, I haven't got all night, Walter—"

"Mr. Sp—Mr. President," Walter said, stumbling over the titles in an agitation he suddenly made no attempt to hide, "please don't take out your resentments on me. Some other time we can discuss that. I really did not call to bandy words, or annoy you, or complicate your problems. I called you because it seems to me I detect something in the country that you ought to be warned about."

The President snorted.

"Glad you detect it," he remarked with something of the scathing sarcasm that had always made Mr. Speaker such a frightening figure for fledgling Congressmen. "Nice to know it's beginning to penetrate."

"Fred Van Ackerman and LeGage Shelby and Rufus Kleinfert were out here this afternoon," Walter said with a dogged determination not to be upset or deflected, "and I am very much afraid that they are planning a lot more violence in connection with the nomination and indeed in connection with many aspects of foreign policy. I think you should know about this. So I am calling to tell you."

"Walter—" the President began, with a real annoyance; but then his voice dropped and, as if to himself, he asked, "Oh, what's the use? What's the use?" in a tired, disgusted tone.

"I thought you should know this," Walter repeated in his heaviest, most pompous manner, and after a moment the President sighed and spoke in a more reasonable

132

tone, which relieved Walter somewhat. He knew the President had problems, but this performance was really hard to understand.

"I appreciate your calling," the President said, more quietly. "I'm sure it must have been unpleasant talking to those three. You can be sure my Administration"—how easy it was to slip into that locution—"will do everything it can to keep order. In fact, by God, Walter, we've *got* to keep order."

"Yes, we have," Walter agreed solemnly. "The question is whether those who are determined to make trouble can be persuaded to refrain from—"

"What will you do to persuade them?" the President inquired without letting him finish. "Write a column or two about it?"

"I will," Walter said seriously. "I think if they can be made to understand that their efforts are unnecessary because the man they support is going to be nominated anyway—"

"Hey, now!" the President interrupted with an ominous gentleness the House knew well. "Is that a fact? Didn't know it was that simple, myself."

"I would say that everything points to it."

"Is that a fact. Well, well."

"Mr. President," Walter said, "surely it is obvious to you that when you recall the convention it will vote overwhelmingly for the man it really wanted. Surely your many years in politics make the situation crystal clear to you."

"Politics are never crystal clear," the President said. "That's what makes it all so fascinating. So you think the convention would do a thing like that, do you? Well, well."

"I am sure of it," Walter said stiffly, his worries about

violence suddenly quite forgotten in the realization that he should be worrying about his candidate instead. What did this wily old man intend, anyway? "You see, many of us who favor his candidacy—many of us who *responsibly* favor his candidacy—are convinced that President Hudson's unfortunate death provides an opportunity to clear the slate and start over."

"What would you suggest, Walter?" the President asked, and although for a second the thought crossed Walter's mind that he might be falling into a trap, he decided that it didn't matter, the President certainly knew where he stood anyway.

"I would end the wars in Gorotoland and Panama at once," he said bluntly. "Be brave enough to say it was a mistake, and get out."

"That's clear enough," the President admitted. "That would be bravery, as you see it."

"The bravery that only the strong can afford," Walter Dobius said solemnly.

"And that's what Governor Jason would do?" the President inquired in a musing tone. "Of course I know it is," he answered himself briskly. "Well, Walter, I'm afraid I wouldn't. And for the time being, at least, I'm the guy who decides, right?"

"Yes, Mr. President, you are," Walter agreed. "But," he added with the assurance that comes with a quarter-century of talking to Presidents, "I would hope that sober reflection would indicate that both the mood of the country and the necessities of world peace require at least some steps in that direction."

"We're ready to make peace anytime, Walter," the President remarked mildly.

"On our terms."

"Not entirely," the President said. "Our terms as long as there's no sign anybody is going to meet us halfway, yes. If they would, I don't feel so extreme about it . . . right now." He allowed a silence to lengthen and then added: "Might, though."

"Mr. President—" Walter began with a sudden determination. And then he too sighed and asked, as if of himself, "What's the use?"

"What's that?" the President asked quickly. "What's that, Walter? Don't want to think I'm upsetting you, here. But of course you know I don't have too many options. Particularly without word from them . . . I tell you what, Walter. How'd you like to write a few columns suggesting to the Communists that *they* negotiate with *us?* How'd you like to propose that *they* give up and get out? How'd you like to tell the world what bastards *they* are? Might be a real help to me, Walter, if you would. Might put the whole thing in perspective. Maybe I could even send you over to negotiate with them and tell them in person. Fred and LeGage and Rufus might like to go too. How would that be?"

For a moment Walter did not reply. When he did, it was in a tone of deeply affronted dignity.

"Mr. President," he said with an immense gravity, "I consider this far too serious for simple humor."

"Not simple at all," the President said. "Not simple at all. I've always wondered why you folks who tell us what to do should be so afraid to go over and see for yourselves. I've often wondered why you back away from taking the slaps in the face that we have to take every time we make an offer to negotiate. Go on over and find out what you're talking about, Walter. It would do you good."

"I called," Walter Dobius said with a frigid courtesy, "to do what I conceived to be my duty as a citizen—to warn you of threatened violence in the country. I did not call to indulge in games about two most serious world problems."

"You misunderstand me, Walter," the President said sorrowfully. "Plumb misunderstand me. No games at all. Just trying to get your help in a most difficult situation, that's all. We leaders need to stand together, seems to me. Let me hear from you any time, Walter. Nice of you to call."

"I think you would be flying in the face of manifest national demand," Walter said in one last desperate, disapproving attempt to bring the conversation back to reality, "if you were to oppose Governor Jason's nomination. I would not, myself, wish to be responsible for the risks you might be taking."

"I'll have to use my judgment on that," the President said, "just as I will on everything else. I've inherited quite a basket of eels. Take me a bit to get 'em sorted out. Thanks for the warning about violence, though. I do appreciate your call. I'll also appreciate anything you can write to help me calm things down. You've had quite a bit to do with stirring 'em up, Walter. Be nice if you could help quiet 'em down, now."

"I am sorry I have intruded upon you at such a time," Walter said coldly. "I did so in all sincerity."

"I understand that. Sincere men will be this country's salvation, Walter. Or its death. Good night."

And he hung up with a contemptuous little smile that might have worried Walter could he have seen it. As it was, Walter put down the receiver in a cold fury—with the President for being such an obdurate man, so hostile to everything Walter believed in, so blind to the dangers he might be plunging the country into if he opposed Ted Jason—with himself for having yielded to the impulse to call him. He had only done so in an attempt to help, and see what good it had done him. He went back to his typewriter and attacked it savagely. There was no question now of the column's not moving swiftly.

"A Chief Executive apparently oblivious to the crisis of violence which gravely threatens the very fabric of the nation," he wrote, "is apparently going to invite and inflame that crisis by an obdurate refusal to accept the fact that Governor Edward M. Jason is the overwhelming choice for President of all those Americans who believe sincerely in the welfare of their country and the future of world peace. President Abbott, possibly giddy with the new-found power that the death of President Hudson has conferred upon him, is evidently unaware of the enormous danger of rising violence—which seems to be prompted—however unwisely—by fears of Jason supporters that the Governor will once again be shunted aside by the conservative prowar faction in the party. Confronted with this deep and obvious threat to the national safety, the President is apparently—"

For some moments after his caller's portentous tones had faded from his ear, the President remained sitting in the worn old rocker that had accommodated his stocky frame so many times during his holidays at his sister's cabin. He was not so much annoyed with Walter Dobius, and with all those elements whose opinions Walter epitomized, as he was simply and honestly depressed. Walter's initial impulse had been one of genuine concern for his country; it had not taken many minutes for it to swing back to concern for his candidate. The way to avoid violence, obviously, was for everyone to give in obediently and accept Ted Jason for President. Otherwise, there would be violence, and God *knows* it wouldn't be the fault of Ted Jason's friends: they would certainly have given everyone fair warning.

He uttered a wry, disgusted, impatient sound, expressive of a mood which was not improved when the phone rang again and his secretary informed him that one of his dearest and most annoying problem children, the Hon. J. B. "Jawbone" Swarthman of North Carolina, was calling.

"God, what now?" he demanded in exasperation, and just then the Chairman of the House Foreign Affairs Committee came on the line and heard it.

"Now, Mr. Speaker—Mr. President, sir," he said in his rapid, colloquial, dumb-like-a-fox manner. "Now, Mr. President, you shouldn't feel that way about me, sir, now you really shouldn't. Old Jawbone just wants to have a little old chat, Mr. Speaker, Mr. President, sir, and you hadn't ought to get that tired old what-in-*the*-hell tone in your voice about your old friend, Jawbone, now—"

"Jawbone," he said in a flat voice that he hoped would interrupt the flow, "what—is—it?"

"Why, I just thought, Mr. President, sir," Jawbone said, his voice dropping confidentially, "that you all might like to know how things are going back here at the home place while you all are out there gallivanting around in that rich, *rich* resort out there, that's all. I been hearing lots of things since I got back to town yestiddy and I thought you ought to know about 'em, that's all. Of course, if you'd rather not—"

"No, no, Jawbone," the President said, "go right ahead."

"Well, thank you, Mr. President, sir—"

"And you don't have to 'sir' me every minute," the President told him with some testiness. "And you don't have to talk corn-pone. You're a Rhodes scholar and one of the smartest men I know, so just pretend I'm still Speaker and give it to me straight, OK?"

"Now, there!" Jawbone exclaimed. "There! You hear that now, you hear that?"

"Who hears what?" the President demanded sharply. "Is someone else on the line?"

"Oh, no, sir," jawbone said hastily. "No, sir, not at all, now. Just Miss Bitty-Bug, she sittin' right here beside me, Mr. President, you know how she is—"

"Yes," the President said, wincing as always at Jawbone's pet name for his wife, "I know how Miss Bitty-Bug is. Why don't you tell her to go nibble on some other tree and let us talk in peace? If you really have something to tell me, that is?"

"Now, Mr. President, sir—" Jawbone began in a shocked voice.

"Tell her," the President ordered sternly. Jawbone clamped a band over the receiver, there were muffled murmurs. Presently he came back on the line with a vigorous cheerfulness. "Well, Miss Bitty-Bug gone, Mr. President," he announced happily. "You know lil' ol' Miss Bitty-Bug, she don't like to get left out of *anything*, but she agreed maybe this time I better talk to you alone. Miss Bitty-Bug sends her love."

"You give my love to Miss Bitty-Bug," the President said dryly. If this weren't the chairman of Foreign Affairs, whose support be needed, and if he weren't President, whose support Jawbone was going to need in his campaign for the Senate seat of the late Seab Cooley, he would have been tempted to tell Jawbone and Miss Bitty-Bug to fly off home and leave him alone. But Jawbone was a good weather vane, among other things. "Now tell me what you hear."

"Well, sir," Jawbone said, "well, sir, Bill, I been talking to some of these National Committee people, now, and they say, Mr. President, they *say,* that they really want that old convention there called back into session. They really do say that, Mr. President. Because there's a feelin', Mr. Speaker, Mr. President, sir, just a wee lil' ol' teensy *feelin',* that mebbe now things all been cleared away, here, it might, it jes' might, be time to take another look at that mighty fine Governor of California out there, *the* Honorable Edward M. Jason. Yes, sir!"

"This wouldn't be just a lil' ol' teensy mite of wishful thinking on your part, would it, Jawbone?" the President inquired, remembering vividly how the chairman had been one of the leaders in the fight against the Gorotoland resolution, and then had gone on to the convention to give active support to the Jason cause.

"No, sir!" Jawbone declared stoutly. "No, sir, not a-tall, now! Why, I just been on the phone with some of 'em, Bill, Mr. President, and—"

"Who?"

"Well, sir," Jawbone said in a confidential tone, "I wouldn't want it to get away, now, I surely wouldn't want it to get away—"

"This is the President, Jawbone," he said. "It isn't going to get away. Who was it, Esmé Stryke and Roger Croy?"

"Well, sir," Jawbone exclaimed in a tone of breathless admiration, "well, sir, if you just don't say the damnedest, if you don't now, Bill, Mr. Speaker, Mr. President, sir! It surely was Mrs. Esmé Harbellow Stryke, that great distinguished National Committeewoman from California, and it surely was that great distinguished National Committeeman from Oregon, Mr. Roger P. Croy, ex-governor of that great state of our great Northwest—"

"I'm not a meeting, Jawbone," the President said. "So it was Esmé and Roger—and that's all."

"Oh, yes, sir," Jawbone confirmed hastily, "but they been in touch, now, oh, yes, sir, they been In Touch. Why, Esmé, she told me she'd heard from at least ten Committee members this A.M. already, Mr. President, and Roger P. Croy, he said he heard from about ten more, and they all, Mr. President, *they all*, are in favor of gettin' together here in D.C. jes' as soon as they *can* and then declarin' the convention reconvened, and have a vote and put Ted Jason on top of that ticket, and go—to—*town!*"

"Mmmmhmm," the President murmured, with a skepticism Jawbone knew from long experience in the House.

"Now, Bill, Mr. President, sir," he said hastily, "you all musn't jes' go 'Mmmmhmmm' at ol' Jawbone here. You all musn't jes' Mmm*hmmm* me, Mr. President, sir! These people, now, Mrs. Esmé and Mr. Governor Roger P. Croy, they know what the mood is, Mr. President, they know what the country wants, and they got pledges, Mr. President—"

"Oh, have they?" the President interrupted sharply. "How many?"

"Well, sir," Jawbone said, and his tone became crafty and uncommunicative, "I couldn't rightly say, now, I couldn't rightly say, but quite a few, I dare say, quite a few. And they and their friends, now, they do want that ol' convention called back, Mr. President. I have a feelin', now, a distinct feelin'—and Miss Bitty-Bug," he added triumphantly, "you know Miss Bitty-Bug, she got pretty good political instincts too, now, and she agrees with me—we got a feelin' that gettin' that ol' convention back is what that National Committee's goin' to want to do when you call 'em into session next week."

"Who said I was going to call them into session next week—" the President began in a deliberately indignant tone, and then dropped it because there was no point in fooling anybody, the realities were clear enough. "Of course you're right, Jawbone, I've got to get them back, and fast. We can't stall it. But I wouldn't be so sure about pledges, if I were you. I don't tell everybody, Jawbone, and I wouldn't want you to, either, but I've been getting a few phone calls myself from the National Committee, and some of them don't agree with Esmé and Roger—"

"Some of 'em don't," Jawbone interrupted triumphantly, "some of 'em don't but some of 'em do, that right, Mr. President? Yes, sir, some of 'em do!"

"Yes," the President conceded slowly, "some of them do. But I haven't tried a head-count yet, Jawbone, and I don't think you should, either. I haven't really had time to get to it, but when I do . . . " He let his voice trail away significantly, and for a moment his ebullient caller was silent too. When he spoke, it was in a quiet, thoughtful tone.

"You fixin' to give that nomination to ol' Orrin, aren't

you?" he inquired softly. "Yes, sir, that's what it is, you fixin' to give that nomination to ol' Orrin."

"I'm not fixing to do anything, yet," the President said calmly. "And I think you'd be making a great mistake to tell anyone I am. After all, Jawbone"—and he made his voice deliberately as forceful, blunt and menacing as he had always been able to make it when dealing with recalcitrant Representatives—"you and Esmé and ol' Roger and your friends, now, you overlook one thing, don't you? *I'm* in the White House, now. *I'm* the President of the United States, now. What makes you so sure, Jawbone," he concluded softly, "that I might not just stay right here where I am?"

"Well, now," Jawbone began hurriedly. "Well, now—"

"Do you think you and your friends can kick me out if I want to stay?" the President demanded. "Maybe you better think about that before you go getting pledges. Maybe I want that nomination myself, now I'm in here. Maybe I like it, Jawbone. Maybe it's fun."

"Then," Jawbone said in an aggrieved voice, "you don't aim for us to call that convention back, do you? You jes' aimin' for a real fight in the Committee, and you don't aim for us to call that convention back. I know it, I know it!"

"I'm not saying what I'm going to do," the President told him calmly. "The Committee has to meet, that's obvious. After that, we'll see."

"Lots of folks just can't stomach ol' Orrin, Mr. President," Jawbone said sadly. "I tell you, lots of 'em just can't."

"If there has to be a fight, there has to be a fight. Thanks for calling, Jawbone. You can be sure I'll have an announcement in a day or two about the Committee. You can tell Esmé and Roger and anyone else you talk to."

"It's going to be a toughie," Jawbone said thoughtfully. "Yes, sir, like I tole Miss Bitty-Bug, it's goin' to be a toughie. She agrees with me, too, Mr. President. She agrees, that Miss Bitty-Bug. A real toughie."

"You tell Miss Bitty-Bug I agree, too. Tougher than any of us imagine, maybe. Might even involve that Senate race of yours in South Carolina, if it comes to that."

"Now, Mr. President," Jawbone began in alarm, "surely, now, Mr. President—" Then his tone changed, and for the first time the President began to be really worried about the outcome of the National Committee meeting. "Well, sir," Jawbone concluded flatly, "if that's how its got to be, that's how it's got to be."

"You really feel that deeply about Orrin Knox and Ted Jason," the President said in a wondering tone. "You really do."

"Miss Bitty-Bug and I, we talked it over," Jawbone said solemnly, "and we agreed. Folks in this country mighty worried 'bout how things goin', Mr. President. They mighty worried. We got a big responsibility in that National Committee. We got a *real* big responsibility."

"And you really feel that Ted Jason, with all his wishy-washy attitude toward the Communists, and all his encouragement of violence—"

"You say wishy-washy, Mr. President," Jawbone objected, "but seems to lots of folks it's not wishy-washy a-tall, just common sense and workin' for peace. Folks want peace, Mr. President, don't you forget that. Oh, my, do they want peace. And *violence?* Why, shucks, a few lil' ol' riots don't add up to much."

"More than a few, Jawbone," the President remarked grimly, "and you know it."

144

"Well, shucks," Jawbone said. "Well, shucks, now. I guess folks got a right to indicate how they feel, now, don't they, just a right to *indicate*?"

"Stop being disingenuous," the President snapped with a sudden anger. "You know damned well what's under way here, and you know damned well it's got to be stopped. You can tell that to Esmé and Roger, too."

"'Course, Mr. President, 'course, now, sir, nobody's goin' to endorse or support unwarranted and unnecessary violence—"

"As distinct from warranted and necessary?" the President demanded. "You crossed the line there, Jawbone. You crossed right over."

"Well, sir, no, sir," Jawbone said hastily. "I don't mean it's ever warranted or necessary, but just the same"—his tone became stubborn and he concluded with a dogged defiance—"just the same, lots of folks want Ted Jason."

"The Committee will be convened in due course," the President said flatly. "And we shall see then what happens."

"Yes, sir," Jawbone agreed. "We surely will, Mr. Speaker, Mr. President, sir."

And so they would, the President promised himself grimly as the conversation ended. Here was Ted Jason again, to complicate his problems: here was the justification for violence, if it could but be tied to a purpose that could be rationalized as good. Again he uttered a wry, disgusted, impatient sound, with such vigorous vehemence that his sister, just going by in the hall, called out and asked if he was all right.

"First-rate," he called back. "Can you bring me a glass of ice water?"

And when she did he tried, as he always had, to erase the worried look on her face with a matter-of-fact, comforting remark that would give her something else to think about besides him and his problems, which now were multiplied beyond even her usual loving concern.

"Ellie," he said, "how would you and Tom like to come to Washington and live in the White House? You could be my official hostess. You're the logical one, and now that Tom's retired there's no reason why you shouldn't, that I can see. Tom could be my unofficial eyes and ears to scout around the government for me, and you could sashay around with Dolly Munson and Patsy Labaiya and the best of them. How about it?"

"Oh," she said, putting her hand to her check in her characteristic way, "I'm sure that's awfully kind of you, Bill, but I'm really not used to that kind of life, with all those glamorous people, and—"

"Now, nonsense," he said with a big-brotherly firmness. "Never let it be said that a child of Leadville can't cope with the world's great. I have: you can. Anyway, Ellie, your President needs you. You know you and Tom will be happy as clams. Let's have no more talk about it."

"Yes, sir," she said with a little smile. "Masterful Mr. Speaker does it again." She frowned thoughtfully. "I wonder if I should even speak to Patsy Labaiya."

"Better," he said with a chuckle. Then the chuckle died. "Her friends will picket the White House if you don't."

"Billy," she said earnestly, "do be careful. Please, be careful."

He gave her a long look.

"As careful as can be. But you know how it is."

"Yes," she agreed quietly. "And it terrifies me."

146

He shrugged.

"The alternative is to run away. I can't do that. It's against my nature and against my job. I'm the only President there is. I can't duck it, even if I wanted to."

"I can imagine you wanting to," she said with a trace of returning humor. He smiled.

"I'm beginning to see its possibilities. I may just stick it out for the fascination of finding out what's going to happen next."

But nothing, probably, could have prepared him for it, either for the telephone call from California or the calls he made thereafter, or the events that followed. It just proved, he told himself wryly now as he sat and stared across the dark water, hearing the sounds of distant parties, the murmur of wind-touched trees, that there was no point in trying to imagine, if you sat in the White House, what might happen next.

Nor was there much point in anybody else's trying. Because the headlines that burst upon the world after the urgent call from Orrin Knox were such as to confound and dismay all those who thought events could be tailored to accommodate the wishes of the naïve and the fears of the timid.

PRESIDENT ORDERS ALL-OUT DRIVE TO CAPTURE GOROTO REBEL CAPITAL, HINTS U.S. MAY SEAL PANAMA REBEL PORT TO WORLD SHIPPING . . .

. . . SOVIETS, BRITISH DEMAND UN SECURITY COUNCIL MEETING, HEADS OF STATE TO ATTEND ON WAY TO HUDSON FUNERAL.

From a log cabin at Tahoe he was shaking the world. I'm sorry, old friend, he told Harley in his mind. I didn't want to ruin your ceremonies. I wanted things to stay quiet until you were decently gone, but you know how it is in this job: they don't give you much leeway. You understand. You were its prisoner, too.

In the morning he slipped away to Reno and flew back to his capital unattended by the press, as he had planned.

6.

IN THE DELEGATES' Lounge of the United Nations, the world was aflutter.

In the Delegates' Lounge of the United Nations, the world was never anything else, but this time it was *really* aflutter.

No sooner had a good many of its members concluded with relief that one American maniac had gone than they were confronted with the fact that another seemed to be in the White House.

It was enough to make anybody flutter.

Not the least concerned, as he stood in the doorway and studied the busy scene—Asians, Africans and Arabs swirling about in brilliantly colored eddies of agitation, the more drably dressed delegates of Europe West, Europe East and the Americas providing darker-suited areas of emphasis as they gathered in worried groups or sat at little tables before the great windows, drinking coffee with a nervous air—was the Ambassador of India.

Krishna Khaleel, as he often told himself and his friends here, who were many, was a man who liked peace and quiet. Yet in all his years in the towering glass monolith on the East River he had never known life to be anything but hectic, chaotic, bothersome and upsetting. Crisis tumbled upon crisis, and with the best good will in the world it was hard for an objective Indian not to feel that nine times out of ten it was the fault of the difficult, obstreperous, unpredictable, unmanageable United States.

It was not that he and his government did not often warn this recalcitrant giant, for they did. India could always be relied upon to criticize American civilization, deplore American morals, oppose American policies, and come running to America for succor when threatened by starvation or Red China. There was a special relationship between these two great nations, and this morning, K.K. felt, it was threatened as it had rarely been before by the persistence of America in doing, with an infallible and inexorable instinct, the wrong thing.

Because the relationship was so special, he did not hesitate now, any more than he had on any other occasion, to convey the alarm and concern of his government to the first Americans he saw. On this Monday afternoon, shortly before the special session of the Security Council that was scheduled to begin at three P.M., these were two, the same two members of the U.S. delegation with whom he had so often discussed the deplorable tendencies of their government. One was stocky and sandy-complexioned, possessed of an engagingly boyish grin and an eye that missed few things, particularly women. The other was a giant young Negro whose normally good-natured face wore now an expression of uncompromising determination.

149

Senator Lafe Smith of Iowa and Representative Cullee Hamilton of California saw him at the same moment as he saw them, and with one accord waved him over to their table by the window.

"My dear friends," he exclaimed, a little breathlessly, for his progress across the buzzing room had been interrupted by effusive greetings from the Ambassador of Guyana, the Ambassador of Brazil, the Ambassador of the Maldives and the Special Delegate from Anguilla, "my dear friends, crisis again!"

"Sit down, K.K.," Lafe Smith said with a kindly air, "and tell us all about it. Today we need the wisdom of the East."

"Which we hope," Cullee Hamilton said, his sober expression relaxing into a smile, "Will be clear, distinct, straightforward—"

"And on our side," Senator Smith concluded for him with a grin. The Indian Ambassador frowned as he took the proffered chair and accepted a cup of coffee from a passing waiter.

"Well, my dear friends!" he said again. "What can I say, what *can* I say? This is all so sudden, so disturbing, so—"

"Out with it, K.K.," Lafe said cheerfully. "So American. I'll bet you all thought that with a new President in the White House things would quiet down and fade away and you could stop worrying."

"I'm afraid," Cullee observed, "they don't know the Speaker."

"We thought," K.K. said with dignity, "that while there would probably be no immediate major change, at least there might be a gradual easing of tensions, a pause, a new approach"—he repeated the phrase, with capitals— "A New Approach—as the result of the tragic death of our late dear friend. But apparently the policy is to rush ahead into new adventures, new escalations, new dreadful flirtations with the peace and safety of the entire world—"

"Now, just a minute," Cullee said. "Just a minute, if you don't mind, K.K. *Who* is it who caused this new escalation? *Who* is it who was going to send in reinforcements and raise the ante? *Who* is it who was planning an all-out assault in Gorotoland and Panama on Wednesday, timed to coincide with Harley's funeral?"

"No doubt that is what the United States will claim," Krishna Khaleel said serenely, "but it is not what most of the world will believe."

"But we have the captured battle plans!" Lafe said indignantly.

"Battle plans, battle plans!" the Indian Ambassador said with an airy dismissal. "Battle plans may be forged, you know."

For a long moment the Americans stared at one another with an air of frustrated disbelief. Then they began to laugh, rather helplessly.

"Why do you laugh?" K.K. demanded. "It is a serious matter, dear Lafe, dear Cullee. It is a terribly serious matter!"

"We're only laughing because it hurts, K.K.," Cullee said. "How conditioned they have you all. It's beyond belief."

"Of course you realize it is not *I* who say the United States is lying, or my government who say it is lying," the Indian Ambassador observed. "I am just reflecting what many here will say, and warning you of it. In any case, it is now rather academic, is it not? The issue has been joined, and we are about to have a meeting. Will the President use your veto again, as Harley did before?"

"I would consider it very likely," Senator Smith said dryly.

"It will be a sad mistake," Krishna Khaleel said regretfully. "There is such an opportunity, now, for A New Approach. It is tragic to see the great United States blindly following the same old anti-Communist pattern. All of these here"—and with a broad gesture which was noted in many corners of the room, he indicated the swirling robes, the huddling business suits, the whole humming, bustling, busy concourse—"are so eager for A New Approach. They are so upset and worried about present events. They wish so much that the United States had only—"

"Had only what, K.K.?" Cullee Hamilton asked with a rising inflection. "Waited until Wednesday when the whole government—the whole country, really—is attending Harley's funeral, and then come away to find out we'd been hit so hard in Gorotoland and Panama that we'd lose them both. That's exactly what your friends in Moscow and Peking were planning for us."

"They are not necessarily my friends," the Indian Ambassador objected stiffly. "And I do not know, of my own knowledge, what they were planning."

"Well, we're going to show you this afternoon," Lafe promised grimly. "It's going to be an interesting session."

"I believe there will be twenty-three heads of state," K.K. remarked politely. "A good showcase for your charges."

Cullee snorted.

"A good showcase for the truth."

"May be," the Indian Ambassador said with an elusive and infuriating air of superior knowledge. "May be."

"K.K.—" Cullee began with a real annoyance, but before he could go further he was interrupted by two other old friends who had been slowly approaching them across the great room through a tangle of extended hands and fervent arm clutches from fellow delegates.

"Don't say it, old boy," Lord Claude Maudulayne said cheerfully. "Just don't say it. Temper never solved a thing, you know."

"Particularly," Raoul Barre agreed blandly, "when one argues a losing case."

Studying the British and French Ambassadors without too much cordiality on this tense afternoon, the Americans could see that they had a certain air of seeing eye-to-eye that they had not always shown in the past.

"I didn't know you two were going steady again," Lafe remarked dryly. "The President's decisions really *have* created a horrible situation, haven't they?"

"They have for us," Lord Maudulayne replied crisply. "This business of interfering with trade and shipping, you know—it's an absolute violation of international law."

"'International law,' whatever that is!" Cullee said. "An absolute violation of some people's desire to trade with everybody. While of course supporting us officially, in Whitehall. How do you do it?"

"I could tell you better with a cup of coffee," Claude Maudulayne said. "Move over." And he squeezed in between Cullee and K.K. with a cheerful blandness while Raoul took a seat next to Lafe. All around them the busy room took note of their little group and buzzed and murmured. "Seriously, we are most deeply concerned. My government is determined that this precedent shall not be allowed to stand."

"My President," Lafe remarked pleasantly, "is determined that it shall. And I would be willing to bet that eighty per cent of the American people are behind him."

Raoul Barre gave him a sarcastic glance.

"'The American people, the American people!' I saw these 'American people' demonstrating in the street as I entered the building just now. They seemed to be carrying big signs which said such things as STOP BOMBING INNOCENT BLACKS! OPEN FREE PANAMA'S PORTS TO WORLD TRADE! One even had a poem"— he took out an envelope, put on his glasses—"which I copied to send to my government as an indication of the mood of the great 'American people': WATCH OUT, ABBOTT/DON'T GET THE HABIT/REMEMBER IF YOU WANT HAPPY DAYS/THE GUN YOU USE CAN SHOOT BOTH WAYS. Rather poor meter," he concluded dryly, "but the thought is clear."

"It pleases you, doesn't it?" Lafe remarked. "You Europeans just love to see us get into the riot-and-assassination pattern, don't you? It puts everybody on the same level. Maybe it can even be the end of America, and that would be what you'd love to have happen, wouldn't it?"

"That is a very foolish remark," the French Ambassador observed calmly. "No one wants the United States destroyed. We just want it to abide by recognized rules of international behavior. However," he added, forestalling Lafe's sarcastic rejoinder, "it does seem that there are very definite threats to your internal stability lately—a

154

progressive deterioration, if you like, which should be checked."

"And when we check it, what will the world say?" Cullee demanded. "'Suppressing legitimate protest' . . . 'Dictatorial methods' . . . 'Shooting down innocent blacks?'" He made a sound of deep repugnance. "Innocent blacks, for God's sake! 'Gage Shelby and his pack of anarchists!"

"First came the Fatuous Fifties," Lafe said slowly. "And then came the Sick Sixties . . . And out of them came the Savage Seventies . . . and out of them—where's it going to stop, Claude? Tell us, Raoul. Enlighten us, K.K. What's at the end of this endless unraveling of law and order and a stable society? Anything at all?"

For a moment, confronted so nakedly with the outlines and implications of the world they lived in, no one said anything, while all around the spokesmen of the mutually hostile races of man gossiped and chattered and exchanged their worried witticisms on the steady decline of a civilization they seemed unable either to strengthen or save. Then the British Ambassador returned to the only safety diplomats know, which is, One Thing At A Time—Today's Issue Today—and, Let Tomorrow Take Care Of Itself.

"Some of us, you know," he said softly, "regard the recent actions of the United States as contributory in major degree to just the endless unraveling you talk about. My government—"

"Your government," Lafe snapped, "fights at our side in Gorotoland, endorses our position in Panama, and is selling arms and supplies briskly to our enemies in both countries. Who is unraveling what, may I ask?"

155

"Nonetheless," Lord Maudulayne said stubbornly, "we do not accept the principle that the United States can unilaterally interfere with our shipping and our trade."

"You assume, you see," the French Ambassador pointed out dryly, "that there was ever a skein of consistency—unless it be consistent inconsistency—in British policy. You assume that integrity is a desirable element in international affairs. How naïve!"

"Yes, we know," Cullee agreed. "France has shown us that."

"The alternative, of course," Lord Maudulayne said, "is to cut off our trade, destroy our economy, impoverish us and make us your international ward. Would you prefer that?"

"We would prefer," Lafe said, "that you try something besides always trading with those who have as their goal our destruction—and your own destruction. You talk about the United States being chained to old policies and old habits! The rest of you are just as chained to them, and the results are just as fatal to any real solution of the world's difficulties. London still operates on the old imperial philosophy of trade-with-anybody, no matter what he stands for, even if he wants to destroy you. That worked when Britain was big enough so that it didn't matter a damn what your customers thought, because you were so powerful nobody *could* destroy you. But my friend, you aren't that powerful now. Now it really does matter if your customers' ultimate aim is to destroy you, because now they have the capability to do it—and you have no capability to stop them. As witness Hong Kong and the pathetic history of 'diplomatic relations with Red China' and a few other adventures based on the old imperial reflex about trade. It's time you learned, one would think."

"The Preaching American!" Raoul Barre said ironically. "The latest development in the never-ceasing pattern of surprises that comes to us from across the Atlantic! If by 'learning' you mean we should all tie ourselves to you with no more independence of action or thought for ourselves, you know very well what our two governments think of that."

"And mine," Krishna Khaleel volunteered quickly. "But, my dear friends, my dear friends!" he added with a nervous brightness. "Such ascerbity of discussion does not advance world harmony, does it? It only aggravates, disrupts, divides. Surely we must not indulge in such carping differences, surely we must stand together!"

"Stand together for what?" Cullee asked moodily. "That's the question we ask. What's the good of standing together if it isn't for something?"

"We intend to stand together, ourselves, for the principles of free trade and free navigation," Claude Maudulayne said with an affronted coolness, "and I think we had best move on, now, and discuss it with those—with the many—who see it as we do."

"Your new chum Tashikov is over by the bar," Senator Smith told him, gesturing down the long room to the end overlooking the East River, where the chunky little figure of the Soviet Ambassador could be discerned surrounded by a dozen gorgeous robes out of Africa. "We shall veto your joint resolution, of course, and you might as well spread the word that there is no point in taking it to the Assembly. We will not be bound."

"We think you are making a great mistake," Lord Maudulayne observed.

"We think we are in good company," Cullee Hamilton replied evenly.

When they were alone again, in a conspicuous isolation that no one else attempted to interrupt as the hour grew closer to the time the Security Council was to meet and take up "The Matter of Increased United States Aggression in Africa and Central America," the Americans for a few moments said little. Lafe stared with a steady glance, which met many eyes and made them drop, around the crowded room. Cullee looked down thoughtfully upon the plaza and the noisy groups of tourists who shuffled slowly along and disappeared through the great bronze doors below. Finally he opened one enormous black hand and closed it again slowly into a tight, unyielding fist.

"Looks like we're in for an unpleasant afternoon," he remarked. "But no more than others we've survived, I guess. The Speaker—the President—apparently isn't going to give an inch."

"And thank God for it."

Cullee smiled.

"He sounded very Presidential when he called us a little while ago, didn't he? It's amazing how quickly they slip into it."

"It's one job where you just haven't got time to think," Lafe agreed. "You've got to be on top of it the minute you're in there."

"The press is certainly having a field day with his trip from Reno," Cullee observed. "But I think he was wise to keep it secret." He sighed. "God knows we couldn't stand another thing like Harley, right now."

"No," Lafe agreed somberly, "we could not. In fact, I don't know just how much we can stand of any other sort of thing either. That damned White House riot, and those murderous fools out there in the street right now . . . Did they give you any trouble when you came in?"

Cullee's expression became somber.

"My wife did, screaming and shouting like a little—"

"Is she still with LeGage?" Lafe asked in surprise.

"Yes," Cullee said. "That little Sue-Dan, I guess she's old 'Gage's secretary and companion and bottle washer and bedmaker *and* bedsharer, way it looks to me. But I don't care!" he exclaimed with a sudden bitter anger, smashing his huge fist into the palm of his other hand. "I don't care two cents for that little tramp! I'm getting that divorce as soon as I win my Senate seat in California."

"And are you going to?" Lafe asked, drawing Cullee away from a topic that always upset him deeply, so much was he still in love with the fox-faced little virago who had left him six months ago because he wasn't militant enough.

"It looks good," Cullee said. "Better if Orrin gets the nomination, but good either way, I think. In spite of all the kooks in California, and a couple of the major non-newspapers out there, and all."

"There's going to be one hell of a fight in the National Committee," Lafe said thoughtfully, giving an absentminded nod to the Ambassador of the Seychelles who was just passing with the Special Envoy of The Free Scillys Liberation Movement.

"There is that," Cullee agreed. "The whole world's going to try to mix into that one. But I still think Orrin can swing it."

"I think Orrin's got to swing it," Lafe said. "After the performance Ted put on at the convention, I can see him

159

even less than I did before. I'm very, very dubious that he should ever be the man for the White House. Particularly since he seems to be playing right along with all the violent elements now, just as he was a week ago. You'd think he'd have learned, but you saw the statement he issued after the White House riot. Two mild little sentences, going both ways: 'All Americans concerned with their country's welfare must deplore acts of violence. Equally must they deplore the fact that many responsible citizens apparently feel that certain policies are so unsatisfactory that the only way to oppose them effectively is by violent means.' In other words, there stands Ted Jason who hasn't changed one bit, thank you very much."

"Helen-Anne Carrew called me last night," Cullee said. "Ceil's left him, you know—Helen-Anne talked to her at 'Vistazo.' And apparently it's because she's completely upset about his condoning violence. Upset and, I gathered from Helen-Anne, frightened. So much so that she'd like him out of the race."

"Did she tell Helen-Anne all that?"

Cullee chuckled.

"No, but you know our demon news-hen. Helen-Anne can take a sneeze, a sniff and a snuffle and write 1500 words of in-depth analysis."

"The whole Washington press corps can do that," Lafe said. He frowned. "So she's actually left. That's going to hurt him."

"That Ceil is a great gal," Cullee said. "A real lady. Left, insofar as she's gone to 'Vistazo,' anyway. I don't think Helen-Anne thinks there's more than that to it, at least right now. She apparently wants him to think about things a little."

"His statement on the riot indicates he's doing so, magnificently," Lafe said. "Good Lord!" he added with a blaze of anger. "That guy is a fool to play around with the kind of dynamite he's playing around with. If Harley hadn't died, he'd be completely discredited. Doesn't he know that Van Ackerman and Shelby and Kleinfert and all that crew are bad, bad business? He's an absolute fool."

Cullee shrugged.

"I think he figures he can handle it. He proved at the convention that he couldn't, but that wasn't enough for him. He has to prove it all over again."

"But he's only encouraging things that may destroy the country—organized by people who really do want to destroy the country."

"Don't tell me," Cullee said. "I know that. He thinks they're doing it for him, poor ambitious fellow. He'll find out. Anybody who goes down that road, in America, is inviting his own destruction."

"But he can destroy a lot of other things as he goes," Lafe said grimly.

"Well, he can't destroy me," Cullee said, his face taking on a sudden pugnacious look that made the Ambassador of Egypt, who happened to catch his eye, give a startled little jump and look quite guilty. "Old 'Gage and his bullyboys, they beat me up once already, you know, when Terry was here six months ago taking Gorotoland away from the British and giving us hell about civil rights. My dear old Howard University roommate 'Gage, he and his friends didn't like the way I was standing up to black racism here in the UN, so they beat me up. But they didn't scare me. And they won't, either!" His scowl increased and the Egyptian Ambassador, after another

161

quick glance, moved hurriedly away down the room.

"They scare Sarah, though, don't they?" Lafe asked, and at the mention of Sarah Johnson, the secretary from the American delegation whom Cullee hoped eventually to marry, the scowl faded and a gentle expression came.

"Sarah's a brave girl," Cullee said. "She knows you take risks in public life, particularly nowadays. It doesn't make her happy, but she knows it's my life, so—that's how it is. How about Mabel?"

"Mabel?" The name of the widow of Senator Brigham Anderson of Utah, whose tragic suicide at the height of the Leffingwell nomination battle had shattered them all, brought a changed expression to Senator Smith's face too: uneasy, concerned, unhappy. "Oh, she's feared and hated politics ever since Brig's death, and the convention only made it worse. She called me from Salt Lake City last night"—he nodded in answer to Cullee's unspoken question—"yes, we talk almost every night, actually—but it was mainly just to urge me again to be careful, and, if possible, to get out of politics." He sighed. "She knows that won't work. I'm coming up to what looks like almost certain re-election in November, and I can't get out. It's my life, too. She knows that."

"I thought maybe being together at the convention—" Cullee suggested, but Lafe shook his head with a glum expression.

"No, it just made things worse—I mean, better as far as we personally are concerned, but worse as far as getting her to marry me and get back into politics herself is concerned. The violence terrified her." He gave a rueful, unhappy smile. "I guess little Lafe," he said with a surprising note of bitterness, "will just have to keep on chasing half the skirts at the UN, just as they all think I do."

"How's the boy?" Cullee asked. "Have you seen him since you got back from San Francisco?"

"I went up the Hudson to the sanitarium yesterday morning," Lafe said. His sad expression deepened at the thought of handsome young Jimmy, son of their late beloved colleague, Senator Harold Fry of West Virginia, locked away by a childhood illness in some silent, unbreachable world of his own. "There was—I thought—a flicker—just a flicker—of recognition again. But hell, buddy, you know him—you know how easy it is to think you get some response, when really it's just that you're wishing so desperately for one that you begin to imagine things."

"We didn't imagine it last time I went with you," Cullee said firmly. "He tried to speak to us. Now, you know that."

"Maybe," Lafe said sadly. "Maybe."

"He did," Cullee said. "*He did*. So stop trying"—he gave Lafe's arm an affectionate squeeze—"to make yourself gloomier than you naturally are."

"Jesus!" Lafe said with a wince, and then a grin. "Watch it, man! You don't know how it feels when you put all 280 pounds into a squeeze."

"Two-thirty," Cullee said proudly, "and losing every day." He grinned too. "I expect this afternoon's session will drain out about another twenty. I get so damned tired of Tashikov jawing away at us and never saying anything but the same old lies that everybody knows are lies."

"And now he has Claude Maudulayne to back him up," Lafe said thoughtfully. "I swear, the British never fail to amaze me. I love them dearly, but they do amaze me."

"I have a hunch," Cullee said, "that the Speaker—the President is going to try to wind up both these wars pretty damned fast, don't you? This all-out attack on Mbuele would seem to indicate as much."

"That will make Terry happy," Lafe said. He smiled, amused as always by the response the name of His Royal Highness Terence Wolowo Ajkaje, the M'Bulu of Mbuele, hereditary ruler of Gorotoland, was able to evoke from Congressman Hamilton.

"That crap artist!" Cullee said in a disgusted tone. "I swear I don't know which of those two pieces of black trash is the worst, old fancy pants Terry or his cousin, Prince Obi. But I guess our choice has got to be Terry, otherwise we won't have a friend left anywhere in Central Africa, and that wouldn't be so good. I wonder," he said thoughtfully, "how Felix Labaiya is feeling down there in Panama this afternoon."

"Encouraged by Russia and Britain, I should think," Lafe said. "Panama is going to be tougher for us, I'm afraid. The Canal—international passage—Communist Cuba to help Felix with subversion—British opposition to interference with trade, even if it is trade with the headsman—Panama is a little more complex. But I think you're right. Apparently Bill's determined to smash right on through and get it over with."

But when the Security Council finally convened, in its customary way, an hour after the scheduled time of three P.M., and then proceeded to drag on into the evening, past

164

midnight, almost to three A.M. before its business was concluded, it became apparent in the reports from Gorotoland and Panama that it was not going to be so neat and easy for the impatient American President. His characteristic and experienced belief that "soonest ended, soonest mended," was evidently not going to be supported by events.

In the Security Council chamber, around the big circular table where so many of the world's problems had been debated, made worse, and swept under the rug, the American diplomatic strategy was clear, simple and successful only when accompanied by a naked application of power. Its first move failed. As soon as debate began on the Soviet-United Kingdom resolution condemning America's escalation of the war in Gorotoland and declaring the Council's opposition to any unilateral interference with trade with Panama, Lafe Smith introduced a substitute United States resolution calling upon all nations to join in a quarantine of both rebel governments. In support he introduced captured Communist plans for simultaneous attacks on Gorotoland and Panama on Wednesday. The United States substitute was vetoed by France and the Soviet Union.

The issue then returned to the Soviet-U.K. resolution. After several hours of angry outcry against "American aggression . . . U.S. imperialism . . . war-mad American leaders . . . deliberate U.S. interference in the affairs of democratic, freedom-loving peoples" and other stirring phrases always ready on the tongue of any well-trained UN diplomat, the resolution was put to a vote. It was defeated on the third American veto in history, cast by Cullee Hamilton after a short and exasperated exchange with Lord Maudulayne, witnessed with an obvious glee by the Soviet Ambassador and a bland smile by many others.

There followed another two hours of bitter attack upon the United States, the gist of it being a series of stern warnings that, in the British Ambassador's words, "No self-respecting nation is going to accept the unilateral attempt to control trade with a government which many members of the United Nations have already recognized as legitimate." Lafe Smith summed up the adamant position of the United States in his openly angry reply:

"The time is coming, and possibly very soon, when the United States may have to disregard world opinion and proceed in the vital interests of its own security to take whatever action it deems necessary to end the dangers to world peace in Gorotoland and Panama."

Furnishing background to all this, the ubiquitous news-tickers in the corridors and lobbies kept up their clicking, clanging, clattering reports, which did not help the American position:

MBUELE BOMBED. U.S. ADVANCE SLOWED BY SAVAGE FIGHTING. RED TANKS, JETS, JOIN BATTLE. LABAIYA WELCOMES TRADE WITH ALL NATIONS.

In all those areas of public opinion and politics in which issues live and have their continuing being long after votes are cast and supposedly "final" decisions rendered, the tide of worried, nervous, uneasy, unfriendly comment continued through the night and into the headlines of the morning of the day on which a President was to be buried.

ARRIVING NATIONAL COMMITTEE MEM-

BERS SPLIT BY WAR CRISIS . . . JASON CONDEMNS EMBARGO THREAT, URGES END TO GOROTO BOMBING . . . KNOX DEFENDS ADMINISTRATION, SAYS CRITICS OFFER "NO PRACTICAL ALTERNATIVE" . . . SENATE, HOUSE FOREIGN AFFAIRS HEADS CALL FOR NEGOTIATION, END TO ESCALATION . . . CROY PREDICTS JASON "INEVITABLE NOW" FOR NOMINATION, MUNSON CLAIMS KNOX "INESCAPABLE CHOICE" . . . VIOLENCE THREAT SEEN IF GOVERNOR NOT CHOSEN . . . PRESIDENT REMAINS SILENT ON COMMITTEE PLANS . . . DEMAND MOUNTS FOR CONVENTION RECALL . . .

And in the world of Walter Wonderful, the comments and editorials, the analyses and advisories, were solemn and severe:

"Even more than before," The Greatest Publication That Absolutely Ever Was said in its lead editorial, "it is incumbent upon the members of the National Committee now gathering in Washington to take most seriously their grave task of selecting a new Presidential nominee. Coming as it does against a background of escalation in Gorotoland, and what seems to us a most dangerous principle of unilateral embargo of Panama, the choosing of a new nominee may well be one of the gravest events of this century.

"Not only is the circumstance in which the Committee meets one without historical precedent—for never has a Presidential nominee died before an election—but the general background of events is such as to call forth the prayers of all thoughtful men upon the Committee's work. Whether it decides to reconvene the convention—

the course that seems to us the most straightforward and desirable—or whether its 106 members reserve to themselves this desperately important task we wish it well.

"There is one other aspect which gives to its deliberations an awesome, even an ominous cast: the possibility that some supporters of Governor Jason may—if thwarted of their right to have the man they want at the head of the ticket—resort to acts of violence.

"Such acts, we believe, would be abhorrent. But, given the depth of feeling which has gathered around this remarkable and gifted man, we can see where some might consider them justified."

And from Walter himself, concluding his column for the day:

"Washington waits upon the man who sits silent in the White House—the man who, having fled silently from his California retreat, by silent means, for silent purposes, has come finally, in silence, to his capital.

"Washington knows what President Abbott will do in foreign affairs, for he has already demonstrated by his actions in recent hours in Gorotoland, Panama and the United Nations, what he will do: more of the same. More of the same dangerous gambling with the peace of the world which characterized the late President Hudson and still characterizes the Hudson-Abbott Secretary of State, Orrin Knox. More of the same use of violence in international affairs which has led, and can only continue to lead, to violence in domestic affairs as well.

"Washington does not know, however, what President Abbott will do with regard to the choice of a nominee to head his party's ticket in November. Washington knows that the choice will do one of two things: if it be Secretary Knox, it will send the nation further down the road of escalation, power politics, unilateral violations of the peace of the world. If it be Governor Jason, it will return America to the course of negotiation, responsibility, collective safety and peace.

"Washington waits upon the silent man in the White House, while the fate of this and future generations hangs in the balance, and while all around us the dark visage and fearful aspect of Violence Unchained threatens the Republic should the wrong decision be made."

But from the White House, as the world howled on and many of the President's countrymen sought to bend the future to their purposes according to their fights, there came no word. The press secretary would say only that the Chief Executive was preparing for the funeral tomorrow, and for the diplomatic reception he would give afterward at the State Department. He would have, the secretary said, no further word of any kind this night.

7.

NOR DID he see, really, why he should have, as another day began, this time far from Tahoe and a relatively calm atmosphere that he never expected to know again as long as he held this office. He had reached the mansion Monday afternoon, and his hours since had been absorbed in such an onslaught of pressures, crises and decisions that he had hardly had a moment to stop and think. As soon as the helicopter had deposited him on the lawn, he had been met by secretaries, Cabinet officers, old friends from the Hill, each bringing good wishes and encouragement inextricably entwined with his own particular problem. All the problems, it seemed, demanded immediate attention.

The President had found that somehow he was supposed to solve them all and at the same time sit down and familiarize himself with the latest news from the battlefronts; send suitable tributes to the funerals today of Air Force One's other victims; brief himself on the most recent developments in the missile race; the status of the American landing-station on the moon which had been established at the time of the Leffingwell nomination and had been growing rapidly in area and manpower ever since; the condition of the national economy; the diplomatic picture all over the world; the progress of negotiations in the shipping and railway disputes; the latest plan for urban renewal; the latest plan for fighting crime; the bill to establish twenty new national park, forest and seaside areas; the alternative programs for either expanding the Peace Corps or finally doing away with it altogether; the progress of the revised foreign aid program; the proposal that the Administration subsidize the so-called "M.M." or "Modi-Missile," the modified passenger missile with which the airlines hoped to replace all their old-fashioned supersonic jets by the turn of the century; the need for new constructions on the Tennessee, the Hudson, the Missouri, the Potomac, the Colorado and the Columbia rivers to serve the almost solid T.R.A.'s ("Triple R Areas"—Residence, Retail and Recreation) which now stretched out in all directions from those principal waterways; whether to increase the anti-missile defense line; the latest "personnel problem" in the State Department, which was the same old problem with only a new group of more or less famous faces to differentiate it from the last "personnel problem" in the State Department; the latest intelligence reports on the Communist Chinese drive toward Indonesia and the white nations beyond; and finally, Harley's death, the call of the National Committee, the planning of the funeral and all its attendant ceremonies and events, not the least of them being the problem posed by Patsy Labaiya who, true to her intention, had livened things up a bit by announcing a reception for the National Committee to be held the day after.

Somehow he had managed to go through all this without losing his temper, with a reasonable serenity, and with a smile for almost everyone. The only time he had not smiled had been when Mr. Justice Thomas Buckmaster Davis, that busy little soul who bustled about the edge of events neglecting his Supreme Court duties in favor of putting two fingers into every political pie, had insisted on seeing him last night. Their conversation had taken place after the American veto at the UN, and Tommy Davis' concern had been about equally divided between chagrin at this shocking new example of Administration intransigence and his ill-concealed glee that the world-wide reaction would help Ted Jason. In fact, after a sufficient amount of burbling, in his determined, fussy way, he had finally come out with the flat statement,

"Now, you know, Mr. President, that Ted stands to gain by this. He just can't escape it. You know that!"

"I do?" the President had inquired with an ominous quiet that would have served as warning to his colleagues on the Hill.

"Of course you do!" Tommy exclaimed triumphantly. "You *know* you do!"

"Now, how the hell," the President asked, spreading his hands flat out on the desk before him and staring at his ubiquitous visitor with all the impatience of Mr. Speaker at his most imperial, "would I know that? I have a country to run, Tommy, I can't be chasing around after little old messy politics all the time."

"*Bill!*" Tommy exclaimed. "Now, Mr. President, my dear boy—"

"I'm only about five years younger than you are, Tommy," the President interrupted. "Some 'boy!' I'm not one of your little legislative scholarship fellows who sits at Mr. Justice Davis' feet and thinks all wisdom flows from there. I know it's just political athlete's foot."

"Mr. President," Tommy Davis said indignantly, "now *that* is hitting below the belt. You are perfectly aware that I only participate in these programs because these fine young people from all over the country ask *specifically* to talk to me. I don't volunteer myself, Bill, you know I've never been one to do that. They always ask to see Mr. Justice Davis. Far more of them, I might add," he remarked with a somewhat waspish satisfaction, "than ask to see some of my distinguished brethren on the Bench. They know who can give them accurate information on what's going on in Washington, Bill. They're not fools!"

"And then they go back home with Washington As Seen By Tommy Davis clutched to their breasts and live in its light forever after. My God!" the President said, slapping one hand on the desk. "It's a wonder America survives!"

"Well, she won't survive, I can tell you that," Justice

Davis said sharply, "if Orrin Knox gets that nomination and becomes President."

"Sound pretty positive there, Tommy boy," the President remarked. "What makes you so certain? For that matter, what makes you so certain Orrin's going to have a chance at it? Or Ted either, for that matter?"

"Now, surely you don't mean—" Tommy began. His dismay became almost quivering. "Surely you *can't* mean—!"

"Why not?" the President inquired blandly. "I'm not doing so badly, Tommy. Maybe I like it here."

"But—"

"After all, it's a nice job. It grows on you. Might be I'll just stick around for a while, Tommy, and take that nomination myself. How would that be?"

"I think you will find," Justice Davis said, recovering with some effort, but recovering rapidly, "that it will not be as simple as you think, Bill. Even *you* will find difficulty in overcoming the great public demand which has centered for many months—and centers still—upon Governor Jason."

"Think it still does, eh? Well, I'm not so sure, Tommy. After that performance at the convention, and condoning all this violence, and all—"

"He issued a statement repudiating it!" Tommy Davis declared indignantly. "He just issued another, after the riot Sunday night. What do you want him to do, for heaven's sake, Bill?"

"It's one thing to issue statements," the President remarked. "This is a very statement-issuing town. It's another, how a man acts. Now, you take Ted Jason, it seems to me I've never seen a more perfect example of trying to maintain with your mouth that your feet aren't going where they're headed."

"He's a great public servant, doing the best he can in a difficult situation—"

"Tommy," the President said, holding up a hand. "I'm a great public servant, doing the best I can in a difficult situation. But when I say something, I *mean* it. That's the difference between the two of us, Tommy, and it doesn't take McCullough versus Tippecanoe to decide *that*."

"Marbury versus Madison," Justice Davis corrected automatically. "The thing is, Mr. President, you have to realize the difficult position that Ted is in vis-à-vis all these radical violent elements in the country—"

"I realize the position we're all in," the President said. "It's damned frightening. We've got to put them down before they put us down. What's your governor doing to help?"

"*My* governor, as you call him," Tommy said with dignity, "is trying to offer a constructive alternative to a foreign policy which seems to many sincere Americans to be leading us straight to the destruction of the world."

"And these sincere Americans will destroy America if they don't get their way," the President said. "Yes." He sat back and surveyed his visitor with a disgusted air. "They're a pack of children. Mean, nasty, evil little children, who will pull the house down if they don't get their way. I despise them!" He slapped his hand down hard again upon the desk. "And I despise anyone who can't see that by rationalizing their violence and calling it a genuine protest against policy he's doing their work for them and endangering—really endangering, Tommy, face it—the very life of his country."

174

"There," Justice Davis said archly. "There, my dear boy, you may get an argument."

"Yes," the President said. "Well. In any event, Tommy, it may all be academic, because, as I say, I may take that nomination myself."

"You can't win it," Justice Davis said flatly, and returned the President's challenging look with defiant head held high, bright little eyes snapping in his keen little face.

"Want to bet?" the President asked softly.

"I don't bet," Tommy said, "but I think you would lose it, all the same."

And possibly, the President thought after his visitor had gone bustling away, Tommy Davis was right, although he wasn't about to admit it to him, or even to himself, really. At the moment he did not have the slightest intention of running, but one never knew. At least he had achieved what he wanted with the threat of it: Tommy had announced defiantly that, late as it was, he was going to telephone his bosom buddy, the general director of the *Post*, "and I think you may find very lively opposition developing, Bill." "That's fine," the President said calmly. "I like a good fight." The more smoke he could throw up, at the moment, the better for the purposes he had in mind.

He had sat for a moment longer at his desk in the upstairs study, and then rose, as so many of his predecessors had before him, and walked out onto the balcony to stare across at the Washington Monument rising immaculate and perfect against the suffocating night. It had been another day in the nineties, no breeze stirred, the heat still lay heavy on Washington. He thought of many things and many men, and sighed. There was never peace in this house. Never.

Why, then, did so many want it, and why did even he, who had come to it unexpectedly and without desire, find himself perilously close to wanting it too?

Now, after a reasonably sound sleep, he had awakened to a day that seemed everywhere, and particularly in this sad house, unusually hushed and still. Everything was muted, there was little of the subdued but insistent stir and movement that he had already, in two short days in residence, come to recognize as characteristic of the White House as day began. His sister and brother-in-law in the next bedroom talked in quiet murmurs as they went about getting up. The knock of the valet on his door was startlingly loud. When the maid came with the breakfast trolley, the clink of silver on china and ice on glass seemed shattering. They ate on the balcony, and in the open air the hush over the city seemed as deep and complete as the silence in the house.

"Well," he said finally, pushing back from the table, "if you'll excuse me, I have an errand to perform."

"Give her our love," his sister said, and he nodded.

"I'll be in my office, after. They want us to be downstairs at the door promptly at eleven-fifteen."

"Yes," his sister said.

Quietly he left the balcony, quietly he went along the corridor to the other wing, smiling briefly but not speaking to the two solemn-faced maids he met along the way, and the two Marines who stood at attention by the stairs. Outside the door he paused for a moment to talk to the Navy nurse who had taken up vigil when Beth Knox and Dolly Munson had finally gone home yesterday morning. Then he knocked gently, heard her soft voice bid him enter. This was what the pomp and circumstance came to, when all was said and done: a sad widow, looking at him with sad eyes.

"Lucille, my dear," he said gravely, bending down to kiss her on the cheek. "How are you today?"

"Not—too bad, Bill," she said, with a little effort but managing. "I think I'm almost ready." She gave him a fleeting, self-deprecating smile. "I've been ready since six A.M., actually." She raised a hand that trembled noticeably and brushed her hair back above her right eye. "Now, isn't that foolish of me?"

"No," he said quietly. "It is not. May I sit down?"

"Oh, yes, of course," she said hastily. "What will you think of me? Sit over there by the window and I'll join you in a minute. The doctor says I'm to finish at least half my cereal, but"—and again the fleeting, sad little smile—"it isn't easy."

"I think he's right," he said, sitting on one of the sofas that faced each other across a rich ruby Aubusson. "It's going to be a difficult day."

At this comment, perhaps too blunt and unvarnished, but characteristic, she looked genuinely amused for a second.

"Dear Bill," she said. "Dear old Mr. Speaker!" Then the animation faded, the sadness rushed back. "I wonder," she said quietly, "if I'll get through it."

"Of course you will," he said; and, deliberately using the name: "Harley would expect you to."

For a moment he thought she might break down, but then it had the effect he hoped it would. She sat up straighter and took another spoonful of cereal with a thoughtful expression.

"Yes," she said presently, "he would. And of course I will. It won't last too long anyway, will it?"

"About two hours," he said. "We ride to the Capitol to get the—where the procession forms—and then back down through town to the bridge and over to Arlington—and then perhaps half an hour—and then that's it."

"That's it," she echoed bleakly. "That's it. Oh, Bill, I—"

"Now," he said, rising quickly, "suppose you abandon the rest of that cereal as a lost cause and come over here with me. We have things to discuss. Come along, now." And he put a hand under her arm and helped her stand up, which she managed somewhat shakily, but dutifully, as though she were an obedient little girl. "Now," he said, when she was seated facing him across the glowing rug, "what are you and I going to do to make sure that this country goes along the way Harley would have wanted it?"

"Yes," she said, and he was relieved to see that she was really considering the question, with an interest that brought back a little of her usual rosy warmth, "yes. I've been doing some thinking about that, Bill. I think you've done very well, so far—what you're doing overseas I think is what my husb—what Harley—would have done. I hope you won't let them scare you out of it."

"Scare *me?*" he asked with a mock-chiding disbelief. "Lucille!"

"Well, I know you won't," she said, with a smile that he was pleased to note was more like herself. "I can't imagine anybody scaring the Speaker out of anything. Particularly now," she added—and for a second she hesitated and he realized that she was making a real effort as she ended firmly—"now that he is the President."

178

"Thank you," he said gravely. "But there are vicious forces loose, Lucille. Vicious and dangerous."

She shivered and her eyes widened with remembered horror.

"Yes, I know. They were outside this house Sunday night. Oh, Bill!" she said urgently. "Do be careful, *do be careful!*"

"I shall," he promised grimly.

"They killed Harley, didn't they?" she asked, and for a long moment he did not answer, staring moodily out the window at the green trees, the Monument, the hot dull sky overcast with intimations of thunderstorms to come.

"I don't know, Lucille," he said finally. "I can't honestly say that. The commission is already finding some strange things. A couple of the crew were involved in a Communist group in Annapolis, there's a lead into the ground crew in San Francisco that may develop something, the body of a man with a gun was found among the victims—"

"No!" she protested in a horrified voice. "Then they—they weren't going to take any chances, were they? If it didn't happen one way, it would happen—"

"Now, Lucille," he said firmly, "you must not, you *must not*, let yourself get into that kind of thinking. All that we actually know is that Air Force One crashed because of some sort of malfunction. We have no evidence as yet of any genuine conspiracy, or any kind of plot, or anything. There are coincidences that are strange, but that's all we know. Until we know more, I don't think you should let yourself brood about it, because that way lies nothing but pain and unhappiness for years to come."

"I think Ted Jason knew about it," she said, almost in a whisper, and again he replied sharply and firmly.

"I think Ted Jason is a fool about certain things, but I don't think—don't think and won't say, and wouldn't want you ever to think or say, either—that he was in any way knowingly involved in Harley's death. Ted's an ill-advised and perhaps ill-fated man in many ways, but I don't believe that he would ever let himself be pushed that far. The irony of it is, of course," he added with a grim little smile, "that if the people who may have been responsible ever find the heat getting too much for them, they'll turn on him and try to make it appear that he did know. That's the type they are," he said with a sudden savage distaste. "Scum of the scum of the earth."

"They're going to cause trouble for Orrin, aren't they?"

He nodded.

"Surely. I think the convention was only the beginning. I think we're going to have many tense times before this is over, Lucille. And perhaps for years after that, if it doesn't come out the way they want."

"How horrible they are," she said softly. "They want to destroy this country, I think."

"I think so too. I took an oath, though, you know, to preserve, protect and defend, and by God, I'm going to do it. And so is Orrin, if he gets it. And even, so is Ted, if he gets it, unless he's absolutely worthless. And I don't think he is."

"No," she agreed with a wan little smile. "I suppose he isn't, really. He's like everything else in America, all mixed up between good and bad. . . . What do you want me to do, Bill? I'll do anything you say."

For a moment he looked at her thoughtfully. Then he smiled affectionately and shook his head.

"Nope. I'm not going to tell you what to do. I've always thought Lucille Hudson was one of the smartest politicians in this town. I expect you'll know what to do when you decide the timing is right. I'll just wait and be surprised like everybody else."

"Well," she said, and he could tell from her pleased expression that for the moment, at least, she was taken out of herself and her grief, "I'll just have to see what seems best."

"I'm sure instinct will tell you," he said. "What will you do, Lucille? Go back to Michigan?"

"Oh, no," she said promptly, and it was obvious that she had been giving this a lot of thought, too. "There's nothing for me there, any more, and here, at least, I can stay in the swing of things and still be part of what's going on. For the time being, I'm going to be with the Munsons."

"Are you," he said. "That will be nice for you. And nice for them."

"Yes," she agreed, looking excited and taken out of herself for a moment by the prospect. "You know that guest house Dolly has at 'Vagaries,' down the slope toward the greenhouse. It's all furnished and ready to occupy, with its own drive and entrance and all, so that I can be close to them and be with them when I want, but not be a burden. And Harley—left enough—so that money's no problem. And also, I suppose I get a—a pension from Congress, so I should be quite comfortable there, I think. For a while, at least. I may get my own place later."

"I think it's an excellent idea. And Lucille—you're always welcome here, you know. My sister and brother-in-law are going to be with me, and we'd all like to have you here just as often as you can."

"Thank you, Bill," she said, her eyes filling with tears. "I have so many good friends in Washington."

"Yes, you do," he said, "and don't you ever forget it. And now, my dear," he said gently, standing up and holding out his hand, "I've got to get back to the office and tend to some things before we go to the Hill."

"Of course," she said, her voice getting shaky again as she accompanied him to the door. "Downstairs at eleven-fifteen, is that right?"

"That's right," he said gravely. "Are your daughters and their families coming here, or do you want us to pick them up at the Carlton?"

"They're coming here in a few minutes," she said, her eyes filling again. "They wanted me to stay over there with them these past three days, but I—I wanted to stay here until—until—"

"Of course you did." He kissed her again. "Now, my dear—be brave for a little longer, and the ordeal will be over."

"It won't be too bad, will it?" she asked in a tiny voice, like a child seeking reassurance.

"No," he said gravely. "It won't be too bad."

But in this, of course, he was mistaken, for it was not a world nor a century that permitted the decent the privilege of being left in peace. It was a world of horrors in a century of evil, and on this day as on some others, all of its pretenses were stripped away and nothing but the glaring skeleton of mankind's hope looked out upon its ghastly spiritual desolation.

However, the funeral of Harley M. Hudson, late President of the United States, began in relative calm and dignity, and for a time it appeared that it would continue so to the end. Lucille was at the door at eleven-fifteen, white and trembling but holding her head high. Her two daughters, her sons-in-law and the five grandchildren were at her side. The President, his sister and his brother-in-law joined them a moment later. Senator Munson and Dolly, representing the Senate (Bob having been elected president *pro tempore* following the death of Senator Cooley) were with them, as were Representative Swarthman and Miss Bitty-Bug, representing the House, which had not yet had time to elect a successor to the Speaker. The Chief Justice and his eight associates came next, Tommy Davis tossing the President an archly defiant little glance as they formed in procession to go out to the limousines. Secretary of State Knox, Beth and his Cabinet colleagues and their wives, followed by the dean of the diplomatic corps and his wife, completed the White House party.

At eleven-thirty exactly, the first limousine, carrying the President, his sister and Mrs. Hudson pulled slowly away from the steps, the others following in evenly spaced procession. Slowly the cortege moved down the curving drive lined on both sides with the men of Army, Navy, Air Force and Marines standing rigidly at attention; turned right past Albert Gallatin and the Treasury, right again and down the short incline, and then left along Pennsylvania Avenue past thousands upon thousands of silent citizens, and the rigid double row of servicemen standing at ten-foot intervals all the way to the Capitol, looming on its hill a mile to the east.

There the members of the White House party left their cars and walked up the worn stone steps to the rotunda where more than half a million people of all races had filed past Harley's coffin during the twenty-four hours it had lain in state there, a tally that rather surprised some of Harley's critics who had thought he was as unpopular with his fellow citizens as he was with them. (Another 110,000 had paid their respects in the East Room of the White House before the body was moved to the Capitol.) Inside in the hushed chamber with the great dome soaring above, the light filtering down upon the catafalque and the grave faces of the dignitaries, the Senate, the House and the heads of foreign states joined the party. Then the flag-draped coffin was carried slowly down the steps and placed on the caisson drawn by eight matched grays. The cortege reassembled in its limousines, orders rang out in the still, humid air; the beat of muffled drums began, and with a slow, implacable, heart-shattering dignity, yet another President of the United States began his last journey down Capitol Hill.

Again the cortege moved slowly, slowly, along Pennsylvania Avenue to the Federal Triangle, past solemn-faced young servicemen and silent thousands (quite a few, reporters noted, were weeping, though it was only for bumbling old Harley Hudson, that poor excuse for a President); slowly it turned left into Constitution Avenue, moved slowly past the great federal buildings and more thousands standing hushed and respectful; turned left and, at Lucille's request, left again and around the east side of the Lincoln Memorial so that for a moment the statue of the saddest of all Presidents looked down upon the somber passage of his distant successor; moved slowly across Memorial Bridge toward Lee Mansion and Arlington National Cemetery on their soft green hills; and there, under the sullen heat of a sullen sky, met the anguish of the age as another procession, led by a hearse and seeming to materialize out of nowhere, shot from the left through the surprised, unsuspecting ranks of military and police and careened alongside the Presidential cortege with horns blaring, riders screaming and placards waving.

In the wild confusion of the next fifteen minutes, reporters and cameramen stationed high on the approaches to Arlington Cemetery were able to discern and transmit to a horrified nation the fact that several of the cars in the opposing group were emblazoned with the flaming torch of KEEP, the clenched fist of DEFY, the stylized white dove of COMFORT; that their passengers, shouting wild obscenities at the Presidential party, were composed about equally of whites and blacks; that the placard affixed to the top of the hearse made clear the purpose of this ghastly intrusion—SYLVESTER SMITH, NEGRO: KILLED AT THE WHITE HOUSE IN OPPOSITION TO THE HUDSON-KNOX WARS. GOING TO A HERO'S GRAVE IN ARLINGTON—and that the hobbledehoy crew in their screeching vehicles, might be perilously close to achieving the intent described in the savage chant that soon filled a hundred million homes:

INTO THE DITCH, YOU SON OF A BITCH! INTO THE DITCH, YOU SON OF A BITCH! INTO THE DITCH, YOU SON OF A BITCH! INTO THE DITCH, YOU SON OF A BITCH!

That the late President's coffin was spared this final horror was due in major part to the quick thinking of his successor, who sprang from his limousine and shouted to the stunned military to close in and protect the caisson, his own and the immediately following cars. It was also due to the drivers of the matched grays, who somehow managed to hold rein on their terrified animals (that evening they would tell their wives that they had thought their arms would be torn from their sockets; but it had to be done, and so they did it); and to the fact that after the first few seconds of stunned disbelief, the military and police did move, the ranks did close, the procession was protected and the invaders were driven off. By some miracle that he was later to thank God for, the President was able to make his own roar of "Don't shoot! Don't shoot!" heard above the melee, and no one did: the invaders were robbed of the martyrdom they would dearly have loved to provoke. But tear gas and nerve gas were available, and were used; and after some fifteen minutes of chaos, they scuttled back to their cars and screeched away toward the cemetery, up the hill and out of sight among the trees, to the spot where, a few minutes later, dutifully recorded by a section of the television crews and reporters who had been quickly reassigned by their alert and fast-thinking superiors to cover this ghastly side show, Sylvester Smith, a veteran of his nation's foreign wars and domestic agonies, was laid to rest.

After such an interruption, the ceremonies for Harley Hudson were concluded under a terrible psychological burden. His wife and family were so close to hysteria that the President was not sure they were going to get through the brief interment without losing control completely. He himself, phlegmatic though he was by nature and deliberate self-discipline, was shattered as he had rarely been in all his life. There hung over the committal of President Hudson's remains to earth a sadness beyond words and very nearly beyond bearing. It communicated itself to the country, where decent citizens wondered with a horrified dismay what was going to happen to America; a wonder made even more frightening when the parallel coverage of the two funerals in Arlington was lent a final terrible note. It was announced about an hour after the cortege had returned to the White House and dispersed that two men wearing masks had run past the sentries at the grave, splashed a bucket of black paint on the headstone and tossed upon the plain white sarcophagus a placard bearing the words, scrawled in blood (of an ox, laboratory analysts at Bethesda Naval Hospital reported later):

SO DIE ALL WAR MAKERS.

8.

OUT OF SUCH horrors the President spoke to his countrymen at nine-thirty that evening, and it was declared, by those who declare such things, that 210,637,209 citizens of the unhappy Republic sat before their television sets and watched him do it. Such statistics were then, as always, a little difficult to prove, but had there been anyone moving in the streets of the hushed cities and the quiet towns, or in the vast empty reaches where only the twinkling lights of an occasional ranch house broke the deepening dusk, he would have seen that the land was silent and listening as it had rarely listened before.

So, too, was the world, linked by satellite into an audience that stretched from Tierra del Fuego to Tibet, from the Cape of Good Hope to Baffin Bay. Wherever men lived, they heard on the "Voice of America" the terse sentences and calm, unhurried tones of the Chief Executive who now led the nation most of them either feared, despised, ridiculed or deplored; and for this he was grateful because he wanted, as he had told Bob Leffingwell a couple of hours ago, to give it to them straight, so that no one anywhere would have any doubts about his intentions, his ideas, or his character. His decision to spell it out beyond mistake had been made in the limousine riding back to the White House with a Lucille Hudson once again on the edge of collapse, and a sister whose white face and strained expression epitomized for him what he knew must be the reaction of millions upon millions of his countrymen. The majority of them, he knew, were decent people, inclined to look upon the world with good will, not perfect always, not tolerant always, sometimes impatient and erratic in their judgments and emotions, but still basically goodhearted and well-meaning. The America they had known—or, idealistically, had liked to think they had known, under all the shabbiness and dross of recent decades—was being whirled away from them by ruthless and despicable men. He could sense that his sister for the first time was genuinely frightened for her country, with a terror and uncertainty she had never felt before. And he knew that many millions—still, he hoped, the great majority—of his fellow Americans felt an equal concern in the face of the acts of the evildoers.

To him fell the task of reassurance. His instinct for timing told him it must be done at once. His instinct for a good speech, the realities of politics and what he believed to be the ultimate good of his country told him whom he should get to help him. Five minutes after commending Lucille to the care of her family and the Munsons, he had detached Orrin Knox from the somber group of dispersing officials and taken him off to the upstairs study. Five minutes after that a startled but perforce compliant Orrin was putting through a call to Arlington Ridge Road. Half an hour after that a startled but perforce compliant Robert A. Leffingwell had joined them. Together they began to draft the speech.

Very promptly, the task broadened.

"I'm going to reassure 'em," he remarked thoughtfully, "but I'm also going to tell a few people here and abroad a few home truths. This is my first speech since taking office and I'm going to let 'em have it. I want to cover violence and the foreign picture and the nomination and a few other things, while I'm at it." He gave a sudden grim little smile. "May not be here tomorrow. Never know, nowadays."

He had then left them and gone off to the State Department for the diplomatic reception scheduled for four P.M., telling Orrin to stay where he was.

"Give Walter Dobius and friends something to think about," he said in the same grimly humorous vein. "They'll wonder where you are. If they only knew. And if they only knew who you're working with. Right, Bob?"

"Right," Bob Leffingwell said, not looking too comfortable, the President thought. He paused at the door.

"If you're not happy about it, Bob, you can go home. No law says you have to stay."

"Oh, no," Bob said quickly. "I didn't say I was unhappy,

Mr. President. I'm still a little numb at being asked to be here, but—if that's what you want—"

"It's what I want," the President said. "We won't tell anybody." He turned to the Secretary of State. "Orrin?"

Orrin looked quizzical, shrugged, then smiled.

"I guess we won't kill each other."

The President snorted.

"I hope not. Keep working. I'll be back here by six."

In the great banquet hall of the State Department the atmosphere was quivering, as he had known it would be. No one dared mention the funeral, everyone expected him to. He took a cold satisfaction from mentioning it not at all. Presidents, kings and prime ministers, most of whom vehemently opposed his actions in Gorotoland, Panama and the UN, many of whom almost certainly relished his discomfiture and that of his country this day, came down the line and shook his hand. He wrapped himself in the formidable dignity of Mr. Speaker, greeted them with exactly the right amount of smile, stared at them with a courteous but inscrutable impassivity, and said nothing of any import whatsoever. "The Caretaker President" became "The Great Stone Face" in the next editions. "A somber and unyielding President Abbott today greeted visiting foreign dignitaries following the riot-besmirched funeral of President Hudson," the first news stories began. Not even the new President of the Sixth (People's) French Republic was able to elicit more than a calm stare when he made some slyly condescending reference to "the difficulties we all face in this difficult world." "Do we?" the President asked, and turned away to greet the next in line.

At no point did he make a comment that might remotely be construed as bearing upon either United States involvements overseas or the dreadful events of the day. By the time he left the reception, shortly before six, he had successfully established an aura of mystery in the minds of his drinking, gossiping, hors d'oeuvres-gulping guests. Orrin's absence nicely compounded it. *What are they up to?* was the general burden of the noisy crowd of famous global leaders upon whom he looked back for a moment with the briefest but most explicit expression of contempt as he departed. The expression of course was noted too. A genuine uneasiness followed his departure. This was, after all, the President of the United States. They did not like to have him acting like a cold and implacable man. It disturbed them, which was what he wanted it to do.

Promptly at six P.M. the press secretary called in the reporters hanging about in the lobby and announced that the President would go on the air at nine. At that point Orrin and Bob Leffingwell had the first draft finished. The President told them to order some drinks and dinner for themselves in the study, took the scribbled-over, crossed-out, written-in pages into his bedroom, propped himself up comfortably on some pillows and began to read and edit. By seven he had it shaped up about the way he wanted it and took it back out to Orrin and Bob, who were, he was pleased to see, in quietly amicable conversation. He called in a secretary, dictated his revised version to the accompaniment of their last-minute suggestions; read it slowly through once again aloud, making a few final corrections in his round, firm hand; sent it down to be typed for delivery. This brought him up to eight-fifteen.

He decided he needed half an hour's rest, decided also that a sudden change of plan would be good for his critics' psychological equilibrium. He told the press secretary to notify the networks that he would speak at nine-thirty instead of nine, which caused great outcries and anguish ("He can't *do* that!" NBC wailed to the press secretary. "He can't?" the secretary said. "Know anybody who can stop him?"). It also made the world even more uneasy about his intentions, which, he thought with a sardonic amusement, was a good thing. He lay down for thirty minutes of instant, deep sleep; was wakened by his valet promptly at nine, got up, washed, put on the freshly pressed suit laid out for him, and by nine-twenty was downstairs in the television room ready to go. The Great Seal appeared on the screens at nine-thirty exactly, a hushed voice uttered the standard, "Ladies and gentlemen, from the White House in Washington, D.C., we bring you the President of the United States," and he was on. He felt grave and looked grave. He also felt powerful and looked powerful. He was in no mood to equivocate.

"My countrymen," he said, looking straight into the cameras, "my first word to you is this: your country is still here. She is going to remain here. Under my administration she is going to do what is best and right for her to do. Neither foreign critics nor domestic guttersnipes are going to deflect her one inch.

"To those who desecrated this sad day, and to those who either by deed or thought supported them, I say: you have met your match. I am sending to Congress tomorrow a message outlining a stringent anti-riot law which will give the Federal Government extensive and necessary powers to protect itself against anarchy—and protect the honest citizen in the honest exercise of his right of dissent *as long as that dissent is peaceable, law-abiding and within the customary norms of decent social behavior.*

"While I hold this office, we will never again tolerate the sort of thing that has gone on in this country too much in recent years. We will never again tolerate the vicious, insane anarchism which has as its sole purpose, not honorable protest, but the deliberate destruction of American government and American society—the deliberate destruction of America herself."

(He stopped to take a sip of water, and in his apartment in Tiber Towers near the Capitol, Fred Van Ackerman turned to Rufus Kleinfert and said smugly, "He'll have a hell of a fight on that one. Listen to the damned liberals yelp!")

"To those honest critics of American foreign policy," the President resumed, "whose reasonable right to protest has been kidnapped by the rioters, the racists"—he paused and gave the next words full impact—"and the rats, I say to you that your government welcomes honest criticism. But I believe, as did the great President we buried today, that you are mistaken and that the present international situation requires us to do the things we are doing.

"Let me spell them out once more, for you and for all those overseas who honestly"—and again he paused and gave his words an uncompromising emphasis—"or dishonestly—oppose what we are doing in Gorotoland and Panama.

"There was a challenge to us, and to human decencies, in Gorotoland. President Hudson warned those responsible. They did not listen. Forty-four American missionaries were raped, murdered, mutilated. American property was wantonly destroyed. A Communist-trained, Communist-financed and Communist-led attempt was made to overturn the legitimate government of Gorotoland.

"In keeping with his repeated warnings to those responsible, President Hudson ordered American intervention. He did so to protect American rights, to uphold the principle of legitimate government, to restore order and stability to a vital section of the African continent; and to stop, if you please, further Communist advances in that continent.

"Three days ago there came into the possession of your government Communist battle plans contemplating an all-out assault in Gorotoland. This assault was to have been timed to coincide with our day of national mourning today.

"Your government," he said calmly, "stopped it. I ordered in additional troops and an assault of our own upon the rebel capital of Mbuele. After early reverses yesterday, that drive is succeeding. I have been informed within the hour that the rebels are abandoning Mbuele and retreating to the highland mountains and plateaus.

"We shall pursue them there," he said bluntly, "until they are beaten.

"In Panama, an adventurer who had been planning for many years to seize the country and the Canal, found Communist support for his dreams and started trying to do it. Again, President Hudson moved. Again, captured Communist battle plans disclosed a proposed all-out attack for today, simultaneous with the one in Gorotoland. Again, your government responded.

"We have not yet," he said—and a certain ironic line came around his lips—"persuaded some of our best and dearest foreign friends to go along with us on the principle that it is better to blockade the Panamanian rebels than it is to bomb them out of existence—something which, of course," he added dryly ("He is so arrogant!" Raoul Barre murmured to the Ambassador of Lesotho. "So arrogant."), "we are completely able to do.

"Still, we have hopes that in time they will see it our way.

"Certainly we do not intend to change *our* policy. Nor will we hesitate to enforce it if we must. ("Oh, dear!" Krishna Khaleel said nervously to Lord Maudulayne in the crowded, quivering delegates' lounge. The British Ambassador murmured, "Quite," with a worried air.)

"We shall restore stability and order to Panama," the President said quietly. "No Communist-backed adventurer will be allowed to seize the Canal." Again the sardonic tone came into his voice. "We shall exercise the first right of nature—we shall survive.

"One further thing I must say to you tonight in this first talk as your President. It concerns the election this fall.

"You all know the situation which confronts my party. It does not now have a candidate for President, though it still has one for Vice President, the Honorable Orrin Knox of Illinois, Secretary of State.

"Both Secretary Knox and the Governor of California ("That's right!" Walter exclaimed bitterly. "Don't name him!") have, as you know, declared their intention to seek the Presidential nomination through the mechanism provided by our party's rules. Those rules have never in history had to be used. Now, tragically, they must be.

"Therefore, by right of the authority vested in me as chairman of the National Committee, and as head of the party, I am tonight issuing a call to the members of the Committee to meet in the Playhouse of the Kennedy Center ("Why there?" Bob Munson wondered aloud to Dolly and Lucille at "Vagaries." Then he said, "Oh, I see.") at ten A.M. on Tuesday next for the purpose of selecting a nominee for the office of President of the United States—and, should events so develop, for the office of Vice President of the United States.

"It is my hope," the President said, "and my expectation," he added firmly, "that the members of the Committee will be able to complete their work swiftly, so that our party and you, the voters, may know at an early date the choices that we will have in November.

"And now," he said, "I conclude this first talk to you as President. I expect to speak to you again from time to time, as may be desirable to keep you fully informed on the purposes and plans of your government. I wish that a tragic event had not put me in this office. But as long as I have it," he concluded quietly, staring straight into the cameras and giving the impression of solid and immovable determination that he had always managed to convey in his long years in the House, "I intend to exercise it to the best of my knowledge and ability, as God sees fit to assist me.

"I ask you to join your prayers with mine that He will do so.

"God bless you, and good night."

PRESIDENT CLAIMS GAINS IN GOROTO-LAND, the headlines said. PLEDGES CONTINUED

FIRMNESS IN OVERSEAS WARS. PROMISES STRONG ANTIRIOT LAW TO HIT "RIOTERS, RACISTS AND RATS." CALLS NATIONAL COMMITTEE TO CHOOSE NEW PRESIDENTIAL NOMINEE . . .

GOVERNOR JASON CAUTIONS AGAINST "UNCONSTITUTIONAL MEANS TO THWART CONSTITUTIONAL PROTEST." PLEDGES OWN PROPOSAL TO CURB VIOLENCE. CALLS ON COMMITTEE TO RECONVENE CONVENTION. CHARGES "RAILROADING IN FAVOR OF HAND-PICKED HEIR . . . "

SECRETARY KNOX REFUSES COMMENT . . .

WORLD ALARMED BY PRESIDENT'S FIRMNESS, DETERMINATION TO GO IT ALONE ON PANAMA BLOCKADE. SOVIETS, BRITISH, FRENCH, TAKE LEAD IN DENOUNCING "DANGEROUS UNILATERALISM." STRONG WORLD SUPPORT FOR JASON PEACE POLICIES SEEN DEVELOPING . . .

And at "Salubria," Walter Dobius, summing it up for tomorrow's column, his fingers racing on the keys:

"Washington is saddened and depressed tonight following the first statement of policy from President Abbott. Not so much because the President has revealed himself, in the opinion of many, to be a self-willed and headstrong man, at a time when America has suffered too much from that type in the White House—but because the policy he offers is so stereotyped, so unyielding, and so dangerous.

"America will continue her attempts to impose her will by force on the small, backward nation of Gorotoland.

197

America will move unilaterally, if need be, to impose an illegal and potentially world-exploding blockade upon the forces fighting to liberate Panama. America will do as America pleases, with the brief and fatal arrogance that history gives to those who think a temporary position of power will last forever.

"Even more, Washington is dismayed by the President's call for what he apparently contemplates as an iron-fisted prohibition on all legitimate protest against his Administration's policies. And Washington links this with his obvious determination to manipulate the National Committee in such a way as to guarantee the election of Secretary Knox as its nominee.

"In that direction lies potential fascism, the iron fist of dictatorship, the hand-picked heir that has always been so repugnant to America.

"Congress must reject this ill-advised and terribly dangerous proposal for a gag-bill. The National Committee must reject this obvious attempt to force it to take Secretary Knox. An end to this gag-bill—and a motion to recall the national convention that it may freely and openly work its will—are the basic things Washington believes must be done now. . . . "

At the White House he talked for a while with his sister and brother-in-law; accepted a few calls, one from Lucille Hudson, somewhat calmer now, and another, quite surprising, from Ceil Jason; read over the first reactions as furnished by the press secretary from the hurrying teletypes in the press room; stood for a few minutes on the balcony, looking at the Washington Monument in the hot, oppressive night which still flickered uneasily with flashes of lightning from the tremendous thunderstorm that had hit the District shortly after seven P.M.; and went in to bed, and almost instantly asleep.

The last thing he watched on television was Frankly Unctuous on his late-news round-up, "The Day Behind Us."

"The President is obviously making it difficult for the National Committee to recall the convention," Frankly was saying in his most pursed-lip, disapproving manner.

So he was, the President thought with a contemptuous satisfaction as he punched the button and watched that round, superior little pudding-face dwindle into nothing.

And what did Frankly and his friends think they could do about it, except bellow?

II

BOB LEFFINGWELL'S BOOK

1.

RETURNING TO HIS empty house after the President's address, he finds a postcard from Louise at Chocorua. "I hope you're happy," it says with the words underlined three times and three enormous exclamation marks after. That is all. There is no indication of what she is referring to. Happy because riots have occurred? Happy because the President has increased the tempo in Gorotoland and Panama? Happy because she isn't there? He shakes his head with a tired, impatient smile. What oblique, elliptical interpretation of things has she come up with this time? It baffles him, as it has so often in the uneasy years of their marriage.

He quickly shreds the card, tosses it in a wastebasket, forgets it. There are other matters for Robert A. Leffingwell to be concerned about tonight, and Louise must retire to that rather neglected corner of his mind that she normally occupies: a rather sad little commentary, but characteristic of many a prominent marriage in the shining capital, which rearranges lives and emotions at whim and often reveals to husbands and wives that they are moving at entirely different tempos than they thought they were, when they and the world were young.

Right now his mind is occupied with the events of the past six hours: the implications they seem to hold for his future, the light they appear to throw on his past, the consequences they may have for his reputation. In Washington, where the care and feeding of the ego often take precedence over love, sex, marriage, hearth, home and health, Bob Leffingwell is following the standard pattern. Where do *I* fit in? What will it mean for *my* future? How do *I* feel about it? How will it affect what is obviously the center of the universe—*me*?

There is in him, however—nearing fifty, handsome, highly intelligent, extremely capable—a saving grace, and he is honest enough to acknowledge to himself that it probably comes to him courtesy of Orrin Knox. Had anyone told him a year ago that he would ever feel for the Secretary anything but a bitter dislike, he would have scoffed the suggestion down with some withering witticism. Nowadays he finds he doesn't make that kind of witticism any more. Something gentling, alleviating, mitigating an old arrogance has entered his being. Orrin Knox gave him a lesson when he defeated him for Secretary of State, and he is finally able to admit the fact to himself. He is even, wry though the thought makes him, beginning to feel the start of gratitude.

In these recent weeks leading up to the convention, he has been going through a quiet personal revolution. Tonight's events have accelerated and advanced it. It amazes him now, as he changes quickly into his swimming trunks, gets a beer from the refrigerator and goes out to his favorite chaise longue beside the pool in the hot, humid night, to think how far he has come from the supercilious public servant who burst out of the Midwest fifteen years ago with all the answers about everything—all of them self-consciously "liberal," all of them arrogant and all of them blindly and ruthlessly intolerant of any other point of view.

In this, he recognizes now, he was suffering from the liberal syndrome of the twentieth century, which said that all knowledge, justice and purity lay on the left and all evil, intolerance and reaction lay on the right. He has learned that nothing on earth can be so intolerant and reactionary as a humorless professional liberal and he understands now as he never did before that out of intolerance and reaction only evil, in the long run, can come.

He and his fellows in all that arrogant, ruthless crew that dominated the thinking of the world in these past decades have a great deal to answer for. That world is in near-collapse. Its societies are in chaos, its laws in disarray, its decencies disappearing, its hopes of survival dwindling fast. How much are the conservatives responsible, for opposing necessary programs for the achievement of a more humane society! But how much also are the liberals responsible, for attempting to impose upon that society an arbitrary form that had no relation to human realities and offered only the most ruthless hostility to those who sought to inject a little human reality into it. How horribly far down the road to destruction has intolerant idealism taken mankind: especially in the hands of those for whom idealism has been only a tool with which to manipulate the naïve for the purposes of the Communist imperialism, harshest and most oppressive of them all.

How many of the sincerely self-deluded—as distinct

203

from the cold, deliberate agents of that imperialism—realize their responsibility and their blame? Not many, he tells himself grimly now. It takes a little humbling such as he has been through to bring about that kind of self-scarifying honesty. Many of them will not be humbled until the final great humbling of us all, when it will be far too late for anyone to make amends or do anything at all about it.

So he is not too sorry to find that bidding farewell to that kind of harshly rigid "liberalism" does not dismay him as it would have done at an earlier time of his life. There are many in the great sprawling city twinkling softly across the lazy river in the hazy night who will go on being true to that concept of liberalism until the day they die—or the world dies. There are many in other great cities, in schools, in churches, in places of power and influence in the press, who will never waver and never relax in their relentless hostility to all who dare expose or challenge the futility and emptiness of their beliefs. The world has passed them by, they are old-fashioned and out of date; but on they go, harsh and rigid and intolerant to the end, trapped in their own pride, unable to make the simple but to them terrifying and soul-destroying admission, "We are not perfect—we may be wrong." Self-limited and self-robbed of the ability to adapt to the realities of human behavior in a changing time, they are as immovable as bugs self-immolated in amber, eons ago.

No longer for him, thank you very much; and as he thinks back now upon that perfect public servant who came to Washington—perfect in everything but tolerance, compassion and an open mind—he thanks God for the change. He has not traveled an easy road in the last two years, but from it he is beginning to emerge with a reasonable peace of mind, a reviving self-respect, and a concept of integrity rather far from that with which he began.

In basic outline the facts of his life have been simple enough, just as Senator Tom August of Minnesota, chairman of the Senate Foreign Relations Committee, described them on that morning, which now seems very long ago, when the committee began its consideration of "the nomination of Robert A. Leffingwell to be Secretary of State."

Forty-nine years old, born in Binghamton, New York, attended elementary and high school there. Graduated from the University of Michigan with a degree in public administration. Received his law degree from Harvard. Taught public administration for four years at the University of Chicago. Appointed to the Southwest Power Administration, becoming director of its public service division four years later. Five years after that, appointed director of the Southwest Power Administration. Seven years ago, appointed chairman of the Federal Power Commission. Two years ago, given temporary leave to accept appointment as Director of the Office of Defense Mobilization.

A year and a half ago, nominated for the office of Secretary of State. Defeated by the Senate after he lied to the Senate Foreign Relations Committee concerning a youthful, innocent and stupid flirtation with Communism at the University of Chicago twenty years ago. Appointed by the late President Harley M. Hudson to the position of director of the President's Commission on Administrative Reform, which he still holds.

Active in international conferences for many years, including terms as chairman of the International Hydroelectric and Power Conferences in Geneva and Bombay; arbitrator between India and Pakistan in their recent water dispute; principal United States delegate to the United Nations Conference on Water, Power and Economic Development of Underdeveloped Areas.

Married to the former Louise Maxwell; two children, Richard, married, of Sandia, New Mexico, and Annette (Mrs. H. B. Sears) of Eglin Air Force Base, Florida. Resident of Manhattan and Alexandria, Virginia. Member of Phi Beta Kappa, the American Bar Association and the Metropolitan Club of Washington.

Expert on government, supremely competent administrator, given numerous awards as "America's outstanding public servant." Somewhat flawed by the past two years, but not, he tells himself with satisfaction as he gets up on a sudden impulse and plunges into the pool, as flawed as he was. . . .

Back in his chair, dripping but perfectly comfortable in the warm unstirring night, he stares thoughtfully across at the city that looks so placid but has such explosive forces roiling in it, and asks himself how he could ever have moved so far from reality as to deny that he had known Herbert Gelman at the University of Chicago. But even as he asks, he knows: because he wanted to be Secretary of State, and all else fell before that overriding desire.

Given the circumstances of those hectic days that saw his nomination, the Foreign Relations Committee hearings, the bitter Senate debate, the tragic death of Brigham Anderson, his defeat, Harley's appointment of

206

Orrin Knox to fill the office he had so fiercely wanted—
he cannot say with certainty even now whether the outcome would have been any different had he told the
truth. His opponents had already charged him with being "an appeaser . . . soft on Communism . . . weak,
wishy-washy . . . willing to compromise America's principles for a temporary respite from tension that will only
be renewed in worse form tomorrow"—and so on. To
have admitted an early flirtation with Communism, however foolish and ineffectual, would only have increased
the outcry a thousandfold. He would have been defeated
anyway.

Or would he? If he had been able to show the esca-
pade for what it was, an outgrowth of a lingering youthful idealism, an empty gesture which meant no harm and
did no harm—if he had been honest about it and thrown
himself on the mercies of the Senate and the country—
would he have lost? And if he had, would it not have
been better to lose that way, rather than to lose after lying to the Senate, and then have Herbert Gelman materialize like a sickly ghost from the past, point the finger
and say, "He did it. I was there."

At least then he would not have defeated himself in
his own heart.

But everyone on his side, of course, had wanted him
to lie at the time. They believed as firmly as he did—
and his belief was quite sincere, and he was not ashamed
of it, and had it still—that he did have much to contribute to the country and to world peace, that he could negotiate constructively with the Communists, that it was
vital that he contribute his talents to saving the world
from war, and do so in the most important Cabinet of-

fice of them all. It had not taken much to move this conviction into the realm of an arrogant, absolute self-confidence that would brook no opposition and accept no other possibility. And of course he had not been alone in this. He would be willing to bet right now that if he had consulted the *Post*—The Greatest Publication—Walter Dobius—any of that powerful group that were on his side in that fight, they would have said: keep quiet about it: if necessary, lie. The President had known about it, after all—that brilliant, effervescent, unfathomable man who had occupied the White House until Harley succeeded to it following his sudden death at the end of the Leffingwell battle—and the President had told him to keep silent. They had all wanted him to win. They were as ruthless for him then as now they were ruthless against him.

So there might have been no difference in the outcome, whichever way he had conducted himself. The only difference would have been in his own heart, which knew, whether his supporters did or not, what he had done to himself when he denied that he had ever known a former student of his named Herbert Gelman.

From that self-inflicted wound it had taken him all this time to recover, but recovery, he knew now, had begun with his defeat by Orrin Knox. It had proceeded slowly, almost subconsciously, for a number of months, as he had begun cautiously to venture forth again. It had come to crisis when a combination of gratitude to Harley for salvaging his public career, and horror at the extremes of violence to which ambition was carrying Ted Jason, had resulted in his leaving Ted's cause at the convention to place Harley in nomination.

And in some curious, almost offhand way, it had settled into what he felt instinctively was to be its final and irrevocable form this afternoon, when Orrin, on the President's orders, had asked him to come to the White House, and he had agreed.

That decision, reached in a moment in his silent house, had been the almost automatic response that most Americans would still give to such a request: if the President needs my help, I'll do it. He had not paused to calculate its effects upon himself, had accepted it almost without thinking. Yet when he was driving, almost as in a trance, over the bridge into town, there had come to him the sudden certainty that he was doing the right thing. By the simple act of asking, the President had resolved many conflicts; and though he has already had, and no doubt will have later, some substantial misgivings about details, in totality he is satisfied. In a sense, shrewd old Mr. Speaker has done his deciding for him, and he realizes that he feels a genuine relief that the struggle is over.

Relief, and a sense of wonder that he suspects will remain with him for a while. Robert A. Leffingwell the liberal—still, he firmly believes, the liberal—falling in line with an Administration that theoretically stands for everything he has always opposed. How can it be that he feels so few qualms and so much peace of mind?

Looking down the convoluted corridors of the liberal years, since his youthful idealism first convinced him that the world must be remade in new ways and new patterns, he recognizes with an ironic—but friendly—smile for that distant believer, that he certainly followed the standard pattern for a long time. In college he was a philosophic leader in all those campaigns that so sternly ordered America to end and the world to get out. He was anti this and anti that, and always what he was against could be related to the established order of things. Yet he did not go as far as some of his contemporaries and opt out of society altogether to go wandering down paths of immaturity and self-destruction that led nowhere. Bob Leffingwell was basically too mature and too convinced of his own destiny to do that.

He had strayed close to what came in time to be described as "the New Left"—that phrase, so beloved of certain segments of the mass media, which really described just the same Old Left with a new generation of stooges to manipulate for its own imperialistic, Commufascist purposes. But he had never quite gone irrevocably over. Even when he had met and fallen in love with intense little Louise Maxwell, who was militant where he was philosophic, emotional where he was basically thoughtful.

How horribly serious and humorless so many of them had been in those days! How far they had persuaded themselves to go in swapping reality for an upside-down, cock-a-hoop vision of the world and society. What a strange psychotic state they lived in, encouraged by a press which tenderly front-paged their every unmannerly public belch and breaking of wind. And how desperately did some of them cling to immaturity still, despite all the evidence of all the years.

It was Louise's intensity, he supposed, which had captured him more than anything else. This was a mate with whom a philosopher might storm the barricades. She did it every day, her bare, strained, not unpretty little face contorted with her bitterness against America. Never had

210

the noisy minority of a generation hated its own country more than Louise and her friends hated America; and with her, as with so many, he could never understand exactly why. She came of a wealthy, established family, had been given the most comfortable of childhoods. She had no reason, but for a long time she was as insensate and unthinking as the rest. It was the fashionable thing to do, in their generation, and so they did it with that herd instinct of a certain segment of the young that stifles all thought and murders all individuality. The vast majority of their generation went quietly along getting an education, preparing themselves for constructive lives, becoming responsible citizens: Louise and her kind, everyday darlings of the media, rode high, wide and handsome in the days of their noisily pathetic youth.

For him it was an intellectual, not an emotional, matter. He kept to himself some basic reservations, for he did not really see for Robert A. Leffingwell any great future in destroying American society. If he had a future, and he believed he did, it was within the framework of that society, not in any chaos that might follow its destruction. And gradually, as time passed and they married and the children came, it seemed to him that Louise, too, acquired a certain maturity and mellowing, though she was still capable of flaring up in a white-lipped, implacable way about her country's policies.

Gradually these outbursts became less, though she was always to be found in the front ranks of the middle-aged spread that overtook youthful rebellion as the years went on. Now her protests took the form of occasional attendance at the meetings of antiwar groups, donations to the Committee Condoning This, the Consensus Against

That, her signature on petitions to Congress and full-page ads in the New York *Times* (moving higher up the list as he moved higher up the government). The barricades did not fit too well with a husband rising in the public service and a five-bedroom house on Arlington Ridge Road.

He had been genuinely surprised, however, that Seab Cooley or some member of the Foreign Relations Committee had not tried to raise the issue of Louise's record and smear him with it during the hearings. No one had, and he had finally concluded, with a certain grudging disbelief that he was now ashamed of, that perhaps United States Senators weren't as bad as he had always suspected. Louise's past could have been a serious handicap to him, had it not turned out, ironically and through his own doing, that his own was quite enough.

Still, she had always furnished the sort of aura that had enabled him to remain in good standing with what he thought of as the "professional liberals." The professional liberals, in his definition, were those who worked at it, for whom there was an unending, intolerant, relentless war against all differing opinion, for whom everything was always my-my and terribly-terribly, even as they too rose to being three-martini and wall-to-wall.

Louise remained, and helped him to remain, dreadfully In with all the Right People; and, as he was shrewdly aware and cynically capable of using, this did no harm to his career and reputation in an era dominated in major degree by certain powerful elements of the mass media, with their ability, through column, syndicate and broadcast, to condition the country coast-to-coast.

He had never told Louise about the days of the rather pathetic little four-man Communist discussion group when he was teaching at the University of Chicago. It had been, as much of his liberalism was, an intellectual exercise, a philosophic experiment, not direct or militant enough for her. She had been as shocked as his other supporters when it had come back years later in a Senate hearing to confront and confound him. He had not considered the episode that important, either when it happened or later. Its only importance, as she and so many who thought as she did were unable to see, was that he had lied about it under oath.

Almost all men, of course, would lie under oath at some point: a few saints perhaps had nothing embarrassing to hide, but not many of them existed in the world of power and press and politics that he knew. It just depended on which side of the table you happened to occupy. If you were lucky enough to be on the asking side instead of the answering side, you could wrap yourself in righteousness and heap coals on the heads of the guilty. If you were on the answering side—and were found out—you became a Robert A. Leffingwell, defeated for Secretary of State.

That was why he had been a little amused, even in the depths of his first despair over the Senate vote, by the attempts of his supporters to convince the country that he had been defeated because he was a "liberal." That phony issue had nothing to do with it, as he knew and they knew: they were just playing the same old game they always played. The country sensed the reality, all right: dumpy little Mary Buttner Baffleburg of Pennsylvania had spoken for the people when she cried "Liar!" at the convention.

Out of the lie had come what he now regarded, in a

way that would be almost mystical in a less skeptical and intelligent man, as regeneration. Out of it too had come what appeared to be the final loss of sympathy that had held together a marriage that had increasingly become, as he matured and she remained essentially the immature rebel of a long-gone day, a matter of calling to one another across an empty room. She had remained rigid, he had become more flexible. He suspected she really despised him because the Chicago incident had been so innocent—she would have respected him more had it really been subversive. A pursed-lipped disapproval had reached its climax in her frantic attempts to persuade him not to support Harley Hudson. He had recognized that this was the final step and, for all the reasons which seemed sufficient to him, had taken it. The result is summed up in a postcard from Chorocua saying, *I hope you're satisfied!*"

Well: he can't worry about that now. More pressing things are on his mind, for he has already had to make the first of those compromises in his new role that all men make, whatever philosophy they cling to.

He had been alarmed by the President's desire to include in his speech a call for a much tighter anti-disturbance bill.

"I don't like this," he had said bluntly to Orrin when the President had gone off to the diplomatic reception.

The Secretary had studied him thoughtfully for a moment, then nodded.

"I don't either. It does go too far. But he has to reply to violence and he has to make it strong. If I know the Hill, the bill will go through a considerable watering-down before it sees the light of day."

"It will bring him an awful lot of criticism from people like me who are in favor of the objective but alarmed at the method."

"I think he feels that a firm response to violence is more important at the moment than criticism from his friends," Orrin said. "It's one of those balancing acts you get involved in here. It's an executive decision." He shrugged. "He's made it. We write it."

"I still don't like it," Bob Leffingwell said stubbornly.

"Just remember that I don't either," Orrin said crisply. "Record that in my favor, if you will. But I see the necessity." He paused and then said, much as the President had earlier, "You don't have to stay, Bob. You can go."

Bob Leffingwell stared at him for a long moment.

"No," he said finally, "I'm not going. Why don't you try writing it out and I'll see what I can do to help."

The moment had been a further step along the way. He did not like it, but he had endorsed it—not only endorsed it but actively participated, for those few sledge-hammer sentences contained a phrase or two of his. The press does not know this now, but it will before long. Somehow, somewhere, through somebody, the story will leak out. (Not from himself, or Orrin, or the President or the stenographer, probably: but the steno-grapher's husband, her girl-friend, her son, her maid, her hair-dresser—who knows where Washington leaks really come from? But they always do.) And when it finally becomes known, the howl against him will be louder than ever from those who oppose the Administration.

But the whole episode has been, as Orrin said, "an executive decision," and for none of them more than for him. All the assumptions of a liberal life had been challenged by the violence at the convention, challenged by the failure of the professional liberals to see the road to lawlessness down which they were taking America, challenged by events of recent years which have finally convinced him that his country must stand and defend on an old-fashioned, inconvenient, awkward, vulnerable but nonetheless valid set of principles, if she is ever to do so. He can see now that he has been circling for a long time around the decision to change his public position on many things. After his evening at the White House, he knows there can be no more hesitations. He is virtually a member of the Administration now, and there can be no turning back.

Nor does he want to, for the shrewd old President has solved something else for him: he has put him to work with Orrin Knox, and out of their forced collaboration has come a sense of relaxation and easiness with one another that comes from shared responsibility and a job effectively done. After the speech was roughed into shape for the President's editing, they had a few minutes together to talk. Later the mere physical fact of eating dinner together had also made its contribution. Subconsciously, he supposed, he and Orrin must always have admired each other's abilities, even in the most bitter moments of their contest in the Senate. In their brief talk in Spring Valley, and even more tonight in the White House, he has discovered to his surprise that apparently they really want to like each other. And they have.

Tonight he has seen another side of Orrin Knox than the prickly, dominant, impulsive, strong-willed politician. The ironic, whimsical, self-deprecating Orrin has also been present: he has found him quite charming, A lively sense of the irony of their collaboration infused many of the Secretary's comments.

"Lord, if Walter and Tommy Davis could see us now!" he had said at one point and had literally stopped to sit back and laugh at the thought. "Who knows," he had added, more thoughtfully. "It may be the start of a beautiful friendship."

Bob Leffingwell had replied with a smile and a cautious, "It may."

Orrin had laughed again.

"Don't commit yourself to anything," he advised. "It's a pretty dangerous thought, I'll grant you."

"I've probably had worse," Bob said.

"There are no worse," Orrin said solemnly. "Absolutely none."

But the idea, finally defined between them, grew of itself. By the time he left the White House, going out the East Gate just as the speech began, so that all the press would be occupied and none would note his passage, he knew they were beginning already to think in terms of a more important collaboration in the days ahead. And he knows now, as he lounges in the warmly rustling night and stares at the city of power still alight across the river, that he is probably already committed.

As he arrives at this conclusion, which perhaps has been implicit in everything he has done since he decided to nominate Harley, the phone rings insistently. After a moment he goes reluctantly to the house to answer. Who can be calling at this midnight hour?

He might have known.

"Sweetie," Patsy says, I HOPE I didn't wake you up!"

"You didn't," he says cheerfully.

"Oh," she says, and he can tell she is a little taken aback at a cordiality she did not expect after her final bitter denunciation of him in Ted's room at the Mark Hopkins. (He can picture that shrewd Jason brain thinking, Now why does he sound so friendly? I thought he didn't like us. What does that mean?)

"Is there something I should know about?" he asks with an innocent interest, pursuing his advantage. "Some crisis, or—?"

She laughs heartily.

"Heavens, NO! Sweetie," she goes on with an intimate urgency, and he gives her credit for sailing right into it, "how would you like to be chairman of Ted's campaign again? You know I'm giving a big reception tomorrow night for the National Committee—"

"I've heard. But isn't it rather soon after—"

"Things move fast nowadays," she says archly. "It will be so wonderful if we can announce that you've decided to return to our side again. You can say that your support of President Hudson was just a personal matter, largely based on gratitude for what he did for you. You can say that you deplored the violence at the convention, just as you know Ted did. You can say that you are satisfied that the violence occurred without Ted's knowledge, and that you are satisfied with his assurances that it will not be permitted to enter his campaign again. You can say—"

"Patsy," he interrupts finally, a trifle dazed by this onrushing outline, "are you reading?"

"No, sweetie," she says quickly. "Us Jasons don't need notes. We think fast, you know."

"I know," he agrees. "But it still sounds—anyway, you have consulted with Ted?"

218

"Ted and I want Ted to be President," she says blandly. "Is it necessary to consult?"

"No, I suppose not. Tell me about the party. Who, what, where—"

"Everybody," she says triumphantly. "EVERYBODY. Six-to-whenever tomorrow night at the Washington Hilton. The entire Committee has accepted, and so have a lot of other people. I want the Committee to meet Washington, and Washington to meet the Committee. I think it should be done in style, don't you?"

"Do you really think you can do a snow job on a bunch of hard-bitten old political characters like that? Surely you don't think this will get you any votes."

"Don't underestimate Washington's glamor, sweetie," she says serenely. "It still has plenty. They'll be impressed. You wait and see. It will help. I think," she adds, her tone more pragmatic, "that you'd better join us while the joining's good."

He laughs.

"You sound very confident, Patsy."

"I am," she says airily. "This will be a real contest on the issues, this time. We've already received lots of pledges. Orrin had better be prepared for a shock. But, sweetie! We're getting off the track. Won't you join us? We need you, and frankly, if you were to come with us again, I'm sure Ted wouldn't forget it when he takes office."

He is silent for a moment and then decides with an ironic smile to give her a shock of her own.

"I would settle for nothing less than a written promise that I would be Secretary of State," he remarks calmly, and he will say for Patsy that she hesitates not a moment.

"SWEETIE!" she cries. "WHAT could be more *perfect?* It's exactly what Ted is planning, I'm sure."

"But you don't know," he says, and then decides to stop playing a game. "Patsy," he tells her in the same calm tone, "I have no intention whatsoever of assisting your brother to become President of the United States. I have left him finally and irrevocably. But I shall of course be interested to attend your party. I expect to have a good deal to do with the National Committee in the next few days."

There is a silence from Dumbarton Oaks. Finally she utters a smooth little laugh which is quite a tribute to Jason will power and self-control.

"Well, well. Sweetie, you DO sound so determined. Of course you can come to the party. We'll be looking forward to seeing you. Bring Orrin, if you like. Ted will be there, and it should be interesting for all of us."

"I just might," he says, and again she laughs.

"You do that, sweetie. I mean it. And—don't issue any statements until you see Ted, all right? I'm sure he wants to talk to you before accepting your decision as final."

"It is."

"I'm sure," she says, "but talk to Ted, OK? You will do at least that much?"

"Very well," he says after a moment. "I will do at least that much."

But when he is once again at poolside, thoughtfully sipping a beer which he has taken rather absent-mindedly from the refrigerator on his way out, he wonders why he should have made that gesture of decent gentility toward a family whose members dismiss the people they have no more use for with a boorishness as

220

ruthless as any he knows. Ted wouldn't do him the courtesy, were the positions reversed. Why did he bother, particularly when it will come to nothing?

He sits for a long time staring at the city over the river. It is almost one A.M. when he goes in. He does not get to sleep easily, and he turns and tosses often through the night in his empty house.

2.

"SHALL WE GO?" Beth asked, at the house in Spring Valley. Orrin smiled.

"You know very well you want to go. As for me, you couldn't keep me away."

"Good," she said; and added with a mock approval. "That's how Jasons fight."

"What's good enough for Teddy," he said, "is good enough for me." He broke into an off-key singsong, accompanying it with a rickety buck and wing. "Oh—what's good enough for Teddy—and his uncle and his aunts— What's good enough for *Patsy—is good enough for me!*"

"All right, George M. Cohan," she said as he finished with a final enthusiastic kick that threatened to overturn a cocktail table, "that's enough of that. Jasons aren't funny."

"It's the only way to take them," he said, puffing cheerfully. "Others worship: I sing."

"Too many worship, for my peace of mind."

"Oh, I don't know," he said, collapsing into his favorite armchair. "Reports of dissension are leaking from the Committee. The press is getting concerned. I have a few friends."

"Bully for you. Can you keep them after tonight?"

"One party? Don't be ridiculous. It isn't going to change anything."

"Better act as though it is," she advised. He nodded.

"They'll know I've been there."

And so they did, though at this particular moment, when members of the National Committee were busily dressing for their big introduction to Washington, and when all over the capital and its environs the really important and the self-designated important were preparing to descend in a whirl of glitter on Patsy's party, nobody could have foreseen quite how the evening would develop. Next day Helen-Anne would vaguely recall that at one point she had shouted, "It's a shambles!" to Bob Leffingwell across the room, and in retrospect that was what it appeared to be. But it took awhile to reach that point, and much had to happen in between.

First there were the arrivals, in themselves always a major event at any Washington political affair. The trio of National Committeewomen whom the press at the convention had dubbed "The Three Disgraces"—Mrs. Mary Buttner Baffleburg of Pennsylvania, Miss Lizzie Hanson McWharter of Kansas, Mrs. Anna Hooper Bigelow of New Hampshire—arrived, as expected, together: Mary Baffleburg plump and belligerent, Lizzie McWharter stringy and nervous, Anna Bigelow solid and acerbic. Mrs. Esmé Harbellow Stryke of California, her dark, pinched little face suspicious and uneasy (looking, as the New York *Times* murmured to the St. Louis *Post-Dispatch*, like a constipated ferret), followed with her co-worker in the Jason cause, the white-haired, dignified, piously shrewd old former Governor Roger P. Croy of Oregon. Bob and Dolly Munson, bearing the Knox banner, as CBS remarked to NBC, as clearly as though it had been painted across their chests, came next. They were followed by Senator Warren Strickland of Idaho, Senate Minority Leader and probable about-to-be Presidential candidate of the other party, obviously enjoying the disgruntlement of his friends in the majority.

A diplomatic contingent entered next, the Maudulaynes, the Barres, Vasily Tashikov and his dumpy little wife, Krishna Khaleel resplendent in white silk coat, trousers and turban with enormous ruby ("Not real, my dear friends," he hastened to tell the Maudulaynes. "Gracious, not real!"). Mr. Justice Thomas Buckmaster Davis and the Chief Justice came in together, the C.J. looking a trifle amused at the company he was keeping. Bob Leffingwell followed soon after with Lafe Smith and Cullee Hamilton (he had just happened to run into them in the lobby, but their entry together was taken as something of great significance by Administration-watchers). Walter Dobius entered with the general director of the *Post*, carefully staying six paces behind Helen-Anne Carrew who came in just ahead of them and looked the other way. Jawbone Swarthman, looking, as always, half-buttoned, though everything seemed to be in order, arrived with Miss Bitty-Bug, jes' the cutest lil' ol' debutante you could ever imagine—at least she had been forty years ago, and still dressed like it to this very day.

With them came Senator Tom August of Minnesota,

chairman of the Senate Foreign Relations Committee, peering about with his usual shyly hesitant yet stubbornly determined air of a surprised groundhog; and after and before and amongst and along with him and all these other distinguished guests there came further members of Senate and House; more members of the diplomatic corps; the other members of the National Committee (only Tobin Janson of Alaska and Jane Smith of Iowa are absent); many members of the press; and several prominent hostesses, all of whom cooed and kissed and cussed Patsy, who once again had obviously pulled off the coup of the season.

Then, finally came the Knoxes, whose entry produced the first real sensation of the evening, for it was heralded by wild applause and shouts from many of the crowd and quite a few members of the National Committee. It was also heralded by Patsy with a widely noted and quoted, "DARLINGS! HOW *GRAND* THAT YOU COULD COME!"

And then came the Jasons, her brother walking in alone, his uncle Herbert and his aunts, Valuela Jason Randall and Selena Jason Castleberry, following quickly in a group a few feet behind; and again the wild applause and shouts, about equal in volume, the press thought, to those accorded the Knoxes.

Toward each of these arrivals, and toward many others who for one reason or another were considered to be indices to political opinion, reporters, photographers and cameramen surged as they entered. Microphones were waved beneath their noses, pencils raced with their frequently vapid comments, their pictures were taken in varying degrees of amiable inanity. The press found members of the National Committee extremely close-mouthed, but enough others were obliging to furnish the basis for a couple of side-bar stories in the *Post* and the Washington *Evening Star.* POLL OF GUESTS SHOWS JASON CARRIES HILTON, the *Post* said, tongue-in-cheek but making a point for the home team. JASON-KNOX STAND-OFF ON COCKTAIL CIRCUIT, said the *Star.*

But it was not in such minor fun and games that the meat of the evening was to be found, of course; and before long it became apparent that the tug of war for the hearts of the National Committee was under way in deadly earnest. The first overt move was what Tommy Davis referred to as "that *marvelous* talk by Ted," and Bob Munson described in an aside to Warren Strickland as, "the speech from the throne."

It came at a shrewdly timed point when everyone was feeling happily relaxed under the weight of Jason drink and Jason food; when the big room was filled with the raucous hum of fifteen hundred voices, each seemingly trying to outdo all the others in the frantically hopeless competition for attention. The party had reached that stage, which comes so quickly and easily in Washington, at which no one can bear anyone else so everyone gives up listening and simply shouts in the general direction of the nearest competitor, a brightly fixed expression on the face, a glazed look in the eye, and an ever more rapidly disappearing sequence of glasses in the hand. Into the midst of this, on the dais that had been decorated with two enormous bronze eagles, two American flags and a papier-mâché arch bearing the words *E Pluribus Unum* ("Not exactly the Presidential Seal," Lafe managed to shout to Cullee through the rising applause, "but a typically quiet Jason substitute"), Patsy stepped forth shortly before eight P.M. She was clad in one of her brightly-colored, garishly exaggerated gowns, a determined look, and a cold sobriety that automatically gave her a position of command over most of her guests.

"Darlings!" she cried, pounding the lectern with a large gavel. "DARLINGS! DO YOU KNOW WHAT THIS IS?" And she held it aloft and waved it, as a sudden murmurous silence fell upon the happy celebrants.

("Now, how did she get *that*?" Helen-Anne demanded loudly of the Ambassador of the Cameroons. "Their money can do *anything!*" The Ambassador nodded and smiled, somewhat blearily.)

"It's from the convention," Patsy announced happily. "And if a certain event occurs that we hope is going to occur, we're going to BURN it!"

There was a smattering of laughter and applause, a little uneasy. Too many bitter memories for the Jasons rode on that gavel, and they were sure she meant what she said. But burning carried a reminiscence of violence that made many uncomfortable. The mood of the room was suddenly very odd, for just a moment. As if she sensed that she had made a mistake (Though when did Patsy ever realize her mistakes, Bob Leffingwell murmured to the Chief Justice in the uneasy quiet) she rushed on to the introductions they all knew were coming, and for a while everything was restored to a familiar basis of understandable political competition.

"On behalf of Washington," Patsy said, "this great capital which awaits—as the whole wide WORLD awaits—what our 106 distinguished guests are going to decide for

226

our beloved country, I wish to welcome the members of the National Committee. We are GLAD to have you with us tonight!"

("They should be," the Chicago *Tribune* remarked to the *Wall Street Journal*. "It's the greatest second chance anybody ever got.")

"We know," Patsy said gravely, "that you will do what you know to be the VERY BEST thing for us all."

There was a burst of applause, quite genuine and heartfelt this time, as if in some curious way, at this curious gathering, official Washington did realize for the first time just how very important its 106 distinguished guests were. The members of the National Committee looked self-conscious and, despite the amount of alcohol most of them had consumed, quite grim: they knew already.

"And now," Patsy said, "I may be prejudiced, but I should like to present to you one whom *I* believe deserves at LEAST a hearing—my brother."

And from somewhere behind the dais, looking tanned and rested, stepped the Governor of California, coming forward so calmly and purposefully into the flashing strobes, the television lights and the sudden wild roar of greeting that very few paused to realize that his wife was not with him. But he knew, and for just a second his face looked quite ravaged, a sad expression that came and went so fast no one really noticed. All they were aware of as he placed one hand on the lectern and began calmly to speak was the handsome, confident, statesmanlike public servant whom so many of them wished so fervently to see in the White House.

"Members of the National Committee," he said quietly, "distinguished guests, my friends: It is good to see good friends having such a good time together!"

Laughter, renewed applause, a sudden warm current of feeling in the room. "I think he's going to carry it off," Lafe said to Cullee, and Cullee shrugged. "Sure, right here. Wait until the cold winds blow at Kennedy Center."

"My family and I," Ted said, "are honored that you have joined us tonight for this happy occasion. May its conviviality be an omen for the days ahead. That they will be serious days, we all know. Yet they need not necessarily be—as some have suggested—days in which our republic is further divided."

("Now who suggested that?" Bob Munson murmured to Orrin Knox. Orrin shrugged. "Must have been me. It's the sort of awful thing I would positively insist upon.")

"No!" Governor Jason said sharply. "That they need not be. I say here and now that they will never be that, as long as I have anything to say about it!"

"Bravo!" shouted someone at the back of the room. The press immediately fell into a bitter argument as to whether it was Ralph Jensen, National Committeeman from Minnesota, or Ewan MacDonald MacDonald, National Committeeman from Wyoming. In any event, it was echoed vociferously from many places around the room, and another tide of applause rolled up.

"Our purpose now," Ted went on, "must be to bind up wounds, not reopen them; to seek unity, not destroy it; to create harmony where disharmony has all too dangerously been allowed to prevail before.

"Our purpose must be to do what is best for America, and do it in accordance with American traditions and American decencies."

His expression became grave, his voice somber.

"Many have deplored the unseemly and disturbing violence which has disgraced and disfigured our political life in recent weeks. I have condemned it before, I condemn it now. I want no such support!"

The applause roared out again, and this time there was in it a certain fervent, insistent note that indicated how much, friends and foes alike, they wanted him to mean it, and how relieved they were to hear him say it.

"But," he said, holding up a hand, and instantly the applause dwindled, and silence, listening and once more uneasy, filled the room—"but, no one man can do it alone. There must be a disposition, on the part of those whose policies arouse violence, to understand why the violence arises—and to make some attempt to accommodate the sincere misgivings which the violence expresses.

"No one could possibly condone the vicious, horrible things that have occurred in this city in the past four days. But"—and the silence became almost a living presence, so intently were they listening—"must we not ask ourselves: why did they occur? What caused the anguish and deep despair of those who organized these things? Why are emotions so high and tempers so hot that protest so easily flames into violence?

"Who is responsible?"

("He's doing a masterful job," Roger P. Croy whispered complacently to Esmé Stryke. "What a trimmer!" Mary Baffleburg hissed to Lizzie McWharter.)

"Obviously," Ted said, and a sternness came into his voice and the set of his jaw, "we need not look far for the answer: the protesters have made it clear enough. It is the present Administration which is at fault. The

229

Administration's policies, and nothing else, have produced the protests."

Once again a surge of applause, but through it, someone shouting, "Are we supposed to swap them for those of a damned appeaser?" The press again was not entirely sure who said this—thought it might be John V. Wilson, National Committeeman from South Carolina—decided it was caused by too much liquor—decided not to print it. But in the room it had its effect: an angry, agreeing sound began to grow. Into it Ted Jason snapped his closing comments in a level, emphatic voice, his head held high.

"Now we have a chance to correct this situation. We have a chance to moderate and accommodate and correct. We have a chance to meet honest objections and honest worries—which have, in some few instances, spilled over into the sort of horrid violence which has demeaned America in these past few days. We have a chance to set things right. We have a chance to chart a new policy—of freedom, of decency, of peace. (JASON CALLS FOR 'NEW POLICY,' the *Times* bannered. EMJ PICKS HIS LABEL: 'THE NEW POLICY' said the Chicago *Tribune*.)

"My friends," he said—and his voice became grave again, and he had, as Esmé Stryke remarked to Roger P. Croy, never looked handsomer—"*will we have the strength to do so?* Will we have the integrity and the courage to accept sincere criticism, meet it halfway, seek a true national unity on the issue of war or peace that now divides us? Will we restore America in the eyes of the world, and in her own eyes, to the position of integrity and honor she used to hold—has a right to hold—must hold again?

230

"That is our challenge.

"That is our task.

"I pledge myself to it in whatever capacity you may deem me worthy to fulfill.

"Thank you."

And he prepared, amid another jumble of sound compounded of the approving shouts of his supporters and the answering, angry murmur of his critics, to step down from the dais. But before he could do so there was a sudden disturbance at a door behind him, a wildfire flare of excitement, a quick tensing as many thought (though there were heavy guards on every door and a hundred cops outside), *What now, more violence?* and then a wave of applause that grew until it filled the room, as the man who was, after all, leader of the party, came forward and stepped up beside Ted Jason.

"Governor," he said, holding out his hand, "thank you for inviting me."

("The old sharpie invited himself," Patsy hissed to her aunt Selena Castleberry. *"HONESTLY!"*)

For a moment Ted looked absolutely taken aback. But he had no choice but to recover, and he recovered fast.

"My pleasure, Mr. President," he said with a fair show of cordiality, shaking hands and drawing the Chief Executive to the lectern. "Members of the National Committee, distinguished guests," he said smoothly, "it is my great pleasure and privilege to present to you the President of the United States."

And again the applause roared up, filled with many things, annoyance and worry on the part of Ted's supporters, amusement and glee on the part of Orrin's, the overriding excitement that grips a Washington crowd

231

when it sees the game of politics being played by masters. This was the kind of blood that Washington really enjoys seeing—political blood—and there could be sensed in the air that happy, delicious anticipation that comes with the conviction that it is about to be spilled all over the room.

For a minute or two, however, the President was in no hurry. He stared slowly about with a stolid, unsmiling air, searching out a face here, a face there, looking it over appraisingly, moving on. By the time he decided the moment was right to speak, he had secured silence and an attention that could not have been more profound. His opening remark was so different from what most expected that an audible gasp of amusement answered it.

"Now that," he said thoughtfully, "was quite a speech." He looked around again slowly, head slightly down, eyes quizzical. "Yes, sir, quite a speech. Don't know who it was about, of course—didn't recognize myself or any of my friends in there anywhere—but it was quite a speech.

"If I were one of your supporters, Governor," he said with a smile, not too unkindly, for the man who had stepped back to the side of the dais, "I think I'd feel as though you'd made it a perfect evening for me.

"Too bad," he said, "that I had to come along and spoil it. Oh, yes," he said quickly, as Ted made a halfhearted gesture of protest, "spoil it. Because I'm going to inject just a fact or two, and then I'm going to ask you to do something that I know you will do, being the fair-minded and decent man you are."

There was a quick, alarmed stirring among Ted's supporters, a peculiar, half-smiling, half-uncertain look from Ted himself. What was the old man up to? They knew

232

from long experience that his political moves were sometimes devastating. He had already proven himself to be a strong and unpredictable President. What was he going to do now?

"First of all," the President said, and his tone became as grave and stern as Ted's had been, "let me remind you of one fact: the violence we have seen in this past week—not only the past four days but the past ten, if you like, back to the convention—has not been any genuine protest against the policies of the Administration. It has been a deliberate attempt to embarrass and disrupt the United States of America itself.

"You say 'accommodate,' Governor," he said, swinging about suddenly to stare at Ted. "You can't accommodate with people who don't want to accommodate with you. You can't reason with people who are operating on an entirely unreasoning level. You can't appease that sort of thing, or it's the end of you . . . The end," he repeated thoughtfully, turning back to the room so that his conclusion was not quite as personal as it might have been, "of you . . .

"God knows," he said, "that nobody wants an end to violence more than I do. God knows I am willing to honor, and try to accommodate, honest dissent. But dissent has an obligation to be lawful and it has an obligation to be constructive. This mindless stuff is not dissent as America has always defined dissent. It is something else. Something else," he said quietly, "that I don't want to play with.

"Others can. Oh, yes, others can—if they like. If that's the way they want to play, others can. But it serves nothing honest, and it doesn't serve this country. What others it may serve, I wouldn't know. But it doesn't serve this one."

("Of all the damnable, slanted, one-sided, self-serving speeches," Roger P. Croy whispered angrily to Esmé Stryke. "My *God!*" "Dreadful," Esmé murmured, her dark little face sharp with disapproval. "Perfectly dreadful.")

"But," the President said, "that's something to fight out somewhere else. That's something we in the National Committee will have to fight out." ("Then he isn't going to relinquish the chairmanship," the general director of the *Post* whispered excitedly to Justice Davis. "Oh, boy, that's going to mess things up." "He'll be right in there working for Orrin every minute," Tommy said in an aggrieved tone. "It's going to be absolutely frightful.")

"Right now," the President went on, "there's another man to be heard from. Knowing you're a fair man, Governor, I know you're going to do the decent thing by him and give him a chance to speak too. Isn't that right?"

And he turned about with a slow, deliberate movement and stared at Ted, who, for a long moment, stared back. Neither made much attempt to hide hostility. ("Wow!" Helen-Anne exclaimed to the Ambassador of Mauritania. "Quelle confrontation!" said the Ambassador with a tipsy smile.)

"So I'll make way," the President said, turning back to the room. "Thank you for your attention, ladies and gentlemen of the Committee. Remember that destruction is not dissent and violence is not a safe thing to play with. I'll be seeing you very soon, I hope. We have things to work out."

("Doesn't he realize," Walter Dobius demanded of Krishna Khaleel in an indignant half-whisper, "that this is a unique situation? Doesn't he realize that the Committee now is as independent as the Constitutional Convention? He still thinks he can control it. It's incredible!")

"Governor," the President said, "thank you for your courtesy. I know you'll be wanting to introduce someone else, so I'll step down, now." And with a quick wave to the room and a tight, sardonic little twist to the corners of his mouth, he did so.

There ensued a pause of several minutes while he stepped back to the opposite side of the dais and looked across with a polite expectancy at Ted. The Governor did not look at him. Instead he stared off over the heads of the swaying, fascinated, unsteady crowd. He made no attempt to conceal the frown on his face or the grim lines around his lips. He was thinking and he wanted them to know it.

For perhaps two minutes the room remained quite still. Just before the tension had to break somehow, his face became impassive. He stepped forward abruptly to the dais, picked up the gavel, brought it down with a single sharp crack on the lectern. Before their stir of startled excitement was over he had said crisply, "Ladies and gentlemen, the Secretary of State," and stepped back to his place, from which he resumed staring impassively over the room.

Orrin came forward on a mounting roar of applause in which Mary Baffleburg, Lizzie McWharter, John V. Wilson and many others could be seen joining with a wild enthusiasm. But his face, too, was as deliberately impassive as his opponent's. And he too, once he was in position on the dais, held his moment and let it lengthen until silence and attention were restored.

"Mr. President," he said quietly, one arm on the lectern, "Governor, members of the Committee: I appreciate the honor. And," he added with a straight face, "I thank you for giving it to me.

"I will save for another time and place, should you care to bear it, the lengthier statement I might wish to give you on the issues that involve us now. For the moment, suffice it to say that I agree with the President."

("There's a switch," Jawbone Swarthman remarked loudly to Perry Amboy, National Committeeman from New Hampshire. "Now, there *is* a ding-danged switch!" Perry Amboy sniffed a disapproving sniff and did not reply.)

"What we have seen in recent days is no one's legitimate protest about anything. It is no sincere attempt to change policy. Any attempt to rationalize it as such is folly.

"Its aim is to ruin and destroy. And it is time to meet it head on."

Applause from his supporters, resentful noises from his critics: about fifty-fifty, the press thought, and so did Beth, standing near the middle of the room with the Munsons. Not conscious that she did so, she moved a little closer to them, as if shielding herself from those who did not like her husband.

"For myself," Orrin said, "I will not appease it, nor will I excuse it, nor will I rationalize it. It is wrong, and it is bad, and I am against it." A wry expression touched his face. "This is old-fashioned, illiberal, simplistic and out of touch with the times. That's me," he said, and the expression deepened, "all over.

"Nonetheless," he said, serious again, "I conceive it to be a valid position and I stand on it. I too want peace.

236

Any man who doesn't is a fool. But I don't want it at the price some people want to pay. I want it with honor ("and with force," the San Francisco *Chronicle* murmured to the St. Louis *Post-Dispatch*) and with some certainty that it will mean something—enough to last for a while, if we can do it. I think we can.

"I too stand ready to serve in any capacity you may deem me worthy to fulfill. But be prepared to take me as I am. Because I am not going to change."

And with a brisk smile for the President, a brisk nod to the Governor, a brief bow to the crowd, he stepped off the dais and into the roar of excited talk that welled up and filled the room again.

"Bob," the President said a few moments later as the Senate Majority Leader saw him to the long black limousine waiting in the midst of its motorcycle escort, engines revving up in little bursts of angry, impatient sound as they walked briskly forward, "I'd like you and Jawbone to start work tomorrow on the antiviolence bill, if you can do it."

"It can't be tomorrow for us," Bob Munson said. "We've got that FTC amendment to complete by Monday. I'm afraid it will have to be Wednesday, which will jam us right up against the National Committee meeting, unfortunately. But that's our situation. I don't know about Jawbone and the House."

"We'll talk to Jawbone," the President said.

"I don't see how Ted Jason had the gall to say the things he did," Anna Hooper Bigelow exclaimed to Lizzie McWharter as they watched Orrin and Beth depart. "He's insufferable!"

"Of all the egregious insolence," Esmé Stryke declared to Roger P. Croy as they turned back to the bar after vigorously applauding the departure of the Governor of California. "I do think Orrin is absolutely insufferable!"

"Sweetie," Helen-Anne Carrew said to Bob Leffingwell as they met in the midst of the swirling, excited, gossiping crowd, "have you made any decisions yet?"

"You'll just have to take me as I am," he quoted with a smile. "I am not going to change."

"But how *are* you?" she said. "That's what I want to know."

"Curiosity killed the cat," he said. She uttered her raucous laugh.

"Not this old tabby! It gives me more lives than I have already."

"I would say," Raoul Barre remarked softly, "that things march toward an interesting culmination."

"I hear they may in Gorotoland," Lord Maudulayne said. The French Ambassador shrugged.

"May—may," he said thoughtfully. "But not in Panama, eh?"

Lord Maudulayne frowned.

"No, I think not in Panama."

"I believe they're here in the hotel," Walter Dobius said quietly to Justice Davis, who looked genuinely alarmed.

"Heavens," he exclaimed, "I wouldn't want to talk to *them.*"

"They aren't pleasant people," Walter agreed. "But I think they can be helpful. And I think also that dealing with them may be the only way to keep them under control."

"But—" Justice Davis began, and was startled to find America's most distinguished philosopher-statesman seizing him suddenly by the arm in a sharp, painful grip.

"*Tommy,*" Walter said in a savage whisper. "*You do not know what is going on in this country right now. You do not know.*"

"Mercy," the little Justice said with a stricken look, "I'm not sure I want to know."

"You're going to have to," Walter said grimly. "Make up your mind to that."

"Say!" The *Post* remarked with some excitement to Helen-Anne Carrew as they met coming out of their respective rest rooms. "Isn't that the Governor getting into the back elevator?"

"After him!" Helen-Anne exclaimed. But he gave no indication he had heard their noisy hailings, and the doors had closed before they could reach him.

They stood for a moment watching the little light blink up the panel. Presently it stopped.

"Twelve," Helen-Anne said thoughtfully.

"Let's go up," *Newsweek* suggested.

"Indubitably," she agreed, prodding the button vigorously. CANDIDATES TRADE VERBAL PUNCHES AT JASON PARTY, the headlines said. NATIONAL COMMITTEE SHARPLY DIVIDED . . . CONGRESS TO MOVE FAST ON RIOT GAG . . . U.S. FORCES GAIN IN GOROTOLAND . . .

And very late, the news breaking just in time for the morning final:

PROTEST GROUPS ANNOUNCE FORMATION

OF NATIONAL ANTIWAR ACTIVITIES CON-
GRESS. SET MAMMOTH CONTINUING D.C.
RALLY FOR OPENING OF NATIONAL COMMIT-
TEE MEETING.

3.

FAR DOWN the tumbling russet hills she could see the breakers curling in against "Vistazo's" shore, their crests stained with flame by the setting sun. Somewhere close, in the dry brown grass, a quail uttered its silvery, turbulent little whistle; farther away in the nearest patch of oaks a branch snapped. Trumpet raised his head and whinnied, then resumed his fruitless search for something green. The pungent mingled odors of sage and bear-clover, baked earth and dried wheat filled the soft, gently moving air. This was the time of day she loved best, when the world turned toward night and all creation seemed to relax and rest from the suffocating heat of central California summer.

Except that for her, there was not as much relaxation and rest as she had thought there would be when she left the convention to come here to her husband's huge ranch north of Santa Barbara. "Vistazo" meant a lot to the Jasons, comprising as it did the remaining acres of the original grant to their Montoya ancestors, filled as it was with the memories and the presence of indomitable old Doña Valuela who had fought for it, saved it, made it the foundation of the fortune whose power now reached over half the world to influence many men and many things. It had come to mean a lot to Ceil, too, in the years of her marriage to Ted, for this was not the first time she had retreated to it to seek renewed perspective on a life, running beside her own, that had increasingly disturbed and worried her as it moved closer to the centers of national power.

It was not, as both of them seemed to understand, that there had been any sharp, dramatic break between Ted as he now was and the handsome, intelligent and capable young millionaire whom she had met one night at the San Francisco Opera and married, in the most photographed ceremony of the year, six months later. The retreat of integrity did not come in any single, inexcusable act; there was always an excuse, and there was always a public front that could be put upon it to conceal its inner realities.

She had seen this suave concealment gradually become a conscious habit with her husband, and she had hated it; but she could not blame him entirely, because his friends and supporters had made it so easy for him. Long before he began consciously rationalizing and protecting his own equivocations, those who wished to see him succeed politically were doing it for him. He had early attracted powerful backers in the communications world, and well before he reached the point at which he could consciously select a course of action that would safeguard a "good image"—Jasons in his time had always been too wealthy and powerful to have to worry about image, and anyway his image in his earlier years had seemed to do all right when he was just being himself— the press had created one for him. He was surrounded and protected by a screen of favorable publicity, headlines and news stories that emphasized his leadership and strength, interpretive analyses that discussed his courage and idealism even as they subtly but steadily attempted to align him with the political point of view their authors favored.

That there might be a price for this when he finally came to make use of it with a conscious deliberation, he never seemed to realize; but for Ceil, who could see it coming, it was not enough to flash a confident grin and declare with Jason self-assurance that you could handle it.

"But that isn't *you!*" she had exclaimed after the first big national magazine discussion of his views on foreign policy.

"It's a good facsimile," he responded with a cheerful smile.

"Is a facsimile all you want to be?" she asked quietly, and he had taken her hand with a sudden genuine earnestness.

"No, of course not. I want to be me. I think that's good enough."

"So do I," she said. "That's why it worries me to see you starting to slip away from it."

He had laughed and kissed her and told her not to worry, but she had not been able to help it, because she loved him and admired him and wanted to continue to respect him. She still loved him, but the admiration and respect were dwindling fast. She realized now, as Trumpet whinnied once again and the sun touched down upon the darkening sea, that she genuinely feared the outcome.

What had seemed to her the steady erosion of character in the pursuit of public office had accelerated prior to the convention, and then in that hectic tangle of ambitions and emotions, had seemed to race dizzyingly out of control. Ted had made his dutiful statements against violence, but the fact of the matter, obvious to everyone on the inside no matter how protectively press and television kept it from the public, was that he had given tacit if not direct assent to the campaign launched by COMFORT, KEEP and DEFY. He had assumed with typical Jason confidence that he could control the situation, and if money and brains had been enough, he would have. But there comes a point in such things when terror takes over, and from that moment money is nonsense and brains do not exist. Terror makes its own rules, and ambitious gentlemen who think they can dabble with it safely find they cannot do so without being consumed in some way or another. The dreadful attack upon Crystal Knox had been the more dramatic aspect of it; but the fact that, even after that warning, Ted had actually been about to let himself be dragged into the vortex of the so-called "Peace Party" movement was, in Ceil's mind, far more fundamental and frightening.

So she had withdrawn into that small fortress of solitude that she had gradually staked out for herself in these recent years while her husband was becoming more and more the ambitious equivocator and less and less the straightforward, honorable man she had married. Now at "Vistazo" she was watching him far-off; and nothing she had heard or seen or could sense in the past five days seemed to give much hope of change. On the occasion of President Hudson's death, after the White House riot, and again this evening at Patsy's party, he had been given the opportunity to break once and for all with those whose terrorism was obviously moving ever closer to a deliberate attempt to destroy the entire fabric of American society and government. He had not done so.

His statement on Harley could not refrain from seeking the support of the Administration's critics even as he paid dutiful, equivocal eulogy to its fallen leader. His condemnation of violence at the White House still kept the door open for the adherence of the violent. His talk to the National Committee (which Frankly Unctuous had been analyzing with warm approval when she left the house) seemed to denounce violence but rationalized its existence in a further bid for the favor of those who fomented it.

Now as Trumpet, giving up at last, responded to her absent-minded tug on the reins and started the long trail back to the rambling old estancia on its ridge above the sea, she feared for her husband greatly. Ceil Jason was terrified of terror too, not only for him but for the country, many of whose citizens, looking to him for salvation, believed him still to be the shining and impeccable knight they read about in their newspapers and heard discussed on their television screens.

In her own way, the only way she felt was open to a wife who loved her husband but believed him to be terribly wrong, she had tried to help him; first, by withdrawing to "Vistazo" in the hope that her leave-taking would jolt him into some fundamental change of direction, and when that failed, by doing what she could to encourage defeat of his ambitions. She knew he would never understand her worried call to the President, her advice to Bob Leffingwell to trust his own judgment, the call she had made this morning to Lucille Hudson with its indirect but quite obvious message of encouragement to Orrin and Beth. These were feeble little efforts to reverse a process that could not be reversed without his active cooperation, and he would probably regard her as a traitor if he ever found out; but she knew she was no traitor: she was doing the best she could to help him. Since ambition appeared to be taking him down a road whose end, she was convinced, could only be disastrous, then he must be prevented from going down that road. She was beautiful, intelligent and clever, but she was not superhuman: these telephone calls were all she could think of to do, aside from pleading in an open and abject way that would only disclose the full extent of her fear and worry for him. The end result of that would be to arouse a certain basic masculine contempt and amusement at feminine weakness, compounded by Jason ego: he would only tell her again that he didn't have to worry because he was Ted Jason, and he could handle it. Anyone else would have been humbled out of this by events at the convention, but not a Jason: she could tell in his voice that he had come back, and come back strong. And so if she pleaded too openly she would lose whatever advantage and influence she might possess.

Her every emotional instinct as a wife urged her to go to him, and it was only by thinking it through in this fashion most carefully, and then adhering to it with a determination as strong in its way as his own, that she was able to remain quietly at "Vistazo." She had gone on several picnics with neighbors and old friends from Santa Barbara; done some swimming, a lot of riding—"Poor old Trumpet, what a workout I've given you!" she said with a smile, reaching down to scratch his neck as they jogged thoughtfully along in the rays of the sunset that had flared up against the banked, innocuous clouds from which no rain would come—a lot of reading—a lot of thinking. She knew she would not go back yet. When he really needed her, when her return might have some effect, then she would. But not yet.

The old servants Manuela and Tomás, children of "Vistazo" whose families had been on the ranch almost as long as the Jasons, had a martini ready for her on the patio. She drank it alone, staring out at the last shreds of sunset as they dissolved in the dusk. The air was still warm and gentle but now the Pacific looked gray and cold.

She shivered.

"Sweetie," Helen-Anne said sharply, "I didn't call to play games with you, I just want to talk to your brother. OK?"

"Darling," Patsy said, "don't lose your temper. Temper, temper, TEMPER! I always say that's your only fault, Helen-Anne, dear, you do lose your temper."

"Yes," Helen-Anne said. "So how about it?"

'Well, you see, dear—" Patsy began carefully.

"What's he doing, hiding under the sofa?"

"He's in his room at the moment," Patsy said with dignity. "What do you want to talk to him about, anyway? Can't it wait?"

"It could," Helen-Anne said, "except that I want to print it and I want to check it out with him and get his comment on a few things."

"Oh?"

"Oh."

"Print what?"

"Never you mind," Helen-Anne said. "Just put me through, please. And don't listen on the line."

"I will if I please."

"Be prepared for a shock then," Helen-Anne told her calmly. "Big Brother has been up to no good."

"Well. WELL!"

"Yes, 'Well, WELL!' Now will you get him to the phone?"

"No," Patsy said with sudden decision. "No, I won't. He's getting ready to go to the White House—"

"Why do you think the President wants to see him?" Helen-Anne inquired. "Because I've already talked to the President, that's why. Don't be naïve all your life, Patsy. Jasons are smarter than that. They're some of the smartest people I know. Only, one of them doesn't know what's good for him, that's all."

"Well, you can't talk to him right now," Patsy said coldly. "I'm sorry."

"You will be sorry," Helen-Anne said, "and so will he. Because I'm going to go ahead and print it as I understand it. One of my distinguished and able colleagues of the press," she added with a scathing sarcasm, "isn't sure yet whether his outfit is going to or not, but I think the good old *Star* will back me to the hilt."

"What is it?" Patsy inquired with an equally scathing sarcasm. "Have you caught one of his assistants in the men's room?"

Helen-Anne snorted.

"Oh, Christ, that old chestnut! No, I have not caught one of his assistants in the men's room. It's a little more important than that. But you don't want me to talk to him, so that's that. Read the *Star*. It'll be in there."

"Print and be damned," Patsy said.

"How grand," Helen-Anne observed. She gave a sudden ribald hoot and used the patronizing tone she knew would infuriate Patsy the most. "You poor Jasons. You'll destroy yourselves yet, if the world will just give you enough rope."

"I am so tired of you," Patsy remarked coldly. "I am so TIRED, Helen-Anne."

"Kiddo," Helen-Anne assured her, "you aren't in it with me. You tell Big Bud that I'm not going to let up on this story, either. I'm going to stay right with it to the end. His end, I hope."

"Well, I hope it's yours," Patsy said viciously. "I just hope so, Helen-Anne!"

"I know you do, love," Helen-Anne said lightly. "But I'm afraid you're all of you just not going to have that satisfaction."

But when she had slammed down the receiver and was staring with an angrily triumphant air around the empty newsroom, puffing a little, looking characteristically disorganized, one strand of hair straggling down over her right eye, another askew on top of her head, she did not feel so confident. For the first time in all her years as a Washington correspondent, in fact, she felt uneasy and perhaps even a little afraid. Great wealth had ways of taking care of difficult matters and never being connected with them at all.

Very big and very ugly things were involved here, and little Helen-Anne, she told herself, was going to have to be careful. Migh-ty careful.

Sometimes, he reflected with a certain somber amusement, a reputation for bluntness could be very helpful when one planned to be the opposite. When his visitor was announced he remained for a moment with his back to him, hands clasped, shoulders hunched, head lowered, staring at the Washington Monument perfect in the night. Then he swung about, stood up, held out his hand with a pleasant smile.

"Governor," he said, "thanks very much for coming to see me at this ungodly hour."

"Your command," Ted Jason said with a smile equally pleasant, "my wish."

"Glad of that," the President said amicably. "Guess if it wasn't your wish, the command wouldn't matter much, right?"

"Oh, I didn't mean that," Ted said, his smile steady.

"Let's sit over by the window," the President suggested, leading the way to a couple of armchairs facing one another comfortably across a coffee table on which cups and a steaming percolator were already set out. "You've no idea how nice it is to get away from that desk. Already. You may not believe it, seeing as how you and some others regard it as the most attractive piece of furniture in the world, but it's a fact. Less than a week, and I'm already glad to sit somewhere else."

Governor Jason smiled and took the proffered chair.

"As long as you retain the option," he said. "That's what makes the difference."

"Coffee?"

"Black, please," Ted said. He looked thoughtfully around the room while the President poured. "Are you going to have it redecorated?"

"Don't imagine so," the President said. "I'll add a few

of my own pictures, of course—I've got about a thousand still up there in the Speaker's office. Going to take me a week or two to dismantle that. Then I'll settle in for a while. I imagine you have a very attractive office in Sacramento?"

"Very pleasant," the Governor said politely.

"Good," his host said, stirring in cream and sugar gently and watching his visitor with a friendly smile while silence grew. Presently Ted put down his cup with a little laugh and leaned forward.

"Mr. President, am I supposed to crack psychologically, or something? Is that the idea?"

"Not at all," the President said blandly. "Not at all! Why on earth would I want you to do that?"

"I really don't know," Ted said calmly. "I really don't. But I thought you might."

"No, indeed."

"Then why am I here?"

"I expect you know," the President said.

His visitor gave him an easy, relaxed smile.

"Pat tells me Helen-Anne Carrew says it's all her doing. The face that launched a thousand inaccurate columns, its owner moving like a noisy gray eminence through the secret paths of government, swaying men to her ruthless desires. See them hop! Senators, Speakers, Governors, Presidents—"

"Not always inaccurate," the President said with an equally relaxed and comfortable smile. "Helen-Anne hits it on the button nine times out of ten, I've found. She's hard-working, clever and astute, and often has the luck that seems to be attracted by those attributes. For instance, she was lucky tonight when she decided to go to the twelfth floor."

250

"Now what cock-and-bull story has she told you about the twelfth floor?" the Governor inquired humorously. "'The Twelfth Floor! It sounds like a good mystery story or a bad novel about big business. Which is it?"

"Neither," the President said, also humorously. "It's just a nice big front-page story by Helen-Anne involving several interesting people."

"Which the *Star* isn't going to print," the Governor said, "because it's only her word, and that can easily enough be knocked down."

"She had company, you know. One of her colleagues was along."

The Governor laughed.

"You won't see a line of it in their pages. Now, if it had been Orrin, whom they don't like, there would have been column after column of sinister speculation. You know how these things are done, Mr. President. But since it's me, whom they do like—Anyway, there was no meeting—nothing sinister—nothing. So what proof does she have?"

"She says she took some pictures of you as you came out."

"No one took any p—" Ted started quickly, and as quickly stopped, while the President gave him a hard, inquisitive stare. "Anyway," he continued after a moment, "it's her word, unsupported, and there is no proof. I doubt very much that the *Star* will print it, with no confirmation from any other source."

"Governor," the President inquired with the quiet curiosity of one who really wanted to know, "why are you still running with that shoddy crew? Don't you see the terrible dangers to you and to the country in what they're doing? Don't you see you're giving them an option on you, even if you only stopped in for two minutes to say hello? They can claim all sorts of things about your approval and your endorsement—maybe even your complicity, for that matter."

"Complicity in what?" Ted Jason demanded sharply. The President shrugged.

"How do I know? Whatever they plan to do. For all I or anyone outside that room knows, you might have been plotting to kill the President. It's been done."

"Not by sane men," the Governor said. The President made an impatient sound.

"Who said we're discussing sane men? Look, Governor"—and he leaned forward and turned on the full impact of Mr. President and Mr. Speaker combined—"there must come a halt to this sort of thing if you wish to survive in American politics, or maybe just if you wish to survive, period. Nobody I know is going to kill you, but your newfound friends might. These things backfire. Violence feeds upon itself; presently all order and all certainty are swept away. You cannot control these forces. I thought you learned that at the convention."

"You and your friends certainly did your best to instruct me!" Ted said with a sudden flash of anger. The President returned him cold look for cold look.

"Somebody had to," he said bluntly. "You refused to learn otherwise. Now I say to you this: I don't know what happened in that room, and I don't know what Helen-Anne is going to print about it—if she does. But I do know that you are betraying yourself—and the people who believe in you—and this republic—if you do not once and for all, unequivocally and forever, repudiate vio-

252

lence as a method of conducting the public business, foreign policy and social progress of the United States of America." He leaned back in his chair and stared out at the Monument with a tired little sigh. "This is so obvious to me," he said quietly, "and, I think, to all sane men who want their country to survive, that I don't see why it has to be spelled out to a man of your intelligence. I really do not."

"You really have it rationalized, don't you?" Governor Jason asked with an equal quietness, an equal wonderment; which, if it was not sincere, was a masterpiece of acting, the President thought. And perhaps it was sincere: he could not tell, so earnestly was it presented. "You really have the world turned around so that the policies of this Administration have nothing at all to do with the excesses of protest that have occurred in the last few days."

"'Excesses of protest,' my God" the President exclaimed, bringing a fist down hard on the arm of his chair. "Is the sort of thing that happened in Arlington an 'excess of protest?' Is the sort of organized disruption we're seeing all across the country these days just an 'excess of protest?' How neatly you rationalize, yourself. How neatly"—his eyes narrowed—"and how well-designed to win you the political support of the disrupters."

"Mr. President," Governor Jason said, "I am willing to concede that there are some forces—"

"Including those you met with earlier this evening."

"Some forces," Ted continued, unmoved, "which are involved in these things, and which are not sincere or genuine or perhaps even loyal to the country. But there are many, many millions more who honestly and earnestly and sincerely deplore and abhor the policies your

Administration is following in world affairs. Now, these people are not," he said carefully, "kooks. They are not crackpots. They are not wild-eyed radicals or subversive Communists. They are decent Americans, deeply and genuinely disturbed. Am I to repudiate them, when they look to me for voice? Am I to say to them, 'Sorry, run along. I agree with Big Daddy, everything's 100 per cent OK and you're just a bunch of disloyal rats?' I cannot do that, Mr. President. I don't believe it to be true."

"What do you believe?" the President asked, as others had asked, and would ask, his handsome visitor. "That's what I don't understand. Perhaps if I could, I'd understand better where you think you're going, and what you think you're trying to do."

"I think, if you will forgive me," Governor Jason said quietly, "that I am going right to that desk over there. And I think what I am trying to do—"

"Is get there."

"Partly that," he agreed, "but even more, I think, I am trying to give these people a voice and an instrument to work out a foreign policy that will really lead this country and the world toward genuine peace—"

"The clichés of peace!" the President interrupted.

"As worn as the clichés of violence," Ted responded quickly.

They gave one another stare for stare until the President finally spoke in a tired, musing tone.

"I wish I could believe you were sincere, Ted. I wish I could believe you know what you're doing, when you run with that pack. I wish I could honestly think your method would bring us through. I might get out of your way if that were the case. But I cannot for the life of me

254

believe you to be anything but overly ambitious, taking desperate chances with the very fabric of the nation, flirting and perhaps even conniving with forces whose capacities for destruction you just don't understand. I think you're the product of your upbringing. I think you think that just because your name's Jason, you can ride any whirlwind, control any holocaust, put any genie back in the bottle. And my friend," he concluded quietly, "I just don't think you can."

"I thank you for worrying about me," Governor Jason said dryly.

"Oh, not you," the President said. "I don't give a damn about you. But quite a lot of my fellow-Americans are involved in what you do—possibly the fate of the country itself is involved. And that makes it a worrisome matter, for me. You have the power to lead or mislead. Right now, you're misleading, in my estimation, because you're misled. By ambition and greed for office and people who are taking advantage of those two weaknesses to trap you into being a stalking-horse for their own purposes."

For a moment Ted did not reply. When he did, it was in a tone of cold and level anger.

"You really think I am nothing more than a stalking-horse for someone else. You really think so."

"That is the most charitable thing I can conclude," the President said calmly. "I wouldn't want to think you were knowingly and deliberately conspiring to bring down your own country."

Again the Governor was silent. At last he shrugged and stood up with a smile that was both tolerant and pitying.

"I must concede your sincerity in these strange remarks," he said, "but I really see no reason to prolong the interview. You obviously really believe that I am a fool, an idiot, a dupe and possibly even a traitor. So I think there's no point in any further communication, except officially. Isn't that correct?"

The President remained seated, staring up at him with an intently appraising air, head cocked to one side, eyes half-closed, shrewd and analytical.

"The only thing I think you are," he said finally, "is an extremely ambitious man who has been gifted by birth with freedom from all restraints, financial, moral or in personal character, upon his ambition. And so I think you're getting into things that may well destroy you, and certainly if carried to their extremes will come pretty close to destroying the country. At least in my judgment. So I guess I have a duty to oppose you, don't I?"

"You haven't been in doubt on that point for six months."

"No," the President said slowly. "But I kept hoping you might see of your own accord where you're headed."

"I told you," Governor Jason said with a sudden, quite genuine smile, gesturing toward the desk. The President smiled too, but there was no humor in it.

"I might say, over my dead body," he remarked softly. "Except that it might be true."

For a long moment the Governor of California stared at him with a look filled with many things, anger and contempt and pity, and a sort of overriding disbelief that there could be such a man, with such an opinion. Then he bowed quickly, said, "You will forgive me, I must go," turned swiftly and left the room.

He could not have analyzed, had anyone asked him, the conflicting currents of anger, emotion, revulsion, determination, which had brought him in Patsy's gleaming black Rolls-Royce to this apparently deserted house at this post-midnight hour. He had given the order to the chauffeur almost without thinking; almost automatically, it seemed, he had acted on the impulse to see the man he had last seen in the heat of anger at the convention. He was not entirely sure why he wanted to see him now, not even sure where the impulse had come from—some urgency developing out of the earlier events of the evening, some headlong rush of decision coming from his tumbling thoughts, something that seemed logical after his bitter, frustrating talk with the President. He had not even known the correct address: the Secret Service man the President had kindly assigned to him yesterday had called Patsy to find out.

Now here they were, and the house was silent and dark in the steaming hot night. For a second only he debated whether to pass on and try to arrange something tomorrow. Then he strode forward up the winding walk, jabbed his finger forcefully and repeatedly on the bell. Somewhere deep in the house he could hear it ringing apparently unanswered. He was about to turn away when he heard the scrape of shrubbery alongside the house.

"I've been out back at the pool," Bob Leffingwell said in a politely puzzled voice. "Did someone wish to see me?"

"I did," he said, and for a moment there was silence from the shadowy figure standing at the corner of the house.

"I'm sorry I didn't turn on the light," Bob said in a voice that indicated nothing. "Watch your step as you come around the walk, here. One or two of the slabs are a little uneven. . . . Sit down, Ted," he said when they had traversed the house, the sloping lawn, and so come to the dim expanse of the pool, its placid surface reflecting a little of the light of the city across the Potomac. "Can I get you something to drink?"

"Ice water, thank you," he said, taking one of the chaise longues beside the water. His host made some sound he could not quite analyze, partly amused, partly, perhaps, quizzical.

"I, too."

When they were both seated, he spoke abruptly and without preliminary.

"What would you think, Bob, if you had just been accused by the President of the United States of conspiring against the country, threatening it with destruction, and perhaps even plotting to kill him?"

For a moment his host said nothing at all, nor could the Governor see in the darkness what expression might be on his face. Actually there was none, for Bob was taking pains to keep both face and voice impersonal.

"I think I might wonder," he said finally, "what could prompt so very grave an accusation from one in such position, and whether I had done anything to warrant it. If I concluded I had, I think I would begin to look around for a way to change what I was doing."

It was Ted's turn to remain silent. When he spoke it was in a half-amused, half-quizzical tone of his own.

"Well, that's straightforward enough."

"I try to be."

"Yes," Ted agreed; and said, with a pleasant edge, "these days. . . . So is he correct, do you think?"

"I wouldn't presume to pass judgment on his judgment," Bob said, his voice impervious.

The Governor laughed without much humor.

"I wouldn't call that straightforward."

"I didn't know you had the capacity to judge—" Bob Leffingwell began quickly, broke it off and started over. "I'm sorry. Yes, in my estimation, he is correct, at least about endangering the country. The conspiring and plotting may have been exaggeration on his part or exaggeration on yours. . . . Though I can see," he added quietly after a moment, "that a fair fear could be raised if things continue as they're going."

"You really think so," Ted said in a thoughtful tone. "You really do think so."

"What you must realize," Bob Leffingwell said with a sudden sharpness, "is that perfectly sensible and intelligent people are very much concerned about the course you're apparently taking. Even though," he added slowly, "other perfectly sensible and intelligent people, I know, approve."

"Exactly," Governor Jason said. "That being so, I have some warrant, I think, for doing what I believe to be right."

"Right for what?" his host inquired, his tone again sharp. "You? The country?"

"Many people," Ted Jason said with the quiet objectivity that in Washington accompanies only the greatest of egotism, "seem to consider the two identical."

"And that justifies anything you want to do," Bob Leffingwell said. "Well . . ." In the dim light the Governor could see his profile as he stared at the city. It indicated nothing. "Well, I suppose that sense of identification is necessary if one is to seek the Presidency. I wouldn't know, thank God. . . . In any event," he added with a sudden firmness, "a fair fear still lies. You haven't reduced it much this evening."

"What have I done this evening?" Governor Jason demanded. "Made a speech to the National Committee. Stated my position candidly to the country. Made clear to the President and Orrin that they have a fight on their hands—"

"Met secretly with a pathological black racist, a paranoic demagogue of a U.S. Senator and an unbalanced right-wing weirdo," Bob Leffingwell snapped. "Isn't that enough to make decent people worry?"

"Oh, that's the problem," Ted said dryly. "Helen-Anne has been talking to you too."

"I haven't seen Helen-Anne since I left the Hilton."

"But she called you."

"She did," Bob Leffingwell said. "It was a damn-fool, stupid, asinine, fantastically dangerous thing for you to do. Who the hell do you think you are, anyway?" he demanded with a sudden, furious disgust. "And what the hell do you think you're trying to do to this country?"

"I am trying to provide it with a leadership that will take it out of this dreadful impasse the Administration has led it into," Ted said quietly. "In that task I need the help of as many good men as I can get. I need yours. That's why I'm here"—and he realized this was true, it was what had really prompted his almost instinctive urge to talk at once to Bob Leffingwell. "May I have it?"

"Well," Bob began, and it was obvious that he was literally at a loss for words in the face of an audacity so great. "Well, I–" And in the dim half-light from the city across the river the Governor could see him shaking his head in a helpless fashion as his voice trailed away.

"The task is difficult," Ted went on in the same quiet tone, "the challenge enormous; but the reward, I think, great. Suppose we can lead America back to sanity, you and I," he said, and his voice became touched with an almost evangelistic fervor. "Suppose we can sweep away all the sickness and insanity, the evil policies that have taken us into wars and divided our country and set us one against the other in senseless, self-destroying bitterness. Suppose we can create policies men can believe in, bring back decency, banish the violence that springs from the conviction that protest is helpless in the face of arrogant power. Help me do that, Bob! Come back to the side you really belong on! Your old friends," he concluded, his voice sinking to a grave conclusion, "await you. Democracy and decency need you. Help me do what must be done to save this beloved land."

For several moments after he finished Bob Leffingwell did not move, uttered no sound. A little wind stirred the dogwood and the tulip trees, an owl murmured petulantly. The traffic over the bridges and along both sides of the river was thinning, the lights on the Capitol, the Washington Monument, the Lincoln Memorial were out. Full night was settling finally on the District of Columbia.

At last Bob shifted position and spoke.

"You are an extraordinary man, Ted," he said quietly. "But I suppose anyone big enough to want to run that town is extraordinary. What makes you think there is the slightest chance that I would want to rejoin you?"

"For the reasons I state," Governor Jason said. "Because obviously you belong with me and not with them. Because you're a political realist and you know mine is the better chance. Because it becomes Bob Leffingwell

261

to be liberal and it goes against his nature to defeat liberalism's cause.

"'*Liberalism's* cause?' *Liberalism*. My God, what an easy word to throw around! To me you're one of the great reactionaries, Ted, ruthless to your opponents, bitterly intolerant of dissent—yes," he said angrily as the Governor moved protestingly in his chair, "intolerant of dissent, honest dissent, *liberal* dissent, any dissent that doesn't dovetail with your own ambitions. You say I belong with you: well, that depends. There is a certain type of self-designated American 'liberal' that I have finally come to have an absolute horror of, because there is no one more vicious, more intolerant, more destructive, more reactionary. And all of that type you seem to have gathered around you: the smug, the superior, the self-righteous, the mindless, the violent, the cruel. That's the way I used to be, and I know. And you know their excesses and you don't repudiate them. God help you, I think you've even begun to condone them in these recent weeks. And now you meet with them in secret to further your own ambitions, and God knows what will come of that. God help you, and us."

It was the Governor's turn to remain silent. When he finally spoke it was in a steady tone that dismissed Bob's comments as though they had never been.

"I understand from Patsy that you would still like to be Secretary of State. Join me and the job is yours."

Bob Leffingwell uttered some strange sound, possibly a laugh, muffled as quickly as it began. His voice came savage and sarcastic.

"In writing, I told her. In writing."

"Get the paper," Ted Jason said indifferently. "I have a pen."

For one insane moment Bob hesitated and almost—almost—let himself begin to think. But he knew instinctively that he must not, that to do so might be to fall back forever from advances sorely won. In some great inner convulsion of heart and mind and emotion that shook his being but came and went so fast he could not analyze it, he knew he must make the break final, and make it now. He stood up so abruptly that he knocked over the little wooden bench beside his chair. The half-empty glass of ice water crashed on the apron of the pool with an explosive tinkle.

"I think you'd better go, Ted. I meant what I said at the convention. I mean what I say now. I can't go with you down the road you're going."

He paused and then with a sigh that made it even more devastating, concluded with the one thing he knew would terminate the interview and the association forever:

"I pity you, Ted. I wish I could help you—I wish it were still possible to help you. But it isn't. And I can't."

"Hi," he said, and again be tried carefully to keep his voice from showing too much emotion, though God knew he had felt enough in these past six hours. "Are you in bed?"

"No," she said, sounding, he thought, a little more remote than even three thousand miles would warrant. "Just sitting out here on the terrace enjoying the night."

"Is it a nice one?" he asked with a politeness almost nervous, almost humble.

"Beautiful," she said, also politely. "Quite warm still. A few traces of color left over the sea, out toward Hawaii."

"We'll have to go there again sometime soon," he said, very conscious of the silence of Patsy's house, hoping she wasn't listening, promising dire things if she were, so awkward and like a pleading schoolboy did he sound.

"Sometime."

"Ceil," he asked after a moment, "what are you thinking?"

He could hear her sigh. Presently she said, "Nothing, really. I'm just sitting out here, as I told you. Manuela and Tomás have gone to bed. I'm all alone. It's very peaceful."

"You must be thinking something," he persisted, hating himself for it. She gave a tired little laugh.

"Must I? About you?"

"Yes," he said. "Me."

"Well," she said with a dry little humor. "I'll admit the subject has crossed my mind."

"What have you decided about it?" he asked, adding in his mind, *Please don't you lecture me, too: I've had enough for one night.* And adding immediately, *Then why call? You know she will.*

Again she sighed; and, finally, "Does it matter?"

"Would I ask if it didn't?"

"You might. You like to go through the proper motions."

"My God," he said, stung into genuine protest. "What kind of man do you think I am?"

"Too intelligent," she said, a little of her irreverent humor bubbling into her voice, "to ask a question as trite as that."

"Well," he said, unamused, "I am asking."

"I think that's something only you can decide," she replied, her voice again polite. "How have you done with the problem tonight?"

264

"Did you hear my speech?"

"Yes," she said, voice noncommittal. "I heard it."

"Did you like it?"

"Why do you ask? If I liked it, you're confirmed in your own concept of it. If I didn't, then you know I'm mistaken. So what difference does it make? No, I didn't like it. I haven't liked any of your speeches in the last few days."

"Things are moving fast," he said with a defensive thoughtfulness. "I have to move with them."

"Do you?"

"Yes," he said crisply. "I'm sorry it upsets you."

"I'm not upset, exactly," she said slowly. "Just—I don't really know. Puzzled, I guess."

"By what?" he demanded. "What's so puzzling about what I'm doing? I'm engaged in a terrific fight for the world's most powerful office. Am I supposed to act as though I'm playing tennis?"

She was silent for a moment, and it seemed to him that he could almost hear the waves on "Vistazo's" shore, though he knew they were three hundred yards below. At last she sighed again.

"I really don't know what good it does to talk about it any longer. You know what I think. You know what I'd prefer to have you do. So why discuss it? You want me to tell you that I think what you're doing is right. I can't. So what's the point?"

"You might at least wish me well," he said sharply, and then his voice changed abruptly. "Ceil," he said humbly, "I need you. I need you here. And don't tell me that's trite, because it's true. . . . I talked to the President and to Bob Leffingwell tonight and they both think—

they both think I'm out to destroy the country. Do you?"

There was a silence and then she started to say something about, "You're so—so—" in a voice that sounded as though she might be half-crying. And then she stopped and the silence returned, and distantly again he thought he heard the surf, though it must have been only the painful pounding of his heart.

"What am I to say?" she asked at last. "I know those two men don't mean that you are deliberately trying to destroy the country—you know they don't mean that. But they're worried about what you're doing, and the people you seem to be depending on for support, and—and that's what frightens them. . . . It frightens me."

"I'm depending upon the National Committee," he said, "and I think a majority is for me. What more do I have to depend upon?"

"*And don't be disingenuous*," she said with a sudden desperate harshness. "You know who I mean, *you know who I mean*. Now, stop it!"

"I'm afraid I don't," he said, and abruptly his voice seemed to be growing calmer as hers became more agitated. "If you mean the legitimate protest groups—"

"'Legitimate!' Oh, Ted!"

"They are legitimate."

"But it isn't legitimate, what they're doing. It isn't legitimate for you to go sneaking off with them and connive at—at—"

"At what?" he demanded, and there was no more supplication or apology in his voice at all. "Exactly what claptrap has Helen-Anne been giving you, anyway?"

"It isn't claptrap," she said. "She told me she saw you go into that room with those men, and just now I heard on the radio that they've formed this National Antiwar Congress to meet when the National Committee does. You told them to do that. And who knows what sort of horrible things will happen when they have their rally? How can you control them? What makes you think they won't control you? Oh, Ted," she said, more quietly, "I am so worried for you."

"I'm all right," he said with a sudden anger in his voice. *"I am all right.* And I'm sorry Helen-Anne is turning into a screaming gossip about all this. She doesn't know who was in that room, or anything about it. She won't file a shred of evidence to support this cock-and-bull story of hers—"

"I suppose you've bought it all up," she said bitterly. "Jason money can do anything."

"What would be the point in 'buying it all up?'" he inquired calmly. "What's so shameful about all this, even if it were true? Can't a candidate confer with his supporters? Has that become illegal now?"

"But such supporters," she said with a sudden sad quietness. "Oh, my dear, such supporters! . . . Well, there's no point in continuing this. You'll do what you want to do, I'm sure. But I fear for you, my dearest—I fear for you. Do be careful. Don't let them hurt you—or the country."

"Now you're dramatizing," he said, attempting to put into his voice a lightness that didn't quite come off. "Now you're being much too, much too serious. Nobody is going to hurt me, or the country either. I can control it. It's just a move in the game that's got to be played out here while the National Committee makes up its mind, that's all. It really isn't anything for you to worry about."

"I hope so," she said in a desolate voice. "Oh, my dear, I hope so."

"Come to me, Ceil," he said softly. "I need you beside me now."

"Good night," she said. "Good night."

"Ceil—" he began with a sudden desperation, but the line went dead at "Vistazo." Slowly he put down the phone in Patsy's silent house. Abruptly the insistent unfounded terrors of the night returned.

In half a dozen hours he had been accused of the deadliest betrayal of his country by his country's President; by a man who now opposed him, but whose opinion, in some curious way, he still respected; and by his wife. From each in turn he had hoped to receive the support that would have enabled him to repudiate and turn away from the vortex they told him he was being drawn into, yet from each he had received only warnings, worries, condemnation. He had not received help.

It did not occur to him, in this dreadful lonely dead of night in Dumbarton Oaks, that the reason they did not give him help might be because he had not made it clear that he was asking help. And perhaps it was just as well that he did not realize this, for if he had, he might also have realized that he had gone so far down his desperate road that it was impossible for him either to ask or accept.

They thought "help" was to persuade him to give up his ambition and retire from the race for President. That was something he would not—could not—do. "Help" in his mind was how to get there without being thrown back completely for support upon the forces of violence active in the country. These in truth seemed to him at the moment to be the most effective and decisive elements in achieving what he wanted, and while he had suffered some misgivings about them in recent days, he no longer felt so uneasy.

He, too, deplored their excesses, but had they not assured him tonight that these were isolated examples? Hadn't Freddie Van Ackerman, much more respectful and obliging than he had been in the convention's closing hours, told him, "Hell, Ted, you have to allow for a little human nature, but we've got it under control now, and it won't happen again"? Hadn't LeGage Shelby, abandoning his stagey, show-off vulgarities about the white man, actually sounded like the brilliant college graduate he was when he had agreed solemnly, "From now on this is going to be dignified protest—*dignified?*" Hadn't even lumpish Rufus Kleinfert nodded ponderously and echoed, "Ve vant to make our pointss like Americanss?" And when he had suggested—or had someone else? He could not be entirely sure, such had been the vigor of their discussion, but he knew he was the one who synthesized and gave it form—the creation of a joint command for all the antiwar, black-racist and neo-isolationist groups in the country, had it not been agreed at once that it would proceed in an orderly and law-abiding manner toward the achievement of its objective, the election of Edward M. Jason as President and, through him, an end to the wars?

The creation of the National Antiwar Activities Congress—"NAWAC"—was, in his estimation, a real triumph on his part, and in fact a very practical answer to just those doubts raised by Ceil, Bob and the President. They had all been so basically hostile to him that he had not been able to explain it—there was, after all, pride, and more than that, Jason pride—but in NAWAC he had produced the formula by which protest could be channeled, legitimatized, made respectable, put back in the mainstream of American society. This had been a major accomplishment, and while he was not yet ready to reveal his participation—which was why he was so deeply annoyed with Helen-Anne for apparently scurrying about trying to get everyone alarmed, without knowing the facts—he was well satisfied. It represented a constructive, sensible and patriotic act, definitely minimizing, if not altogether removing, the influence of the Communists, kooks and crackpots whose violent outbursts had in recent days so seriously upset the country and his own campaign.

Granted, not everyone could put the genie back in the bottle. But he was about to prove that he could. And would.

Nothing now could shake his confidence in himself. He was doing exactly what Ceil and the others wanted him to do: control the violence. And they wanted him to abandon the cause just when he was about to re-establish his command!

Why were they so fearful, so unimaginative, so obtuse?

And why, in Patsy's silent house, was he suddenly shivering himself?

And who, in the haunted two cities in the ominous night, was walking on whose grave?

4.

NATIONAL COMMITTEE MEMBERS ON SOCIAL, SIGHTSEEING BINGE AS THEY AWAIT BIG DAY, the *Star* headlined Helen-Anne's column on their activities three days later; STAND-BY PERIOD MEANS "RED-CARPET WHIRL" FOR FATEFUL HUNDRED AND SIX.

"Washington," she wrote, "has rarely thrown the like of the round-the-clock party it is giving this week for the most important hundred and six people in the world—the members of the National Committee who are awaiting the start of the fateful meeting at which they will select a Presidential candidate to succeed the late President Harley M. Hudson.

"From Alabama's Helen M. Rupert and Henry C. Godwin to Wyoming's Alice Lathrop Smith and Ewan MacDonald MacDonald, the national Committeemen and women are having a red-carpeted whale of a time.

"So far they have enjoyed:

"1. The sensational reception given by Patsy Jason Labaiya at which the two top contenders, her brother, Governor Edward M. Jason of California, and Secretary of State Orrin Knox, plus new President William Abbott, laid down the battle lines for the contest to come.

"2. A dinner party at 'Sots Hollow,' fabulous Revolutionary-days estate of Mrs. Hattie Hamill Johnstone, ageless duenna of Washington society, at which Committee members first dined on diamond-studded gold plates, then whooped it up at an old-fashioned square dance amid seventeen cows, twenty-three horses and fifty-eight tons of hay flown in especially for the occasion.

"3. A Potomac cruise to a White House reception at Mt. Vernon, given two days ago by the President and the full Cabinet—this one very sedate with no fireworks, thank you very much!

"4. A reception given by the dean of the diplomatic corps, His Excellency Willem van der Merwe, at the South African Embassy, attended by fifty-one nations that are presently speaking to South Africa.

"5. A reception given at the Embassy of Ethiopia by His Excellency Ras Tafari Tudwa, attended by sixty-seven nations that presently are not speaking to South Africa.

"6. A joint dinner given by the Ford and Rockefeller Foundations, the National Committee for a More Effective Congress, and the Over All Study Group on Improving Just About Everything in Washington.

"7. Innumerable receptions, cocktail parties, dinners, brunches, teas, lunches, given by the various Congressional delegations for their respective National Committeemen and women.

"This capital, which does half its business at social functions and lives in a perpetual daze—and haze—of sociopolitical entertaining, has never seen the like.

"If Committee members don't start their rendezvous with destiny next week with the biggest hang-over in history, it won't be Washington's fault. Everybody is doing his, or her, best!"

But there was, of course, a darker side; and as she sat at her cluttered desk in the Monday-morning-noisy newsroom, she reflected thoughtfully on how little the country was told, sometimes, about what actually went on in the beautiful city where its fate was decided. She was not the only reporter in Washington who had been tipped to various strange events in the past several days: ominous, anonymous telephone calls to certain Committee members urging their support for Ted Jason, more open attempts to influence them through direct interventions by powerful political and financial leaders in their states, even, in three or four cases, veiled but unmistakable threats of physical reprisal if they did not support the Governor's cause.

She was not the only reporter, but she was still the only one who was almost certain she knew where and when this new spurt of underground activity had begun. Or at least, she thought with a contempt that twisted her mouth suddenly into an ugly line that startled a passing copy boy, the only one who was prepared to print what she knew.

Prepared but uncertain, at the moment, whether she was going to be able to. She had not yet discussed it with her editors, but she was not entirely sure, for all her bravado to Patsy last week, that the *Star* really would back her up and print the story. Especially since the story was getting rather more sensational, as she dug deeper, than she had at first dared imagine.

Her inquiries to the hotel, as she had expected, had met with a bland, blank incomprehension. No, no one at all had been in Room 1223 that night. No, no one on the staff had seen the Governor anywhere except at the reception downstairs. No, nobody had any knowledge— certainly no record—of the presence on the premises of Senator Van Ackerman, Mr. Shelby, Mr. Kleinfert, other than at the reception, of course. Actually, that room had been reserved for a Mr. and Mrs. Hjalmar B. Poulsen from St. Paul, Minnesota, but they had not appeared and so the management regretfully was going to have to bill American Express for it; perhaps if madam would care to check with Amer—"I just might!" she had snapped before banging down the receiver.

But it had not been necessary to collect one more lie: by one of those happenstances that occur quite often in the capital, her maid happened to have a sister who happened to have a son who happened to work as a waiter at the hotel. He just happened to have been the one to take drinks a couple of times to Room 1223, the first time while the Governor was there, the second after he left. From him Helen-Anne was able to find out a good deal of what she wanted to know. She had learned from long experience covering Congressional hearings, political crises and social scandals, that there was almost always one little link somewhere that somebody forgot to take care of. If you could just find it, most things fell into place, even though when she called the hotel again, the response was equally bland. No, no one had seen that gentleman either, except at the reception, of course.

Yet she was convinced that now she had a good deal of the story and could piece together intuitively, in the fashion of most experienced Washington correspondents, much of the rest of it. She was planning at this moment to do two things. One would probably not produce much response, but would be interesting as a further insight into a character she was coming to dislike and fear as she had few others in a long reportorial life. The other could be downright dangerous. The gaps in what she knew were such that she had to tackle the dangerous one before she would be fully briefed for the other. She made a quick telephone call, elicited prompt if surprised assent from the party on the other end of the line. Then she drew a deep breath, pushed her wayward hair back under the rim of a rather rakish green hat she had purchased just yesterday at Woody's, tossed a terse, "I'll be on the Hill," over her shoulder to the city desk, and started forth.

Already a shimmering opacity lay over the sprawling city. It was going to be another exhauster of a day. How the government had functioned without air conditioning, he would never know. How it functioned with it he would never know. Somehow, he reflected with a sardonic little smile, it managed.

Standing on the narrow balcony rimming the top of the New State Building, staring, with both hands on the railing, across the jumble of trees, parks, government buildings, rushing traffic, placid river, he could see the Hill where he had worked so long, the White House, almost hidden, where he hoped to work. He was supposed to go there in a short while to tell its new occupant the news from Gorotoland, and he hoped that this, when officially released, would brighten things a little for the country. But of course it would not for those who opposed the Administration, who wanted nothing less than American surrender, and whose joy, in this odd age, was not reserved for America's victories but for America's defeats.

The dead weight of their doggedly sterile hostility weighed him down this morning; indeed it weighed him down all the time. The security detail was still on duty at the house in Spring Valley, and he supposed it would be until the National Committee had rendered its decision, at which time, if the decision was in his favor, the Secret Service would take over. If it was not in his favor, he supposed he would still have to have guards for a while, so venomous and unrelenting were his critics.

From Walter Dobius' most recent column to the episode at the house at three o'clock this morning, he had certainly received full proof of this since Patsy's reception. Walter had been at his smoothest, providing what to his friends, supporters, idolators and true believers must have been just one more of his brilliantly sound and balanced discussions of national realities:

"Washington," he wrote, "is awaiting with a somber unease the meeting of the National Committee. A mood of deep sobriety lies upon this restive and worried capital.

"It wants a solution for its crisis, but it doesn't want a catastrophe.

"It wants a leader, but it doesn't want a misleader.

"It wants a President, but it doesn't want Orrin Knox.

"Thus the task which confronts everyone here is how to keep things on an even keel while at the same time aiding the Committee to reach the decision that will be best for the nation and the world. Perhaps not since the Constitutional Convention of 1789 has a handful of Americans borne a greater responsibility than the fifty-three men and fifty-three women of the National Committee bear today. Washington is doing what it can to assist them in reaching a sane and sensible decision.

"What this troubled city is trying to do is show the Committee that there is a way out of uncertainty that will not create more uncertainty; that there is a policy of accommodation which is not a policy of appeasement; that there is a policy of firmness which is not a policy of fatuity; that there is an answer to violence which will remove the causes of violence."

And from there, in a straight line, the column went on to one more endorsement of the Governor of California, who would provide all these balanced and alliterative alternatives and in the process remove from government the ominous and destructive influence of the late Harley M. Hudson, his successor, and above all, the dreadful and dismaying Secretary of State.

In any ordinary context, Orrin would have dismissed Walter as he had dismissed him so many times before, as the bellwether of a certain element and a personal enemy who had been after Orrin as a matter of spite ever since the Secretary rejected his advice in the first Gorotoland crisis six months ago. In the context of present events, he possessed more significance.

All through the body of the column there had run the smooth rationalization of violence—and the smooth implication that violence must be appeased by a drastic change in Administration policy, or it would grow worse—which Orrin had come to recognize as the hallmark of the new Jason campaign. How directly his opponent was involved in this, he did not know; but from what he had learned of Ted during their contest in the convention, he had arrived at a concept of a man rather far from the steady, unshakable, responsible leader whom Walter and his friends were so busy re-establishing for the public on the eve of the National Committee meeting.

This newly restored hero of certain columns, networks, newspapers and magazines, this suddenly revived colossus, who stood astride the Committee's path like some leader gifted to the nation by Heaven, was not the man Orrin knew. Nor, he suspected, was it the man Walter knew. Walter was too shrewd a Washington hand to be fooled for long by the caliber of the men he wrote about; only his obsessive fear of the consequences of a Knox victory could be dictating his columns now. That, and perhaps things more sinister, which the Secretary could suspect though he did not know them for sure.

Like Helen-Anne and many others in the deceptively placid capital that lay sprawled before him in August mid-morning, he too had heard rumors of pressures on the Committee, and of course he was a practical politician: his people were just as busy lobbying the Committee as Ted's were, he wanted them to, and he had told them to go to it. Every possible source of appeal was being exerted to influence the Committee members who were either, to believe Helen-Anne, headed for "the greatest hang-over in history," or, to believe her ex-husband, awaiting with "a mood of deep sobriety" their day of destiny.

But he did not think—in fact, he was certain—that the nature of the pressures was the same from his supporters as it was from some in the Jason camp.

Down below the customary surface of political battle—the calls from state and local leaders, the pressure from financial and professional figures, the appeals to self-interest the promises of future preferment, the desire to be with the winner that were all part of the fair game of politics—something deeper and more frightening seemed to be underpinning the Jason campaign now as it had in the convention. Ted had not shaken himself free from the vicious and the violent, for all his statements and speeches of the past few days. The statements and speeches had never really closed the door: violence still grinned like a deaths-head behind the mask of reason.

And it had grinned like a death's-head at his own house, where Beth had brought him awake just before three A.M. with a hand on his shoulder and a whispered, "Don't move, but I think there's someone at the window."

"How could there be?" he had demanded, instantly awake, in an answering whisper. "The guards are all around the house."

"Just listen."

And presently he had heard it, a very gentle, very furtive *scrape, scrape, scrape* as though someone were doing—what?

Trying to attach a bomb to the sill, it had turned out two minutes later, after he had reached out very slowly and carefully to touch the buzzer over the bed that connected with the impromptu command post in the garage. Instantly the floodlights had illumined the house, there had been a concerted rush by the four men on duty. A sullen Negro had been captured and held for questioning. (A good thing the episode was unknown to the press, he thought now with a dry smile: it would have been absolutely horrid for them to have to contemplate the fact of the culprit's race. He would have appeared in their pages as "a man," and his membership in DEFY and his close personal relationship with LeGage Shelby, which had been developed this morning in the investigation, would have required an evasive delicacy of treatment that all too many of them had learned how to achieve in these recent dishonest decades.)

So there it was, confronting him in Spring Valley, confronting him in the final great political contest of his life, confronting him in the National Committee. Neither he nor Ted had been idle in these past three days: much more than the giddy garland of social fripperies reported by Helen-Anne had occupied the attention of the "fateful 106." Both he and his opponent had managed to hold highly secret conferences with nearly all of them; and while he had not emerged with any very clear picture of how the majority intended to vote, it was very clear that they were deeply disturbed, and in many cases, downright scared, by the menace that seemed to be in the air around them.

This was what Washington had become, in the current climate: a city of fear in a nation of violence. It was not a prospect that reasonable men could contemplate without the gravest misgivings.

Nonetheless, he must go forward along the road his destiny seemed to have laid out, and he had to do it with all the vigor and courage at his command—with what Seab Cooley in the Senate had long ago referred to as "Orrin's leetle extra—he drives and drives and drives and just when you think you have him beaten, he gives it jest a leetle extra—jest a leetle extra." He would need the leetle extra now, for the options open to his opponents were many, and he would have to be alert for all of them.

The least they could do would be to provoke a nasty riot at the opening of the Committee tomorrow; the most, something such as had occurred in Spring Valley, carried to its final extreme. He knew that he, Ted, the

President and their immediate families were all under guard; but as history had proved, guards were only as good as they happened to be at the moment they were needed. There might well be attempts to assassinate him, there might be attempts to get at him again through his family: what had happened to Crystal was warning enough, had any of the Knoxes been cowards. But they were not, any more than were Jasons. The difference was that the Knoxes did not create situations in which people could be killed.

Yet here he paused, turned back by the innate sense of justice that had made him such an effective leader in the Senate. He was quite sure that Ted would not consciously desire his death, or even remotely give anyone cause to think he would like to have it brought about. He would simply let things slide into a situation in which such an event could occur, and even as he did so, would be maintaining to himself that he was innocent of desire, guiltless of intention.

This paralysis of foresight and moral will, taken with a policy the Secretary could only regard as one of dangerous and possibly fatal appeasement of those who wished to destroy the country, made Ted in Orrin's estimation a dangerous man; about as dangerous, he thought with a wry smile, as Ted probably considered him. Ted was also one whose quick recovery from his low point at the convention had brought back to his side all the major elements of the communications world which had assisted him so powerfully before. Again Orrin faced the hostile establishment he had faced in San Francisco. But perhaps foolishly, as he stood above the city, he was not discouraged or downhearted. In fact he was quite lighthearted, exhilarated by the prospect of the battle ahead, encouraged and lifted up by a number of signs of support, both from within the Committee and from less expected quarters. Ceil, for one. She had sent her cautious message via Lucille Hudson, but its import was clear enough: she too was trying to save the country from Ted, and Ted, though he would never acknowledge it, from himself.

At least, Orrin reflected as he cast one more glance at the distant Capitol before going in—a glance that touched his face, though he was unaware of it, with an instant's wistful regret for days in the Senate when life, while highly contentious, had somehow seemed so much simpler—at least the pattern of the next few days was reasonably well set.

The Committee would meet at ten A.M. tomorrow. On the Hill and in the world, events would be moving in favor of the Administration. Inevitably he would profit from this.

Or so he thought, as he stood for one last lingering moment staring out at the lovely city where ambition and apprehension lived, before going in.

"Now, Mr. Speaker, Mr. President, sir," Jawbone Swarthman said in his usual hurried way after a quick glance around the Oval Room, "now, Mr. President sir, looks to me like you all are jes' gangin' up on ol' Jawbone, it surely does, now."

"Sit down, Jawbone," the President said. "Wouldn't dream of doing a thing like that to you. Isn't that right, Bob? Cullee?"

"Absolutely correct," Senator Munson agreed.

"Anyway, what's to gang up about?" Cullee Hamilton

inquired cheerfully. "Far as I know, everything's going just the way you want it to. Big campaign against the anti-violence bill, that takes care of that. Big antiwar demonstration coming up tomorrow, that takes care of that. Lots of stirring around in the Committee lining up votes for Ted, that takes care of *that*—"

"Not doing any stirrin' 'round," Jawbone declared stoutly. "Not at all, now! Anyway," he added defiantly, "can't nobody say I'm the only one doin' it, now, can they, Mr. President, sir!"

"I expect we've all been doing our share," the President said calmly. "Can't blame anybody for trying. Must confess, though, I don't get a very clear picture at the moment, do you? Looks to me like you haven't made much of a dent, can't say as I have either. Maybe we're losing our touch."

"No, sir, Mr. President," Jawbone said, "I don't think it's that at all, now. I just think that ol' Committee's jes' not about to let anybody know what it's going to do. Those members, they're as independent as a hog on ice, seems to me. They got that bit in their teeth and they're runnin' and ain't nobody, not *nobody*, goin' to tell 'em. what to do. No, sir!"

"I think also," Bob Munson said with a sudden gravity, "that many of them are downright scared. Of their responsibility, and of—other things. Have you been coordinating your efforts with Ted's threateners, Jawbone?"

"I swear," Jawbone said. "I swear now, I never heard the like of this. What do you mean, now, 'Ted's threateners?' I don't know anything about that. I'm not a threatener, now, Bob, you know I'm not, and you hadn't ought to imply it, now."

"But you know it's been going on, don't you," Senator Munson said quietly. "You've heard about it. Everybody in town's heard about it."

"Well, sir," Jawbone said, sitting back with a sudden solemn dignity, "well, sir, I never. Is that why you all called me in here, to put the squeeze on me about what some little ol' crackpots may be doin' around the Committee without anybody at all, anybody at *all*, knowin' about it or havin' told 'em to do it? Is that it?"

"All right," Senator Munson said. "Maybe 'Ted's threateners' is to harsh, but *somebody* knows about it, Jawbone, and *somebody* is telling them to do it. Now, you know that as well as we do, so why don't we drop the phony indignation and discuss it for what it is, a damned serious thing?"

"Well, sir," Jawbone said, "if anyone had told me that an old friend like you, an old colleague, an old *comrade-in-arms*, would practically accuse me of lying, I just wouldn't have believed him, Bob! I just wouldn't have thought for one minute—"

"Jawbone," Cullee interrupted, "do you agree that it's a damned serious thing, or don't you?"

"Well, now," Jawbone said. "Well, now. If by any chance it were true that somebody were really doing something *sinister*, then I'd say: Sure! I'd say: Get 'em! But, now, you know, now, there isn't any real proof of this, leastways not any proof anybody *responsible's* behind it. Good gravy, Aunt Melissa! You mean to tell me, Mr. President now, that we all got to go scurryin' 'round like little ol' rabbits with our tails between our legs just because some screwy crackpot or other is using the telephone—"

"And the mails," the President said, tapping a manila folder. "I've got a few examples right here."

"—the telephone and even the mails," Jawbone said, "to try to put over some crackpot ol' idea? Can't even keep crackpots from operatin' in this country, Mr. President. They got a right to be crackpots jes' like you and I got a right to be serious citizens, isn't that so, now?"

"Not dangerous crackpots," the President suggested. "Not evil and threatening crackpots. Not crackpots with murder on their minds."

"What have they done except threaten?" Jawbone demanded. "Nothing at all, Mr. President, nothing at all! Now, surely, I'll grant you some little ol' lady Committeewoman from some little ol' state out West, Mr. President, she's probably all shook up about a phone call or two, but shucks almighty, we know in public life you get that stuff all the time. Now, we all know that, Cullee and Bob! We've all had our share of it. What's it mean, now, what's it mean? Nothin', that's what, just not nothin'!"

"Jawbone," the President said with the ominous quietude of Mr. Speaker fed up. "Stop being disingenuous. You know, because you're apparently pretty close to the Governor—"

"Just think he's the best man to lead us back to peace, that's all!" Jawbone said with a defiant promptness.

"—that there are some strange and really quite sinister things going on. Now, you *know* that, just as a good many people in this town do. Because you are a supporter of the Governor's, you're in a better position than a lot of us to find out who's doing it, and tell them to stop. And that's what I want you to do, Jawbone. I'm giving you a little commission. Call off the crackpots. That's your job."

"Well, now," Jawbone said hastily, "Well, now, Bill, Mr. President, it's mighty fine of you to put all this trust in me, but I repeat, I just don't think they're all that important, now, I truly don't. Why!" he exclaimed. "Even assumin' there were such people, Mr. President, how would I know where to find them? How would I know where some little or screwy crackpot's hangin' out in this big ol' Federal City? How would I know—"

"You aren't afraid of them yourself, are you, Jawbone?" Cullee asked softly. "I'm going to do some talking. You're not afraid to, are you? You wouldn't want us to think that, surely."

"Now, see here," Jawbone said. "Now you see here, Cullee, don't you talk to me like that! I'm not afraid of anybody, I just don't think they're all that important, now. And I keep *asking* you, where would I find them, anyway? Just where would I, now? *Say!*" he cried with a sudden brightness, "I thought the reason you all wanted to see me was so we could have a little ol' conference on takin' up that antiviolence bill tomorrow, Bob. I thought that was what this was all about, you and me decidin' what the Senate and House are goin' to do tomorrow! What about that little ol' bill, now? What we goin' to do about that?"

"*You*," the President said after a while, "aren't going to do anything, Jawbone."

"But I'm the Acting Speaker—" Jawbone began indignantly.

"And you've already made it perfectly plain to me," the President said, "that you oppose the bill. So I'm turning it over to Cullee to handle on the floor. Nobody elected you Acting Speaker, Jawbone, we just had to have somebody to represent the House at the funeral. Cullee'll do just as well now."

"You'll never get elected Senator from California handling that bill!" Jawbone said with a sudden triumphant inflection.

"I'll take my chances," Cullee told him calmly. "Want to lead off for the opposition?"

"Might do that, now," Jawbone retorted. "Might just do that. But, here, now! We all are talkin' jes' like enemies, 'stead of like ol' friends from the Hill! Why'd you get us so all-fired mixed up, Mr. President? We're not enemies! We're friends!"

"Are we?" the President asked quietly. "I don't know whether this tangle right now is going to leave anybody friends. Bob," he said with a sudden brisk air, beginning to shuffle the papers on his desk, "Cullee —we take her up tomorrow, then. And Jawbone: I'd appreciate it if you'd take word back to whoever you know, wherever they are. Tell them there's a lot of toughness here, too. And we aren't afraid to use it."

"I don't know what you mean, Mr. President," Jawbone said solemnly. "I truly don't, now."

"Tell them, all the same," the President suggested, rising to see them out. "Perhaps they don't, even now, really understand."

Nor should they, he told himself as he returned to his desk, experiencing annoyance that he could hardly keep from being bitter: look what they had been fed in the past week. Everybody from the Pope to Jawbone's Aunt Melissa had entered the act.

The Pope, a slick old politician who had recently oozed his way onto Peter's throne and had immediately begun to dabble in everything under the sun as busily as Alexander Borgia ever did, had been first crack out of the box on the day after Harley's funeral with a speech to a mammoth peace demonstration in St. Peter's Square.

"O children of the earth!" he had cried, his reedy voice whistling out through a hundred amplifiers while his audience dabbed and sweltered below him in the heat, "O children and leaders of all the peoples! Let us have no more of warfare, O ye who are powerful! Let us have compassion, O ye who hold the reins of mankind's future!"

Then he had come down to cases, and his exhortations, of course, had been addressed to the United States, apparently the only power on earth that was ever guilty of anything:

"We say to our beloved children in the United States, Let us have peace! We say to them, Be not too proud to undertake negotiations! Do not indulge yourselves in clever diplomacy which twists and turns and rejects the hand offered in friendship! Be not too clever and harsh against those who offer you an end to battle and surcease of pain! Let us end these horrible wars, we beg of you! And may those who have it in their power to confer a new leadership upon this dearly beloved, troubled land, bear always in mind the blessedness of peace and the eternal salvation granted the peacemakers!"

Since these noble sentiments hit the headlines just as the President was studying the flat rejection by Prince Obi of the latest offer of negotiations made by the United States, he had not been too impressed with the fervent papal injunction. It had sounded to him like one more politician trying to make points by beating America over the head. God knew he had enough of that in his own country.

There had been, for instance, the retired Air Force general, the former Assistant Secretary of State, the "intimate Presidential adviser" who once had functioned on the outer fringes of a brief but forever-ballyhooed Administration, the famed evangelist whose moralizings were as well-publicized as his morals were well-concealed, the famous doctor whose heart transplants automatically made him an authority on all aspects of world affairs—they too had been heard from, as they called a press conference to issue one more of those pompous, arrogant, self-righteous and self-serving statements by the pseudo-great that had cluttered every national issue since the end of World War II. As usual in such cases, their solemnly portentous press conference had received a full five minutes coverage on all the evening television newscasts. Their message had of course been highly critical of Administration policy, and they had most earnestly urged the National Committee to select a candidate "with the integrity, the decency *and the will* to accept honest offers of negotiation and meet halfway those who have clearly signaled their desire to end a futile and foredoomed attempt to dominate them by force of arms." The networks had given them full coverage, morning, noon and night.

There had also been the five youthful defectors from the Marines in Gorotoland, who had stayed in service just long enough to qualify for the loving attention of the press and then had fled to Tanzania and from there (where the coverage and publicity were not very good) to Paris. They had appeared at a crowded press conference to be photographed peering out with innocent baby-eyes above pouting baby-mouths that spewed forth bitter damnations of their own country. Thirty thousand of their fellow Marines were valiantly doing their jobs, but the Pouting Five were the ones who got the full treatment from the media.

And now on the eve of the National Committee meeting there had either appeared or were scheduled to appear:

—A round table of correspondents on Network X, entitled "A Candidate for President: Peace or War?" In pompous and all-knowing tones, our White House Correspondent, Our Overseas Correspondent and our National Observer would agree with Our Chipmunk-Cheeked Moderator that yes, indeed, America was in bad odor everywhere and the only way she could save herself would be by electing a man who would most speedily and forcefully terminate all her positions of principle.

—A special presentation on Network Y, entitled "Hour of Decision," on which Network Y's counterparts of Network X would offer a worldwide roundup of all the areas and all the peoples who didn't like America. It would feature the youthful despisers and the senile haters of a dozen nations, maybe no more than ten in a riot providing they threw enough rocks and screamed enough screams, and at the end of it no American watching would have any reason at all to be proud of his country or to believe that there was any good at all in anything she was doing. All Americans would be made to feel, not in so many words but simply by a shrewd selection of news clips and a suavely undercutting commentary, that only "a man of peace—of honest peace—of *genuine* peace" could possibly save them. That man, it would be clear, would not be Orrin Knox.

—An hour-long interview with Governor Jason on Network Z, in which a panel of three Washington correspondents (The Greatest Publication That Absolutely Ever Was, the Los Angeles *Times,* and the network's own) would gently and skillfully lead Ted from one favorable answer to another, their admiration and encouragement so obvious that a lesser man might well be embarrassed: except that lesser men do not become President, nor do lesser men get invitations to ask questions on such impartial and objective programs.

—An hour-long interview with Secretary Knox immediately after on the same network, in which a panel of three Washington correspondents (the *National Observer,* the Los Angeles *Times,* the network's own) would ask a series of smoothly worded questions designed to anger, harass and trap their victim into as many damaging answers as possible. Orrin would field them all, but inevitably a hundred million living rooms would be left with the indefinable but unsettling impression that here was a man short-tempered, ill-prepared, dangerously warlike and quite irresponsible.

—Innumerable articles, headlines, photographs, editorials, columns, commentaries, which would pay the briefest inescapable tribute to the Secretary's courage and integrity, heap the most fulsome praise upon Ted's.

—And to further set the climate in which the decision must be made, in major newspaper and television offices there would be selected photographs and film clips of GRANDMOTHER FLEES ADVANCING U.S. MARINES . . . VILLAGERS DRAGGED FROM HOMES

AS U.S. CLEARS AREA . . . CHILD CRIPPLED BY U.S. SHELL FIRE.

Carefully there would be considered the few—the very few, since very few were all that the wire services sent from the battlefronts—pictures of loyal natives hacked to pieces by rebel soldiers, loyal villages burned by rebel invaders, the naked bodies of U.S. Marines strung up by their heels with their genitals burned off by rebel torturers.

Carefully these would be considered, in the offices that decided what the country was to be allowed to see, and carefully they would be withheld from the American public. To print them would be to destroy the public's objectivity, and that just wouldn't be fair.

So it had been in America, over and over and over again in recent decades. So it would be today, tonight and tomorrow, world without end.

Until the end came.

Underneath, there was of course the working political level, and the President's comment to Jawbone was a truthful one, if rueful: he could not tell on the eve of the Committee's meeting how much effect his own lobbying, Orrin's, Jawbone's, Ted's, had had with the members. Some stubborn independence, fortunately inherent in most Americans still, had seemed to be withstanding both the massive barrage of media propaganda and the quieter, more practical methods of political pressure. The President had not been able to detect, nor had such of his lieutenants as Senators Powell Hanson and Lafe Smith who had been canvassing the Committee for him, any real shifting of sentiment up to a couple of days ago. Then the uglier pressures, not reported though a great many knew about them, had begun: and suddenly all was hurry, scurry, confusion and mystery.

And fear.

All that he had said to Ted, all that anyone else had said, was perfectly true: there was a restless, uneasy, worried, apprehensive mood developing in the Committee: by so much had the rioters, the demonstrators, and all the vicious trash clustered around the antiwar movement achieved their purpose. The country was still suffering from the traumatic shock of Harley's death—he made a mental note that he must call in the investigating commission soon and find out what it had discovered so far— and it was still suffering the even deeper shock of the horrible episode at the funeral. The cruel and ruthless had created exactly the atmosphere they wanted: a sick atmosphere, a savage atmosphere, in which many worried citizens could logically believe that anything, no matter how extreme, might happen.

This might not be so, but if they thought so, that was all that mattered for the purposes of the destroyers.

Intimidation was in the air, as palpable as the heat haze that lay over the Potomac basin.

For who knew what would happen next? Newspaper articles, television schedules, fatuous statements by fatuous people—these were predictable and customary, these were the standard aspects of life and government in late twentieth century America. But nobody knew what might be unscheduled and unpredictable—where or when a riot would flare out, a theater be blown up, a restaurant be bombed, a school be burned, a sniper's bullet slam home, poison strike. The incident at the funeral had finally convinced the country, if more were needed, that it really had entered upon an era in which no crime was too unthinkable, no horror too ghastly, no inhumanity too obscene. Quite conceivably the ominous telephone calls some members of the Committee were receiving could be translated into dreadful fact if the sane forces of society were not constantly alert against the insane.

The rock on which civilized behavior rested was no longer steady. It was being turned over, and the crawling things were coming out and making their bid to take over the world.

Whether the process could be arrested, the President could not say, nor, he suspected, could anyone. He had fellow citizens, white and black, who at this moment were somewhere, in secret rooms or well-publicized demonstrations, spitting out their savage hatred for him and for the government and the orderly society his office represented. Some of them, he was quite sure, were absolutely convinced that they were going to bring America down. What would become of the miserable fools when they did so, he could not imagine, for they would be left to hug their venom in a wasteland, if they lived at all, which was highly doubtful. But still they would persist, until they provoked sufficient force to meet force; after which there would be blood, and quietude. Hopefully not on their terms.

In the meantime, what must the good and decent do, abandon their principles and beliefs, run and hide? Some would, of course, and among some members of the Committee he could detect the beginnings of a disposition to do so. But many, he hoped, would not. Many, he hoped, would be brave enough to oppose the equivocal hero out of California for what he was, the prisoner of evil and the thrall of forces beyond his control.

He realized with a self-deprecating little laugh in the serene coolness of the Oval Room that he was thinking of Ted Jason almost as though he were Lucifer incarnate, the contest between him and Orrin as though it were some medieval battle between absolute good and absolute evil. But Ted was only a man, and so was Orrin: so even were the wreckers and the vicious and the violent. They were all human—or were they? He was no longer so sure.

Nor were they at "Vagaries," that lovely white house in Rock Creek Park where Dolly Munson had presided over so many brilliant social events, some of which had played a not insignificant part in deciding the course of nations and the destinies of men. Today her guests were few, and perhaps not quite as earthshaking as on some other occasions: or were they? It had been three years since she had come to Washington as a wealthy divorcee who had made up her mind to be a famous hostess and had wound up being not only a famous hostess but the wife of the Senate Majority Leader. She had discovered that you never knew what might happen at Washington parties. Sometimes the guests who seemed least likely to generate sensations did so. The potential was always there.

Not that her guests today were so unimportant, of course. She was honoring Lucille Hudson, after all, and in addition to the wife of the Secretary of State she had also invited the wives of the British and French Ambassadors. And, with that knack for the bizarre and unexpected which in less skillful hands could ruin a party but in hers always produced some unique and ineffable effect, she had also invited the unique and ineffable character who was just now alighting, with a grimly determined air, from her Rolls-Royce under the porte-cochere.

"Patsy, dear," Dolly said cordially, stepping forward through the stately doors and holding out her hand, "it is so nice of you to come."

"This HEAT!" Patsy exclaimed, giving her hostess's hand the slightest formal pressure as she brushed on past into the gracious coolness of the house. "The price Washington makes us pay for living here!"

"But we wouldn't leave, would we, dear?" Dolly inquired gently. "My goodness," she added thoughtfully, surveying the enormous orange and red concoction swaying forward ahead of her, "that is certainly *some* hat, Patsy. Where on earth did you get it?"

"At 'Yes-Sirree Bob's' in Georgetown," Patsy said proudly. "He's just opened, you know, with the sweetest little friend, and they have the most SUPERB things. Isn't it an utterly ridiculous name? But it makes you remember him."

"Which is the name of the game, in Washington," Dolly agreed. "Do come along into the drawing room. I expect Lucille will be over in a moment."

"Does she know I'm going to be here?" Patsy inquired, and for once Dolly thought she detected a slight trace of nervousness in that usually monumentally assured voice.

"Oh, yes," she said cheerfully. "I told her."

"And she didn't mind?"

"Do you?"

"No."

296

"Neither did she," Dolly said. "She said she thought it was time to find out what you're up to."

"It seems clear enough," Patsy said, settling into one of the velvet-covered armchairs with an air of satisfaction. "I'm helping to nominate a President."

"Yes, we know."

"Well?"

"I think Lucille is interested on a somewhat deeper level than that," Dolly said. "But there's the bell again . . . Patsy's already here," she confided with some amusement to Beth Knox as she stepped from a State Department Cadillac at the door. "Be prepared."

Beth chuckled.

"I'm always prepared for Patsy. I wonder if that girl knows how obvious she is."

"Only a complete unawareness of self could possibly carry it off," Dolly remarked. "Here comes Embassy Row," she added as two more Rolls-Royces, the first carrying a small Union Jack on the fender, the second a tricolor, entered the gates on Woodley Road and began the curving climb up the dogwood-covered hill. "You go on in and brave the lioness in her den while I greet them."

"With pleasure," Beth said . . . "Patsy," she suggested, forestalling a courtesy Patsy showed no signs of conferring, "don't get up. You look so comfortable sitting there."

"I must say," Patsy remarked without bothering to say hello, "I DO wonder about Dolly's taste in this room, I always do. It's so GAUCHE, somehow."

"Sad," Beth agreed, looking at the hat. "Gaucherie is exactly what one strives so hard to avoid. How is the campaign coming?"

"Reasonably well," Patsy said airily. "Reasonably well.

But here," she said, hoisting her gangling, long-limbed figure out of the clutching depths of the armchair, "come Kitty Maudulayne and Celestine Barre. So we don't have to struggle any more to make conversation, do we?"

Beth laughed with a quite genuine amusement.

"Speak for yourself, dear. I never struggle. I just listen, wide-eyed and open-mouthed, waiting to find out what I will hear next."

"Hmph!" said Patsy, giving her a sudden sharp glance before she turned away to greet Lady Maudulayne and the wife of the French Ambassador.

"Darlings," Kitty Maudulayne said with a calm cordiality, "how nice to see you both. Claude and I were saying only last night that it had been too long."

"We, too," Celestine remarked, and gave the sudden, grave little smile which made her conversation, so much of which was conducted in silences, the pleasantly intriguing and faintly mysterious thing it was.

"We hope," Patsy said, "that things will develop so that you will be able to feel welcome, TRULY welcome, in Washington. We hope there will presently be policies which will make you feel really AT HOME."

Lady Maudulayne looked surprised.

"Oh, I feel quite at home in Washington. I've felt at home here for five years. I don't see how I could possibly feel more at home, do you, Celestine?"

"No," Celestine said, and smiled.

"But you will feel more at home," Patsy said, "when things are brought back to a basis of sense, when we have a really sane policy in the government again and stop all these—these—"

"Don't work at it, dear," Dolly suggested calmly. "We

all get your point. I think I hear Lucille coming—yes, here she is." And she stepped forward gracefully to take the hand of the former First Lady, who had just entered through the conservatory, looking somewhat tired but otherwise quite calm and self-possessed.

"I'm sorry to be slow about it," Lucille Hudson said, "but I was just talking on the phone to one of the National Committeewomen and she proved to be rather long-winded."

"Oh?" Patsy said.

"Yes," Lucille said. "I talk to quite a few of them nowadays. And some of the Committeemen too. I find them a very interesting group."

"Everybody," Kitty Maudulayne said cheerfully, "seems to be talking to the National Committee. Simply everybody. I believe even Claude has spoken to a few—at their request, of course," she added hastily. "I wouldn't want you to think we were volunteering. And Vasily Tashikov, too. And no doubt Raoul—?" she suggested to Celestine. But Celestine only smiled.

"I'm afraid we're all going to turn the poor old Committee's collective head," Dolly said, "giving it so much attention—"

"Nothing on earth is more important than that they DO THE RIGHT THING!" Patsy snapped.

"You're so right," Dolly agreed calmly. "I think perhaps we can have a cocktail now, if we'd like." And when they had ordered, Lucille and Beth asking for Dubonnet on the rocks, Kitty and Celestine taking dry sherry, Dolly an old-fashioned and Patsy a martini straight up, Dolly turned to the guest of honor and said gently,

"Lucille, dear, we are so glad you felt like being with us."

"And we are so glad you feel able to talk to the National Committee, too," Beth said. "I'm sure they want your advice and I'm sure you are being very helpful to them."

"Very helpful to SOMEONE," Patsy observed with a savage gulp of her martini.

"I want to do what I can," Lucille said gently. "It is so difficult for them right now. They are under such pressure, from the whole world, really. I believe many of them don't know what is the right thing to do."

"Is there any question?" Beth asked. Patsy responded on cue.

"WELL! If you *of all people* don't know—"

"It seems to me," Beth said innocently, "that everything's going along very well. Particularly with this news from Af— Oh, dear!" she exclaimed with a show of dismay. "I wasn't supposed to say that."

"What news?" Patsy demanded. "What are you talking about?"

"Nothing," Beth said. "Forget it. Forgive me. My mistake. All thumbs. And it hasn't even been formally—"

"What ARE you talking about, Beth Knox?" Patsy insisted. "You certainly aren't being very fair."

"I said 'nothing,'" Beth repeated blandly. "I just meant that everything is going so well everywhere, the world is in such a settled state, the country has never been calmer, everybody is so happy—" She paused and in spite of her attempts to keep a straight face, a little humorous line came around the corners of her eyes. "Kitty Maudulayne," she said, "what are *you* smiling about?"

For a moment the British Ambassadress gave her a direct candid look.

"But of course there's still Panama, isn't there?" she said.

"There are still a million things, aren't there?" Dolly said firmly. "I think we can go in to the table, now. Lucille, dear—" And she was on her feet assisting the former First Lady, and her guests perforce were following, even Patsy silenced for the moment. But when they were seated in the gracious gray-green dining room amid the beautiful Minton, the glistening Steuben, the softly gleaming warmth of the vermeil, she rounded sharply on Lucille and said in a challenging voice, "All right, then, Lucille, what HAVE you found out in the Committee? Are they going to nominate my brother?"

The former First Lady looked at her with a rather wondering, pensive air. Then she said quietly,

"I'm sure I don't know. They seem very uncertain about it. I should hope, however"—and she paused and stared down the charming room as though seeing many things—I should hope that they would not. Nothing, it seems to me, would be more detrimental to the United States."

For several minutes no one spoke, though Dolly had the hostess's impulse to fill the gap. Then she thought, *Oh, the hell with it. She deserves it. Let her take it.* With a polite interest they all stared vaguely past one another's ears while the maids provided a welcome interruption with the soup. When they had vanished as silently as they had appeared, Patsy, who had been sitting transfixed, put both hands against, the table edge, looked straight ahead at Celestine who looked politely back, and said flatly, "I have never been so insulted in my life."

"Try losing a husband," Lucille suggested in a voice

that almost broke, but didn't. "That can be rather insulting, too."

"Lucille Hudson," Patsy said, literally gasping with indignation, "are you insinuating that my brother had anything at all—had anything—had anything to do with—with—*are you insinuating* THAT?"

"I'm not insinuating anything," Lucille said, her eyes beginning to fill with tears but her voice steady. "I'm saying your brother is responsible for encouraging the atmosphere in which it could be done. I'm saying you Jasons go through the world knocking people out of your way and encouraging forces you don't know anything about. I'm saying your brother bears a major share of the blame for my husb—for the President's death—whether he realizes it or not. I think he is a bad man, and I think he should be defeated."

"How dare you say that to me!" Patsy said in a violent whisper. "How DARE you! Who else created this atmosphere!" she demanded, her voice rising. "Isn't anybody else responsible for it? How about precious Orrin Knox, there"—and she flung out a hand that knocked over one of the stately goblets, snapping its stem with a tiny clean sound—"how about precious Orrin Knox and that old FOOL who sits in the White House? What have THEY done to create the atmosphere in which people get hurt? Why aren't THEY responsible? Why don't you sit here and say terrible things about THEM? I'm going," she said, getting somewhat unsteadily to her feet, "I'm sorry I broke your glass, Dolly. I'm sorry you all had to stand my awful presence. I'm sorry I agreed to be with you. But I hope my brother wins this nomination and I hope he becomes President because then this country will be run the way it ought to be. Goodbye!"

And without pausing for Dolly's hasty, "Wait a minute, Patsy, I'll see you to the—" she was up and out, stalking blindly through the gorgeous rooms to the great doors, the porte-cochere and her startled chauffeur, who took her rapidly away in her gleaming Rolls-Royce.

Into the silence that fell, Celestine Barre presently remarked in a politely analytical tone, "You know, I believe she was actually crying. I never thought I should see it."

"It was rage," Dolly said shortly. "Nothing with them ever goes deeper than that."

"Perhaps it was more than that," Beth said. "I'm afraid I did tease her unmercifully."

"Why should anyone be merciful?" Lucille Hudson asked in a cold and distant voice. Then her expression changed and became regretful. "I'm sorry. I suppose I shouldn't have been so harsh. But they are bad people. They are encouraging awful things—*awful* things." And suddenly she too began to cry, and with a hurried, "I'm sorry. Forgive me, forgive me!" rose abruptly from the table and disappeared.

"Well," Dolly said a few minutes later when, the awkward luncheon finally completed, they were standing at the door waiting for the cars to come up, "I can't claim that this was one of my more successful ideas."

"It's just the times," Kitty Maudulayne said quietly. "Everything is out of joint."

"Isn't it too bad," Beth said wryly. "One can't even have a nice, normally catty luncheon any more."

Kitty nodded.

"Even that is ruined now."

Beth looked at her thoughtfully.

"Nothing new on Panama?" she asked.

Lady Maudulayne gave her a direct, unblinking glance.

"The times are out of joint, but not *that* out of joint. Don't you agree, Celestine?"

But Celestine, who had contributed her sentences for the day, only smiled.

After they had departed in their respective limousines, Beth turned to her hostess.

"I'm sorry for the shambles."

Dolly shrugged.

"Don't be. It *is* the times."

"Let me offer you a diversion," Beth suggested. "Come to the airport with me and meet Hal and Crystal. They're coming in at three to join us for the big push."

"Gladly," Dolly said. "Let me just run up and get a hat. . . . Don't call Helen-Anne about this," she called over her shoulder. "I don't want to read about it in the *Star!*"

"I won't," Beth promised, "but you know Helen-Anne. She may get it anyway. That girl flies on sheer instinct and the seat of her pants."

But it was not on instinct or the seat of her pants—except as instinct told her she was going into danger—that she was flying now, as she stood in the great echoing rotunda of the Capitol and listened absentmindedly to the guides herding their throngs of wide-eyed, camera-hung, sloppily dressed, heat-weary, awe-struck Americans. In fact, she wasn't flying: she had rarely felt so depressed.

She had seen and covered many things in Washington, stretching back over such other savage issues as Vietnam and the First and Second Korean Wars, but never had there been quite the note of almost frivolous bestiality that characterized the present uproar over Gorotoland and Panama: as though certain of her countrymen had undergone some final, irrevocable leave-taking of their sanity, their decency, their heritage.

Evil strode the land, so that virtually every hour on the hour there was some new flare-up somewhere of mindless violence or rabid outburst, an almost carefree viciousness that in its ultimate form was close to simple anarchy, destruction for destruction's sake.

Except that in the minds of some of her fellow-Americans, and in the minds of those others who organized and financed many of their outbursts, destruction had an object: America. Such was the aim of the destroyers. Such was the aim of the nasty character she was planning to see in the next few minutes.

She sighed deeply, and pushed her hair nervously behind her ear in a characteristic gesture just as someone said, "Boo!" She literally jumped and then found to her surprise and annoyance that she was trembling. It was only when the Congressman from California put an enormous black hand on her shoulder and said gently, "Slow down, slow down!" that she did so.

"Lord, you startled me!" she said.

"You act as though you're seeing ghosts right here in the old rotunda," Cullee said with a smile. "Is it that bad?"

"Almost," she said. "And you know it."

He sighed and his face became somber.

"Yes, I do know it. I've been getting it hot and heavy too, you know."

"I'll bet you have," she said with a sudden sympathy. "Are you safe, Cullee?"

"Not very," he said with a grim little smile. "But I've taken a few steps. I've closed up my house out Sixteenth Street and old Maudie and I, we've moved to River Towers, temporarily. But of course the house isn't very safe empty, and as for me, I suppose I'm a sitting duck. But, hell!" he said with a sudden scowling anger that made two passing tourists give him a startled glance and caused him to lower his voice. "Can't waste all my time running from the black trash. They beat me up six months ago when Terry was here, and I suppose they may try it again, one of these days. Hasn't stopped me, much."

"For God's sake be careful," she said, her voice also dropping cautiously, her own worries forgotten for the moment in concern for this good friend. The Congressman smiled again, a little more relaxed.

"Oh, I will. I'm not exactly standing still and waiting for it. But it's just there, in our country right now, and any of us who dares oppose it is fair game, I suppose. Who're you waiting for?"

She looked at him thoughtfully for a second and then decided to tell the truth.

"Bob Leffingwell."

"Good place for a rendezvous," Cullee observed with a smile. "If anybody looks suspicious, you can always join a tour."

"I could lead one," she said, "I've heard that routine so many thousands of times."

For a minute or two they stood silent, looking around the enormous echoing room, a little sentimental expression in their eyes at the thought of this old building in which so much of their lives had been spent.

306

"Who are you going to see?" Cullee asked quietly, and after a moment she told him that, too; adding quickly, "You don't want to come along, do you?"

"I would like to," he said, looking somber again. "I really would like to talk to that slimy son of a bitch. But I can't, unfortunately. I'm going to be seeing another one. I'm just on my way to the House, and then to my office, right now. He'll be there, if he doesn't chicken out."

"Be careful," she said, her voice still low. "I think he's a very dangerous man. I think they're all very dangerous."

"Why do you want to see Freddie?" he asked.

"Why do you want to see LeGage?"

"Scare him off," he said grimly. "If I can. And you?"

"Confirm something, and scare *him* off. If I can."

"We can't," he said with a grimly sardonic smile. "What do you want to confirm?"

"I'll tell you if I confirm it."

"All right," he said. "Just don't take any chances, though. If you're really onto something, the more people you tell the safer you'll be, in this climate. Don't wait to get a scoop in the *Star*. It isn't worth it."

"You're asking me to go against the training of a lifetime," she said with an attempt at lightness that didn't quite come off.

"Don't take chances," he said earnestly. "That's an order, Helen-Anne."

"You're sweet to worry," she said, "but I think I'll be all right."

"Just watch it."

"I will," she said. "Here comes Bob."

"Hi," Cullee said, holding out a hand. "I understand you're on a secret mission. I'd join you if I could."

"I wish you could," Bob Leffingwell said, his voice also instinctively lowered as another group of tourists straggled by. "I don't really know what it's all about; but Helen-Anne commanded, and here I am."

"As you should," Cullee said. "I've been telling her," he said, his amiable expression fading and his voice confidential, "to be damned careful. I want you to take care of her."

"That's what I'm here for," Bob Leffingwell said, equally low-voiced.

"How strange it is," Helen-Anne said with an odd, distant thoughtfulness, "that a United States Congressman, a distinguished public servant and a Washington newspaperwoman should feel they have to lower their voices and talk like conspirators in the rotunda of the United States Capitol. What are we all afraid of?"

"Nobody knows," Bob Leffingwell said. "And that's why everybody's afraid."

"Take care, you two," Cullee said. "I've got to run. Be *careful.*"

"You, too, for heaven's sake," Helen-Anne said. "He's going to see LeGage," she confided as they watched his tall, powerful figure go swiftly away with the college athlete's lightness of stride that he had never quite lost. "He's the one who needs protection."

"More than we do, with the character we're going to see?" Bob asked with a humorous wryness. "Helen-Anne, don't overestimate the power of a woman."

"Sweetie," she said, "I don't. My feeling, most times nowadays, is: God help us all."

Whether God was on the job today, however, was something of a moot point. Certainly He was rather far from both the presence and the thoughts of the ominously scowling individual who sat in his office on the fourth floor of the New Senate Office Building and waited for his visitors. Fred Van Ackerman, junior Senator from the State of Wyoming, was not in the mood to waste much time on what he regarded as two feather-headed, hysterical boobs. Helen-Anne had been a pest ever since his first run-in with her. She had begun digging around in his personal affairs soon after he took office, and although she never really found anything, she had put a couple of things in her column that had probably helped to start the trail of vindictiveness that had led to his censuring by the Senate at the time of the Leffingwell nomination. As for Bob himself—that mealy-mouthed, hypocritical pantywaist for whom Fred had done so much during the nomination battle was now deserting Fred's candidate and thus was deserting not only Fred himself but that crusade for world peace and justice that the junior Senator from Wyoming conceived to be his particular mission in life.

The Leffingwell nomination! It had happened more than a year ago, and still its bitter divisions and suspicions were racking the Senate and influencing in a thousand subtle ways the conduct of American policy. It was amazing how such an event could continue to eat away at the American system like some constantly recurring cancer that one had thought to be excised but which apparently possessed a life of its own. So major a tangle of emotions, ambitions, likes, dislikes, ideals, nobilities, cupidities, braveries, cowardice, took a long time dying in Washington. There had been a few such back down the decades, great legislative battles that had split the Senate, the government and the country, and it was usually not until the major participants had passed from the scene that the ramifications and repercussions died away. In this instance, most of the major participants were still very much alive and kicking.

Out of the spiteful inability of some of them to accept the fact that he and Ted Jason really represented a major section of the country's thinking had come many of the bitter aspects of the fight over the visit of Terrible Terry to the United States and the United Nations. Out of them had come most of the bitter hostility to Ted and his cause at the San Francisco convention. And now, finally, there came still the adamant and implacable opposition of such men as the President as Ted was about to try again in the National Committee for the prize that history, simple justice and the desperate need of the world said should be his.

It was what you could expect of the sort of half-assed, half-baked minds that were coming to see Fred today. Certainly the fact of his own political survival was proof enough that the cause he espoused was the right one. For a time, true enough, it had seemed to be nip and tuck, but he appeared to have won out quite all right. Maybe he had been a little harsh on poor old AC-DC Brigham Anderson, and certainly no one could have foreseen that the pathetic little weak sister would commit suicide under pressures that Senator Van Ackerman regarded as no more than legitimate political hazing. After all, if a guy wanted to play around with the boys on the beach in Hawaii, he deserved what he got, in Fred's book. Fred had enough brains to be discreet, and he didn't have much respect for someone who didn't.

There had been a fearfully bitter reaction in the Senate when his part in blackmailing Brig to the point of suicide had become known, but, hell! They had censured him, and even now he could sometimes brood in furious anger on the dreadful injustice of that, but, hell! Bob Munson and Warren Strickland had raised the rafters with stern warnings about what they would do to "get him," but, hell! They hadn't really dared to lay a finger on him, in actual practical fact: the tradition of the Senate kept them from being too harsh on a member, even a member in disgrace, because there was always the uneasy feeling that his constituents, after all, had elected him, and the Senate couldn't really overrule them until they had a chance to pass on him again. And more than that, the practical political fact of it was that he spoke for a group so powerful in the country that Bob and Warren and all the rest of them just didn't have the guts to defy it.

He would admit that this year they had scrounged around Wyoming until they had come up with Representative Harvey Elrod, a young sucker who was taking on the task of trying to beat Fred in his campaign for re-election. But it wasn't going to work, for a simple reason: more people in rich, comfortable, cotton-padded America liked the easy Nirvana of peace, any kind of peace, than liked the hard choices and harsh sacrifices of war. Lenin had said, in effect, that the dollar would be the death of them, because they'd do anything to get it and keep it, and maybe he had been right. Certainly it made a great many of them suckers for the type of peace campaign he and Ted and their friends were conducting now.

And why shouldn't they be, anyway? Was there anything wrong in wanting to put a stop to these endless petty wars that were draining away the substance, the unity and the purpose of America? He had thought a year and a half ago that Bob Leffingwell was really going to be the man to do it, and that was why he had fought for him so viciously in the Senate and why he had really, for a while, had such faith in him. This had held firm even through the disclosure that Bob had lied to the Foreign Relations Committee, because, hell! Anybody could lie to protect himself in politics. Fred did it all the time. One little lie or another wasn't going to affect a man's abilities to lead the crusade for final peace. He survived: Bob could have survived, if he hadn't turned out to be such a two-bit weakling and traitor to everyone who believed in him.

Fred didn't have any respect for weaklings who let their effectiveness be destroyed by moral considerations. It was a tough game these days, particularly if you were right out there on the firing line, and you couldn't afford to let niceties cripple you.

This was what he often told his friends in the Committee on Making Further Offers for a Russian Truce. COMFORT had seemed to come from nowhere to support him in the nomination fight, and even now he didn't know exactly where all its money came from, but he knew it was an invaluable ally and a perfect sounding board for him in the crusade for peace. One thing he liked about it was that he didn't have to spend any time persuading COMFORT to be tough: it was tough, as witness these demonstrations its members were joining in now all over the country. He liked that. None of this damned wishy-washy hesitating round-and-round-the-mulberry-bush Bob Leffingwell type of thinking about what was right and what was wrong. COMFORT, like DEFY and KEEP, meant business.

And why shouldn't they? Their aim was peace, and what higher aim was there? It justified everything. The alternatives were so frightful that it justified anything that had to be done to stop the damned destroying fools who were leading the country and the world down the road to doom.

So he rationalized it, and for him it was an adequate rationale. So adequate, in fact, that sometimes he could almost forget the rest of it. He could right now, that was for sure, as his phone rang and his secretary announced his visitors.

He stood up and waited impassively behind his desk as she ushered them in, making no attempt to smile or speak or indicate the slightest warmth of greeting. He had long ago found this to be an effective trick, and apparently it was effective with them, for he was pleased to see that Bob Leffingwell looked openly annoyed, and Helen-Anne, for all her attempt to hide it, decidedly flustered. He decided he wouldn't even offer them a chair and see how they liked that the war-loving, reactionary bastards. He didn't permit his inner glee to show at all when Bob Leffingwell finally remarked in a frigid voice,

"I assume we are to be allowed to sit down."

Then he finally spoke, with that cruelly humorous overexpansiveness he loved to display to his opponents on the Senate floor.

"Why, bless your hearts," he said with a fleering, exaggerated cordiality, "of course you can sit down. Anywhere you please. On the floor, Bob, if you like."

To this they made no reply. Instead Helen-Anne looked at Bob and said, "I'm sorry I inflicted this on you. I shouldn't have."

"Oh, yes, you should," he said grimly. "It's a good study in abnormal psychology, if nothing else. But we'll leave if you—"

"Oh, no," she said quickly, sitting down in one of the two armchairs facing the desk. "My idea. . . . We'll see it through."

"Yes," Bob agreed, taking the other. "I think we should."

"When you two get through playing your little word games," Senator Van Ackerman remarked in a bored voice, slumping into his own chair behind the desk, "maybe we can get to it. What's this all about?"

"It's about a country," Helen-Anne said, and added immediately, "Oh, hell, that's too damned pompous. It's about your meeting at the Hilton and what's going to happen if the plans aren't changed."

"Oh?" Fred Van Ackerman said, and a dangerous sound came into his voice, deliberately menacing, deliberately soft. "What meeting was that?"

"I suppose there are so many you don't want to admit to—" Bob Leffingwell began with a dry sarcasm, and at once Fred was off into one of the rages that his Senate colleagues knew so well and could never quite analyze, some, like Lacey Pollard of Georgia considering them "Fred's damned phony stunts," and others, like Powell Hanson of North Dakota, saying with genuine alarm, "That fellow ought to be committed."

"Who the hell do you think you *are?*" he demanded, his voice edging toward the high, hysteric whine it acquired so often on the Senate floor, "you pious, pompous, pathetic son of a bitch? Just who do you think you are, you two-bit pantywaist who hasn't got the guts to stand up and fight for what he believes in, you double-crossing, lily-livered, worthless, two-timing *tramp?*"

"Bob," Helen-Anne said warningly, and her companion managed a smile, though a tense one.

"I know," he said. "Don't worry."

"Let me tell you something, you poor pathetic bastard," Fred went on, "you have a hell of a nerve to come in this office about anything, after what you've done to the greatest fighter for peace this world has ever known—"

"We call him the Prince," Bob Leffingwell said, his sense of humor suddenly reviving in a way that startled him, it seemed so outside himself. Instantly Senator Van Ackerman leaped to his feet and began striding up and down behind the desk, face suffused, hands clenching and unclenching at his sides.

"*You!*" he said. "I might expect some kind of smart-ass humor like that from *you!* What are they going to do for you, Bobby boy, now that you've betrayed Ted and gone over to dear, precious Orrin? Thirty pieces of silver wouldn't be enough for you, would they?" he demanded, his face contorted in a contemptuous sneer. "How about thirty-six?"

For a long moment Bob Leffingwell fought obviously for self-control; achieved it with a great effort; managed to respond quietly.

"You always try to create a diversion, don't you, Fred? We aren't here to talk about me—"

"No," Fred erupted savagely, "but *I'm* here to talk

about you. And a sorrier subject for discussion I can't think of. I didn't mind you crapping out on the Foreign Relations Committee, the silly bastards don't deserve anything better from anybody, but then to have you turn on the only candidate who really wants peace, the only one who offers any hope for the world—why, hell! And *you* come here to lecture *me!*"

"Fred," Helen-Anne said quietly, "I know about that meeting."

"And as for you, you damned busybody," Senator Van Ackerman said, swinging around the desk with an air that made Bob half-rise to his feet as Fred stopped scarcely a foot from her, "I've had just about all the crap from you that I'm going to take. You've been out to get me ever since I came to Washington—"

"And maybe this is the time I'm going to do it, too!" she snapped with an anger so sudden that it made him pause in mid-sentence. "You get back behind that desk," she went on in a furious tone, "and don't you come near me again, you hear?"

"Well, well," he said, stepping back involuntarily. "Well, well, listen to Little Miss Scoop."

"I'm warning you, Fred," she said, more quietly. "You're not the only one who's had all the crap she can take. So have I, up to here. I've got a story ready to go—"

"Who's going to print it?" he asked contemptuously, returning to his chair, leaning forward with one hand on the arm, elbow out, head lowered, scowl on his face. "Who in the hell is going to touch your damned pipe dreams? Not the *Star*, certainly. They've got too much sense.

"They aren't pipe dreams," she said quietly. His exaggerated contemptuous smile deepened.

"Oh, no? Who's got the proof, Weak-Willed Willie, here?"

"Bob doesn't know anything about it." She paused. "Yet. I asked him to come with me as a witness, and for my protection. Frankly I didn't know what insane thing you might do."

"So now I'm crazy," he said, turning away with a gesture that invited the world to marvel at such imbecility. He snorted. "Like a fox."

"Like a sick fox," she said. "That's the pity of it."

But, as always with Fred, one could never be sure how he would react. Instead of going through the ceiling as she expected, he gave her a quizzical stare and said, "Pity! My God, pity! If anybody needs pity, it's you, girlie, spreading these wild rumors all over town—"

"I haven't spread any rumors," she said, "but I'm sure as hell going to spread a story all over the papers, buster, unless you think maybe it would be wiser to call off the things you have planned."

"Oh, ho," he said softly. "You hear that, Bob? I thought I was the one who threatened, but lo and behold! It's Miss Purity of the Press. You're the witness, Bob, that's what you're here for. You heard her."

"I think you'd better listen," Bob Leffingwell suggested. Senator Van Ackerman's mouth twisted in a thin, sarcastic line.

"What game are you two up to, anyway? Is this some sort of blackmail?"

"You ought to recognize it," Bob Leffingwell said swiftly, but again, Fred baffled them. Instead of going into a ranting rage he simply sat back and laughed, with a complete and apparently genuine scorn.

"If you two don't take the cake!" he said. "If you don't win all the prizes in town! Coming here with some phony cock-and-bull story, trying to scare me with these phony threats! Me! *Me!* Don't you know better than that?"

"Fred," Helen-Anne said earnestly, as to a fractious, willful child, "you must pay attention to what I am saying, because I do know that there was a meeting at the Hilton after Patsy Labaiya's party at which you—and LeGage Shelby—and Rufus Kleinfert—and Ted Jason—and probably a fifth party—"

"But you aren't absolutely sure of it, are you?" Fred interrupted with a cold spitefulness. "You're just fishing, like all you damned reporters. Why don't you stop this and run along?"

"You and Rufus and LeGage and Ted," Helen-Anne repeated, "and you sat down with an enemy of this country and you planned—"

But this time Fred did react, his face suddenly livid, his voice snarling upward, his body shaking with the quivering rage they had seen him display in moments of crisis on the Senate floor.

"Now, see here, you prying bitch!" he said. "You don't know anything about any damned meeting, you don't have any proof of any damned meeting—do you?" he demanded quickly as Helen-Anne despite her best efforts was unable to suppress a flicker of expression. "Do you? God damn it," and he jumped suddenly out of his chair and again started around the desk, *"do you?"*

"Stand back!" she shouted, jumping up and raising her enormous handbag ludicrously above her head as Bob also surged to his feet, "Stand back, you *raving maniac!* Yes, I *do* have proof. Yes, I *do* know who was there. Yes,

I *am* going to print it unless you call it off. Now, damn you, *sit down!*"

"I think you'd better, Fred," Bob Leffingwell said quietly into the silence; and presently, glaring at them both and breathing like the heavy in an early film, he did so. For several minutes he stared at them, his expression gradually changing from rage to his usual one of settled contempt for the world in general and them in particular.

"Let me get this straight," he said presently in quite an ordinary voice. "Somebody has come to you with some crazy story about a meeting, and you haven't anything better to write about, so that's the project for today. Now, who"—and his eyes and voice became speculative in a way that suddenly made Helen-Anne's skin crawl—"could have told you a fairy-tale like that?"

"I've got my sources," she said hurriedly, "and they're no concern of yours."

"Somebody," he said thoughtfully. "Now, who—?"

"What I want to know is," she said loudly, "are you going to call it off or aren't you?"

But Fred was in some private world of his own, the clever, crooked mind working like lightning.

"Who—?" Then suddenly the speculative look was gone, his expression was instantly bland and innocent.

"I think what you'd better do is just forget it," he said, not unkindly. "And you, too, Bob. Somebody must have had some kind of delusion. There wasn't any meeting. You'd be better off too, Helen-Anne, if you just didn't think about it any more. Thinking too much isn't healthy," he said with a sort of amiable inanity. "We all know that in this town." He stood up.

"I warn you, Fred," Helen-Anne said loudly. He waved her absently to her feet.

"I'm sorry, but I've got to get over to the floor."

"Then you aren't going to do anything to stop it?" she asked, and to her intense annoyance sounded almost pleading. Fred smiled, a smile that for once seemed genuine and quite satisfied.

"What's to do," he inquired innocently, "when it's all a figment of your imagination, anyway?"

But when they had left he turned at once to the telephone; and outside in the corridor Helen-Anne looked frantically around for a public booth. His call went through at once. Hers took ten minutes, while Bob Leffingwell stood by with a worried frown and held her handbag.

"You know," Beth said thoughtfully as they stood by the window and watched the beautiful and terrible machines roar in and out, "I've been a little leery of watching planes land ever since—"

"Now, now," Dolly said firmly. "Calm, constructive thoughts, please. It rarely happens and when it does there's usually a reason."

"What, I wonder? Have you people heard anything definite?"

Dolly shook her head.

"Only the usual rumors. The dead man with the pistol, the two subversives on the ground crew, the Army mess boy in the cabin with the blank-faced little wife he married in Albania—"

"That I hadn't heard," Beth said.

"Oh, yes. If you could add it all up, it could prove very

interesting. But of course with the great, instinctive American disbelief in plots—nobody's *that* bad, you know, although of course they have been, for a very long time—it probably wouldn't be accepted. It would just start another book and play industry—"

"Thereby putting dollars to work helping the economy, and contributing substantially to the Gross National Product," Beth remarked. "It's probably worth doing, for that alone."

"How cynical you've grown in Washington's sunny climes. I believe that must be the kids, just taxiing in."

"I believe so," Beth agreed, looking pleased.

"How are they?" Dolly asked. "Should I be prepared to—"

"Just be prepared to be yourself. It's always more than enough."

"I don't know whether I quite understand that or not," Dolly said. Beth laughed.

"Persiflage and hyperbole."

"Hmm," Dolly said thoughtfully. "That may be the ticket the National Committee is looking for: Rutherford B. Persiflage and Oscar W. Hyperbole. 'So Good They're Unbelievable.'"

"Now you're being nonsensical."

"No," Dolly said. "Just a little excited at seeing your wandering chicks again."

"If you're excited," Beth said, "guess how I feel."

But when Hal and Crystal came along the ramp, Crystal walking a little slowly, Hal supporting her with a protective arm around her waist, Beth was all brisk, comfortable good-humor, just as always. For a second both the children looked as though they might cry, but Beth and Dolly promptly smothered them with kisses and jolly welcomes and the moment became like any other warm family homecoming. Except that of course it wasn't, quite.

"How are you feeling, Crystal?" Dolly asked quietly when Beth and Hal had gone to see about the luggage. Crystal managed a reasonable facsimile of a smile.

"Not too bad. The doctor says I can have another baby, you know, so—"

"Oh, *wonderful*," Dolly said. "I am so pleased for you all. That ought to make recuperation a breeze."

"Yes," Crystal said, the smile fading, "except that we seem to be coming back to just—more of the same. At least before there was some consolation that it had all been settled in the convention, but now because of poor Uncle Harley, we have it all to do over again."

"I don't think your father-in-law needs to worry about the outcome," Dolly said firmly. Crystal's eyes darkened with the thought of many things.

"It's not the outcome," she said. "It's what happens while you're getting there. A funny thing happened on the way to the—" And suddenly her eyes began to fill with tears and Dolly said hastily and sharply, "Stop that. Now, stop it!"

"I try to," Crystal said, "but it keeps coming back."

"Well—" Dolly began, and fell silent, unable at the moment to think of anything to say that would erase the horrible memory of that swirling fog-bound night outside the Cow Palace in San Francisco only ten days ago.

"I'm sorry," Crystal said presently. "How do things look here?"

"About what you've been reading in Carmel, I imagine. Unpleasant, there's no use in pretending. The Knox house is under guard, and so are we. Lucille Hudson is staying in the guest house, and the very night she moved in somebody got over the wall on the park side and threw a bucket of sewage all over the front door—"

"Oh, *no.*"

"Oh, yes," Dolly said grimly. "That's the kind of people we're dealing with in America these days. If they don't kill you, they defile you. . . . So," she went on, more gently, "I'm afraid, my dear, that you're quite right. You're going to have to be careful here, too. All of you. But I still believe the prospect for Orrin is bright. The National Committee is under great pressures, but I think its moving his way."

"Dear Dolly," Crystal said, a grateful smile returning. "You're always so kind to us poor old beleaguered Knoxes. And, in fact, to everyone."

"I'm sure I'm right," Dolly said firmly.

"I want to think so," Crystal said. "Maybe it's because Daddy's been in the Senate twenty years and I've been around politics all my life, but I just don't feel as optimistic as you do." She smiled again, rather wistfully. "I'll try, though. I really will try, Dolly."

And at the luggage counter Hal was trying, too, though a lifetime of growing up in politics was making it as difficult for him as for his wife. Nor was his mother's practicality much assistance. Beth, as always, was shrewd and objective about her husband and his chances.

"How's Dad doing?" Hal asked as soon as they had left the others and started through the crowded concourse.

"Fairly well."

He frowned.

"That all? Only fair?"

"The Committee's being very close-mouthed," Beth said. "Actually, some of them are plain scared. But inevitably, things come out. There's the same Jason group there was at the convention, led principally by Roger Croy of Oregon and Esmé Stryke of California, and they've made quite a bit of headway in the preliminary sparring. The Knox forces, as usual"—and despite her quite genuine air of pragmatic humor, a little expression of pain and annoyance did come into her eyes—"are well-meaning, hopeful, busy and disorganized." She smiled dryly. "Mary Baffleburg and Lizzie McWharter aren't exactly the world's most dynamic leaders, you know. And so far, nobody much has come forward from anywhere else to get things moving. Stanley's done a little work sounding people out, but his heart isn't in it any more."

"No," Hal said somberly, thinking of his father-in-law, the Senate Majority whip, Stanley Danta of Connecticut, devastated and disheartened by what had happened to his daughter at the convention. "That pretty well threw him for life, I'm afraid."

"But it hasn't you," Beth said, giving her son a sudden shrewd glance. He shrugged.

"I'm young. You know it did for a while, but—I guess you can adapt to almost anything when you're our age. Knowing we can have another helps, of course. It would be pretty awful without that."

"How's Crystal been this past week?"

"Better," he said slowly. "Much better. She's still . . . afraid."

"Coming here won't help," Beth said. "This town isn't very safe, right now."

"What place is?" Hal asked. He gave her a sudden shrewd look that was an exact copy of her own. "What kind of deals is Dad going to have to make to get this nomination?"

"Why should he have to make any?"

"He may," Hal said. "He may . . ."

"None have been proposed and none have been offered," Beth said.

"But they will be," he suggested. "And what he does then will tell a lot of things."

"Do you doubt him?" she asked, and they might have been alone in a desert instead of in the middle of the hurrying concourse, so intent were they upon their conversation.

"I never have," he said finally.

"Then don't now."

"OK . . . if you say so."

"If you believe so," she said. He stared at her for a long moment and again said:

"OK."

"I think your bags are coming along now," she remarked, her tone becoming businesslike. "That's Dolly's car out there, ask the chauffeur to help you. I'll go get the others and we'll—get on home. You'll be wanting to see your father."

"Yes," he said, his smile suddenly warm. "I will."

"Bob," Helen-Anne said, "would you do me a favor? I can't seem to reach their house and the city desk doesn't seem to be able to find anybody who can help me at the moment. Would you go to the hotel for me while I go to the house?"

"Damn it, Helen-Anne," he said, "stop being noble and use sense. You're not going to a neighborhood where there may be bloodshed if we can't head it off, and let me go to a nice, safe hotel. Now, be sensible, damn it. I'll go to T Street, *you* go to the Hilton. OK?"

"But there's no point in exposing you to—" His expression stopped her.

"Stop being Fearless Girl Reporter and start being scared, will you?"

"All right," she said with a sudden meekness that indicated more than words how scared she really was. "Why don't you call me at the paper around three? I'll go back there as soon as I know everything's all right."

"I will," he promised. She started to turn away and then stopped abruptly and fished in her handbag.

"Here," she said hurriedly, holding out a sheaf of folded copy paper. "Keep these for me until—until we see each other again."

"Oh, now," he began, "don't—"

"Just keep them for me," she said. "OK?"

"All right," he said slowly, putting them in his breast pocket. "Be careful."

A sad expression touched her face.

"'Be careful,'" she echoed, a bitter twist to her lips. "It's getting to be the password of the age."

And now he realized that he must be prepared for unpleasantness, as he turned the familiar corner in the empty corridor of the Old House Office Building and came to the massive door that bore the once-magic words (and still magic, in spite of all the disillusioning years that had passed since he first saw them):

MR. HAMILTON
California

On the other side of them today sat trouble. Or rather, as he saw in a glance as he entered his office, noted the frightened expression in his receptionist's eyes, and became aware of the tall, rangy figure near the window, stood—talked—paced—glared—trouble.

Deliberately he paid it no mind at first, asking his receptionist with a fair show of matter-of-factness, though his voice trembled slightly, "Any calls for me?"

"A few," she said. "The Agriculture Department wants you to call on that Hempstead matter. The Secretary of State has been trying to reach you—"

"Oh, well, then—" he began, moving toward the phone, but she held up a hand.

"No, I told him you were expecting a—a visitor—and he said don't bother, he'll call later."

"That was after you told him who the visitor was," LeGage suggested with a sour smile, and she lifted her head defiantly and gave him stare for stare.

"Yes," she said. "Assuming it's any of your business."

"Why don't you invite your old buddy Orrin over, Cullee?" LeGage suggested, deliberately turning his back on her. "Us old buddies might have a real cozy chat together. The damned war maker!"

"Maybe you'd better come on in my office and get your vomiting over with," Cullee said coldly, "so I can get back to my work. Get on in there!" he added sharply as LeGage gave him a furious scowl and hesitated. But finally he shook his head with an angry impatience and stepped swiftly inside. Cullee followed and closed the door.

"Now," he said, leaning back against it and looking his ex-friend, ex-political adviser, ex-Howard University roommate, thoughtfully up and down, "why in hell don't you try to act civilized, black boy too big for your britches? Or are you still getting your kicks from doing the jungle bit?"

For a moment he thought LeGage might spring at him and he could feel his muscles tense instinctively for it, welcoming it, wanting it, hoping 'Gage would give him the opportunity to administer a beating that would somehow assuage all the unhappiness and pain he felt because of Sue-Dan's leaving him and going to LeGage, because of 'Gage's opposition and dislike and all the bitter-hurtful things that had grown from their once-close friendship. But as always in their arguments, LeGage was too clever to give him the excuse. Instead he turned away with a contemptuous disgust and flung himself into a chair.

"Not the only black boy who's too big for his britches," he remarked, staring out at the tourists straggling through the stately trees and gentle lawns of Capitol Plaza. "Not the only black boy who needs setting down. Could be old Better-Than-Anybody Cullee needs a lesson too."

"You and your trash tried to give me one," Cullee said, moving to his desk, sitting down, propping his legs up on a corner of the desk. "Didn't take."

"There could always be another," 'Gage observed. Cullee abruptly dropped his legs to the floor, swung around full-face and leaned forward across the desk, staring intently at the clever, sullen face across from him.

"You won't be happy until you kill me, will you?" he asked softly.

"I don't want to kill you," 'Gage said. "You're worth

too much to us, if you'd just decide to be with your friends instead of against them."

"Friends!" Cullee echoed bitterly. "Crazy Fred and Lump-Head Rufus! Is that what you're calling your friends nowadays? Seems a long way to come from the old days."

"Oh, I had a friend once," LeGage said with a sort of brooding thoughtfulness. "Helped him get elected to Congress, had us some big dreams, thought he might be Senator, Governor, even Vice President someday, maybe, if everything went right. Had us some grand dreams, all right, until he went off with Whitey."

"And his old pal went off with his wife," Cullee said harshly. 'Gage gave him an odd look somewhere between sadness and smirk.

"I didn't make that little Sue-Dan come to me," be said. "She just got bored with you, Cullee baby. You just weren't man enough for her. That little gal needs lots of man, sure enough."

"Well, she knows by now she doesn't have it in you," Cullee snapped, and again for a second he thought his old friend-enemy might swarm across the desk. But after an angry glare for a moment he sank back and looked both tired and sardonic.

"I know you won't understand it," he said, "but she really believes in what we're doing in our campaign. She doesn't like me as much as she likes the idea. She knew she wasn't ever going to get anything but empty talk from you, so she went where the action is. We've got it, baby, in case you don't know it."

"Yes, I know it," Cullee said grimly, "and a hell of a fine action it is, tearing up your own country and ruining America—"

"Is *that* your hang up?" 'Gage demanded with an elaborate surprise. "Is *that* what's got you crying, poor old Congressman Hamilton Our Black White Hope? Well, well. Well, *well*."

"What are you getting out of it?" Cullee asked, and he really wanted to know. "You hoping to be the Black Commissar for the United States or something?"

'Gage uttered a contemptuous snort and turned again to stare out at the beautiful lawns, the peaceful trees.

"That's typical," he said. "That's so damned typical. We're going to burn this country down, and you and your whitey friends go around mouthing phony slogans like 'black commissars'! My God! Don't you *know* what's going on in your own country, Cullee? Don't you know what's happening in your own race?"

For several moments the Congressman simply stared at him, chin on hand, expressionless. Finally he shrugged.

"I know fools like you have been talking like that for quite a few years now," he said, "and you've done a lot of damage and misled a lot of innocent people who haven't known any better. But I'm damned if I see what you've done for the Negro race except stir up a lot of white hatred and make things even tougher. But I guess that's what you want, isn't it? To make 'em so tough that when the big reaction comes it will all go smash and everything will be ruined for everybody. Then maybe you can crawl out and be king of the ruins." He sighed and concluded with a puzzled shake of the head and a genuine bafflement that couldn't possibly have infuriated LeGage more: "Poor, sick fool."

"Oh I am, am I?" LeGage shouted, leaping to his feet and beginning to pace up and down before the window, so angry he could hardly see. "So I'm a poor, sick fool, am I? And what are you, Mr. Pompous-Self-Satisfied-Know-It-All stooge for Whitey? If you aren't the saddest son of a bitch that ever pretended to be a black man—"

"At least I'm not a murderer," Cullee snapped, getting on his feet, too, and planting himself solidly beside his chair. "At least I'm not a bloody betrayer of my own country who goes around beating up pregnant women and trying to burn down everything for everybody. Now, you listen to me, Mr. High-and-Mighty-Pompous-Self-Satisfied-Know-It-All, yourself! You haven't got a patient man in the White House any more, or one who's scared of you or of anybody's 'opinion.' You've got a hard-nosed old son of a bitch who's every bit as tough as you are, and when Orrin Knox succeeds him you'll find he's the same. They've got your number, and they're fed up and they mean business. And I'm here to tell you, you'd damned well better cool it, and fast. Take that back to your crazy boyfriends and see how they like it!"

"So that's it" LeGage said, pausing abruptly at the edge of the desk. "So that's the damned game! You're supposed to pass the word and scare us off. Good Christ! You have no more idea what's being planned for this country—"

"I suppose Ted has told you just what to do!" Cullee said with a deliberate innocence and instantly an expression of scowling contempt came over LeGage's face.

"Ted! That pathetic egomaniac! Ted has no more idea—" Then his expression changed again, the crafty curtain came down. He shrugged. "Ted is quite a boy, all right. But you!" he said, beginning to generate steam again. "We're talking about *you*, you—"

"*Listen,*" Cullee interrupted, and he put into the word

such a weight of anger and dislike that Gage stopped in mid-sentence. "I'm saying one thing to you, smart boy, and that is that whatever your pretense of helping your own race, and however much you can sell the pretense to the white fools you want to destroy, what you're really out to do is bring down America. And it isn't going to work, because this society wants to survive and it isn't going to let a minority throw it down the drain. It may take a while for it to really resist, but, brother, watch out when it finally does. You'll be consumed."

"Maybe," LeGage said softly. "But I plan to do a little consuming, first."

"I was asked to warn you," Cullee said with equal softness, "and I have. What you do now is your own problem."

"Just watch me," LeGage said with the same almost singing softness. "Just you watch."

After that, the ringing of the telephone came as something of an anticlimax; and even Orrin's message, which Cullee could not resist passing along triumphantly to 'Gage, did little to change it. LeGage was set on some collision course from which nothing would deflect him, and his reaction was much like Lady Maudulayne's. With one last stagey, but nonetheless ominous, warning that Cullee "had better not walk alone through Capitol Plaza after dark," he swung angrily out of the office and went away. Cullee called the White House, conveyed his congratulations to the President, who seemed pleased to have them, and reported the discouraging outcome of the visit.

"One interesting thing, though," he said. "Whatever is in the wind, Ted apparently doesn't know about it."

"He thinks he does," the President observed.

"That's a tribute to his ego, not his sense. He doesn't."

"Should we try to warn him again?" the President asked in an idle tone that indicated how little he thought of the idea. Congressman Hamilton made an equally skeptical sound.

"He's been warned enough. I'm through having anything to do with him."

"Suits me," the President said. "See you at the Committee meeting tomorrow."

"I'll be there. Is everything ready?"

"I think we're in pretty good shape," the President said, "or will be, after my announcement at the opening." Then he added, in a reflective tone born of many and many a hectic battle in the House, "But of course, you know, you can never be sure of anything in this world."

Which was just as well; for it was only three o'clock in the afternoon, and by nightfall, on certain days in Washington, quite a lot can happen.

Certainly it was happening for Bob Leffingwell, who even then was nearing his destination on T Street, Northwest. He was not alone, for he had prudently stopped at a precinct house and picked up a policeman, and now as the patrol car moved cautiously along through the hurrying traffic, the boy was talking earnestly about the situation in the country. Bob was gratified to find that he was not a follower of DEFY, nor a hater of the whites, nor a worshiper of false gods foreign or domestic. Instead he was a quiet, determined and worried youth who took his life in his hands every time he stepped out the precinct door, but who went ahead and did his duty because he had some concept of America and his responsibility toward it which told him he should. It was enough to make a man cry, Bob told himself, to see the gap between the gallantry and decency that could exist below, and the cupidity, ambition, reckless hatred and greed for power that flourished in the upper levels he had just come from. In fifteen minutes he had moved out of one city into the other; except, of course, that the two cities were always and eternally one.

Unconsciously he sighed, and at once the boy broke off in mid-sentence and said politely, "Sir?"

"I'm sorry," Bob Leffingwell said. "I'm afraid I was momentarily distracted by my own thoughts." He smiled. "I'm afraid that wasn't very considerate."

"It's easy to do," the boy said with an answering smile. "I find I do it a lot. There's so much to think about nowadays."

"Yes, there is. What were you saying when I drifted away from you, officer?"

"I was saying that I don't really see where people like LeGage Shelby and some of these other radicals get away with saying the things they do about America," he said, his smile fading and a troubled expression coming into the large dark eyes. "I just don't understand how they *think*."

"I don't either," Bob Leffingwell confessed. "But, then, I'm white."

"Well, I'm not," the boy said belligerently, and then smiled again at his own vehemence. "As I guess you can see. And I don't understand them. Mind you, I don't say things are perfect, who'd be such a fool? But they're— well, they're bad and they're not bad. I mean, there's some hope, a lot of things have improved in recent years. We can make it if we just have the guts to stay with it."

"Do many?" Bob Leffingwell asked, not sure just when he was going to dry up this flood of confidence with his questions, but thinking that he hadn't started it, his companion obviously wanted, maybe had, to talk.

The boy frowned.

"Not as many as we need," he said honestly. "Of course, it's a big problem. You take people in some of the conditions we have here in this city, conditions like we have in Harlem and Detroit and Chicago and other places like that, and you can understand how they never get out of it and why something like DEFY appeals to them. They climb up a little, and just as they begin to make it they run into a wall of some kind. And they fall back. They don't keep fighting. Or if they do, it's just frustrated fighting, riots and snipers and mobs in the streets, and nothing but hate, hate, hate, all day long and all night, too." He rubbed his forehead and squeezed his eyelids with a tired gesture. "I don't know," he said moodily. "Sometimes I think maybe I'm making a mistake to stick with society and law and order. Maybe I'd be better off out there on the other side of it tearing down instead of trying to hold together and eventually build up. But then I think—I don't really think that. It doesn't add up to anything in the long run. Once the riot's over, what have you got? A television set you looted from some store, maybe, and a lot more hatred from the whites. And just more frustration and more despair. And if Shelby has his way," he concluded grimly, "just a new set of bosses. Black, maybe, but still pushing you around, just like before."

"It seems to me," Bob said cautiously, as they turned into R Street and headed west, planning to double back at Fourth and go up to T, "that someone like—oh, say, Congressman Hamilton from California, for instance—does more for your people than someone like Shelby."

"Mr. Hamilton is a fine man," the boy said promptly, "but he gets attacked too, all the time. I'll bet you if you could see his mail and listen to his telephone calls, you'd find he takes a beating from Negroes nine-tenths of the time. A lot of people I know around the area here don't think much of him; they think he's too pro-white. But, Mr. Leffingwell, he only tries to be honest and do what he can to make things work. And things have got to work if any one of us is ever going to get anywhere. We've got the best country anybody ever handed a people, and we've got to preserve it and make it work, all of us together. We've *got* to."

"I couldn't agree with you more," Bob Leffingwell said, more moved than he cared to show—and yet, why not show it, wasn't part of the trouble a timidity of communication, a fear of being honest? He held out his hand, and after a second's surprise, the boy took it and they exchanged a solemn handshake. "I think you're great," he said simply. "Just great. Don't ever change."

"Oh, I expect I won't," the boy said, grinning suddenly and speaking more lightly. "My mother always says when I get on something I stick with it. She says I'm the hardest-headed child she's ever known."

"You stay hard-headed just the way you are," Bob advised. "We all need you, just like that."

"I'm going to," the boy said. "Can't say it's always easy to do, but—oh, oh!" he said sharply as they turned into

T Street, and suddenly he wasn't a boy any more, but an officer of the law with every sense alert. "What's going on down there?"

"It looks to me," Bob Leffingwell said bleakly, for here was the world undone again, "like a fire."

And so it was, smoke pillaring straight upward into the still, steaming air, flames already leaping high over the simple one-story dwelling they were relentlessly consuming. People were running, the street was becoming choked with traffic. The officer touched his siren and they started slowly through as a fire truck began to push noisily into the block from the other end.

"I think that's the place we're looking for," Bob said, and the officer nodded and said quietly, "I believe it is."

"They got here first," Bob said with a sort of bitter tiredness, and again the officer nodded.

"I guess they did," he agreed, and his eyes and voice were very sad.

When they were as near as they could safely go, he stopped the car and they got out. Bob Leffingwell was aware of shouts, screams, voices, heard from a couple jostling past, "—fellow say he from DEFY, he say we all better watch out that what happen to enemies of DEFY—" "—heard from someone else—" "—believe they an old lady with arthritis still in there—" and was aware suddenly that his companion was no longer at his side but was running blindly, instinctively, headlong toward the flames.

"Come back!" he shouted frantically. "Don't go in there! Officer! Stop him, somebody! Stop him!"

But all he got were blank, impassive looks.

And a heavy voice saying, "You crazy, man? That fuzz."

And another heavy voice saying, "We don't stop no fuzz, man."

And a heavy, subdued, almost sullen chuckling, all around.

"There he is!" Helen-Anne cried as the taxi neared the trade entrance of the Hilton. "Driver, let me out! Quickly!"

And she thrust a dollar bill into his hand, yanked open the door, scrambled out slammed it shut behind her and started hurrying toward the hotel.

As she did so the tall young Negro walking ahead of her suddenly lifted his arms convulsively, a bright pink flower bloomed in the air where his head had been, his body spun around once and fell to the sidewalk.

Helen-Anne, still running forward, her gray hair askew, her short legs churning, began to scream. Then the screaming stopped in a strange, choked gargle. And then the street became filled with the clatter of many feet, the clamor of many voices, and the sound America was coming to know too well, the heavy, insistent pulse of sirens, moaning in the hot, still air.

FAMED *STAR* COLUMNIST SHOT TO DEATH AT HILTON, the *Star* cried in an extra half an hour later. NEGRO BUS BOY ALSO SLAIN: BURNING OF HIS HOME MAY FURNISH CLUE IN MYSTERY KILL-INGS; POLICEMAN DIES IN FUTILE ATTEMPT TO SAVE WOMAN IN HOUSE.

And in a small Page 1 box accompanying the main story, it noted:

"Police believe a laser gun was used to kill Helen-Anne Carrew, *Star* columnist, and a bus boy at the Washington Hilton Hotel this afternoon.

"Control of these silent long-range weapons has been under study by Congress ever since they began to find their way into private hands six years ago. Despite numerous hearings on Capitol Hill, no legislation to keep them out of the hands of unauthorized persons has been forthcoming. . . . "

Outside, somewhere faint and far off, he heard a sound of sirens and shivered a little, though the kind of world sirens represented always seemed very far away from the hushed, luxurious chambers of Mr. Thomas Buckmaster Davis. Now and again, usually prompted by some occurrence in the swarming Negro areas north of the Capitol, out toward R Street and beyond, an ambulance would race down past the Supreme Court, or a police car would race up. Occasionally when things were as quiet as they were this afternoon in the beautiful building, they could be heard, just faintly, inside: intimations of the world's pain, mortality, love or hate, that always made the wispy little Justice pause for a second and feel uncomfortable before returning to his books, his papers, and his incessant telephoning.

The world was getting to be a horrible place, Mr. Justice Davis thought with a sigh, and there didn't seem to be much the Court could do about it, except lessen the bonds of legal restraint more and more and hope that the innate goodness of human nature would reestablish those curbs upon man's baser instincts which he and his colleagues simply could not uphold on any reasonable Constitutional grounds.

Now he wondered idly what drama lay behind the siren (actually, it was all very conventional and had happened a thousand times: a liquor store had been held up in Q Street and the proprietor, who had foolishly attempted resistance, had been shot in the stomach with a .45) and then put it briskly from his mind. Not his worry: he had troubles enough. Right now, he was expecting a visitor, and it was most important to give him the courage and the determination that Tommy Davis knew he needed on the eve of the climactic battle of his political career.

Tommy had no doubt that he was the man to provide the deciding element of spiritual comfort and encouragement required by the occasion, and that was why he had suggested the appointment.

Rather ironically, though keeping his feelings to himself because he knew Tommy carried great weight with the *Post*, Frankly Unctuous, The Greatest Publication That Absolutely Ever Was, Walter Dobius, the New York *Times*, and all the rest whose powerful support he had and needed—and because there was going to be a use for Tommy—Governor Jason had accepted.

That he should feel such irony was something the busy little Justice simply could not imagine. He had been such a vital and vigorous part of Washington's political life for so many years that he honestly, by now, did not know how it could proceed without him. It is true that some people occasionally made a little fun of him, but when it came from his friends he could accept it for the affectionate joshing it was, and when it came from his enemies he could dismiss it for its obvious stupidity. Those who began by laughing usually ended by granting full recognition to his brains, resourcefulness and perspicacity.

He felt himself to be, and now and then was, one of

340

the major figures in a landscape where most people consider themselves important and some are.

In the present instance, he had spent the past ten days worming his way into the center of things. Mr. Justice Davis, too, was one of the many who had been in contact with members of the National Committee. Ten or fifteen—and he congratulated himself that they were among the most influential—of that besought, besieged and bedazzled 106 had received a phone call, a little note, a confidential chat from Mr. Justice Davis. He was confident his activities had helped Ted greatly, and he was deeply gratified. For he was one of those who were sincerely, completely and absolutely convinced that the Governor of California was the only hope for world peace and the only political leader who could possibly prevent the final holocaust toward which the Administration, and above all Orrin Knox, were inexorably driving the nation.

There was nothing phony or sinister or self-serving in Tommy's support for the Jason campaign. He believed in it; and now, with all the drive and devotion that his essentially lonely soul could muster for the causes to which it gave itself, he wanted to offer his services in any way he might be useful.

Promptly at four-thirty his secretary notified him that the Governor had arrived, and with a pleased little smile he came forward from his desk with hand outstretched.

"My dear Ted," he said in his brisk, clipped fashion, "my dear boy! How delightful to see you, really how delightful."

"My pleasure and honor, Mr. Justice," Ted said. His host beamed in a fatherly fashion.

"Call me Tommy," he directed. "Everybody does."

Then he gave a merry little laugh. "Well, almost everybody. There are some—including your distinguished opponent—who call me other things. On occasion. But even he, I am happy to say, calls me Tommy face to face."

"But you don't really like each other," Governor Jason suggested with a smile, taking the chair toward which the Justice urged him.

"No, indeed," Tommy said crisply. "I regard Orrin Knox as the greatest living danger to this country and the world. And he regards me as—what?" A mischievous twinkle came into his eyes. "A fussy little busybody? An inveterate meddler in areas where he has no business? A part-time Justice and full-time dabbler?"

"You're quoting," Ted suggested, and his host uttered a delighted little laugh.

"At one time or another in his Senate career," he acknowledged, "Orrin said every one of those things about me. I wrote them all down in my diary and now and then I copy one and send it to him on my official stationery, without any comment, just my name on the letterhead."

"That must amuse him."

"It amuses me," Justice Davis said. "I don't care what it does to him. Well, then," he said with a businesslike briskness, "so tomorrow is the big day. Are you ready for it?"

"I think so," Governor Jason said calmly; and, noting his host's crestfallen expression, added quickly, "But I think there is much that you can advise me about— Tommy. I need," he said with a simple candor, "your help."

"My dear boy," Justice Davis said, brightening visibly, "that is exactly what I hoped you would say when I asked you to come here. I haven't been idle you know, in these recent days. I've been talking to members of the National

Committee, I've been planting a word here and there, I've been working for you. And gladly."

"I appreciate it," Ted said, "more deeply than I can say. I know I shall be needing your help even more in the next few weeks. May I rely upon it?"

"You may, my dear boy," Tommy said gravely, "you may! You see before you one who is completely convinced of the worth of your cause and entirely ready to devote such poor energies as he may possess to it, in every way. I seem to detect, however, some uncertainty: you say 'the next few weeks.' You think it may be a little protracted, I gather."

"It could be quite protracted," Ted said soberly. "There will be attempts to delay, to confuse—"

"Orrin won't stop at anything," Justice Davis said. "He is absolutely ruthless."

"—there may be stratagems and devious methods. We may find it necessary"—and Ted's voice dropped significantly—"to fight fire with fire." He paused and stared at Tommy with an earnest intentness that made the little Justice feel, deliciously, that he was about to be taken into the innermost secrets of Jason strategy, as indeed he was. "Do you think you could find it in your heart to assist us, if it came to that?"

"Tell me how," Justice Davis said solemnly; and when Ted had, he shook his head with an admiring air.

"My dear boy—my dear Governor—my dear Mr. President!—I think you have devised a positively brilliant strategy. I don't see how it can fail."

"You are the key," Governor Jason assured him gravely, and was ironically amused to see that Tommy was almost visibly glowing with the excitement and importance of it all.

"I shall do my best," he said with an equal gravity. "Providing it goes as planned, below—"

"It will."

'Then I see no real reason why there should be any doubt. I haven't researched the precedents—"

"There are none," Ted said and Tommy laughed.

"Of course not! Then I shall go down in history by creating one! And in an absolutely worthy cause."

"I was sure we could rely upon you."

"Completely, my dear boy. Completely."

"Good," Ted said, starting to rise. "Then I won't take up more of your valuable time—"

"Not at all," Justice Davis said, waving him down again. "Do sit and chat for a moment. There's really nothing going on here today—"

But in this he was mistaken, for there was a sudden commotion in the office outside, the door flew open and Bob Leffingwell strode into the room with Tommy's secretary hanging on one arm.

"But you mustn't," she was crying frantically. "But you *mustn't*—"

"Oh, yes, I must," Bob said in a tone of such cold rage that she stopped with a gasp and let go of his arm. "Tommy!" he snapped. "Tell this sniveling woman to get out, and then stay where you are. I have something to say to this—this"—and he gestured toward the Governor—"now that I've managed to track him down, and I want you to be witness. Are you going to get out?" he demanded, turning on the secretary.

Justice Davis said hastily, "Yes, yes, do go! It's quite all right, I'm sure, quite all right."

"Shall I call the guards?" she quavered from the door. Bob Leffingwell uttered an angry laugh.

"That won't be necessary," he said, "but if you'd feel better, by all means do. Just keep them outside until the Justice calls for them, though. We don't want to be interrupted."

"Yes, sir," she said, giving him a terrified glance as Tommy said, somewhat shakily, "Yes, do that, my dear. It's all right. Just keep them out there. I'm sure I won't need them . . . And now," he said after she had hurried out, slamming the door behind her in her nervous haste, "*Now*," he said with an attempt at restored dignity that came off pretty well considering the circumstances, "what *is* this?"

"Apparently you haven't heard," Bob said, flinging the *Star* extra onto the desk so hard it skidded and knocked over an antique inkwell that was one of Tommy's joys. Fortunately it was empty.

Ted got up at once and came to stand beside the Justice as he obediently spread out the paper. For quite some time no one said anything. Finally Tommy Davis said in a hushed voice,

"My goodness. Oh, my goodness."

"Yes, 'my goodness,'" Bob echoed harshly. He glared at Ted. "What do you know about this?"

"I don't know anything about it," Governor Jason said flatly. "Why the hell should I?"

"Because she was onto something involving you," Bob said in the same harsh tone, "and the crowd you're running with these days kills. That's why you should"—he bit off the title—"Governor!"

"I don't know what you're talking about," Ted said quietly. "Suppose you sit down, and let us sit down, and we can try to find out what this is all about."

"It's obvious what it's about," Bob said, refusing to take a chair though Ted and the Justice slowly resumed theirs. "It's about murder. Three of them. And a fire. And it's also about the death of a hard-headed child whom we couldn't afford to lose. But you wouldn't know about that. I think maybe you do know about the murders and the fire."

"Bob," Governor Jason said, and this time his solemnity was genuine, "I swear to you before God and this witness that I do not know what you are talking about. I honestly *do not know.*"

"Look," Bob Leffingwell said bluntly, "even in times like these it is not customary for a famous correspondent and a colored boy to be gunned down together on the streets of Washington, D.C., at the same time the colored boy's house is being burned and his grandmother killed. That isn't quite commonplace yet, though you and your friends are fast getting us to that condition. Therefore there must be a reason. I think I know what it is, and I think you do too, oaths or no oaths, God or no God. *God?*" he repeated bitterly. "I'm surprised He takes the time to bother with this country any more."

"Now, Bob," Justice Davis said nervously, "now, Bob, that kind of language isn't going to get us anywhere—"

"You be still and listen!" Bob Leffingwell ordered, so sharply that the little Justice literally seemed to shrivel in his chair.

"Yes, Tommy," Governor Jason said quietly, "we might as well. Apparently this is not going to stop until it has run its course, no matter what the truth is, no matter what proof there may be that I know noth—"

"Proof!" Bob snapped, pulling several sheets of folded copy paper from his vest pocket. "I don't know what proof you have, but I happen to have a little."

"Of *what*?" Ted demanded with a genuine exasperation. "That's what I'm trying to find out."

"Of a meeting at the Hilton at which you and your friends conspired with a deadly enemy of the United States—"

"Now, see here!" Governor Jason said angrily, and now he too was on his feet, as Justice Davis seemed to shrink back even further behind his desk. *"I attended no such meeting.* I swear to you by—by anything you want me to swear by—that I attended no—such—meeting. Nor," he said, more quietly, "do I believe that any such meeting ever existed, except in the inflamed imagination of a poor woman whose journalistic fantasies finally, apparently, led her into a fatal situation. But I didn't create the situation, and I didn't lead her into it, and in simple fairness, if nothing else, I don't think you should say that I did."

"What a strange man you are," Bob Leffingwell said slowly. "I suppose you have the mind—the divided mind—that is necessary for power. So that you can create a climate—or not prevent one being created in your name—in which awful things can happen, and still pretend to yourself that there is no connection between the climate and its consequences . . . so that while you may vaguely admit to yourself that you might have had something, remotely, to do with the climate, you can simply absolve yourself of all responsibility for the consequences. I suppose those who rise very high in government, or business, or whatever have to have something of that, don't they? Otherwise they couldn't bear the thought of the abyss on whose edge they stand all the time."

"Bob—" Justice Davis began nervously, but Bob Leffingwell gestured him to silence almost absentmindedly.

"You are a very strange man," he repeated in a puzzled, thoughtful voice. "A very strange man . . ."

"Do you believe that I do not know of any such meeting?" Ted asked quietly, and after a moment Bob nodded.

"Yes, I believe you. But I'm wondering how it is that you don't know."

"Do you believe that there *was* no such meeting?" Ted asked, and this time Bob shook his head slowly and lifted the sheaf of copy paper.

"I know there was."

"I say there was not!" Ted said with a sudden anger, and with an equal anger Bob shot back,

"You met with Shelby and Van Ackerman and Kleinfert after Patsy's party. I don't know what you plotted, I expect it was bad enough, but then after you left, so that no one could say you were directly involved, someone else joined them and the discussion really got down to cases. That is what Helen-Anne's investigation disclosed, and that is what I believe."

"No!" Ted said sharply. "No, no, *no!*"

"How do you know?" Bob demanded, and for several seconds the Governor stared at him without speaking. When he did it was with a calm simplicity.

"Because I got worried myself that there might have been some further meeting after I left, and I asked them."

"And what did they tell you?"

"All three assured me that no such meeting occurred."

"And you believed them," Bob Leffingwell said with a genuine wonderment. "You *believed* them."

"What proof is there that I should not?" Ted asked reasonably. "Were there any witnesses?"

"There was one," Bob said bleakly, "but he died this afternoon outside the Hilton."

"Very well—" Ted began, but Bob again held up the sheaf of notes.

"And there was one very competent reporter who investigated and made extensive notes."

"What are you going to do with them?" Governor Jason asked with a sudden savage sarcasm. "Sell them to *Life*?"

"No, I am not," Bob Leffingwell said; and he turned abruptly to Justice Davis, listening with a nervous intensity, and tossed them onto the desk in front of him. "I am going to give them to this witness, a Justice of the Supreme Court of the United States—"

"Oh, dear," Tommy said weakly. "Oh, *dear*."

"—whom. I believe to be, essentially and in the final analysis, an honest man, and I am going to ask him to retain them in his safekeeping, as an earnest that the Governor of California will from this point forward disengage himself from people whose fundamental and overriding aim is the destruction of the country whose Chief Magistrate he wishes to be."

Again there was a silence, during which Tommy said, "Oh, *dear*" several times but did not touch the notes.

"That was quite a speech," Governor Jason said at last. "Quite a speech. Are you going to accept these papers, Mr. Justice?"

"Oh, *dear*," Tommy said again. "I don't know what—I just don't know—I just—"

"I would suggest that you do," Ted said calmly. "I can

think of no more reliable and trustworthy repository."

"Well—"

"Take them," Bob Leffingwell said. "Take them, and after we leave, read them and then put them in a secure place. . . . Go on," he ordered with a sudden impatience. "Take them!"

"I really think you should," Ted said; and after a few more seconds of uncertainty the Justice did, picking them up slowly, turning to a wall safe set into the bookshelves behind his desk, concentrating for a minute on the combination, opening it, putting them in, closing it again with a quick involuntary shiver that seemed to shake the whole of his frail little body.

"And now," Bob said, turning to the Governor, "I would advise you to leave these people—to cut them off completely—to free yourself and your campaign from everything having to do with them. Because the proof rests there"—he pointed to the safe—"and the witness is here"—Tommy instinctively stepped back a pace— "and if you go ahead as you are doing, he and I will know that from now on it is deliberate choice, and you will know that there are two people in the world who can never again accept any pretense that you are not part and parcel of whatever evil may befall this country."

"And not part and parcel of whatever good may befall it?" Ted inquired with a musing bitterness. "How blind and one-sided you are! How willfully you twist everything to suit your own interpretation of me and of those who don't agree with this Administration's policies. How neatly you have it all worked out . . . Understand me!" he said with a sudden commanding strength. "I shall continue to do what I believe best to save this nation and

I shall continue to accept and welcome the support of all sincere people who genuinely wish to assist me in changing a course that can only end in terrible disaster for us and all mankind. *I will not swerve one inch,* and no witches' tales of sinister influences and secret meetings and deep, dark conspiracies can make me do so. . . . So guide yourself," he concluded softly, "accordingly."

For a long moment he and Bob Leffingwell stared at one another without expression; and then Bob said quietly, "You can be sure I will," turned quickly, opened the door, brushed past the still wide-eyed secretary and two elderly and apprehensive Court policemen, and was gone.

"My goodness," Justice Davis said automatically. "My goodness."

"Don't worry about it, Tommy" Ted Jason said. "Everything is going to work out all right."

"But, my *goodness*—"

"Everything," the Governor repeated firmly, "is going to be all right."

And was able, with a combination of faith, determination and sheer Jason will power, to say it and believe it.

"And so you see," Lafe Smith typed laboriously at seven P.M. in his silent office, after his staff had closed up and gone home, "things are really in an awful mess here. Helen-Anne was such a good reporter and such a good pal to so many people around town, that none of us can really take it in, yet. The rumor is—you know D.C.—that she was onto something that could possibly have had a really damaging effect on Ted. So a lot of people, at least on our side, are saying some pretty frightening things. According to our Iowa National Committeeman, it has scared some weak ones on the Committee even more than they were already.

"I still think, though, that it is going to go well when the Committee meets. I wish you could be here, Mabel, as its really going to be a (an?) historic show. Isn't there a chance you could get away? We could arrange a nice apartment for you somewhere nearby for a couple of weeks, and there are plenty of baby sitters who could look after Pridge. Say you will. It would be a lot of fun to have you here. And another thing (always have to be the politician and think of all the angles, don't I?) it would be a real help to Orrin, too. Your name and Brig's carry a lot of weight in the West, and Orrin needs all the help he can get. It looks good for him, I think, but we can't afford to relax for a moment. So: he needs you—I need you. How can you resist? Write and say you'll come.

"Love to my two girls in Utah

from

Lafe"

At "Salubria" in Leesburg another typewriter was busy, its version of events somewhat different from that of the junior Senator from Iowa. The time had come, on this eve of the National Committee's fateful meeting, for someone to put events in perspective as they really were. For such a task there was no one, he knew, better equipped than America's leading statesman-philosopher of the press. Walter Dobius frequently felt the heavy responsibility of guiding the nation as it should go, and never had he felt it more than he did tonight, in the long hot twilight of this long hot day.

Perhaps he felt it so deeply now because in some strange, unexpected way he was feeling the death of his ex-wife so deeply. Like most of the official Washington through which she had pushed, shoved and cussed her quirky way for so many years, he still could not really believe that Helen-Anne was gone, or gone in such a horrible, mysterious and ominous fashion.

It was not that he still loved her, for all that, if it ever really existed, had been destroyed by her obvious hostility and her raucous sarcasm about his own position in the world. He could see now that she had been always a competitor, never really a wife: she had always intended to have her own column, she had never been able to understand that one famous member was all a Washington marriage could stand. She had never realized that Walter Dobius' wife must love, serve and respect Walter Dobius.

Particularly respect. That was what had finally driven Walter up the wall. She just had never realized how important he was to the country, how good he was in his own right, how necessary it was that Walter Dobius, of all people, not pick up the *Star* and see his wife's picture grinning back at him over columns that quite frequently were as sharp, as astute and as well-informed as his own. Helen-Anne had always thought she had a perfect right to be as capable and as famous as he was.

How could you possibly have a loving and lasting partnership on that basis?

Furthermore, it would be a long time, perhaps never, before he could forget their dreadful last argument in the press room at the San Francisco Hilton after the attack on Crystal Knox. She had bitterly assailed every assumption on which his entire life had been built, and she had done it with such hysterical savagery and sarcasm that he knew some of her phrases would ring in his mind until the day he died. And yet the *Star's* lawyer had called a little while ago and told him with a dryly disapproving economy that she had left him everything except her diary and private papers, which were to go to the Library of Congress. The estate was not very much, and he could not escape the quick, ironic little thought that of course she wasn't going to take any chances that he might destroy her diary and papers, but nonetheless it did indicate something. It indicated that if she had only been a different and more understanding person—if only she had been less egotistical and less *competitive*, that was the main thing—their marriage might have held up very well.

Why weren't you like that? he thought with a sudden, agonized, bereft feeling that startled and amazed him with its intensity. *Why couldn't you have been my nice wife instead of my competitor? Why did you have to be so unfair to me?*

And why, more practically, did she have to go meddling into matters that had produced such a disastrous conclusion? He reflected now, his mind welcoming the diversion from a momentary sentimental weakness, that he himself had received from Ted Jason, prior to Patsy's reception, some hint of a meeting to be held later. In fact, he had transmitted the knowledge to Tommy Davis, because even at that stage Ted was beginning to formulate some idea of using the little Justice in his plans. Walter had told him it was a beautifully shrewd strategy and had encouraged him to do it. But Helen-Anne had not been content to find out about the meeting and let it go at that.

354

She had apparently kept digging and probing and worrying at it, in her haphazard but tenacious way, until she had stumbled onto something that had brought swift and terrible retribution.

What was it? He had already considered and rejected a number of possibilities. His own reportorial instinct, which was among the three or four best in the capital, had not told him yet that he had found the right one. He knew already that if it did—when it did—he would not pursue it further. For he knew that it must be something very dangerous, and he suspected it might lead into areas of the Jason campaign where he did not wish to go. To do so might be to throw into question his entire support for that campaign, and this would not be right. He considered Ted's success absolutely imperative for the country. If there was some reason why the Governor should be defeated that even he could accept as valid, he did not want to know. It could mean political disaster for Ted; and the knowledge of it could even mean for Walter what it had meant for Helen-Anne.

No. Better to put Helen-Anne and her dark mystery with all its dark implications out of his mind now, because tomorrow's newspapers were waiting and there was a column to write. Great events were marching, and all across the land many millions were waiting to know what Walter Dobius thought about them. His views, as always, might well have some direct effect. With an almost physical sensation, as though he had closed a door, or gone to a window to shut it against the cold winds of the world, he said goodbye to Helen-Anne and moved forward into that future for whose shape he bore such a responsibility:

"WASHINGTON—Today the nations stand hushed

and expectant as the most powerful of all begins the dramatic and painful process of selecting the man who will guide its destinies for the next four years.

"To say that the American nation will select this man might seem to those beyond our borders an enormous oversimplification. Yet in some mysterious, ineffable way that defies analysis, it will be true that all the nation will participate in what will appear to be the deliberations of only fifty-three men and fifty-three women. For in the million subtle segments that go into the making-up of America's mind, we will all be joining in the deliberations of the National Committee.

"Never, perhaps—even when the first small group met in Philadelphia more than two centuries ago to frame the Constitution—has such a handful of citizens of this Republic had such a heavy charge laid upon it. Never, perhaps, has a more awesome decision had to be made under such desperate conditions for us all.

"Here in this city, which has seen so many great crises and great men come and go, there is the hope—the hushed and fearful hope—that the Committee will select for us a candidate who will have the courage to break free of the futile policies and crippled thinking that have tied America down in these recent bloody years. Hushed and fearful hope, yet singing, too.

"Hidden beneath the sultry summer heat that has Washington under its iron fist, there is an almost springtime mood of freshness in the air.

"Great things are expected.

"Great things must be done.

"The choices which confront the Committee are simple: one who represents the new, one who represents

356

the old. In Gorotoland and Panama, the United States is fighting two indefensible wars whose outcome can only be further failure and disgrace for outmoded, insupportable policies. How can these conflicts be ended? By more of the same? Or by a new approach that will find new solutions, new bases for negotiation, new humanities to replace the old inhumanities and the old futilities—the old gray commitment to more war, more death, more waste of national substance?

"True it is that the Committee meets in an atmosphere that can perhaps only be described by the word 'ominous.' There are reports of sinister doings here in Washington, fleeting rumors of dangerous events that could surround the deliberations of this fateful handful of Americans like you and me. Tragedy has struck in the streets. One of Washington's"—here Walter paused and stared at the blank wall above his desk. How should he describe her, what would be fair? Suddenly as on a television screen her face leaped out at him, some japing disrespectful mockery on her grinning lips. He typed hurriedly on "better-known correspondents has been killed, along with others who may or may not have been involved in some violent plot. What the plot may be, or even if there is one, no one of any substance seems to know. Yet the event together with other pressures brought to bear upon Committee members, has served to increase the tensions under which the great decision must be reached.

"It is one of the unhappy ironies of an unhappy era that while both candidates deny all knowledge of the origins of violence, the responsibility for it must inevitably come back to the doorstep of the one whose policies have inflamed the country to the point where violence is becoming almost a political fact of life.

"It is not the Governor of California, history will submit, who has eagerly assisted two Presidents on their war-bent way. It is not the Governor of California who has dismayed a great many of his countrymen to the point where they feel their only recourse is to take to the streets in riotous fear and frustration. It is not the Governor of California whose solution to the world's ills is the old stale recipe of war and more war.

"No: upon the Secretary of State there rests a heavy burden, and the National Committee has no choice but to take account of this. It is late—too late—to rehearse the rights and wrongs of policy. But the rights and wrongs of violence are everywhere to see. The Committee must ask itself whose nomination would reduce violence and restore decency—and whose would increase violence and send America hurtling still further away from her traditional decencies. The answer would not seem difficult to perceive.

"America, the world and history await the outcome. To lead the nation back to sanity and peace—or to light the way still further down to dusty death. No men and women ever carried a heavier charge than the men and women of the National Committee do today."

He struck the final words with a satisfied "thwack!" that sounded startlingly loud in the silent old house; ripped the paper out of the typewriter; picked up the telephone and prepared to dictate to the copy boy who always transcribed his column at the *Post*.

In Gorotoland and Panama as he did so, the belligerents were fighting on toward conclusions that events

358

of the past few hours had made inevitable; in Moscow and Peking, Paris and London, everywhere around the globe, men in places of power and in the streets were discussing with curiosity, apprehension, wonderment or dread, what might be going to happen in the unpredictable republic beyond the seas; and at fifteen or twenty parties in Washington, in a last, almost hysterical, fling before their ordeal began, the members of the National Committee chattered and gossiped and tossed off tensely merry remarks in futile attempts to conceal their worry, their foreboding and their terrifying realization that they were about to stand exposed and vulnerable to the cold blast of history.

5.

AND NOW—finally, and yet with an astounding and awesomely sudden impact upon its members—the day of the National Committee has come.

That it is more likely to be "days" is of course apparent to them all, and it is with some sense of entering a state of siege that they are now proceeding, on the morning of this eleventh day since Air Force One precipitated them into history, toward the Studio Playhouse at the Kennedy Center. There on the banks of the Potomac they will make their decision; and as they come nearer to it from their various hotels and temporary domiciles, they begin to understand why it was chosen, and to realize that "state of siege" is perhaps not too dramatic a term to use.

For, as Senator Munson perceived immediately at Patsy's reception when the President announced his choice of site, the Kennedy Center, and particularly its Playhouse, is defensible. Entered by three broad avenues that can be easily closed off, flanked on the land side by open park and on the other by Theodore Roosevelt Island and the sluggish moat of the lazy river as it bends along the city's edge through Georgetown Channel, it is almost ideally suited for the purpose to which it is to be put, in an age in which that purpose could easily give rise to the most violent consequences.

Indeed it is precisely because of this that the President selected it; and now that NAWAC—the "National Antiwar Activities Congress"—has declared its intention to hold a mammoth around-the-clock rally for the duration of the Committee meeting, the choice appears even more astute. Already the Chief Executive has quietly arranged for 500 riot-trained soldiers to supplement the District of Columbia police in throwing a cordon around the entire land boundary of the Center. An inner ring of 500 riot-trained Marines has been assigned to guard the perimeter of the Playhouse. Theodore Roosevelt Island and Theodore Roosevelt Bridge have been closed. Across the river a strip a half mile long and three hundred yards deep has been sealed off to all traffic. In the channel two small armed Coast Guard cutters lie at anchor just off the esplanade. Overhead five helicopters are on regular patrol over the entire area, and at "Checkpoint Alpha," sole entrance for Committee members, visiting dignitaries and the press, the most rigid security procedures have been established.

The Playhouse seats 500 people, and its selection has

caused a world wide outcry, fanned by press and television and joined by many who oppose Administration policies, on the ground that both coverage and attendance will be inadequate. "Where, in this miniscule meeting room" the New York *Times* demanded only yesterday, "will there be accommodation, not only for sufficient press and television, but for those legitimate and reasonable petitioners who may be invited by the Committee to appear and tender their advice?"

It is exactly this that the President intends to avoid: a mammoth circus in which every agitator with the flimsiest of credentials can appear and broadcast his vitriol to the world. He is determined, if possible, that none shall be permitted to appear at all; though that is one of the points that may have to be conceded if a majority of the Committee decides to make it an issue. He has been arguing for a week with members that they should not do so, on the ground that the more people, the more confusion; but he is not confident what will happen should it be put to vote. At least he has made sure that it will be physically impossible to accommodate very many.

He has also made sure that the media will have to pool their coverage, which he also considers a gain. He has, in fact, reduced the seating capacity to about 400, for he has requested the Kennedy Center's directors (who have complied with some grumbling) to remove several rows of seats so that each member of the Committee may have a desk. These have been placed in a half circle facing the stage. On the stage itself there is a lectern and desk for the chairman, a desk to the left for three official stenographers, a desk with microphones to the right in case the Committee decides to call witnesses.

Behind the Committee the remaining seats will accommodate 300 visitors. A day ago he called Ted and with an impersonal courtesy offered to let him name 150 of them, but the Governor declined as impersonally. "I wouldn't want the responsibility if something went wrong. You have screening procedures I haven't got. I'll trust you not to stack the audience." Then he had laughed, a humorless sound. "Wouldn't do you any good, anyway." "That's right," the President had agreed, sharp in spite of himself. "It isn't going to be decided by applause meter."

Partly his tight control over the size of the gathering is prompted by a desire for security, manageability and speed of decision, but partly also, as the media are well aware, it is a method of preventing Ted's supporters from turning the Committee's deliberations into a worldwide spectacle in which it would be quite impossible to arrive at a thoughtful and objective conclusion. Being the shrewd old veteran he is, he knows that such a circus would also, almost automatically, make it much more difficult for his candidate to win, but he doesn't talk about that: any more than Ted's supporters talk about the fact that such a circus would, almost automatically, make it much easier for Ted to win.

The President, in fact, doesn't talk about the situation at all. All complaints to his press secretary, all global indignations, have been blandly turned aside with, "No comment." He learned long ago in the House that nobody can make him open his mouth when he doesn't want to. He is using silence now as effectively as he always has.

Not that this diminishes the clamor, of course. Preparations for the tight security around the Center have been conducted, on his strict orders, after midnight, yet it has of course been obvious to late-passing motorists that intensive preliminaries have been going on. The *Post*, the *Star* and the New York *Times* have all run pictures, taken from across the river, of the Center under floodlights, barricades being put in place. Editorial outrage has been increased by a White House announcement that Committee members, for the duration—"for their personal safety, and since they are, in effect, the jury of the nation at this moment"—will be housed in the visiting Officers' Quarters at nearby Fort Myer, Virginia, and will be transported to and from their meetings in Army cars. And in Washington, which leaks like a sieve, the *Post* has just this morning published a copy of the Pentagon order posting the troops at the Center.

"What is this military spectacle?" the accompanying editorial has demanded in an anguished tone. "Is this how democracy chooses its candidates, or is this how dictatorship prepares to squash all opposition?" The President has been tempted to call the general director and say, "Oh, come on, now!" But a remark like that presupposes a sense of humor on both sides, so he abandons the idea.

He has not, however, abandoned the idea that his inspiration about the Playhouse, which occurred to him at breakfast the second morning at Tahoe, is a thoroughly sound and prudent one. NAWAC's first statement, issued in the early morning hours after the Hilton meeting, promised a rally on the opening day of the Committee. At six P.M. last night a terse communiqué, militant and military, extended the program for the duration of the meeting. Immediately—so immediately that it was obvious the influx had actually been planned for several days—the advance thousands who had reached the city were increased with new multitudes who descended from every plane, train, bus and freeway. This morning they are still coming, and the President and Secretary of Defense have been advised just a few minutes ago that the crowds which press aga: 1st the barricades on the land side of the Center and swarm in hastily erected tent-towns at the edge of the barred zone across the river now number close to 100,000.

At the moment their temper seems ostentatiously sullen but not actively disorderly. Obviously they are waiting, and it is clear from the walkie-talkie directions they are receiving—intercepted and reported by the shabbily dressed infiltrators sent in by military intelligence—that their leaders' plan is to be tough enough to scare the country but not tough enough to bring reprisals. At this point they apparently feel that their candidate may need only the threat of violence to put him over. For that, at least, the President is thankful, though he has made up his mind that if they want martyrs, he will oblige.

So goes the morning and the mood in the command centers; what of the mood in the Committee? There is one sizable segment, perhaps best summed up by Mrs. Lathia Talbot Jennings, National Committeewoman from South Dakota, as she arrives at Checkpoint Alpha. "Good heavens!" she cries, her ample jowls aquiver with nervousness. "I wonder if any of us is going to get out of here alive!" But there is another segment whose attitude is epitomized by Pete Boissevain, National Committeeman from Vermont. Turning back to look for a moment at the encircling troops and the vast crowd beyond with its obscene banners and determined dirtiness, he snaps tartly, "Guess they don't know Vermont if they think they can scare *me!*"

Fortunately it appears at the moment that more members are inclined to be defiant with Pete Boissevain than tremble with Lathia Jennings; or so it seems to the news-pool representatives who greet each new arrival with microphones, cameras and pencils poised. "An awful lot of members seem to have chips on their shoulders," the St. Louis *Post-Dispatch* muses in a puzzled tone to CBS. "I can't imagine why," says the listening Chicago *Tribune* cheerfully, "but *I* think it's just great."

For the spokesmen of the opposing factions in the Committee, Checkpoint Alpha provides one final opportunity before the battle.

"It is obvious as we begin these historic deliberations," says Roger P. Croy of Oregon, his stately white head erect and challenging in the already suffocating heat, his mellow voice confident and serene, "that Governor Edward M. Jason of California should and will be the nominee of this party for the office of President of the United States."

"Will you be his running mate, Governor?" someone asks, as someone did at the convention when it appeared Ted was on the high road to victory; and now, as then, Roger P. Croy smiles a graceful deprecating smile and waves a graceful deprecating hand.

"One thing at a time, my friend," he says with a comfortable smile that implies a rosy future. "One thing at a time, if you please."

From Mary Buttner Baffleburg of Pennsylvania, who is singled out by the media as the Knox spokesman they want to feature, there comes, as expected, an indignant and nicely laughable blurt:

"Everything I've heard points to victory for the greatest Senator and Secretary of State this country has ever had, Orrin Knox of Illinois. And don't think you people of the press and all your friends"—and she gestures wildly off in the general direction of the restless crowds—"can scare us out of it, either!"

"Mrs. Baffleburg, do you really think that the press—"

"Yes, I do!" she cries, her normally florid complexion turning even redder with indignation and heat. "You've been absolutely mean to Orrin!"

Too late, Lyle Strathmore of Michigan hurries up to Checkpoint Alpha and tries to interject a more calm and reasonable note for the Secretary of State, but of course the damage has been done. On television and radio the Croy-Baffleburg statements have been transmitted live, and one of the dominant public memories of the first session will be Roger Croy's stately white-haired confidence and Mary Baffleburg's red-faced, squawking indignation.

Very soon, however, the opportunity for such last-minute fun and games is over. It is now close to ten A.M., and over the Kennedy Center, the vast crowd around it, the city, the nation, and to a considerable degree the world, an almost palpable hush is beginning to fall.

Outside, the well-disciplined throngs are silent, listening attentively to the loud-speakers and television sets which have been set up by COMFORT, DEFY and KEEP to broadcast the proceedings. Inside, the members of the Committee—all 106 are now on hand, though Tobin Janson of Alaska, just out of Bethesda Naval Hospital after an emergency hernia operation a week ago,

366

looks white and shaky—are settling at their desks with a subdued but nervous rustling that indicates how heavily the tensions of this moment are finally crushing in upon them. Behind them in the few rows of seats remaining, the 300 visitors, among them Bob and Dolly Munson, Beth Knox, Lafe Smith and Cullee Hamilton, Jawbone Swarthman and Senator Tom August of Minnesota, chairman of the Foreign Relations Committee; a handful from the diplomatic corps, Lord Maudulayne, Raoul Barre, Krishna Khaleel, (Vasily Tashikov, invited with a grave irony by the President, has declined), the Ambassadors of Guinea, Malawi and Tanzania, Patsy Labaiya and her aunt Valuela Jason Randall (Herbert and Selena are carrying banners outside.) And behind them, and along the sides of the little room, the banked cameras and narrow, microphone-filled tables of the media, its members still grumbling and unhappy with their cramped and awkward working conditions, furious with the man who put them there but knowing they have met their match and cannot budge him.

Now it is two minutes to ten, then one minute; and suddenly they are aware that they have all stopped talking. The minute holds, seems to lengthen unbearably. The electric clock on the wall goes "Click!" distinctly into the silence: many jump. It is ten A.M.; and far off in the distance there begins the swelling chorus of sirens which this time herald, not disaster, but the heavily guarded approach, from the White House a mile away, of the President of the United States.

It is a swift approach, and the hostile crowds which stir and shake their angry banners—but, because they have been instructed not to, make no sound other than an instinctive, irrepressible murmur of hatred and hostility—do not even catch a glimpse of the old man they detest sitting far back in the cushions of the armored limousine. Almost before they know he is upon them, he has passed, along the approach where armed servicemen stand side by side, facing out against their bitter countrymen. Then, abruptly, he is out of the limousine and quickly inside, and a great sigh of released tension seems to come from all over the watching world.

In the Playhouse, they turn and stare up the aisle, almost forgetting, in the impact of the moment, the courtesy due his office. Then Senator Munson rises and quickly they all follow suit as the President enters alone and comes with a steady stride, his face in sternly thoughtful lines, his eyes looking at the carpet before him, neither right nor left, down to the stage. He climbs the little access stair with the same deliberate gait, walks to the lectern, turns and faces them.

"Ladies and gentlemen," he says, hardly raising his voice, for it is really a very small room, to hold such a weight of destiny, "please remain standing until the invocation has been delivered. It is my pleasure and privilege to request this kindness of our good friend and colleague, Luther W. Redfield, distinguished National Committeeman from the state of Washington."

With a pleased if somewhat rusty air (for he has not been a practicing minister for twenty years, since he retired to become president of Walla Walla College) Luther Redfield says, "Let us pray . . . " and then delivers a wandering homily, filled with emotion and overlong, but concluding with an obvious, deep sincerity: "May You guide us, Your servants, dear Lord, to do the best we can for our beloved country."

After he has concluded and they have resumed their seats, an intent silence falls. The President looks about him for a moment, studying the room, their waiting faces, the cameras, the microphones, the hot white lights. Then he lowers his gaze to some notes he has pulled from his pocket and placed upon the lectern, and begins to talk slowly and thoughtfully in a quiet, conversational voice.

"By virtue of the authority vested in me as chairman," he says, raising a small ivory gavel without a handle and bringing it down with a sharp crack! upon the lectern, "I hereby declare this special emergency meeting of the National Committee to be now in session for the purpose of selecting a candidate for the office of President of the United States, and"—he uses again the phrase he used in his speech to the country after President Hudson's funeral—"should events so develop, a candidate for the office of Vice President of the United States."

("And he's going to make them develop that way if he can, all right," the Denver *Post* whispers to the Los Angeles *Times*. "Reactionary old bastard," the L.A. *Times* whispers back.)

"I came here just now, as did we all," the President goes on, "through streets guarded by the armed forces of the United States whose mission, on my orders as Commander-in-Chief, is to restrain and, if necessary, shoot down, citizens of the United States of America."

There is a gasp from somewhere in the room (and in the crowds outside, as he intended, a sudden hesitation). He lifts his head and stares at them.

"I hope that no one thinks it is my doing that this sort of precaution should be necessary. But I also hope that no one, at this particular point in our history, is so naïve as to think I should not take the precaution.

"Murder and civil disturbance stalk our streets. In this city alone, four deaths yesterday, sudden, mysterious, horrifying, attest to the fact that things are sadly amiss in America. Still another mysterious and horrifying death, eleven days ago, has brought us to this spot. Riots, terrorism, threats against the country and against some of us in this room, have occurred, are occurring, and in all probability will continue to occur.

"We meet, with a heavy responsibility, in a tragic and ominous time.

"It is not for me to say"—and he pauses and stares thoughtfully down upon Roger P. Croy, straight-backed and attentive at his desk—"where the loyalties lie of those who are behind these things. There are some"—Roger P. Croy stares impassively back—"who are perfectly loyal to the United States. I think this is probably true of the great majority of misguided citizens who let themselves be persuaded into a type of protest which is very far from decent, democratic dissent. It is probably also true of that sizable segment of the press"—and he pays no attention to the little stirring that runs along both sides of the room—"which consistently condemns and obstructs every attempt the United States makes to protect freedom by opposing Commufascist imperialism. It is probably also true of candidates who fail to make clear that they dissociate themselves from violence whose ultimate aim, I am convinced, is the destruction of the Republic."

("*Probably* true!" Esmé Stryke hisses to her fellow Committee member from California, Asa B. Attwood at his adjoining desk. "*Oh!* I could *scream!*")

"But there are those," the President goes on, "who are not loyal to the United States. There are those who have

370

as their plan and final goal the conquest of America—
first by destroying our society, and then by taking it over.
Some of these are native-born. Some are not native-born,
and come here, or are sent, to stir whatever disruption
and destruction they can.

"Nearly all have been inflated by press and television
to an influence out of all proportion to their personal
value or their original weight in this land. They are cre-
ations of news story and tube, and those who created
them, if they have a conscience, must have them on it.

"All of this little inner group who prey on the emotions and ideals of the naïve, the innocent and the foolish," the President said quietly, "I believe to be actively
working in conjunction with a worldwide conspiracy to
destroy this nation."

("Christ!" *Newsweek* murmurs to the *National Observer.* "How antiquated and reactionary can you get!"
"No limits, apparently," the *National Observer* smiles
back. And from outside, coming faintly to the room like
the distant howling of a fetid wind, 100,000 voices scream
their derision in a prolonged and bitter, "Booooooo!")

"We cannot, in this Committee," the President continues calmly, "ignore the fact that what we do here will
have a very direct bearing upon what happens to the stability and safety of the United States. At the moment,
things are quiet outside"—a slight ironic line touches his
lips—"relatively quiet outside, and generally over the
country today, they are quiet. But that is only because
the cold-blooded strategists in charge think that it is in
the best interests of the candidate they favor that it be
quiet. They will be in the streets in an hour if we do
something they don't like."

("Honest to *God!*" the *Post* hisses with an infinite disgust to Walter Dobius. "He is senile," Walter says flatly.)

"Does that frighten you?" the President asks quietly of the intent faces looking up at his, the faces plain, earnest, simple, clever, shrewd, honest, crafty, decent or corrupt, as America has sent them here out of all her diversities. "Does that mean that you are going to be afraid to do what is right? I hope not, because if that is the case, then the destroyers have won and America as we have known it is not going to be here much longer.

"If you honestly favor their candidate," he says slowly, "and I am perfectly well aware that some of you honestly and sincerely do, then by all means vote for him. If he wins, it will be his problem to handle, and more power to him. But I beg of you, do not vote from fear, because if you do that, you might as well not vote at all. . . . And now, I have perhaps presumed too long on my advantage in being chairman, so I shall soon conclude. Perhaps I shouldn't have spoken at all—"

("You can say that again, you old fool!" Patsy whispers viciously to Valuela Jason Randall.)

"—but there are no precedents for this situation, so we have to feel our way. And I do have some responsibility now"—he smiles somewhat wryly—"to try to tell you what I think best for the country.

"In any event," he remarks, and his tone becomes businesslike, "there are just a couple of things I want to place before you before I conclude. The first is a letter, addressed to me as chairman, from a lovely lady—"

("Oh, oh," Dolly whispers to Beth. "Here it comes." In front of the television set in the den at Dumbarton Oaks, a wild, fantastic, sickening thought suddenly hits the Governor of California so hard he actually thinks for a second that he may be physically ill.)

"—whom many of us know, love and admire. She writes:

"'Dear Mr. President:

"'I have been giving a great deal of thought in recent days to the choice which confronts the National Committee. I thought at first I would not say anything, but then I decided that my husband would have wanted—'" (At Dumbarton Oaks the Governor sits back in his chair and expells, with a long, whistling sound, the breath he was not even aware he was holding) "'—me to speak.

"'I believe the issue to be simple: a continuation of the policies of firmness and steadfastness that my husband always tried to uphold during his time in the White House, or a surrender to all the enemies who are attacking our beloved country abroad and at home.

"'I have honestly tried to decide which of the two men you are going to consider is better equipped and more deserving to be President—which would be braver and more honest. Because I think America needs a brave and honest man in the White House more than she needs anything else.

"'I do not believe Governor Jason to be this man. I think Orrin Knox is. I believe Secretary Knox would carry on firmly and with great integrity the policies my husband believed best for America.

"'I hope he will be nominated.

                    "'Sincerely and affectionately yours,
                    "'Lucille (Mrs. Harley M.) Hudson.'"

For a moment, as the President quietly concludes his

reading, there is such a stirring and movement in the room that it seems some Jason supporter must jump to his feet and shout an angry protest. But Roger P. Croy, the logical one to do it, the one to whom others quickly look for some indication of the course they should follow, is curiously silent, an oddly impassive, almost waiting, expression on his face. So the protest dies in dismayed rustles and murmurs, and the President briskly continues.

"One other thing, and then we will proceed, in any way the Committee deems best to bring the issues and candidates before it.

"I have been notified by the Secretary of State, who this morning has received official confirmation from General Kroner in Gorotoland of word we first began to receive yesterday, that the rebel government has collapsed and is suing for surrender—"

("Oh, *no!*" the New York *Post* exclaims in an anguished tone to *The New Yorker.* "What can you do?" *The New Yorker* says with a sad shrug. And from the fetid wind outside comes a long, sighing groan.)

"Prince Obi has fled to Tanzania and apparently intends to go from there to Moscow and then to Peking to seek support for renewing the war. But in actual practical fact, the war is over. And," he adds with a calm bluntness, "the policies of President Hudson, myself, and the Secretary of State, have been proved correct.

"We are informed that the Soviet Union, Britain and France have demanded an urgent Security Council meeting tomorrow to discuss this sad event, and Panama. But on that, too," he adds with an equal bluntness, "the actual practical fact of it is that we have indicated our position with three vetoes so far, and will, if necessary, indicate it again."

("The arrogance of it," Raoul Barre murmurs to Lord Maudulayne. The British Ambassador shakes his head with a sad and worried look.)

"And now it would seem to me," the President says, once more businesslike, "that perhaps the best way to proceed would be to have nominations immediately, to be followed by a roll call. We know the men. We know the issues. We need a candidate, and we shouldn't delay. Perhaps if someone would like to make a motion—"

And now Roger P. Croy does hold up his hand, a long, flowing, imperious hand at the end of a long, flowing and imperious arm. The President looks a little amused, as though he had expected this.

"The distinguished National Committeeman from Oregon," he says, and Roger Croy rises and turns gracefully so that he is half-addressing the chair, half-addressing the cameras, microphones and pencils eager to record something at last that will bring a little balance back into these sickeningly one-sided proceedings.

"Mr. President," he says graciously, "I rise for the purpose of requesting a small delay. Since we are cut off here completely from the outside world—is there even a telephone in here?"

"Are you asking me?" the President inquires. "Yes, there is, up here on the stenographers' desk. And there are three more in private booths we've had set up backstage. I'm sorry, I didn't know anyone wanted to call. No one has called in," he adds with a smile, and a little wave of amusement breaks the tension somewhat.

"Oh, I don't," Roger Croy says. "Everything is in order, I believe. It's just that I would like to know exactly when the U.S. marshal is going to be here—"

"What U.S. marshal is that?" the President asks in an ominous tone, and over the little room a sudden rush of excitement and renewed tension surges.

"Bearing the order, I believe—" Roger P. Croy begins gently, but doesn't finish, because suddenly, so suddenly that it makes many in the audience gasp, the phone on the stenographers' desk does ring, shatteringly loud and insistent.

"Get that," the President orders, his voice beginning to show a little strain in spite of him. One of the stenographers, looking frightened, does so.

"It's for you, Mr. President," he says, and holds it out at such nervous arm's length that the President can't help but look amused. Again the tension eases a little. But the amused expression doesn't last long as he listens carefully and then snaps, "Let him through!" He replaces the receiver and returns the phone to the still apprehensive stenographer. Then he turns back to the lectern, places his hands firmly upon it and leans forward to stare directly down at Roger P. Croy.

"Very well, Governor. Your man is on the way. I don't think we need a formal recess—"

"Oh, no," says Roger Croy graciously.

"So," the President says, still staring down at him with an ironic and quizzical expression, "we shall just wait. It shouldn't be more than two minutes, ladies and gentlemen."

And just about two minutes it is, long enough for a fearful tension to build again. Then there is a stir at the door. Committee, guests, press, television, cameras, microphones, lights and all, swivel around as though moved by the same mechanism. In the doorway stands an earnest little man, wearing a salt-and-pepper suit ("What, no ten-gallon hat and six-shooter?" the New York *Times* has time to murmur with a wild irreverence to the AP) and a nervous but grimly determined expression. In his hand he holds high a folded piece of paper. And there he stands, paralyzed, until the President says, impatiently yet not unkindly, "Come in, marshal. It's quite all right, you've got your duty to perform. Come ahead."

"Yes, sir," the marshal says, starts down the aisle, almost trips in his excitement, catches himself and hurries forward.

"Right up here," the President says, waving him up the steps and holding out his hand. The marshal thrusts his paper into it, and suddenly and quite genuinely, the President laughs.

"I just wanted to shake hands, first," he remarks. "But thanks anyway."

At this there is a burst of laughter, also quite genuine, from the room, and for a moment they are all chortling together, friends and enemies alike. Then the marshal steps back, the President opens the paper, and abruptly all is silence again.

"This appears to be"—the President says slowly, "—it is—a temporary restraining order—a preliminary injunction—from the District Court for the District of Columbia. It purports to be"—he stares over it once more at Roger P. Croy, bland and attentive below "—it is—issued pursuant to a suit filed at ten A.M., just about an hour ago—how clever you have been, Governor, how clever—by attorneys for the distinguished National Committeeman from Oregon and the distinguished National Committeewoman from California, Mrs. Stryke, joined by attorneys for the National Antiwar Activities Committee. The suit seeks a permanent injunction that would prohibit further proceedings of this Committee to select a nominee for President and/or Vice President, and directs the Committee to reconvene the convention—"

"My *God!*" somebody says from the press benches, loud and clear.

"—with instructions to select the nominee for President and/or Vice President.

"The preliminary injunction directs that this meeting be suspended until the case has been decided."

For quite a few minutes after that, there is pandemonium in the room, and on the wind from outside, faint but distinct, there comes a great rushing sound of cheers and jubilation. In the room, reactions run from Krishna Khaleel, who is practically hugging himself with excitement—what *will* these Americans think of next!—to Cullee Hamilton, who tries to remain impassive but cannot prevent an annoyed and disgusted scowl from crossing his face. Temporarily, at least, the Knox forces are in obvious dismay and disarray, the Jason forces are quivering with excited triumph and anticipation. Into the hubbub Roger P. Croy once more raises a graceful arm and the President once more says, this time with a considerable irony in his voice, "The distinguished National Committeeman from Oregon."

"Mr. President," Roger Croy says, "I move this committee stand in adjournment, pursuant to temporary injunction, until the pending suit has been decided."

"Second! Second!" cry many voices, and "Question! Question!" cry many others. There is some suspicion that the voices are not entirely confined to bona fide members of the Committee, but in any event it doesn't matter, because the President brings his gavel down with a crash on the lectern.

Abruptly it is still again.

"It seems to me," he says firmly, "that while the Committee is legally bound by the terms of this temporary injunction pending decision of the case, nonetheless the Committee as a collective body also has a right to decide what legal course it should take in this situation, over and beyond simply adjourning, which is a perfectly valid motion under the circumstances.

"Now, the only time and the only place in which the Committee is gathered as a committee, and can be under this injunction, is right here and now. This is the only chance we will have, if we disband pursuant to call *after* decision of the case, to decide what we should do as a collective body. Therefore, if Governor Croy would be willing to withhold his motion for a moment, so that we might decide—"

There are cries of, "No! No! Abide by the law, abide by the law!" countered by shouts of, "Put it to a vote! Let's decide! We have a right to decide!"

Again the President terminates the uproar with his gavel.

"I am aware," he says with a certain comfortable irony, as a trained ear tells him that sentiment is beginning to move his way a little, "that the President of the United States is in a somewhat questionable position defying an injunction, and I am not defying it. I am simply saying that we have a right now, while we are still together as a body, to decide what course we should pursue in the new situation posed by the injunction.

"Now, we can have a vote on the motion to adjourn, but I am not sure it would carry, Governor. In this purely procedural situation, the chair would hold, if the Committee will support me, that a simple majority vote of the membership must prevail. When it comes to selecting a nominee, as you know, each state's vote has the same numerical value as it had in the convention. But here, I should think, a simple majority must prevail. Does that seem unreasonable?"

He pauses and inwardly holds his breath; but by some miracle, nobody challenges. "Very well. On that basis, Governor, do you wish to press your motion to adjourn immediately?"

He stares down again upon Roger P. Croy, stately, handsome, and obviously doing a lot of thinking. In a moment the thinking produces a slow shaking of the head and the thoughtful comment:

"Not, perhaps, at the moment Mr. President. Possibly there is some logic"—and he raises the graceful hand again as protesting murmurs break out here and there—"to considering this carefully for a moment. It is certainly a situation without precedent, and perhaps we should give it thorough consideration while we are, as the President says, gathered in one place as one entity."

("That's a mistake," Walter Dobius whispers with an angry dismay to Frankly Unctuous. "Oh, that's a mistake! Don't do it, don't do it!")

But Roger P. Croy, persuaded by no one knows what considerations, possibly just the calm reasonableness of the President who seems so calm and so logical as he skates on legal thin ice and emotions which could at any moment take the meeting out of his hands, has already done it.

The President wastes no time.

"Very well. Does anyone wish to speak or make a motion on this issue?"

Out of the babble and talk Lyle Strathmore of Michigan is first on his feet.

"Mr. President!" he says, and his voice rings out commandingly. "I move that this Committee take an immediate appeal against the temporary injunction to the U.S. Circuit Court of Appeals."

"Second!" screeches Lizzie Hanson McWharter as the room again explodes in angry sound.

"Question!" caterwauls Anna Hooper Bigelow.

'Now, just a minute!" shouts Roger P. Croy, coming suddenly out of his curious complacency which apparently has not been curious at all but part of a shrewder strategy than the President's. "I move to amend that motion to state that this Committee take an immediate appeal to the Supreme Court. Specifically, since the Court is in summer recess, to the presiding justice of the District Court for the District of Columbia."

"Tommy!" Bob Munson says explosively to Lafe Smith. *"Christ!"*

"Second!" screams Esmé Stryke, and "Question!" shouts Milton S. Oppenheimer of New York.

For just a moment the President hesitates, but he knows there is nothing for it. Under parliamentary law the amendment must be voted upon first.

"Mrs. Bigelow," he says with a fair show of calmness, as though by pretending the vote will go the way he wants it to, he can make it so—a tactic that sometimes works in the House, and just might here—"I would appreciate it, and I am sure we all would, if you would repeat the role you filled so ably at the convention. Would you please act as secretary of the Committee and call the roll?"

"Mr. President," Anna Hooper Bigelow protests, "Please let someone else—" But there is a return of amicability for a moment as they all cheer and clap, and finally Anna, looking flustered, comes forward and takes her place beside him at the lectern.

"The vote is on the motion of the distinguished National Committeeman from Oregon," the President says. "All those in favor will say Aye, those opposed No, the Secretary will call the roll."

"Alabama!" says Anna Bigelow, and at once the deep divisions here flare into the open for all the world to see.

"Madam Secretary," Helen M. Rupert says in a voice that remains steady with some difficulty, "on this motion, as it was in the convention, Alabama is divided. I cast my vote Aye."

"Madam Secretary," says Henry C. Godwin at the desk beside her, "I vote Nay."

And as Anna Bigelow goes on down the proud parade of states, it swiftly becomes apparent that the bitter differences on policy, which became so clear in the many split delegation votes on the nomination of Harley Hudson, are just as strong today. Many of the smaller states remain consistently united for either the Jason cause or the Knox—Tobin Janson and Mary V. Aluta of Alaska voting firmly No, Henrietta McEwan and Elliot B. Whitaker of Nevada voting firmly Aye, the President and his colleague Jessica Edmonds Clark voting No for Colorado, Alice Lathrop Smith and Ewan MacDonald MacDonald voting Aye for Wyoming. Many of the big states are consistent too—consistently divided. From

382

California, where Esmé Stryke defiantly votes "Aye!" and Asa B. Attwood defiantly counters "Nay!", through Illinois, where Ruth B. Stillson votes No but Malcolm N. Sherman votes Aye, to New York, where Milton Oppenheimer votes Aye but Janette Wilkins Vandervoort votes No, it is obvious that the Committee, like the convention, is a horse race.

As Anna proceeds, however, the excitement grows, for it begins to appear that this time a trend may be developing. Some states that were divided before, such as Minnesota and Ohio, are not divided today; and although they don't even think of it, so intently are they concentrating on their own concerns right here in this small room, outside on the sweltering lawns, in the city, across the nation, over the watching world, the tension again becomes almost unbearable. For it appears that in a handful of four small—small? Fantastically large—votes, the fate of Roger Croy's motion, and perhaps the fate of his candidate, will be decided.

"On this vote," the President says quietly, confirming what the world has already counted, "the Yeas are fifty-five the Nays fifty-one and the motion of the Committeeman from Oregon to amend the motion of the Committeeman from Michigan is agreed to. The vote now comes"—he raises his voice above the excited noises that at once break out—"the vote now comes on the motion of the Committeeman from Michigan, as amended. All those in favor—"

But Mary Baffleburg is on her feet:

"I don't think that any vote we take in this Committee should be by voice vote! It's all too important! I demand a roll call!"

There is, for once, unanimous agreement in the National Committee with Mary Baffleburg. A shout of approval goes up, the President nods and directs Anna Bigelow to call the roll. Again the tension rises, but the Jasonites find they have no worries.

"On the motion of the Committeeman from Michigan, as amended," the President says, "the Ayes are fifty-five, the Nays fifty-one. The motion is agreed to and an immediate appeal will be taken to the presiding Justice of the District Circuit.

"The chair," he says, with an amiable smile which serves to restore at least a temporary good humor to the proceeding, "would love to appear before the Supreme Court himself, but he does have a few things to tend to at the White House. Obviously, however, arguments will be heard and counsel will be necessary.

"Now, you understand, all of you, I hope, that in the very act of taking an appeal to the Court, there is implicit the Committee's official position that it is opposed to the injunction and its terms. But obviously"—he raises his hand as good feeling vanishes again and angry murmurs begin—"obviously, if I may be permitted to say so, this does not reflect the very closely divided sentiments in the Committee.

"The motion is simply a mechanism, I take it—you will correct me, Governor," he says dryly—"simply a mechanism for getting it before the Court in the hope that the Court will deny the appeal and thereby uphold the injunction and force us to reconvene the convention.

"Therefore, both sides, it seems to me, will undoubtedly wish to be represented by counsel. If I may be permitted to speak for those who oppose the injunction"—

he pauses with a questioning look; there are no objectors—"I think perhaps we should meet in caucus to select—" But his attention is attracted by a hand in the audience, moving quickly and then as quickly stilled. His eyes search for and find its owner, who nods, almost imperceptibly but with a calm, almost fatalistic determination.

"I think," the President says smoothly, "that perhaps by virtue of the authority vested in me as chairman of the caucus—"

("Chairman of a caucus that hasn't even been held!" The Greatest Publication exclaims, torn between helpless laughter and rage. "What a railroad!")

"—I may now make our selection. I hereby appoint the Honorable Robert A. Leffingwell—"

"Oh, *no!*" cries Mary Baffleburg, and there are several other Knox supporters who cry out with an equal dismay. But a majority seems willing to accept the President's judgment, or at least unwilling to offer an open challenge to it.

"—as counsel representing those members of the Committee opposed to the injunction. I assume those favoring it will select the distinguished gentleman who offered the amendment."

"We want Roger P. Croy, if that's what you mean," says Ewan MacDonald MacDonald of Wyoming in the clipped brogue his children call "Playing the Old Country."

"That's who I mean," the President agrees with a smile. "And now, Governor Croy, if you care to reintroduce your motion to adjourn—"

But again the telephone rings, and he breaks off with a wry, "Somebody must be watching."

The stenographer, still looking perturbed, picks up the receiver, listens for a moment, holds out the instrument without a word to the President.

"Hello?" the President says. "Oh, hello, Tommy!"

The room is instantly silent.

"Yes . . . Yes . . . Oh, I would think so. Yes, that should be time enough for adequate preparation, I would think. Anyway, you're the boss, now: you name it, we'll be there . . . OK, fine . . . Fine, Tommy . . . Fine, Tommy . . . Yes, *fine*, Tommy. Thank you!"

He hands the telephone to the stenographer, turns back to the Committee, the guests, the cameras, the microphones, the pencils, the city, the nation, the world.

"That was Mr. Justice Davis," he says, with only the slightest hint of amusement in his eyes. "Justice Davis informs me that he will hear arguments on the appeal in his chambers at two P.M. tomorrow. And now, Governor—"

"I move," says Roger P. Croy, "that the Committee stand in recess, subject to call of the Chair after decision has been rendered upon the appeal."

"Without objection," the President says, "it is so ordered."

And the Committee, preceded by the President, who is whisked swiftly away in his limousine to the White House, passes gossiping and exclamatory back through the heavily guarded Center (which will remain under twenty-four-hour security for the duration) to the waiting Army cars, which whisk members swiftly away to their heavily guarded quarters in Fort Myer.

And the guests and the media hurry back by their own various routes and means to their respective homes and offices, there to tell, retell, write, rewrite, broadcast, re-broadcast, the events of this dramatic day.

And the crowds, not so sullen now, more lighthearted, almost festive as they seem to see their candidate's apotheosis ahead, begin to break up into little groups and go wandering off among the trees along the river, there to bring out picnic lunches, strum guitars and sing, or to go straggling on toward the center of the city, where they will wander aimlessly through the stores and along the broad, hot avenues until night comes and they can sleep in preparation for their rendezvous tomorrow.

And the world—except for that little handful of it which is preparing for tomorrow's bitter debate in the Security Council, returns to the business of living filled with wonder about what will happen next.

And the nation—except for those 535 who comprise the Congress of the United States and must prepare themselves for tomorrow's bitter debate on the antiriot bill—gradually unwinds and relaxes and goes back to its normal pursuits, though it too is filled with wonder and a deep, unshakable apprehension.

And the focus of history narrows down to Mr. Justice Thomas Buckmaster Davis of the United States Supreme Court, who, notifying his secretary that he will see no one, finally takes from his wall safe a sheaf of copy paper he has not touched since he put it there, settles back in the quiet of his hushed, luxurious office and slowly, carefully, begins to read.

6.

IT WAS MORNING in the home of George Harrison Wattersill, and already there was the stir that developed when Daddy had a big case. Today the stir was greater than usual, and it had been going on most of the night, which made it seem even more important. Strange cars had come and gone at the handsome old twenty-room house on Foxhall Road (result of a thousand cases in the Right Cause for the Right People at the Right Time) ever since mid-afternoon yesterday, and in them had come and gone a strange parade: LeGage Shelby, Fred Van Ackerman, Rufus Kleinfert; Roger P. Croy and six fellow members of the National Committee; Walter Dobius, Frankly Unctuous, and several other prominent columnists and news commentators; several members of Congress; a deputation of ministers; a delegation of students and professors from Georgetown Law School.

There had been conferrings in muffled voices behind the big oaken doors of Daddy's study. Sometimes the voices had surged upward in heat and anger, sometimes they had sunk to a murmur so confidential that it hardly seemed anyone was talking at all. Afterward most of the visitors had gone out on the steps to pose for pictures and be interviewed before they went away.

"This is probably my biggest case," Daddy had told the *Post* when it called yesterday afternoon right after Roger Croy announced his selection to head the Jason team when it appeared in Justice Davis' chambers. And Daddy, with his sure instinct for drama which had won him so much fame, was milking it for all it was worth.

For Daddy was indeed a famous man, and carefully

filed in his study, he had the articles, the headlines and the picture layouts to prove it.

"GALAHAD IN THE COURTROOM," *Look* had called him when he had secured release of the saboteurs who had ruined two moon shots at Cape Kennedy: "George Harrison Wattersill Fights for the Defiant and the Dissident." "WATTERSILL FOR THE DEFENSE," *Newsweek* had burbled at the time he sprung four flag desecraters and six draft-card burners: "A Daring Advocate Upholds Freedom's Cause." "DEMOCRACY'S DEFENDER," The Greatest Publication described him admiringly at the time he was successfully conducting the defense of three union leaders who had tied up 100,000 tons of war matériel and thereby caused the unnecessary deaths of American soldiers. "G.H.W.," *Life* had reported only last week: "Washington's Most Dynamic Young Lawyer Saves Its Most Wanted Rapist."

On George Harrison Wattersill's shelves could also be found the writings with which he had embellished and given further status to the glamorous and glorious career that had shot him into orbit at the age of twenty-six, never to fall.

There was the sober study of "Rules of Evidence," for the *Journal of the American Bar Association*. There was the article for *Reader's Digest:* "What *You* Can Do If Your Teenybopper Gets Into Trouble." There was the thoughtful piece in *Fortune:* "Has the Law Become Too Big a Business?" There was the swinging piece for *Seventeen:* "Hey, Kids, Stay Clear of the Fuzz!" And there was the book, published only three weeks ago and already soaring to the top of the nonfiction best-seller list on a wave of flattering reviews from the *Times*, *The New Yorker*,

Time, Newsweek, The Greatest Publication, and *Book World.*
MY CLIENT, LIBERTY: The Story of "Democracy's Defender," by George Harrison Wattersill.

It was said, and truly, of George Harrison Wattersill, that his clients, whether they be rapists, saboteurs, draft dodgers or common murderers, had one trait in common. They were Against—against law, against order, against common decency, against society, and against their own country. They were the sick of an anarchic age, and so, perhaps, was he, for all his beautifully tailored good looks and his aristocratic courtroom manner. And because he had very early in his career perceived that the Against were the darlings of the media, he gave them his abilities and they automatically gave him the publicity and prominence that meant fame and fortune.

There were some critics, both at the bar and outside it, who marveled at how adeptly George Harrison Wattersill could twist his conscience and his principles to fit his clients and his reputation. But solemnly he would repeat in interview after interview the sentence that had become his trademark:

"Freedom is indivisible. It is indivisible for you, for me, for the rapist and for the demonstrator. [Slowly and gravely] Freedom . . . is . . . indivisible. If you live by that guidestone, all else falls into place."

"How marvelous, how brave," cried all his admirers as they boosted him still further up the ladder of publicity. "How shrewd and smart for Georgie Watters," darkly murmured his detractors as they tried to pull him down.

But it couldn't be done.

"Georgie is our darlin', our darlin', our darlin'," they

had caroled at the most recent Gridiron Club show. "Georgie is our darlin', our Young Cavalier!"

The sentiment was well-nigh universal in all the opinion factories that Really Count.

George Harrison Wattersill could happen, probably, only in America in the latter half of the twentieth century. But there was no doubt that he had happened, and happened big.

So now at thirty-eight "this most brilliant young lawyer anywhere," as *Commentary* had called him, this "gallant defender of the indefensible" as the *Saturday Review* (perhaps not quite saying what it had intended) hailed him on the occasion of his guest editorial urging a treaty to restrict nuclear weapons to the twenty-seven mutually hostile and suspicious nations which now had them, was approaching his biggest case.

It would be, he thought, short and sweet. Given Tommy Davis for a target, he and his clients were confident they knew exactly the approach they should take, because after all, wasn't it all set anyway? All they had to do was help the Justice put a respectable face on it—"Give him enough arguments to make him look good and satisfy the boobs," George had remarked, with a certain disrespect for the great American public whose freedom he so gallantly defended every day of his life—and it would all be over in two hours' time.

"Just leave it to me," he had assured Governor Jason when the Governor telephoned a little while ago to check on progress. "We're going to be so smooth they'll never know what hit them."

"Don't underestimate Bob Leffingwell or Bob Munson," Ted had advised. "And don't go in overconfident about Tommy."

"Overconfidence is not my habit," George Wattersill had replied crisply. "But you have talked to him, I understand?"

"Oh, yes—"

"Well," George said, dismissing doubt. "It worked with old Hempstone on the District Court, didn't it? He handed down that injunction quickly enough."

"Not without a price," Ted replied. He uttered a dry little chuckle. "I suppose the perfect pay-off would be when Tommy retires—"

"Tommy will never retire," George Harrison Wattersill said with a laugh. "He likes that job too much."

"Well, I repeat," Governor Jason said. "Don't go in overconfident. We can't afford any slips at this point in the game."

"Leave it to me," George Harrison Wattersill said calmly. "I know my town."

And as Washington, or those very few of it who were going to be privileged to squeeze into Justice Davis' chambers, began to arrive at the Supreme Court shortly after one P.M., it appeared that George Wattersill did. He had assistance, of course, for again NAWAC was out in force, its massive contribution to the week's events transferred from the troop-ringed, but temporarily deserted Kennedy Center, to Capitol Plaza and the streets around the Court. Here his skillful hand was immediately noticeable, for today the aspect was solemn, dignified, respectful, polite, and the banners were far from yesterday's obscenities, which had been stored temporarily at COMFORT headquarters downtown. Now in place of such things as ONE SHOT, TWO SHOTS, THREE SHOTS, FOUR/THE CAUSE OF PEACE HAS PLENTY

MORE, and the infantile but satisfyingly offensive F.*old* U.*p*, C.*razy* K.*nox!*, they offered only such mild suggestions as FAIR PLAY, MR. JUSTICE—AMERICA COUNTS ON YOU, and, LET LAW DECIDE/NOT FRATRI-CIDE. It appeared to Bob Munson and Bob Leffingwell as they arrived, to be greeted by a few mildly resentful murmurs but no overt outburst, that there were even a few relatively clean shirts and serapes in the front rows, a few faces that looked as though they had actually been washed.

"Georgie wants everybody respectable today," Senator Munson remarked.

Bob Leffingwell snorted.

"It isn't going to do him any good inside."

It certainly, however, did him and his cause some good outside, because the nation and the world, again largely immobilized and attentive, today had an impression of orderly, decent, responsible protest. The dignified atmosphere was increased by the arrival of George himself, accompanied by Roger P. Croy, who, as Lafe Smith had remarked to Cullee during the convention, would manage to look dignified in a Japanese massage parlor. The combination of George's alert, intelligent face and Roger Croy's imposing white-topped visage, gave world viewers an instant feeling of solidity, determination, strength and supreme confidence. The two Bobs, in contrast, while looking solid, determined and strong, also looked worried, somber and actively concerned about their cause.

By five minutes to two, everyone who had a reason to be there was in the leather-lined, book-filled, comfortably cluttered room where Mr. Justice Davis was accustomed to discuss pending cases with his clerks, entertain his friends at little private luncheons, write his opinions, or just sit and read. With a firmness that matched the President's, and had quite surprised, puzzled and upset the media, he had sharply reduced the number of people and the amount of equipment that might be in the room. At best it was tiny and would hold no more than fifty comfortably. He had reduced it even further by announcing that he would permit one pool cameraman, one sound man and one reporter for television; two radio correspondents; two still photographers and two reporters from each of the two wire services; and three newspaper correspondents. These had been chosen by lot at emergency meetings last night of the Congressional gallery committees for the various media. The outcry was not as bitter against Mr. Justice Davis as it had been against the President, because Mr. Justice Davis, after all, was one of the Good Guys; but his decision did make for a lot of practical difficulties in coverage, there was no doubt about that. But Tommy, though they did not know it, had made up his mind on certain things and intended to stick to them.

For this brief moment, the power of America rested with him. He was, as the President had told him, the boss. And literally nobody on earth could overrule him.

Add to the fifteen media representatives, himself; an official stenographer for the Court; a stenographer for each side; two of his young law clerks (thrilled almost to the point of tears at the opportunity to participate in this historic occasion) to keep water glasses filled and scratch pads replenished; the four lawyers for the disputants; and the Marshal at the door, and he had what he considered a manageable group of twenty-six individuals.

This, he thought now as he peered quickly around at them while the bailiff closed the door and locked it, was quite enough. He cleared his throat, took a sip of water, and, somewhat nervously yet firmly, began to speak.

("I don't think he looks very well, do you?" the New-ark *News*, one of the three newspapers chosen, whispered to the Arkansas *Gazette*. "He's really on the spot," the *Gazette* whispered back. "Oh, is he?" murmured the Boston *Herald* in some surprise. "I thought it was all cut and dried.")

If this was indeed the case, there was no indication from Justice Davis. His opening remarks were brief, impartial and straight to the point.

"Petitioners," he said, for once enunciating slowly and distinctly as if conscious of the uncountable millions whose eyes and ears were upon him, "appear here pursuant to a decision of the National Committee Yesterday, to appeal the temporary injunction issued yesterday morning by the U. S. District Court for the District of Columbia.

"Said injunction required the suspension of National Committee proceedings pending decision of the suit entered in the District Court on behalf of the National Committeeman from Oregon, the Honorable Roger P. Croy, and Mrs. Esmé Harbellow Stryke, National Committeewoman from California. This suit has been joined by a newly formed organization known by the acronym 'NAWAC,' which this Court understands to mean, 'National Antiwar Activities Committee.'

"The temporary injunction has been complied with by the National Committee, which now stands in recess pending decision of present appeal to this Court.

"The suit filed by Governor Croy, Mrs. Stryke and NAWAC, seeks a permanent injunction prohibiting the National Committee in its own right from selecting candidates for President and/or Vice President and requiring the Committee to recall the convention which adjourned in San Francisco two weeks ago, and to direct said convention to select said nominee and/or nominees.

"The effect of overturning the temporary injunction on appeal would of course be to free the National Committee to resume its deliberations immediately and to decide by its own free vote, if it so pleases, whether to reconvene the convention, or to dispense with that procedure and select nominees in and of its own right to do so under the rules governing the party.

"Therefore, this Court would hope that appellants and counter-appellants would address themselves today not only to the validity of the temporary injunction and whether or not it can, in fact be issued legally by the court below; but also, and perhaps more importantly, to the basic questions raised by the pending suit in the court below.

("He doesn't have the right to go into that, does he?" the AP murmured. The UPI gave a snort, swiftly suppressed as Justice Davis, Bob Leffingwell and Roger P. Croy all gave him sharp glances. "This Court can do anything," he whispered. "Anyway, who's going to stop him? God?")

"In a situation which has to create its own precedents, because there are none," Tommy went on, "the first seems to be, I gather, that there are no counsel present for the official position of a majority of the Committee as defined by its vote yesterday—namely, in favor of the appeal against the injunction, but in reality *for* the injunction, and for the suit. Rather than designate counsel for this rather topsy-turvy situation, the Committee has simply split into its two factions and each has selected its own counsel.

"This would seem a further justification for the position"—he looked quite severely at the tiny press table, then smiled as the UPI put his arm over his face in mock contrition—"taken by the Court, that it should hear the merits of the case which prompts the temporary injunction, as well as the merits of the injunction itself.

"Now: since we have to have some order of procedure, the Court is going to arbitrarily make the selection of the first speaker on the basis of positions vis-à-vis the appeal. Therefore the Court will now call upon the Honorable Robert A. Leffingwell to open the arguments for the appeal, and such other arguments as he may wish to present against the case below.

"The Court will then call upon Mr. George Harrison Wattersill, to argue against the appeal, and to present such other arguments as he may wish to present for the case below.

"After that the Court will recognize the distinguished Majority Leader of the United States Senate, the Honorable Robert D. Munson, if he desires to supplement or expand the remarks of Mr. Leffingwell, to be followed by the Honorable Roger P. Croy, to supplement or expand the arguments of Mr. Wattersill.

"Each side will then have the opportunity, through a single spokesman, to rebut."

("My God," the Newark *News* whispered, "We'll be here all night." But Tommy had thought of that, too.)

"Because of the great—I might even say, the overwhelming—concern in this matter," he went on with a somewhat hesitant smile that George Harrison Wattersill immediately decided to act upon, "and because of the great necessity to expedite it so that the National Committee may know immediately how to proceed hereafter, the Court is arbitrarily"—he paused, took a breath and then licked his lips in a nervous little gesture that only confirmed George Wattersill in his intention—"the Court is arbitrarily going to restrict arguments on each side to one and one-half hours, to be apportioned internally as counsel may decide between themselves, and rebuttal to one-half hour for each side. In this way—"

But George Harrison Wattersill was on his feet, every line of his body rigid with disapproval, his face suffused with a respectful but overpowering indignation.

"Now, Mr. Justice," he said in a tone that nicely mixed sharpness and supplication, "if Your Honor please! This is indeed, Your Honor, a most overwhelmingly vital matter, in which the future fate of this nation and the fate of the world insofar as this nation contributes to or affects it are involved, as Your Honor most truly says. How, then, are we to present—on either side, if I may speak for my able friends opposite—the facts and the arguments upon which this Court may reach a fair and just decision? Now, I do not say, Your Honor," he added with a respectful haste, "that Your Honor cannot reach a fair and just decision on brief arguments, but is it fair to the two sides here? Is it fair to the candidates—to the nation—to the world—to restrict us to such arbitrary and hampering limitations? I submit respectfully this is hardly a democratic procedure, if Your Honor please!"

"Your Honor," Senator Munson inquired in a dry

drawl from his side of the table, "who said this is a democratic procedure? Isn't it true—need I stand, incidentally?"

"No, certainly not," Justice Davis said promptly. "Considering the quasi-informal nature of a hearing in chambers, and considering"—and he gave a sudden twinkle that somehow disturbed George Harrison Wattersill a great deal—"your advanced years, the Court thinks all counsel may remain seated if they wish. If they wish to stand, that is all right, too. It is up to them."

"Thank you, Your Honor," Bob Munson said, interpreting Tommy's humorous mood exactly as George Harrison Wattersill did. "As far as I'm concerned, I'll let George, here, do the leaping, even if I'm not quite as ancient as you think."

("Oh, God," the general director of the *Post* said savagely to Walter Dobius in front of the television set in his office downtown. "Isn't everything so God-damned *chummy!*" I don't like it," Walter said with a worried frown.)

"I was going to say, Your Honor," Senator Munson resumed, "that of course this is not a democratic procedure, in the sense that anybody can take a vote on whether we talk at length or not. Now, counsel knows that as well as I do. This Court has absolute constitutional authority to set any rules it pleases. This Court isn't democratic—it's an *arm* of democracy. Counsel knows that."

"Counsel will not split hairs, I will say," George Wattersill snapped, "with the distinguished Majority Leader. I am simply saying that we on our side are going to be very seriously restricted if we are subject to any such close and arbitrary course of procedure. While I know," he said with a grave worry, "that such is not the intention of the Court *at all,* still I am very much afraid this can only be interpreted by everyone who is watching or listening as being simply a fortuitous, gratuitous, and I am sure most highly welcome, advantage for the Secretary of State, Mr. Knox."

("Tommy won't like that," Orrin remarked with a sudden amusement to Beth, Dolly and Lucille in front of the set at Vagaries. And Tommy didn't.)

"Well, now!" he said with a tartness that told George Wattersill he had gone too far, "I think counsel has gone too far. There is no intention to give anyone any advantage about anything. There is an intention to expedite this and get it over with, in the national interest and the world interest. This Court resents any implication or imputation of such a motive. Counsel knows better than that."

George Harrison Wattersill looked positively crushed.

"I apologize most humbly, Your Honor," he said with a confused, beseeching air. "I am afraid my desire to present a well-rounded case—a desire which Your Honor, as a lawyer, surely cannot criticize—led me to protest too vigorously. We on our side do have, we believe, a well-rounded case to present. Of course," he said thoughtfully, "those who have fewer facts perhaps understandably need less time. (The two Bobs stirred, but decided simultaneously to hold their tongues.) It will be difficult to present the sound arguments we believe we have, but of course we will be bound by Your Honor's wishes. I do apologize, Your Honor, most humbly. Most humbly."

And he sat down, shaking his head in a sad, bewildered fashion. Roger P. Croy leaned over and put an arm around his shoulders with a fatherly, comforting air.

(WATTERSILL CHARGES KNOX COURT AD-
VANTAGE, the next edition headlines said. Throughout
the country and around the globe, many millions agreed.)

"Counsel should watch his language," Tommy said,
more mildly. "Now, if Mr. Leffingwell wishes to present
his arguments, perhaps we can begin."

"Your Honor," George Harrison Wattersill interrupted,
contrite and humble still. "I do appreciate your courtesy
and kindness to one who perhaps allowed a certain—I
can hardly say youthful"—he smiled exactly the right kind
of smile, a little shy, a little abashed, a little boyish, a little
self-deprecatory—"perhaps lower-middle/middle-aged
might be better—enthusiasm and impulsiveness to run
away with him."

"Yes, yes," Tommy said with just the faintest show of
a rising impatience. "Please let Mr. Leffingwell begin
now."

"Georgie, I think you'd better," Lafe Smith remarked
to Cullee Hamilton in the Delegates' Lounge at the UN.
"The last time that boy let impulsiveness run away with
him was when he couldn't control himself at the age of
six months. After that one initial mistake, he's known exactly what he was doing, ever since."

"I've always found him an awfully tiresome character
when he's been before House committees," Cullee agreed.
"I get awfully fed up with this fake humility and these
fake blunders that always wind up in such propaganda
advantages. Look at them over there," he said with some
disgust, pointing to a group in front of one of the television sets that had been placed around the enormous

room for this momentous day. "Japan, Congo Leopoldville, Ceylon and Bolivia think he's absolutely great."

"They all think he's great," Lafe said. "Look at all those eager, happy, laughing faces, all around the room. I don't see how they can tear themselves away for the Security Council meeting."

"When we're the target," Cullee said dryly, "they'll manage. Anyway, the general services people have put ten sets in the room next door, so I dare say we'll all be nipping in there when things get dull in the Council."

But contrary to his expectation, things did not get so very dull in the Council, for no sooner had they taken their places than they became aware of a rustling and a murmuring and a behind-the-hand gossiping around the big green circle which seemed to promise some surprise for the arrogant, overconfident, deplored and mistrusted United States.

It must be, they decided, something more than the resolution introduced by France and the Soviet Union which urged continued recognition of the Obifumatta government in Gorotoland and dispatch of a UN force to reopen the fighting. They were pretty sure they could count on Britain to veto that one, and knew that if Britain didn't, they would. So it did not worry them particularly.

Nor were they much more concerned about the second resolution, introduced by Britain, France and the Soviet Union, condemning the threatened U.S. blockade of Panama and pledging "all efforts of this organization, both collectively and in the realm of individual members acting within their rights upon the seas," to break it. That, too, could be vetoed if necessary. But it might never have

402

to be if the resolving powers could be convinced that America meant business in her drive to defeat Felix Labaiya's "Government of the Panamanian People's Liberation Movement" and its threat to the Canal.

As the meeting prepared to pull itself cumberously together, late as always in typical UN fashion, it appeared that this last might take some doing, for the British Ambassador, easing quietly into his seat beside Lafe, looked as upset and affronted as he had the last time they had seen him.

"Claude," Lafe said with a challenging good humor, "good afternoon. How are you?"

"Quite well, thank you," Lord Maudulayne said crisply. "Better, since it appears that the National Committee is going to be permitted to select a reasonable and responsible candidate."

"Oh?" Cullee said, his tone beginning to bristle as he leaned forward to talk around Lafe. "Is that how he looks to you?"

"Anyone," Lord Maudulayne said with a sort of strangled indignation. "*Anyone*, to break this damnable chain of wars and more wars, crisis on top of crisis. Don't you people realize *the world must have peace?*"

"Oh, my God," Lafe said in a weary voice, making no attempt to conceal his tired disgust from Vasily Tashikov, watching alertly from across the circle. "Not you, too."

"Yes, we too!" Claude said sharply. "My Government are sick of it. Sick of it, sick of it!"

"Well, don't get hysterical," Cullee said in a deliberately blunt tone. "We know you're frustrated, but don't let it get you down."

"We are not, I submit," Lord Maudulayne snapped,

"as frustrated as an Administration whose answer to everything is war and more war."

"And you honestly believe," Lafe said slowly, staring thoughtfully straight at Tashikov, who finally looked away, "that America lives and functions entirely in a vacuum: that no one else in this world commits aggression or upsets the peace of the world: that no one else in this world ever does anything to bait or provoke us: that no one else in this world is ever guilty of anything detrimental to peace: that we have no genuine interest whatsoever in preserving peace: that our only motive is conquest and aggression: that it is all the bad old United States, exclusively and entirely the only evil-doer in all the world." He turned to stare at his seat-mate. "You honestly and truly believe that."

"Well," Lord Maudulayne said, looking down and shuffling the papers on the desk in front of him. "Well! Naturally not. Naturally not! Only fools believe that. But I do believe, and my Government believe, that in recent decades it has become too easy for you to resort to force."

"*Easy* for us, my God?" Cullee demanded. "With the number of Americans we've had killed and the amount of money we've spent and the way we've spread ourselves around the world to pick up where you left off? *Easy* for us? Oh, come on, now!"

"Nonetheless," Claude said stubbornly, "the face you show to the world is the face of war and the policy you follow is the willingness to make war. And you frighten the world, and you accomplish little."

"All we accomplish," Cullee said bitterly, "is to save you all from being overrun. And what in the hell thanks do we get for it?"

"Why shouldn't we go our own way?" Lafe asked quietly. "What do our friends—strange friends!—do to help us? Why shouldn't we just follow our own policy, for our own self-interest, do what we think is right *for us*, and let the rest of you sink? Is that what you'd like? Vasily over there would be very happy to take you all over if we didn't spend our lives and substance to stop him. Why should we continue to protect you? Can you think of one good reason?"

"But that's ridiculous," Lord Maudulayne said. "Now, that is ridiculous."

"No, really," Lafe said. "I'm not kidding. I want to know."

"If it isn't obvious," Lord Maudulayne said coldly, "I'm afraid I can't explain it."

"Somehow, Claude," Cullee said dryly, "we just knew you couldn't."

"I believe we have a session to attend to," the British Ambassador said, still coldly, as the Ambassador of Cymru, this month's President of the Council, gaveled for order.

"I believe we do," Cullee said with a sudden attentiveness. Cymru said in his inimitable accent,

"The Council is now seized of SC/127, introduced by France and the Soviet Union, on the situation in Gorotoland. I believe the People's Free Government of Gorotoland has petitioned to address the Council, and I believe"—he peered around brightly with his sharply twinkling little eyes—"I believe that government's special envoy is ready, is it?"

"Is it, indeed," Lafe remarked as Prince Obifumatta, gorgeous in his giant height and flaming robes, stepped suddenly into the excited, buzzing room and came with his long, loping stride to take his seat at the table. "Yes, yes. Is it, indeed."

"Now, Mr. Presiding Officer, Mr. Temporary Speaker or whatever you are, sir," Jawbone Swarthman cried as a packed and worried House began consideration of *A Bill to Further Curb Acts Against the Public Order and Welfare*, "now, Mr. Presider, sir, I want to state right here and now at the beginning that this bill, this measure that comes here under this pious title, sir, is repugnant to every instinct of a democratic people! Yes, sir, it is plumb, downright repugnant, and this House ought to toss this crazy ol' bill right out the window, sir, I submit it just should toss this ol' bill right—"

"Your Honor," Bob Leffingwell said, and from his comfortable smile no outsider could ever have guessed the mood or the conditions in which he and Tommy had faced each other last, "I think I too shall avail myself of your kindness to the aged, and remain seated. It is not that I don't value the dramatic advantages of being on my feet, and perhaps may avail myself of them before my time is up, but I don't really feel, Your Honor, that a sound case needs too many dramatics.

"I do believe," he said quietly (George Harrison Wattersill and Roger P. Croy shifted in their chairs and looked suitably superior), "that the case I represent is sound.

"You are aware, Your Honor, that it has been a good many years since I actively practiced at law. And yet it seemed to me that this was an issue in which a certain personal dedication might overcome any slight rustiness. It is also an issue in which common sense, a modicum of fairness, and a reasonable care for the habits and customs of this democracy, would seem to equip almost any decent citizen to argue this side of it."

("Throwing a few knives today, isn't he?" the Arkansas *Gazette* whispered to the Newark *News*. "And Georgie Wattersill isn't?" the *News* inquired.)

"We are confronted here with an attempt, quite blatant, to make use of Your Honor and this Court simply as mechanisms to secure a political advantage. It is quite clear that those who are manipulating"—and again he ignored the restlessness of George Wattersill and Roger Croy, except to repeat calmly—"those who are manipulating—the very narrow majority which existed in the National Committee yesterday are not really interested in appealing against the temporary injunction. They are here in the obvious hope that Your Honor will overturn the appeal and thereby uphold the injunction, which would, of course, paralyze the Committee until such time, possibly much later in the summer, when the pending suit might be decided in the court below.

"But, Your Honor, even if there should be a swift decision by the court below, say even within a week, directing the Committee to reconvene the convention, is anyone so naïve as to think that the sentiment within the Committee which I represent" (At 'Vagaries' Orrin said softly, "Good man.") "and am proud to represent—would not immediately appeal from that decision? And there we would be again, with who knows what delays then, and who knows when there might be a chance, then, to select candidates?

"No, Your Honor. This is the time it will be decided, right here and now, once and forever. Consequently we on our side intend to be brief and, I hope, both pertinent and constructive.

"As Your Honor truly says, this is a matter of overriding importance to the country and the world, and to judge it fairly it must be placed in context. Context of a most bitter convention, lately concluded, at which the delegates freely made their choice" ("By damn," 'Gage Shelby remarked to Sue-Dan Hamilton at DEFY headquarters downtown, "listen to that man lie.") "context of the tragic and unexplained death of the late President of the United States—context of a war"—and his choice of the singular was not lost upon the world—"context of carefully managed and completely unprincipled violence through the country and in this capital—context of other recent tragic events"—and he stared thoughtfully at the little Justice, who for just a second looked sad, worried and harassed, but the camera did not swing to him quite quickly enough to catch it—"with which Your Honor has lately been made familiar."

("Now, what do you suppose he means by that?" the AP asked of no one in particular.)

"It is against this background that the appeal, the injunction, and the case below, must all be considered.

"Now, Your Honor," he said, and his aspect was still calm, comfortable and relaxed as though he were at his own poolside, "we do not intend to dwell upon facts which are known to everyone. The basic fact is, of course, that the convention, freely and regularly called, legally bound at every point by its own rules of procedure, did in fact select the late Harley M. Hudson as its candidate for President and the Secretary of State, Mr. Knox, as its candidate for Vice President. No challenge can ethically or legally be laid against that proceeding. The convention was open, democratic, and free" ("Oh, come *on!*"

408

the general director of the *Post* exclaimed. "Come *on*."
"George will take care of it," Walter Dobius promised.)
"as all American Presidential nominating conventions,"
Bob Leffingwell went on blandly, "are open, democratic,
and free, and I think that too can be stipulated on the
face of it. Certainly to open up a line of argument to the
contrary," he said softly, "would be to force us to produce
evidence of various attempts to intimidate, harass,
threaten, and—in the case of the daughter-in-law of the
Secretary of State—actually to beat a pregnant girl and
cause her to lose her baby. This would not, perhaps, be
a profitable line of argument for opposing counsel to pursue."

Again George Wattersill and Roger P. Croy bristled
and stirred, but there was something about the way they
did it which indicated that this physical restlessness for
the record would be their first and final comment on that
particular point.

"It is clear, Your Honor," Bob Leffingwell continued,
not even bothering to look at them, "that the convention
faithfully reflected its own majority opinion as conventions do. There is no reason now, except political adventurism, to try to establish the thesis that the opinion of
the majority of the delegates somehow was not their
opinion, or that their opinion has substantially changed
as a result of the tragic and unexplained death of President Hudson.

"Therefore, there is no reason or need to reconvene
the convention. More fundamental than that, there is not
only no reason to reconvene, there is no authority whatsoever, vested in this Court, the court below, any court
or any body of any nature whatsoever, to direct, com-

409

mand or require the National Committee to do so.

"The National Committee, Your Honor, stands supreme under its own rules and regulations. If it wishes to reconvene the convention, it may do so. If it wishes to dispense with that procedure and reserve to itself the choice of new nominees, it may do so. Each method is democratic, each guarantees a free democratic vote, each provides exactly the same democratic choice.

"Now, Your Honor, *if* one method were dictatorial and the other democratic, there would be a genuine argument. But both are democratic. The sole difference lies in the number of votes to be cast, and even that is for all practical purposes a quibble, since in choosing nominees under these circumstances, the votes of members of the Committee are given a weight equal to the number of actual delegate votes cast by their states in the convention.

"So, Your Honor, the choice is equal, and it is a choice which the Committee has a perfect and unchallengeable right to make. *The matter is entirely in its discretion.* It is a private body, not subject to the jurisdiction of any authority as long as it abides by its rules, faithfully conducts the party business according to those rules, and does not engage in any financial malpractices in the use of party funds.

"No evidence has yet been presented here, nor, I suspect, can be presented, supporting any challenge to the Committee on any of these three points.

"What the opposing side seeks to do by engaging in this action, and what its argument, I venture to predict, will attempt to support, is to establish the entirely new thesis that the National Committee not only can be held

410

accountable for misdeeds under its own rules—which is not in dispute—but can actually be forced to choose between two options which its own rules clearly and absolutely confer upon it with no restrictions whatsoever.

"True, Your Honor, the Committee under its rules is required to select new nominees in this situation. This it *must* do, and if, for instance, it were to gather again tomorrow and vote that it would adjourn and go home without selecting anyone, then, certainly, we would be here side by side with our friends across the table seeking an injunction. And an injunction could be fairly laid.

"But that is not the issue. The Committee *is* going to select new nominees. That is as certain as that we sit here. The sole issue is our friends' contention that, being given two options by its own rules—rules freely adopted, freely established and sanctified by many years of unchallenged and successful operation—the Committee can arbitrarily be forced to choose one of them.

"This, we submit, is bad logic and disastrous doctrine. We do not say it is bad law, for no law has ever touched this point. Nor, we submit can it touch it, as long as both options open to the Committee guarantee an equally democratic selection of nominees."

("It's just that some democratic options are more democratic than other democratic options," the Boston *Herald* whispered to the Newark *News*.)

"That in essence, Your Honor," Bob Leffingwell said, sitting back and stretching his legs comfortably, "is our case. We will reserve the remainder of our time on argument, for the time being."

Mr. Wattersill?" Tommy said promptly.

"Yes, Your Honor," George Harrison Wattersill replied,

and once more he was on his feet, flexing his arms and shooting his cuffs like some dandified prize fighter. "We shall now show that opposing counsel's arguments are unfounded, untenable, undemocratic, and hostile to the hopes and wishes of the nation and the world."

"Mr. Chairman," Prince Obi said in his clipped, British-African accent, looking like some gorgeous elongated beetle in his flowing robes against the somber business suits around the table, "distinguished delegates to the United Nations Security Council: you are all aware of the sad result of American aggression in my country. American imperialism, intervening in a situation which was none of America's business, has temporarily halted the advance of the liberation of the free people of Gorotoland.

"American imperialists have won a battle.

"Only if your distinguished body concedes them an easy victory will they have won the war.

"I am here today, distinguished gentlemen, to appeal to the collective conscience of mankind against this vicious, inexcusable, horrible American imperialistic aggression. But more than that"—he stared straight at Cullee Hamilton, who returned the look with an impassive distaste—"I am here to appeal to the collective conscience of the American people at a moment when America is deciding whether she will choose a man of peace or a man of war to guide her destinies.

"Yes, in this fateful moment I am here to say to America: give us your man of peace! Give us your statesman! Give us your great leader who wishes to save mankind from further war and trouble!

412

"Do not give us—your warmonger! Do not give us—your imperialist! Do not give us—your world criminal, who has launched aggression and encourages aggression—and expands aggression—and separates America from all her friends around the world—because he loves aggression—because he loves war—because he loves hatred and bitterness—and horrible things—against innocent people!"

"Oh, Christ," Lafe murmured with a tired disgust. "Everybody's in the act aren't they?"

"Why not?" Lord Maudulayne inquired dryly at his side. "You're in everybody else's."

"Now, Mr. Temporary Speaker, sir, or whatever you are," Jawbone Swarthman cried, while the crowded House and crowded galleries chuckled, "what is the main feature of this in-ex-cu-sable bill, this monstrous ol' measure that comes in here bearin' the endorsement of the White House, though I suspect, Mr. Presider, yes, I do suspect, that somebody else had a hand in it. I do suspect that there might be what-we-used-to-have-an -expression-for in the woodpile; yes, sir, I do suspect that. And I suspect his initials are O.K., Mr. Temporary, sir, but I tell you he is *not* OK. He is not OK at all, particularly when he uses our sweet old innocent unsuspecting President—"

But this was too much for the House, and a roar of genuine laughter interrupted him.

"You may laugh," he cried undaunted, rushing on, "you may laugh now, yes, distinguished members here may give ol' Jawbone the ol' haw-*haw*, but the fact is, the fact most certainly is, that our beloved former Speaker who now by tragic fate sits in the White House could not possibly have sent us such an *evil* bill, such a *monstrous* measure, if he hadn't had Mr. O.K. hisself doing the dirty work, there, puttin' in these little bitty words and clauses that just twist and turn it and make it something this free democracy just can't stand.

"Why, I ask distinguished and honorable members, what is distinguished and honorable about this bill? Just take two clauses, here, Mr. Temporary, sir, just two: this one that says a National Riot Control Board got to be set up to approve use of any facilities within one mile of any Federal building or installation for gatherings of three or more people, for instance; and this other one that says any gathering of three or more people is illegal 'if there is obvious intent to create civil disturbance and/or riot.'

"Now, Mr. Presider, what kind of antidemocratic, anti-Constitutional stuff is that! Where's our right of peaceable assembly gone to, there, Mr. Presider, sir! Who's to decide 'intent to create civil disturbance and/or riot?' We all been writing legislation here for years, now, some of us for *many* years, and we *know* 'intent' is the hardest thing in the world to prove. We know 'intent' is the bugaboo of legislation. We *know* that, now!

"I suspect, Mr. Temporary Speaker, I suspect this is just a little ol' scare tactic, that's what it is, this whole bill, and particularly these two clauses. I don't think our sweet old President wants to do something like that to this great free country, any more than he wants to fly to Mars, now. But I suspect there's some as does, Mr. Temporary Speaker. I suspect there's one in particular does, and he's not OK, Mr. Temporary, he—is—not—OK. He wants to

414

do things to this grand old Republic that we just can't stand, Mr. Temporary, we just surely cannot stand. We all been watching on the television screens out there in the Members' Reading Room just how things going over there across the Plaza in the Court, and we just hopin', Mr. Presider, we're just hopin' they're not goin' to go in the direction of dictatorship and disaster to our democracy, like this bill which comes here initialed 'O.K.' but is *not* OK, my dear friends, it is *not* OK."

SWARTHMAN CHARGES KNOX AUTHORED GAG BILL AS PART OF DICTATORSHIP DRIVE, the headlines said. "Good *God*," the Secretary of State said with an absolute weary disgust when they were brought him in his office a few minutes later.

"Your Honor," George Harrison Wattersill said in a tone of patient forbearance, "this Court and the world have been treated here this afternoon to a rather extraordinary legal—or should I say, quasi-legal—or parti-legal —or rusti-legal"—Bob Leffingwell grinned amicably and gave him an ironic little bow—"tergiversation on the issues involved with, and pertinent to, this appeal.

"Now, my friend across seems to have the idea that the circumstance in which we meet can be completely ignored. He talks much of context, but the most important context of all—the context of peace or war, democracy or dictatorship, he ignores completely.

"We submit, Your Honor, that quasi-legal niceties must not be allowed to confuse the basic and overriding issue—and that is the issue of the kind of country we are, and want to be. It is all very well to talk of National Committee rules and regulations, and practices hallowed by centuries, and necessities without precedents, and all the rest of it. But the essential thing to talk about is the choices the Committee confronts.

"And contrary to my distinguished and able, if somewhat rusty, friend, the choices are not between methods of procedure, but between men.

("How's that?" the UPI whispered. "Don't interrupt the flow," the AP whispered back. "It always gets better. It's guaranteed.")

"If it were simply a matter of method, Your Honor," George Wattersill said, "we on our side might very well find ourselves in agreement, or at least willing to waive any contention. It is clear enough that in one way or another the Committee must, and will, select a candidate to take the place of the late, tragically fallen, President of the United States. This is so apparent that I am a trifle surprised"—and he paused and looked down with a quizzical, slightly pitying air at Bob Leffingwell and Bob Munson, the latter chin-on-hand with an aspect of absolutely rapt attention belied by the elaborate wink he now gave George Wattersill—"that counsel," George Wattersill continued with dignity, "should consider it so important that he must waste the time of the Court with a labored explanation of the obvious. In this—but in this only," he said graciously, "does he reveal that he has, indeed, been some time away from the law.

"But he has not been, Your Honor, away from the mainstream of American life and American politics; the whole world knows how intimately he has been involved with them. Therefore it is somewhat puzzling to find him concentrating on issues which can only be considered ancillary, instead of discussing what all know to be at the heart of this dispute, namely which method of choice of candidate will result in choice of the best candidate.

"There, I think can be found legitimate ground on which to stand and contend. If we were to accept the position of counsel for the opposing side, we should presuppose a method by which this choice is left, not to the great, open, free, democratic considerations of a convention numbering well over 1000 souls, but to a very small, very select, very—shall I say?—impressionable—"

("Better not," the President remarked with a smile to the Secretary of Defense as they watched in the Oval Room. "They won't like it.")

"—group of only 106 men and women. Now, Your Honor: if we were to accept the theory, obviously held by my distinguished opponent, that democracy improves as it is restricted, and that the fewer you extend the franchise to, the purer and finer and more effective the franchise becomes, then that would be one thing. But that is not the concept of democracy upon which the United States of America has grown great. That is the Athenian concept of democracy restricted to the few who know best for the many; and here I would say, if Your Honor would indulge me, beware of Greeks."

("Better not," the President said again. "Anotis Spirotis of Pennsylvania won't like it.")

George Harrison Wattersill looked straight into the television camera and a stern disapproval appeared upon his handsome face.

"That concept, if I may use the strong language it deserves, Your Honor, is repugnant, unworthy and downright evil. It would place an almost unthinkable, an almost omnipotent power in the hands of 106 men and women—highly intelligent men and women, yes—highly qualified men and women, yes—highly trustworthy men and women, yes—but still only 106 men and women. And that, I submit, Your Honor, is not enough for a decision so grave, upon which the fate of great states and nations, yea the great globe itself, may well depend."

("Yea!" the Boston *Herald* whispered with a cheerful grin at the Arkansas *Gazette*. "Swing it, baby!")

"I venture to state, Your Honor," George Harrison Wattersill said solemnly, "that if we could bring them before us here today, place them before this camera and the world, put them under oath in this Court, a majority of these fateful 106 would cry out, 'Nay! Torture us not! Let this dreadful cup pass from our lips! We are worthy of your trust but we wish it not! We wish to share it with our brothers and sisters of the convention! Let us recall them to aid us in this dread task!'"

"You really think they would say that," Justice Davis observed gently, and for a moment George Harrison Wattersill's mouth literally hung open. But only for a moment. Then it closed firmly, regrouped itself, and re-opened for more of the same. But it was obvious that he was shaken by the Justice's intervention, nor was he the only one. In many clever minds Tommy's quiet little comment was interpreted as a warning signal. George Wattersill took a deep breath and swiftly rearranged his strategy.

"They would, Your Honor. They would! Because they would know, as we know"—and he went into another of his famous soaring cadenzas —"as the nation knows—as the world knows—that by so doing they would be opening the door not only for a truly democratic procedure, but they would also be increasing the possibility that the man the majority of them clearly want—the man the nation clearly wants—the man the world clearly wants—could win the nomination free from the pressures which presently surround the proceedings of the 106.

"Why, Your Honor!" George Harrison Wattersill cried, and a fine, fervent indignation suffused his words. "Who anywhere on this globe who had access yesterday to television screen or radio set does not recall the tragic—the frightening—the *un-American* spectacle, if you please, that occurred at the Committee's opening session?

"Military troops with bayonets drawn and ammunition ready against their fellow citizens! The Kennedy Center, that lovely memorial filled with grace and culture, turned into an armed camp! The Commander in Chief of the armed forces, deploying his janizaries with all the shrewd skill and ruthless power of a Caesar about to conquer Rome!"

("Oh, my, Georgie," the President said. "Oh, my, oh, *my!*")

"There was your Committee, counsel!" he cried, turning suddenly upon Bob Leffingwell and flinging out an accusing finger within an inch of his nose, which of course made him visibly flinch. "There was *your* method of selecting a nominee! There was the fine, democratic atmosphere that surrounded that fine, democratic group—*cowed into submission by the show of military force!*

"Your Honor," he said, abruptly solemn, "I think that never in my lifetime have I felt that America was so close to military dictatorship as I felt yesterday when the world was shown this sad spectacle—and as I shall feel tomorrow—and the day after—and the day after—and the day after, until the sorry tale is done—unless Your Honor's ruling frees the Committee from its bondage—shows it that, yes, it has a friend, the most powerful friend that liberty has, this great Supreme Court—shows it that it need not be afraid to do what a majority of its members want—reconvene the convention so that there may be nominated the man of peace and hope whom America and the world desire!"

"Is there anything," Tommy inquired in the same quiet voice, "which prevents the Committee from making that decision of its own uninstructed will? Does it not now have that authority? Why are the injunction and the suit pending below necessary? Could this not be regarded as an attempt, as Mr. Leffingwell says, to narrow its options, foreclose its choices, restrict its freedom rather than expand it? Could you respond to that point?"

"Indeed I could, Your Honor!" George Wattersill cried. "Indeed I could! The Committee does have that option now, true enough, but"—and his voice came with a low, confidential rush, and his eyes were fixed upon the Justice's in a stark, hypnotic stare—"*it is a frightened Committee*. It is not a truly free Committee, happy and glorious in its democratic right—*it is a frightened Committee*.

"It dares not move because it knows that over it stands the Commander in Chief, his troops surrounding it, his military might brooding ominously over its deliberations.

"True, the bayonets are fixed—outward.

"True, the guns are pointed—outward.

"But, Your Honor"—and his voice became husky with emotion—"bayonets that are fixed outward—*can be turned inward*. Guns that are pointed outward—*can be turned inward*.

420

"Who knows, Your Honor"—and now he was down almost to a whisper, ominous and nerve-tingling—*"who knows when the order may be given?"*

("To use a word I practically never use," the President said slowly in the Oval Room, "what—utter—crap.")

But, WATTERSILL CHARGES PRESIDENT'S ARMED MIGHT MAY FORCE COMMITTEE TO TAKE KNOX, the headlines cried; and all over the nation, yea the great globe itself, many sincerely worried people were frightened and dismayed by the specter he had so adroitly created.

"Your Honor," George Harrison Wattersill said solemnly, "we too will reserve the balance of our time. I defer now to my distinguished friends across the table."

"Are you actually going to vote for this damned thing?" Lafe murmured to Claude Maudulayne as the Ambassador of Cymru polled the Council on the Soviet-French resolution to condemn U.S. aggression in Gorotoland and urge dispatch of a UN force to reopen the fighting.

"Abstain!" the British Ambassador said clearly.

"Very well," Lafe snapped with an equal clarity that rang across the crowded room. "The United States votes No."

"On this vote," Cymru said, "there are eleven votes Yes, one abstention and one No. Since the No is cast by the United States, the resolution is defeated, is it?"

"Is it," Lafe agreed. "What further surprises do you have for America this afternoon, Mr. President?"

"The Ambassador of Panama," Cymru announced, not without a certain relish, as Felix Labaiya-Sofra came soberly down the aisle to take his seat, his small, trim presence and dark, perfectly tailored business suit forming a nice contrast to giant Obifumatta, glittering and coruscating in the light beside him.

"The Council is now seized of SC/128," Cymru said, "introduced by Britain, France and the Soviet Union, to protest the proposed blockade of Panama by the Government of the United States and to pledge all efforts of the United Nations and of individual member states to exercise their rights upon the seas with respect to said proposed blockade. The Ambassador of Panama and President of the Government of the Panamanian People's Liberation Movement has requested permission to address the Council. If agreeable he will do so, is it?"

"No objections here," Cullee said as there was a general nodding around the circle. "What must be," he added with a wink at the Ambassador of South Africa, who winked back, "must be, is it?"

"Mr. President," Stanley Danta said, and the emotion in his voice brought an instant hush to the crowded Senate and galleries, "it is, as you know, with a special interest that I rise to speak on the pending bill.

"Normally, I might regard with some misgivings a bill 'to further curb acts against the public order and welfare.' But, Mr. President"—and he passed a hand that visibly trembled across his forehead in a slow, bone-weary gesture—"I have had more occasion than most to appreciate the vicious things that are alive in this country today.

"I will not," he said, while his colleagues listened intently, "burden the Senate at this point with a recapitulation of recent events. Suffice it to say that you all know what my"—his voice threatened to break for a second, but he went on—"what my daughter has been through. Nothing could more clearly indicate the necessity for any and all measures that will curb once and for all the beast which has been let loose out of the gutters of America to prey upon decent, innocent people.

"Mr. President, the pending measure is, perhaps, drawn too broadly in some sections, and it may well be that the Senate will wish to examine the bill, as introduced, very closely, and perhaps amend it. We may wish to do the same thing with the House version when it is passed and reaches us. But the essential purpose, I think, is something we must come to grips with, and something we must take action upon.

"There is too much, Mr. President," he said, and again the emotion was very close to the surface, "there is too much going on these days in America which is alien to our traditions and our spirit, which is desperately dangerous to all our laws and stability, but which is more than this: it is simply and truly evil, and as such it must be rooted out of our country if our country is to survive.

"We all know, Mr. President, that these things exist in the subterranean depths of the human spirit, but we also know that if society is to survive, these things must be curbed and driven back and driven out. All societies have known that; all intelligent men have known that, through recorded time. The measure of the decline of nations can be found in the rate at which lawlessness and viciousness were allowed to come to the top. When they got there, it was all over, except for the dying throes, which may have gone on for a few more years or even decades. Once the process was allowed to get out of hand, no society has ever succeeded in reversing it. The end has been inevitable. It will be here, too, unless we stop it while we can.

"Now, as I say, Mr. President, I do not know that all features of this bill are desirable; I rather suspect, from a quick first reading, that they are not. It would be a rare piece of legislation if they were. But I do know that the essential purpose, to curb this growing evil of deliberate, coordinated, vicious violence which is aimed at the very destruction of America itself, is one which we must endorse and support.

"We have means, through fair debate and open discussion and public consideration, to change the things in our country and our policy which this violence claims to be trying to correct. These means are slow at times, but they are orderly: they preserve what must be preserved in any human society unless it is all to go down, namely stability.

"I for one, Mr. President," he said quietly, "do not want it all to go down. I want it to remain stable, for the sake of my country and for all those I hold dear. I want my"—he hesitated, the emotion returned, his voice trembled but he finished firmly—"I want my grandchildren to have a decent country to live in, and to know all the wonderful things about it that we have known, underneath the sad things and the unhappy things which are here. Because the wonderful things are here also, and more of them, if we can only save them.

"And we must, Mr. President.

"We must."

And he started to sit down. But before he could do so a familiar, near-psychotic whine came from a desk near the back of the Senate, and at once the tension in the room shot up as Senators turned to see their most unmanageable colleague standing in the aisle calling on a rising note, "Mr. President! Mr. President! *Mr. President!*"

Lacey Pollard of Georgia, in the chair, looked about desperately for someone else to recognize, but the Senate had been caught short: no one else appeared to be ready.

"The Senator from Wyoming," Lacey said in a voice which made no attempt to conceal his impatient annoyance. Fred Van Ackerman of course took him up on it at once.

"Now, Mr. President," he said sharply, "the Chair knows he has no right to recognize me in that tone of voice. The Chair knows—"

"The Chair knows he has recognized you," Lacey Pollard said. "Does the Senator wish to speak or does he not?"

'Yes, I do!" Fred said angrily. "But I will say to the Chair that I resent this impatient, offhand, disparaging manner in which he recognized me. The Chair is required by the rules of the Senate, I believe, to show a decent courtesy to a member—"

"There is no such rule," Lacey snapped. "Senators get the courtesy they earn. The Senator from Wyoming doesn't have much in the bank. Does the Senator wish to speak on the pending bill?"

"Yes, the Senator wishes to speak on the pending bill!" Fred said with a sneering mimicry. "He wishes to ask the *distinguished* Senator from Connecticut if he will yield for a question?"

"Don't do it, Stanley," Johnny DeWilton of Vermont

said in a low but clearly audible voice, and the galleries laughed. At once Senator Van Ackerman was off.

"I am not asking for smart-aleck comments from other Senators, I will say to the distinguished Senator from Vermont! I am asking the Senator from Connecticut if he will yield. Does the Senator yield? Does he? I am asking!"

For a moment Senator Danta hesitated; and then, without looking at Fred, but straight ahead at the Chair, he spoke in a cold and measured voice.

"If the Senator expects love, affection, admiration and respect if I yield to him," he said, "then I am afraid he will be disappointed, since I regard the Senator as being one of those responsible for what happened to my daughter." There was a gasp from the galleries, a stirring in the Senate. He went on inflexibly. "And I do not know what else. If he is willing to settle for a minimal courtesy, I shall talk to him, yes."

"Very clever," Fred said bitterly. "Very clever. The Senator is so busy making points about his daughter—"

"My God, have you no decency at all?" Stanley Danta cried, swinging around then and staring at him, as so many of his colleagues had at one time or another, as though he were looking at an insane person, as perhaps he was. "What *are* you composed of, anyway?"

"I am 'composed of,'" Fred said, perversely and characteristically becoming quieter as his victim became louder, "a United States Senator who is deeply concerned about this vicious and inexcusable bill which would take this country a long way toward dictatorship. What is the Senator concerned about, I will ask him, except trying to impugn the motives and integrity of those who disagree with his hysterical endorsement of this monstrous and inexcusable gag bill?"

Senator DeWilton got up quickly, came down the aisle and slid into the seat beside Senator Danta. "Don't let him throw you off balance," he cautioned softly, but Stanley was too upset to pay attention.

"I am interested in trying to save this country," he snapped, "which is something I sometimes think is rather far from the Senator's mind!"

"Mr. President," Fred Van Ackerman said calmly. "Now, Mr. President. I submit that the Senator's language—"

"The Senator from Connecticut will take his seat," Lacey Pollard said promptly, for there was obviously nothing for it but to go through the standard formula used when tempers grew too hot and language unparliamentary. Stanley sat down, grim-faced.

"Mr. President," Johnny DeWilton said, "I move that the Senator from Connecticut be allowed to proceed in order."

"The Senator will proceed in order," Lacey Pollard said, and Stanley got up again.

"I apologize to the Chair," he said, controlling his temper with an obvious effort, "but I have made perfectly clear that I have misgivings about some aspects of this bill. But the main thrust of it namely to control the violence growing in the country—violence with which, Mr. President"—and for a mild man, his tone became savagely sarcastic—"I think I may safely say the Senator and his associates have had some connection—I am one hundred per cent for, I will say to the Senator and I make no apologies for it.

"Why is this bill here, anyway, Mr. President?" he inquired with a sudden exasperation. "It is here because the violence is here, not the other way around. Stop trying to confuse the issue! Now did the Senator have a question to ask me, or was his request that I yield, a while back, just a typical maneuver?"

"*Careful*," John DeWilton murmured, but this time Fred chose to ignore it.

"Mr. President," he said blandly, "of course I had a question. To wit: is the Senator aware that this bill contains two very odd clauses, the first of which would establish a National Riot Control Board to approve use of 'any facilities within one mile of any Federal building or installation' for gatherings of three or more people, and the other defining as illegal any gathering of three or more 'if there is obvious intent to create civil disturbance and/or riot?'"

"I am aware, I will say to the Senator," Stanley Danta said. "I think I have covered them in my previous remarks."

"Does the Senator think that this bill, with these clauses, when taken in conjunction with the enormous military display the President is putting on at the Kennedy Center—"

"Now the Senator is taking his cues from television," Stanley said, and again there was a titter from the galleries.

"Oh, the Senator can scoff," Senator Van Ackerman said softly. "The Senator can sneer and joke and poke fun. But the fact remains, our good friend Mr. Wattersill—"

"Not mine," Senator Danta snapped, and the riffle of laughter spread across the floor as well.

428

"—has a point, you know. He does have a point. Does the Senator think that this bill, taken in conjunction with the military display put on by the President, indicates the beginning of a real dictatorship in the United States of America? Doesn't he think possibly that this is an evil as great as any he professes to see in a little genuine protest against our stupid and foredoomed foreign policy?"

"What genuine protest?" Senator Danta demanded. "If you mean the organized riots and carefully controlled violence whose only aim is the deliberate destruction of this Republic—"

"Mr. President!" Senator Van Ackerman cried.

"*I have the floor,*" Stanley Danta said angrily. "Whose vicious and only aim is the deliberate destruction of this Republic—is that what you mean when you say 'genuine protest,' Senator? How naïve can you be? Except that you aren't naïve, are you? You aren't naïve at all. You know exactly what these people are doing, because you are one of them. So much for 'genuine protest.'

"I yield the floor."

And he sat down abruptly. There was a little ripple of laughter and applause through the galleries, and at once Fred Van Ackerman was off again.

"Mr. President!" he cried, and when Lacey Pollard gave him the floor:

"Mr. President, listen to them laugh. Listen to the great American boobs laugh!" There was a sudden hiss and at once his voice sailed up into its high, psychotic register. "Yes, Mr. President, laugh and hiss, laugh and hiss! That's all some people know how to do, but thank God, Mr. President, they are few and getting fewer in America! Thank God we do have genuine protests, by sincere and troubled citizens who want to stop this insane policy of war, war and more war! Thank God there are great patriotic leaders like the great Governor of California, whose nomination is even now being assured by the Supreme Court of the United States—"

"Mr. President," said Powell Hanson of North Dakota, but Fred swung around and shot him a savage glare.

"No, Mr. President, I will *not* yield to the Senator from North Dakota! The Senator from North Dakota is typical of all the blind, mixed-up Americans who follow the present incompetent incumbent of the White House and his guide and mentor, the Secretary of State. The Secretary of State! Why, Mr. President—"

"Mr. President," Powell Hanson said loudly as he sat down, "what about Helen-Anne Carrew, who was buried today?"

Fred stopped short, and for a few moments there was a shocked and startled silence in the chamber. Then Senator Van Ackerman smiled, a savage, humorless grimace.

"So typical, Mr. President," he said. "So typical of all the elements who are supporting this crazy, dictatorial attempt to place iron military bonds on this country and prevent free, genuine protest! Drag in a name, Mr. President! Hint something ominous, Mr. President! Create a sinister atmosphere, Mr. President! Imply all sorts of who-knows-what, Mr. President! All right," he said, and his tone became heavily sarcastic, "I will say to the Senator: what about Helen-Anne Carrew? Does he know something we ought to know?"

"No, Mr. President, if the Senator will yield," Powell Hanson said, "I just wanted to know what you know about her? She was buried today. I thought the Senator might be able to enlighten us, that's all."

"How should I know?" Fred inquired contemptuously. "I thought she was just a reporter who got onto the wrong story. It happens. It's probably going to happen more from now on, if the press gets curious about the wrong things."

"Is the Senator threatening the press?" Senator Hanson asked sharply, looking up at the Press Gallery above the Chair. "Is that the next step?"

"I'm not threatening anything," Fred Van Ackerman said, still with the contemptuous smile, "and I'd suggest the Senator stop trying to raise bugaboos and red herrings here. Yes, Mr. President," he cried, and his voice suddenly shot up again, the moment passed, the ominous undercurrents were pushed aside, he concluded as he wanted to conclude, "I suggest to the Senator, and the Senator from Connecticut, and all Senators, stop trying to confuse the issue and concentrate on what is best for this country, for a change! I suggest we kill this monstrous, dictatorial gag bill whose only purpose is to further the purposes of Orrin Knox and his captive President, which all decent Americans protest and deplore! I suggest we fight dictatorship before it's too late, Mr. President! Now's the time to do it, not after pious Orrin and his captive President have slapped it on us!"

("I wonder what he meant by that reference to the press?" The Greatest Publication murmured to the *New Republic*, a trifle uneasily, as they went out together to the telephones. The *New Republic* shrugged and grinned. "Who knows? That guy never makes sense except on the Big Issues. But he's So Right on them." "Yeah," the G.P. agreed, and relaxed.

(VAN ACKERMAN FANS DICTATOR CHARGE,

they headlined the story he telephoned in. UPHOLDS RIGHT OF PROTEST AGAINST ADMINISTRATION WAR POLICIES.

("Earlier," the story said, in one short paragraph toward the end, "Senate Majority Whip Stanley Danta of Connecticut warned of 'lawlessness and viciousness' which he said were endangering the values and stability of American society.")

"Mr. President, members of the Security Council," Felix Labaiya said in his quietly efficient voice, its accent modified into a liquid, only slightly Spanish, version of English by his years of diplomatic assignment in Washington and New York, "it is my purpose here today, as it has been the purpose of my valued friend and colleague the legitimate head of the government of Gorotoland"—Obifumatta bowed gravely—"to call to the attention of the United Nations and the world the iniquitous crimes and unforgivable aggression of the United States of America.

"I do not in any way, gentlemen of the Council, seek to minimize or diminish the gravity of United States crimes against Gorotoland. Yet I think that perhaps we will all agree that in Panama the crime is even greater and more dangerous to the peace of the world, because in my country the United States is issuing, and has issued, a challenge to the sovereign rights of all nations to free and unhindered passage of one of the indispensable tradeways of the world.

"Not only has the effect of the United States attempt to overthrow my government been to close off the Canal temporarily but effectively to the free passage of the

432

maritime nations of the world, but now it is proposed by the"—and for the first time he raised his eyes from the notes he had placed before him and stared directly at Lafe and Cullee—"temporary Administration of the government of the United States"—he dropped his eyes to his notes again—"that a blockade be instituted to seal off my country from access by the sea. This universal denial of the rights of maritime nations to free passage upon the seas, and incidentally but no less importantly to free passage of the Canal, is to be instituted, apparently, as a means of overthrowing my government.

"Other means," he said, and at his tone there was a little rush of agreeing laughter from the crowded galleries and from a number of delegations at the table, "appear to have failed.

"What this new move contemplates, as my friends from Britain, France and the Soviet Union have shown themselves vividly aware in the pending resolution, is to most blatantly and ruthlessly violate international law and to propose to close unilaterally the seas upon which all maritime nations, and indeed all nations, have an historic and absolute right.

"This, I think," he said quietly, "makes it even graver than a ruthless, but in a strange sense conventional, attempt to strangle the Government of the People's Liberation Movement of Panama.

"Mr. President and members of the Council, the PLM is well-equipped to withstand any such attempt. We have means of getting supplies which are well-known to the world, and to the United States. It is no secret that we are receiving assistance overland—overland but underground," he said with a smile that again brought laughter from his friends around the room, "if I may employ the curious but wonderful English language in all its delightful contradiction—as well as supplies by airlift from elsewhere in Latin America and the Caribbean. Our good friends in Cuba, in particular," he said with a bow to the Cuban Ambassador, who nodded and smiled approvingly, "are particularly helpful."

("And where Cuba gets her supplies," Lafe murmured to Cullee, "we can never guess." "In the curious but wonderful warlike way of peace-loving people's governments," Cullee agreed.)

"Mr. President" Felix said, "the PLM will get along. We have managed now, with reasonable success, to withstand the assaults of the United States for approximately two months. During that time our many friends around the world have come valiantly and unstintingly to our assistance. We can hold out. Even with the blockade, we can hold out. But I wonder, Mr. President and members of the Council, whether the world can hold out against the arbitrary, unilateral decision of the temporary Administration of the government of the United States to establish an illegal and completely unprincipled ban upon world passage of the seas. That is the consideration which should, and I am sure does, govern delegates as they approach this resolution this afternoon.

"Mr. President," he said, and something about his change of tone brought an even more attentive mood upon the room, "there is one other matter upon which I might make some comment. In the past, as we all know, there have been instances in which representatives of foreign states have commented directly or indirectly upon the United States political scene. Such comments, which the United States has always chosen to regard as offensive if not downright hostile intervention, have perhaps not been warranted or right.

"But, Mr. President and members of the Council, the United States occupies in the world today such a position of power to do good or, as in the case of my country, evil that we cannot sit idly by while the internal politics of the United States threaten the peace and well-being of the world.

"My brother-in-law," he said blandly, and since they all knew that Patsy's divorce action was in its final stages and that his relationship with Ted Jason was accordingly tenuous at best, the term brought some amused stirring from his audience, "my brother-in-law is, as you know, a candidate for the Presidential nomination of his party. I will not pretend," he added with a smile that told them it was all right to laugh, so many did, "that my personal relationships with the Jason family are of the best at this moment. Nonetheless, Mr. President"—and his tone became somber—"the selection of a candidate for President of the United States is so important to the world at this particular juncture that I cannot refrain from comment.

"We all know the situation as it presently stands. The one constant factor in two Administrations, now, has been the Secretary of State, Mr. Knox. There have been two Presidents but in Foggy Bottom there has been only Mr. Knox. It is not an exaggeration, I think, to say that the war and aggression policies of the United States Government have been for a year and a half, now, the war and aggression policies of Orrin Knox.

"Now, Mr. President, Mr. Knox is a brilliant and able, and to those of us who have had some personal contact with him over the years, a likable man as well. But," he said gravely, "on any basis on which peace-loving men can judge him, he is a danger to the world.

"It is my earnest hope, Mr. President and members of the Council, that the proceedings now going on at this moment in the Supreme Court in Washington, proceedings which all of us have watched and will continue to watch as the afternoon progresses, will permit a free and democratic selection of a candidate by the convention originally called for that purpose.

"I am confident that if that is the case, my brother-in-law will be selected. Thereby the peace of the world will be saved."

("*Jesus!*" Lafe murmured. Claude Maudulayne looked a quizzical "Well?" but did not quite say it.)

"Mr. President and members of the Council," Felix concluded quietly, "I commend to you the British-French-Soviet resolution. We should pass it as a stern warning to the announced aggressive intention of the temporary Administration of the Government of the United States to institute a unilateral, illegal blockade against the right of free passage upon the seas.

"I waive consecutive translation."

"The next speaker on my list," the Ambassador of Cymru said, "is the Union of Soviet Socialist Republics."

Vasily Tashikov leaned forward, sharp little black eyes snapping, indignation and contempt in every line of his chunky little body.

"Simultaneous translation, please," he said in Russian. "Mr. President! Members of the Security Council! Today we are seized with the question of ruthless armed aggression by the United States against freedom of the seas and the small, struggling—but destined to be triumphant, Mr. President, destined to be triumphant!—People's Liberation Movement in Panama. Tomorrow we may be seized with U.S. aggression against the world. The time to stop it is *now*, Mr. President, *now*. Otherwise we shall fall one by one, like dominoes, before this ravenous, imperialistic, aggressive power.

"Mr. President and members of the Council, my government will not waste many words upon these Orrin Knox-style warmongers. We share the contempt of the world for their horrible actions in Gorotoland, which this Council would have condemned just a few minutes ago—in fact, which all but two members of the Council did condemn. The United States, by its inexcusable use of the veto, evaded the formal condemnation which its actions deserve. But the judgment of the Council is clear.

"We share the universal contempt for the United States for what it has done in Gorotoland, but even more we share the contempt for its vicious and worthless attempt to blockade the high seas. Mr. President and delegates, the Soviet navy now sails all those seas, from one end of the earth to the other. The days when warmongers in the United States could ignore the Soviet navy are gone, Mr. President. While they slept we built and while they pretended for their own comfort that their eyes did not see what their noses could smell, we entered their oceans. And now we are upon them all. And we do not propose, Mr. President"—and the translator's tone faithfully became as sarcastic in English as his was in Russian—"we do not intend to permit the dying naval power of the United States to dictate to the rising naval power of the Soviet Union.

"We say flatly to the warmongering imperialist aggressors of the United States, Mr. President, we say to Mr. Knox and all his friends: do not try this foolishly dangerous blockade. Do not try to cripple the Soviet Union on the high seas. The days when you could bluff us back from Cuba are gone! The days when you could bluff us out of the Mediterranean are gone! We are here, America! And here"—his voice dropped dramatically—"we stay."

He shifted in his chair to stare straight at Lafe and Cullee, who stared impassively back.

"Mr. President and members of the Council: we urge adoption of this resolution. We warn against vetoes of it. Vetoes are undemocratic. They are against the spirit of the United Nations—"

("How many have they used?" Cullee asked Lafe. "Three hundred or so," Lafe told Cullee. They grinned cheerfully at Tashikov, who glared ostentatiously and became even more emphatic.)

"Vetoes are useless. Vetoes, Mr. President, are a Mr. Knox trick. Mr. Knox started these wars, Mr. Knox would veto his way out of them. We must not let him, Mr. President. We must educate Mr. Knox, who will soon be beaten, who will soon be a discard of history, that vetoes are no good. As Mr. Knox himself is no good.

"My government, too, Mr. President, hopes Mr. Knox will soon be forgotten. My government, too, hopes Governor Jason will be selected. It would be nice, Mr. President," he said with an elaborate sarcasm mimicked by the translator, "to deal with a peaceful United States government, for a change. The world has suffered enough from the other kind!"

438

There was a frenzy of applause from the audience, and he looked up, smiled and applauded vigorously in return.

"I am authorized, Mr. President"—an aide sitting behind him slipped into his hand a sheet of paper which he placed on the table—"on behalf of my government, the government of the French Republic and the Government of the United Kingdom, to make the following statement:

"'Irrespective of the outcome of the vote today in the Security Council and irrespective of any action the United States may take with regard to its threatened blockade of the Government of the People's Liberation Movement of Panama, the Government of the U.S.S.R., the Government of the United Kingdom and the Government of the French Republic, jointly and severally declare:

"'The principle of free navigation of the high seas is inviolate and must be preserved at all times.

"'Our governments can accept no infringement or modification of this principle in any extent or degree.

"'Any attempt to infringe or modify this principle will be met with appropriate action.'

"Mr. President and members of the Council, my government urges a favorable vote upon the pending resolution. But it also calls the attention of the United States to the statement I have just read."

And he sat back, his little eyes gleaming, his expression triumphant as the audience broke into a murmurous, approving confusion.

"Members of the Council," the Ambassador of Cymru said, "I find that there are no further speakers on my list—"

"Aren't you and Raoul going to speak?" Cullee asked.

"No," Lord Maudulayne said quietly.

"You're actually going to let him speak for you," Lafe said in disbelief.

"For the time being."

"A strange day for Britain," Cullee remarked.

"Stranger still for America," Claude could not resist.

"Mr. President!" Lafe said, raising his hand as Cymru was about to call for the vote.

"The distinguished delegate of the United States," Cymru said.

"Mr. President," Lafe said, "I shall not take long to respond to the mouthings of the self-interested and the ravings of the subverters of peace. (Tashikov turned his back with a great show of indignation, and side by side Felix and Obifumatta straightened in their seats and stared with an affronted anger.) It will not take long to present the position of the United States, and to offer the proposal my government has instructed me to make to the world.

"Why is there talk of blockade, Mr. President? Because the United States finds that those who profess to be its friends—at such times," he said dryly, "as the friends find they need help, financial or military—are now, as always, helping those whose attacks upon world peace and stability the United States feels it must oppose if world peace and stability are to be preserved.

"My government has tried patiently for many years, Mr. President, to point out the need for collective action to maintain the peace of the world. Much lip service has been paid to the idea by members of this organization. Every time it has come down to a matter of actually doing something about it, old friends have turned tail and run. Not only have they turned tail and run," he repeated calmly as the British Ambassador fidgeted beside him, "but they have pitched in and given aid and comfort to the enemies of the United States and the enemies of world peace.

"On various occasions in the past, for various reasons having to do with an oversensitivity to world opinion and the subtler realms of self-paralyzed national will, the United States has permitted this situation to continue. This time we happen to have in office in Washington an Administration which will not.

"The distinguished delegate from Panama says his rebel government has been able to 'withstand the assaults' of the United States for two months. Is he, or anyone, Mr. President, so naïve as to think that those 'assaults' have represented the full strength of the United States? That is nonsense, Mr. President, and he knows it. There has just been an example in Gorotoland of the application of the full strength of the United States. The Administration—the 'temporary Administration,' if it satisfies something in the delegate to use that locution—decided it was going to finish the business quickly. It put in the necessary strength and the business is finished—despite," he added acidly as Prince Obi glared, "the curious relics of the battle who still appear to be drifting about on the international scene.

"The same thing could happen to Panama ten minutes from now, Mr. President,"—Felix remained impassive—"if the United States so desired. Panama could be wiped out in an hour so that not a stick would remain on a stick or a stone on a stone. But that is not the way

441

of the United States. And you can thank God it is not. It is the way of some. When there is a challenge to the Soviet Union by some small, weak power, Soviet tanks and planes appear, Soviet guns fire, Soviet bombs drop, and it is over.

"Sometimes, Mr. President, I think the Soviet Union is smart. It talks a lot about world opinion but it ignores it whenever necessary in its own self-interest.

"A little of that is now prevalent in Washington. It is unlikely that it will be more, because that is not really the way of the United States. And distinguished delegates who clamor and cry can be profoundly grateful. The United States for the most part, Mr. President, shows an extraordinary forbearance in such matters. It shows to the world a forbearance that no other power on the face of this earth, with the possible exception of the United Kingdom, has ever shown, will ever show, or could ever show.

"So we get a little tired, Mr. President, of all the cry and clamor. We think it is pious and hypocritical nonsense. And for the time being in Washington, at least, we aren't scared of it. And we are going to do what we think is right in the cause of world peace.

"Now if delegates are so worried about blockade, the United States offers you a chance, as we say in our possibly undignified but pertinent fashion, to put up or shut up.

"My government has instructed me to offer the following amendment to the pending resolution SC/128:

"'Strike all after the preamble and insert:

"'And, whereas, events in Panama pose a serious and continuing threat to world peace, and

"'Whereas, this threat will continue as long as the Panama Canal remains both a matter of contention between nations and a vital necessity to world commerce and well-being,

"'Now, therefore, be it resolved:

"'That the United Nations create an International Waterways Organization and invite all member states possessing any rights, title, interest or control in or over the following international waterways to transfer those rights, title, interest or control immediately without reservation to such International Waterways Organization, to wit:

"'The Panama Canal.

"'The Suez Canal.

"'The Dardanelles.

"'Gibraltar.

"'The St. Lawrence River.

"'The Rhine River.

"'The Danube River.'

"In pursuit of the objective of this amendment, Mr. President," Lafe said, "and in the interests of permanent world peace, my government herewith states that it is ready to turn over to such a body, as soon as it is created by the United Nations, all rights, title, interest or control the United States may now or in future possess in the Panama Canal.

"The United States suggests, Mr. President, an immediate favorable vote on this amendment, so that the United Nations may proceed at once with the great, constructive task of placing these world waterways under world control for the benefit of all and the assurance of world peace.

"Mr. President, the United States requests that the Chair call the roll—"

But his concluding words, of course, were lost in the uproar of voices shouting for recognition and it was not until Raoul Barre managed to catch Cymru's eye and Cymru hastily cried, "The distinguished delegate of France!" that a semblance of order began to return.

"Mr. President," Raoul said with a certain sardonic expression as he caught Lafe's eye and received a bland smile, "this very interesting proposal is, of course, something entirely new, and it seems to my government that it would be best to consider it quietly for a little while. Therefore, Mr. President, I propose an adjournment overnight—"

"Until Monday," Lafe interrupted firmly; and Raoul agreed with a graceful promptitude, "Until Monday."

"Is there objection to the motion of the distinguished Ambassador of France?" the Ambassador of Cymru asked hastily. "The Chair hears none," he added hastily. "The Council stands adjourned until Monday, is it!" he said hastily, banging down his gavel with an air of relief.

"Is it, all right," Cullee said to Claude Maudulayne, who managed only a distant, glacial smile as they stood up and stretched and prepared to go. "Yes, sir, you can say that again. Is it, sure enough."

"Your Honor," Bob Leffingwell said, still comfortably relaxed after three hours of argument, "the afternoon is getting on, now, and we have reached, as Your Honor has just pointed out, the time for rebuttal and conclusion.

"I rather regret that our pleasant discussion must now come speedily to an end, for, frankly, I have enjoyed it.

It did my heart good to witness our brilliant friend across the way, Mr. George Harrison Wattersill, display the virtuosity and forensic talent that have made him a household word . . . in some households. (George Wattersill bowed ironically.) I was equally impressed to hear the eloquence of our other good friend, the former Governor and present National Committeeman of Oregon, the Honorable Roger P. Croy—eloquence which was not only eloquent but even, I thought, magniloquent. (Roger Croy, who had started to look pleased, looked less so.) My own—if I may use the affectionate possessive—good colleague, Senator Munson, shrewdly and astutely reinforced and buttressed and, at many points, improved upon my arguments. (Bob Munson shook his head with a humorously deprecating air.)

"But now the time has come to conclude it all. . . .

"Your Honor," he said, and slowly and deliberately got to his feet, "our side has not stood during these discussions, but I think now perhaps I will, for what it may be worth in lending emphasis. I do not intend, as has Mr. Wattersill, to allow my voice to soar—and dip—and whisper—and alarm. I do not intend, as has Governor Croy, to make my voice thunder—and roll—and blast—and shrivel. Like my friend and colleague the distinguished Senate Majority Leader, I shall simply—as we have throughout—talk: on the issues and, I hope, to the point.

"Now, Your Honor, to refresh the memories of our viewers and listeners in this country and throughout the world, we are here pursuant to a temporary injunction issued by the presiding judge of the U. S. District Court for the District of Columbia, pending decision of a suit filed in the District Court that would direct the National

Committee to reconvene the nominating convention which was concluded in San Francisco two weeks ago and turn over to it the task of nominating the candidate to succeed President Hudson, and a Vice Presidential candidate to run with him.

"It is our belief, Your Honor—though we have refrained from making it our contention—that the granting of this temporary injunction was irregular, unfounded and not based on the law: perhaps prompted by considerations known to the judge of the court below who handed it down, but not known to us. The justification for it, the soundness of it, the integrity of the premise upon which it was granted, are matters for Your Honor's wisdom to decide and his conscience to accommodate."

("Wowee," the Boston *Herald* whispered to the Arkansas *Gazette*. "That ought to make old Hempstone squirm." "That bird?" the Newark *News* sniffed. "He's too dumb to know what he was doing." "Dumb like a fox," the Arkansas *Gazette* retorted. "He got some payoff. Or will. That's for sure.")

"Sometimes, Your Honor," Bob Leffingwell said gently, "good politics is bad law. So our side feels it to be, in this instance.

"We also feel it to be in the instance of counsel who have spoken for the other side. We have heard a great deal about world peace and justice, and about freedom and liberty, and about which candidate can best save suffering humanity from the fate which it sometimes seems determined to bring upon itself."

("Does the bastard think it's funny?" 'Gage Shelby demanded of no one in particular, slamming a fist into a palm with a bitter, frustrated gesture. "Ah, Christ!")

"We do not say that these considerations are not valid," Bob Leffingwell said calmly, "nor do we say that they should not weigh decisively with the National Committee when it is again permitted to proceed in an orderly fashion to do its work. But we do say that they are not pertinent to the narrow issue which confronts Your Honor: namely, whether the National Committee can be forced to choose one of the two options which it is given without restriction by its own rules.

"On this, Your Honor, we believe that our argument must stand unchallenged—because it has not been challenged. Instead, counsel opposite have wandered all over the lot of political partisanship, emotional prejudice and inflammatory intimidation, without ever once meeting head on this absolutely fundamental point.

"Meanwhile, in the world outside this little room, there has been what almost seems a conspiracy to bolster exactly these tactics; to place the whole matter on an emotional, strictly political, basis; and to create a climate in which, were we not relatively isolated here, and did Your Honor not possess such wisdom and such sense—"

("Let's hope he has," Orrin remarked to the Undersecretary for Latin American Affairs.)

"—might very well have a major effect upon the atmosphere in which Your Honor must decide.

"During the fifteen-minute recess just past, which Your Honor most graciously allowed, for instance, there was thrust into my hands by several reporters outside as I was trying desperately to find a haven of relief, editions of the afternoon newspapers which carried such headlines as: SWARTHMAN CHARGES KNOX AUTHORED

GAG BILL AS PART OF DICTATORSHIP DRIVE . . . VAN ACKERMAN"—for just a second a genuine distaste, so strong that it came across to startled millions of viewers, transformed his easy expression—"FANS DICTATOR CHARGE . . . UN SPEAKERS FLAY KNOX, URGE JASON AS ONLY HOPE FOR WORLD PEACE.

"I did not allow," Bob Leffingwell said with a return of amiability, "indeed, could not allow, these intrusions to interfere with my urgent and necessary quest. Yet it was apparent, even in those brief glimpses accorded me by our friends of the waiting press, that we are everywhere surrounded by a most insistent and oppressive campaign seeking to pursuade and, if you please, intimidate, both this Court and the National Committee in pursuit of your respective duties.

"Now, Your Honor, I know that you will not be swayed, as I know a majority of the Committee will not be swayed. And therefore I think we can safely leave such arguments to the side which has originated and is encouraging them.

"We return, as we have returned frequently this afternoon, and now do for the last time, to the only issue which to us is valid as a point of law: the question of whether the court below, or this Court, or any body anywhere, has any legal authority whatsoever to instruct the National Committee as to which of its two options, equally free and equally democratic, it must choose.

"We believe that no such directive can be given the National Committee. We believe that all arguments political—emotional—national—international—are completely invalid and completely extraneous to this one basic *legal* issue.

448

"With faith in Your Honor's wisdom, integrity and courage, and with thanks for your infinite patience and kindness, we rest our case."

He smiled briefly but cordially and sat down.

"Mr. Wattersill," Tommy Davis said quietly, and democracy's defender was on his feet.

"Yes, Your Honor," he said briskly. "We too believe we can be brief.

"Counsel attempts here, in these final moments of this historic hearing, a hearing which a desperately concerned and worried world has been privileged to follow through the marvels of television and radio—and press," he added hastily as the UPI cleared his throat with a significant "A-hem!"—"this historic hearing which could very likely, Your Honor, be the first step in separating the quick from the dead—counsel attempts here, in these closing moments, to once again narrow proceedings to a quibble concerning which there is, really, no argument."

("What's that?" the Arkansas *Gazette* asked the Newark *News* in a startled whisper. "Keep calm," the Boston *Herald* advised. "Georgie will get out of it somehow. Georgie has a plan. Georgie always has a plan.")

"Certainly, Your Honor," George Harrison Wattersill said reasonably, "there can be no dispute that the Committee has the option under its rules of either selecting the nominees itself or reconvening the convention. We thought that was clearly understood. We have been surprised in fact, that counsel opposite have thought it worthwhile to spend so much time this afternoon in pointless repetition. The issue has never been the Committee's rules: it has been whether the Committee would be free to exercise its option under those rules, or whether the arbitrary and hurtful decision of a temporarily inflamed and excited majority would prevent it."

("Ah," said the Arkansas *Gazette*. "So that was it." "I told you," said the Boston *Herald*.)

"It is to make impossible just such hasty and ill-advised action, Your Honor," George Wattersill said earnestly, "that we on our side have contended throughout this hearing that the matter must not be left to chance. It must not be left to a capricious and uncertain impulse of a majority of the moment whether or no the Committee is to select the nominee or whether or no the convention is to select the nominee. It must not be left to the passions and the pressures which can afflict 106 men and women, Your Honor, however noble, however honest, however decent and responsible. It must be left to the great, free, open, democratic decision of the full convention, once more called together in all its solemn majesty, its libertarian dignity—"

("Is that what we saw in San Francisco?" the AP whispered. "W-e-e-e-llll," the UPI replied with a grin.)

"—its sober dedication—"

("Not that!" protested the Arkansas *Gazette*.)

"—its profound and moving devotion to the eternal principles of this great Republic, its deep and somber realization of the importance—to *all* humanity—of what it does.

"That is all that we have contended, Your Honor. That is all we want. We want the great responsibility to rest, not with 106 men and women, however honorable and however worthy—and no encomiums of mine can increase what the world already knows to be their manifest integrity, their supreme competence—but with the even greater integrity and still greater competence of the

450

great convention—to which, after all, Your Honor, all these 106 did belong and will belong again, so that their voices will by no stretch of the imagination be silenced.

"This, we think, Your Honor, is the purpose of the suit pending below, of the temporary injunction issued below, of the argument here. We submit that our only purpose and our only aim is to secure, not a narrow, limited, possibly emotional democracy of 106, but a vigorous, active, solemn, broadly based democracy of more than 1000 drawn from all the broad reaches of this broad land, bringing to their awesome deliberations not just a handful of hearts and minds, Your Honor, but many hearts and minds to represent *all* the people.

"We have so argued, and we do so argue, Your Honor: not to restrict or hamper the National Committee—not to control it—not to command it—not to interfere with its free exercise of its free choice—but to help it—to encourage it—to assist it to do what mankind cries out for it to do.

"The Committee needs your protection and your strength, Your Honor. It needs this Court to free it from pressure and from fear so that it may make the truly democratic choice. 'Help it!' cries the nation. 'Help it!'"— and his voice sank once more to its low, husky, nerve-tingling appeal—"*Help it!*' cries all mankind. . . .

"Your Honor," he said presently when, after a great and obvious struggle, his emotions were once more under control, "we too thank you for your patience, your kindness, your decency, your attention. Never was democracy better served by better servant than it has been served today by the Honorable—the very Honorable— Mr. Justice Davis.

"Your Honor," George Harrison Wattersill said quietly, "we rest."

"Thank you, Mr. Wattersill," Tommy said with a courtesy so impersonal that no one could interpret it though millions tried, "thank you, Mr. Leffingwell, Governor Croy, Senator Munson. Thank you, too, our friends of press, television and radio, and thank you, Mr. Marshal, the clerks, the secretaries, the official stenographers, for your patience. Thank all of you for your patience during this long, tiring afternoon.

"Thank you all, everywhere"—and for a moment he looked straight into the camera with a small, shy, somewhat hesitant smile of vague politeness and benign good will—"for your patience and attentiveness too. We hope you have received some understanding of how our democracy works. It is not very perfect, but it does work."

("We hope," the Boston *Herald* whispered as they gathered their notes and prepared to go.)

"The Court would suggest to all the press," Tommy said, "that it be prepared for a decision later this evening, possibly around ten P.M. in the main chamber of the Supreme Court. The Court does not feel that this matter should be delayed.

"This hearing is now concluded."

"So what do you make of it?" the President asked half an hour later, when the Majority Leader, as requested, called from "Vagaries" where he and Dolly were entertaining Lucille Hudson, the four Knoxes and Bob Leffingwell for dinner.

"I don't quite know," Senator Munson said thoughtfully, "but I have the impression he's on our side, surprisingly."

"So do I," Bob Leffingwell said from the extension phone in the study.

"And so do I," the President agreed, "but of course we could always be mistaken. There's a powerful pull in the other direction, and he's not particularly noted for going against his political convictions."

"More 'social convictions,' isn't it?" Bob Munson suggested. "In the sense of social welfare, that is. On the whole, I think Tommy's pretty fair-minded, at heart." He chuckled. "And certainly he couldn't have been more judicial today. My goodness! He did the Court proud."

"It goes with the office, you know," the President said. "Look at me, now, old stumbling, bumbling Bill Abbott, still got straw in his ears, still got the lead of Leadville in his pants after forty years in this town, doesn't know which fork to use at your wife's parties—"

"Sure, sure," Senator Munson said.

"—but when I'm on the job here, by George—or rather, I should say by somebody else, after the performance George put on this afternoon—by Tommy, I really haul on the mantle and get dignified."

"That's what happened to Tommy," Bob Leffingwell agreed. "At the moment he's the Supreme Court of the United States, and that's a body with a good deal of dignity, in working hours. He's no mean Justice, when the occasion requires. He just called me a minute ago, incidentally."

"Oh, did he," the President said.

"Yes, we told him where we'd be in case he needed any further clarifications. He wants me to come see him at eight o'clock."

"Before the decision. Alone?"

"Alone."

"Do you know why?"

"I think so," Bob Leffingwell said slowly.

"Can you tell me?" the President asked.

"Not now," Bob Leffingwell said. "I will . . . I'm glad you went to Oak Hill Cemetery this afternoon," he said, apparently without connection. The President of course got it at once but made no comment.

"Yes. I thought perhaps I should emphasize a few things just by being there."

"Was Walter?" Senator Munson asked.

"Lots of newspaper people and a good many from the Hill, the diplomatic corps and the Green Book," the President said. "It was a sizable funeral. Flowers only, from Walter. Big ones, but that's all. I suppose he couldn't face it."

"A funny man," Bob Leffingwell remarked.

"Hysterically," the President said. "How are the Knoxes bearing up?"

"Feeling good," Bob Munson said. "I think they're slightly hysterical too from Orrin's day of being the world's punching-bag."

"Relieved me of the pressure a little, anyway," the President said with a laugh. "Give them my love. And Lucille. And Dolly. And also, Robert A. Leffingwell, give my love to Tommy, too. Tell him I think he did a magnificent job of conducting the hearing, win, lose or draw on the decision. And tell me what you can later about your mystery. She never told me all the details, poor gal. So you do it."

"I shall," Bob Leffingwell promised. "Good night, Mr. President."

454

"Good night." There was a click from the extension, and: "Bob Munson—"

"Yes, sir, Bill, Mr. Speaker, Mr. President, sir?"

"That's my problem," the President said glumly. "Jawbone still had the House stalled when they adjourned an hour ago, and your friend Van Ackerman successfully did the same to the Senate. At least he didn't threaten violence, though. It was all pro-peace and antiwar, with the threat left out."

"Everybody was arguing on a noble plane today," Senator Munson said dryly. "That was part of the strategy. The violence will come back tomorrow if the decision doesn't go the right way. . . . What do you want done on those two sections of the bill, incidentally?"

"I want them modified, naturally," the President said. "But," he added grimly, "I want a few people scared fitless, first."

"I'm not sure we can hold them in line," Senator Munson said thoughtfully. "There's a very strong sentiment, particularly in the House, for going all the way. Whether we can scare people as you want but still get enough amendment to make it reasonable, I don't know. They may want all or nothing."

"Well, try," the President said.

"You know I will, Bill."

"I know you will. Incidentally, I think you two did a magnificent job yourselves, this afternoon. I was proud of you."

"Be proudest of Bob," Senator Munson said. "He did the most—and also had the most to lose, and the most to live up to, in doing what he did."

"I've changed my opinion of him a lot in recent days," the President said.

"So have many people," Senator Munson said. "Some for the better, some for the worse."

"I hope he values the ones for the better."

"Oh, he does. He's come a long way."

"And may go further if we can get this country straightened out and back on the right path again."

"We must," Senator Munson said.

"We must," the President agreed.

"What we *must* do," George Harrison Wattersill said earnestly in Patsy's enormous living room in Dumbarton Oaks, "is get this country straightened out and back on the right path again. That is what you will do, Governor," he said, beaming down upon Ted from his position beside the grand piano, where he stood with a Scotch-on-the-rocks in his hand.

"I hope so," Ted said gravely. "I hope so. I am not so sure, after this afternoon, that it is going to be so simple."

"Why is that Governor?" Roger P. Croy asked with some surprise and a trace of alarm. "Were you dissatisfied with—"

"Oh, no," Ted said. "Not at all, Governor. I thought you both did a magnificent job."

"We tried," George Wattersill said modestly. "We tried, because we are both so deeply aware of the enormous importance of your cause, and the great—I might say, the desperate—necessity that you win this battle. Not only the nation but the whole world needs you, Governor—"

"Yes," Ted interrupted, "you've stated that, George. We know that. Thank you. Don't think I'm ungrateful," he added quickly, as democracy's defender looked a little crestfallen. "I am most humbly grateful for all that you both did. No, it was Tommy who puzzled me a little. I think," he said carefully, "he's got something on his mind."

"I thought he presided very fairly," Patsy said, coming in with a tray of hors-d'oeuvres she had decided to serve herself, rather than let the maid do it, because this was a very confidential talk that shouldn't be overheard by outsiders. "Having to put up with all that nonsense from Bob Leffingwell and Bob Munson would be enough to drive ANYBODY around the bend. But he remained perfectly calm and pleasant, I thought, even when they were doing their best to confuse the issue."

"They did try," Roger P. Croy said with a reminiscent smile.

"But we wouldn't let them," George Wattersill said with satisfaction. "We kept returning to the single, fundamental point. I really thought Justice Davis was impressed. Aside from that one early question, he said very, very little."

"Perhaps that's what worries me," Governor Jason said with a smile. "It's so unlike our little friend to be so silent."

"Well, you must remember, Governor," Roger Croy said, "he was representing the Court, of course; in fact, he *was* the Court, at that moment. That is quite a responsibility for a single Justice, and I am sure any undue gravity"—he also smiled—"was due to that."

"I suppose you're right," Ted said; and then, lightly, because he knew his sister could sense what the others would not, that he was genuinely worried, "Pat, what on earth have you cooked up there to make us fat?"

She gave him a quick, shrewd glance.

"Just some odds and ends to tide us over. I know Roger and George will have to be back up at the Court before long to hear the decision, so I thought we'd just have a few nibbles now, and then go to the Jockey Club or the Gangplank or some place like that where we can be *seen*, for the victory dinner afterward. I think," she said with a certain grim relish, "they should SEE us being victorious. Some of them DESERVE it!"

"You sound quite Madame Defarge-ish," George Harrison Wattersill said with a laugh, helping himself as she brought the tray around.

"Pat's my commander in chief when we go over the barricades," Governor Jason said. "Incidentally," he added, more seriously, "I do want to commend you on the demeanor of the crowds outside the Court. I understand that was your doing, and I thought it was very sensible. I trust it marks the beginning of the end of the sort of outburst that has disfigured this campaign to some extent."

For just a second both Roger Croy and George Wattersill looked at him with curious expressions, half-puzzled, half-quizzical. Then Roger Croy said carefully,

"You did not transmit the order to George through Senator Van Ackerman, Mr. Shelby and Mr. Kleinfert at his house this morning? They gave him to understand that—"

"No, I saw no necessity," Ted said, taking a plate and several hors-d'oeuvres as Patsy came to him. "They had already assured me that from now on they were going to control their people and not permit things to get out of hand. I saw no reason to reaffirm this with them. Apparently there was no reason to. They did it, didn't they?"

"Yes," George Wattersill agreed quickly, dismissing whatever doubts he might have in favor of the cause he believed in, "and it was a most shrewd decision, which I am sure they would not have reached had it not been for the prior discussion they had with you. It showed not only an astute appraisal on your part of the realities of presenting a good image to the country and the world, but it also was a gesture of genuine responsibility, I thought. It is the sort of thing which makes your leadership so valuable to the cause of world peace. And makes me," he said with his flair for gracious phraseology, "so humbly grateful that I have been selected to work, in some small capacity, at your side."

"No small capacity at all," the Governor said. "An indispensable capacity, I should say. We will want you with us for the duration, if you would be willing."

"Nothing," said George Harrison Wattersill gravely, "would please me more."

"Well, good!" Patsy said, setting down the tray, taking up her own Scotch and soda, raising it high. "Let's drink to THAT, and to the gathering of all good friends and the confounding of all Ted's enemies!"

"And to Mr. Justice Davis," Ted said, lightly again but still, she could sense, uneasy. "May he do the right thing."

"For US," Patsy said.

"For us," he echoed.

And with a hearty laugh they all did drink to Tommy Davis, who of course would do the right thing. They knew he would, because, as Patsy added a moment later, he simply HAD to.

"Miss Wilson," he had said quietly over the intercom when the Marshal had escorted him back to his office through the deserted, echoing marble corridors shortly after six P.M., "will you please have the kitchen send up a small bowl of tomato soup, a chicken sandwich, and some vanilla ice cream. Tell them to knock and leave it, please. Thank you."

And ten minutes later when he had heard, first the chink and tinkle of china and silver on the cart, and then the dutiful knock, and then the silence left by someone going away, he had gone to the door and brought it in himself, because he did not want anyone or anything to destroy his concentration in these final hours when he was alone with his case, his conscience and his God.

He wondered now, as he pushed back his half-eaten snack and stared in profound thought at the sheaf of notes from a dead hand which lay before him on the desk, what they were all doing, while the world waited for him to speak; and knowing his Washington, he could guess fairly well.

He could imagine that the two sides, confident yet worried, were talking and speculating—as they were. He could see members of the National Committee at Fort Myer or, with their Army escorts and guards, visiting friends or attending parties around Washington to await his decision—as they were. He could see his friends of press and television, already gathering in the chamber, gossiping nervously, jockeying for vantage point and position as the harassed press officer of the Court tried to find space for everyone and keep everyone happy: and this was happening. He could visualize the steamy thousands of NAWAC, still outside on the lawns, singing or drinking or even, behind the hospitable bushes of Capitol Plaza, making love—and this was occurring. And all across the country and the world—what George Harrison Wattersill, that flamboyant young man, had called "yea, the great globe itself"—he could imagine his countrymen and all the scurrying races of man, trying to tend to the business of ordinary living that must be done, but not able to concentrate very much because their minds were occupied so intensely with him—and this, too, was the fact of it.

For these few remaining hours, no man on earth was more important, or more obsessively on the minds of other men, than Mr. Justice Thomas Buckmaster Davis of the United States Supreme Court.

And how did he feel about it? Well, certainly not egotistical, he could say that honestly. Certainly not self-important for his importance now transcended self. Certainly not worried, for here, too, the demand upon him was so great that he could not afford worry. And certainly, he told himself, and was quietly surprised and pleased to find that it was true, certainly not afraid, either of history or of himself.

Once long ago when Mr. Justice Davis was a very small boy, his father, who had been a lawyer before him and had been chief justice of the New York state supreme court, though he had never risen as high as his son, had said to Tommy: "Don't be afraid of what life may bring, for men of character find that they have the strength to do what must be done."

And he had always found this to be true for under his gossiping and his busy-bodying and his bustling about among the famous men and issues of his time, Tommy, in

461

his own fussy, quirky, inimitable way, was a man of character, and he had found his father's statement to be sound.

He thought with some amusement now that he had probably confounded them all with his demeanor at the hearing. They had probably expected him to be as voluble and gossipy as his reputation said he was, and as his friends privately knew him to be. Perhaps Bob Leffingwell had expected him to be as nervous and upset as he had been on the day Bob had given him that sheaf of notes. But he hadn't been, because he had conducted himself as what, after all, he was: Justice of the Supreme Court.

And also, he had read that sheaf of notes.

He could reconstruct very vividly now, for in fact he still felt it, the horror and dismay that had swept over him when he had gone patiently through Helen-Anne's scribblings to the end. At first he had experienced a little difficulty with her slap-dash reporter's abbreviations and rusty, catch-as-catch-can shorthand, but his days as a law clerk had come to his rescue and it had not taken him long to piece together what she had to say.

The unholy trinity of violence in the streets had held a meeting, right enough, first with Ted Jason and then, after he had left, with someone else; and Tommy could understand, after he had read through the details as an excellent reporter had been able to piece them together, both why Bob Leffingwell could have been so upset in his office and why Governor Jason could have been so calm and confident.

Ted was a dupe, but he was something more: he was a dupe whose egotism and self-confidence were so great that they made it almost inevitable that he should have become a dupe. No wonder he could accept denials from Fred, LeGage and Rufus: he was so supremely sure of himself that he was tailor-made for their purposes. He honestly did not know about the later meeting, but more than that—and much more disturbing to Justice Davis as he sat alone in his utterly silent wing of the beautiful building—was the fact that he quite obviously did not want to know about it, and in fact *would not let himself know*.

The revelation that a meeting had occurred, and one sufficiently dangerous in its implications to justify the concern of both Helen-Anne and Bob Leffingwell, had in a sense not been nearly as shattering for the little Justice as this revelation of the character of the man whose political cause and personal integrity he had believed in so completely. Somebody's money—probably, he suspected, Patsy's—had been given freely to buy the silence of all—except one—who could bear witness to the individuals who had gone up to the twelfth floor that night. Whether Patsy knew this, he was not sure: in all likelihood not. Someone she recognized as friendly to her brother had probably said funds were urgently needed for the campaign, and she had dashed off a check and that was it, as far as she was concerned. From buying silence it had spread to—he didn't want to face it, but there was no way to avoid it—Helen-Anne and a busboy dead in the street. And it could spread much, much beyond; and the only man who could really repudiate it and stop it was Governor Jason, and he evidently was unable or unwilling, which was much more serious, because consciously or subconsciously, that made it a deliberate decision—to face it in all its implications.

To do so—and here also Tommy had to force himself to go on, but he did it—would be to jeopardize the effective foundations of Ted's campaign and very likely terminate his ambition to be President.

Beyond that point in his thinking, Mr. Justice Davis, at this moment, did not want to go. What it did to his whole concept of the Jason cause, what it did to his whole concept of Ted himself, what he himself should do from now on about both Ted and his cause, he did not know right now. That would require a very careful thinking-out, and one in which he would have to struggle with his heart and conscience, and with many very deep-seated convictions about many things. It was not something he wanted to tackle now, nor did he have to: but he knew it was waiting for him, as soon as these hectic hours of his dubious and difficult fame were over.

At eight o'clock, as he had requested, Robert A. Leffingwell knocked on his door; and after he had told Bob about his reaction to the notes, and his thoughts about them, and to some degree about Ted Jason, and about Bob himself, Bob had shaken his hand gravely and gone away, still uncertain what Tommy's decision would be, but thinking perhaps he had helped him clarify it a little.

And shortly before nine one other, perhaps the only one who would think of inviting himself at such a time, appeared and did what he could to clarify Tommy's thinking, from his own point of view, more angrily than George, more vehemently than Bob; and also shook Tommy's hand and departed uncertain, but not before the little Justice had said, "Please see me after the decision. There is a visit I want to make, and I would like to have you accompany me." The other, almost as though he guessed where—though how could he, it had only that moment popped into Tommy's head—had said with a wary caution, "We'll discuss it when I see you."

And now it was time for him to write his decision. Placing a large pad of yellow legal note paper neatly before him on the desk, he did so in no more than fifteen minutes, for it had really been inevitable from the first.

With that completed, he did one more thing, which in some curious way was a linkback to old, unhappy events; something which he recognized, with a little prickling of the hair on the back of his neck, as a penance, a payment, a settling of accounts with the gallant, unhappy ghost of Brigham Anderson, whom he had joined with others to drive from life a year and a half ago.

He took an envelope, inserted Helen-Anne's notes, sealed it, franked it with his signature; opened his door and took it himself, though the waiting bailiff offered to do it, to the nearest mail chute and dropped it in.

It would reach the addressee tomorrow. Mr. Justice Davis had no idea at all what he would do with it. But that he should have it seemed right and just and somehow a thing that would make not only that earlier unhappy ghost, but Helen-Anne's as well, rest more easily this fateful night.

Then he went back and asked his secretary to notify the press officer that he would appear in the chamber in fifteen minutes' time, at ten P.M. sharp, to deliver his decision.

"Damn it, *stop shoving!*" the Los Angeles *Times* said in exasperation to France-Presse, and from the row behind Reuters leaned forward to poke them both in the back.

"Let us have more international friendship and cooperation," he suggested. "And also, if both of you would please lean to the left so that I can see past—"

"We're so squeezed in we can't lean either way," the L.A. *Times* tossed over his shoulder, still sounding annoyed but beginning to relent a little. "Anyway, what makes you think we would both want to lean left?"

"I'm not thinking of your preference but my view," Reuters said. "What a mess!"

And so it was, for not even on the most dramatic of Mondays, the day the Court traditionally hands down its opinions, had the dimly lit, dark-paneled chamber known such confusion of reporters, photographers, lights, cameras, correspondents, commentators, publishers, editors, hangers-on. The rule that prohibits photographs and television in the chamber had been relaxed (the Chief Justice, vacationing in Switzerland, had cabled his approval this morning in view of the magnitude of the event; and also, because he wanted to watch it himself via satellite) and a room that normally accommodates 500 comfortably was jammed with almost twice that number, plus equipment. And as they pushed and shoved and squeezed and turned uneasily about, trying to find positions of greater comfort, trying to free their arms from their encroaching neighbors' so that they could take notes, or broadcast, or, like Walter Dobius, just observe, they gossiped and argued and speculated and shouted back and forth across the chamber to one another with such uninhibited enthusiasm that to Tommy Davis, approaching along the Court's private hallway with a bailiff in attendance, it sounded like the distant angry hum of giant bees that grew ever louder as he neared until it seemed it must drown out the universe and thought itself.

Then, as he stepped, still unseen, into place behind the red velvet curtains that form a backdrop for the nine battered old leather armchairs which house the nine supreme judicial bottoms, the noise ceased so abruptly that it seemed a giant hand must have reached down and chopped it off. Out front, at his high desk to the right, the Marshal had suddenly appeared. In his clear, measured tones, he cried out in the old, traditional way:

"The honorable, the Associate Justice of the Supreme Court of the United States!

"Oyez, oyez, oyez! All persons having business before the honorable, the Supreme Court of the United States are admonished to draw near and give their attention, for the Court is now sitting!

"God save the United States and this honorable Court!"

And Tommy parted the red velvet curtains and stepped through, as the Justices do, almost before they knew he was there.

For a moment he stood where he was, alone in the eye of the world, trying to find his particular friends but unable to do so in the harsh glare of the lights.

Then he stepped forward, his expression grave and thoughtful, in a silence broken only by the steady whirring of the television cameras, and sat down in his chair, two seats to the right of the chair of the Chief Justice.

He placed several sheets of yellow legal note paper neatly before him on the burnished desk, fussed with them for a moment or two, then folded his arms, lifted his head, leaned forward slightly and began to talk, in a rather thin but steady voice that was carried to the ends of the earth.

"First of all," he said, "the Court wishes to apologize for the confusion here, even though it is perhaps inevitable considering the nature of the occasion. The Court hopes you are all reasonably comfortable and may be able to do your work without undue interference by the various extremities of your neighbors."

There was a spatter of laughter, tight with the tension of great events that afflicts even the most experienced of correspondents; yet friendly, for most of them liked Tommy Davis.

"The Court also regrets," he went on, "that it has been impossible to prepare printed copies of the Court's opinion"—here was a groan but he responded with a certain testiness that silenced it at once—"but the Court, after all, has not had long to consider this. The Court felt that it was more important to announce a decision swiftly than it was to make easier the work of the press. The Court is sorry, but that is how it is.

"Members of the press," he said, more amicably, "will simply have to revert to being working reporters for the evening. I don't think it will hurt you."

There was a general murmur of amusement and even, though this, too, was against Court rules, a smattering of good-natured applause. The atmosphere became more relaxed and so, for a moment, did he. Then he sat straighter in his chair, his expression again turned grave and thoughtful, again only the whirring of the cameras broke the intent, devouring silence.

"The issue before the Court is this—" he began, and

for five minutes, simply and clearly, he laid it on the record: the temporary injunction, the case below, the National Committee's decision to appeal, his own decision to hear arguments at the earliest possible moment "to expedite a matter in which, it seems safe to say, there is an almost universal interest."

"So, as you know," he continued, "a hearing was held in chambers this afternoon, attended in physical fact by only a very small handful of individuals; but attended through the wonderful mediums of press, television, and radio, aided by the worldwide communications-satellite network, by a great many peoples of the earth. In fact, I would suspect, the great majority.

"During the hearing, as all who viewed or heard it are aware, counsel for one faction in the National Committee argued, in essence, that neither the court below, this Court, or any other body of whatever nature anywhere, have any legal right whatsoever to force the National Committee to choose one, as distinct from the other, of the two free and equally democratic options given it by its own rules.

"The other faction argued—

("Come on Tommy, come on," the Boston *Herald* whispered impatiently. "We know all that." But the Court record, as always, had to be made.)

"—that to permit the National Committee to exercise its option freely might be, in effect to pre-empt its choice anyway, by making possible a decision by a majority of the Committee to select its new nominees through what counsel chose to refer to as 'a narrow, limited, possibly emotional democracy of 106' rather than 'a vigorous, active, solemn, broadly based democracy of more than 1000 drawn from all the broad reaches of this broad land.'

"Whatever one may think of arguments of counsel on this side of the issue," he remarked with a little smile that brought some uneasy laughter, for many were not sure but what he might be making a little fun of George Harrison Wattersill, and they didn't like that, "it must be acknowledged that his language is colorful and added much to the interesting nature of the hearing."

And he peered over the edge of the bench and did succeed in finding George Wattersill, seated directly down front with Roger P. Croy, who had Senator Munson next to him, and then Bob Leffingwell. George bowed and smiled, clamping an iron control on his suddenly rising uneasiness and appearing as cheerful as could be while the cameras zoomed in on him to find out how he was taking it.

"Essentially," Tommy went on, "the Court feels that these two points of view do represent the major, and indeed perhaps the only valid, arguments that the Court can consider in this proceeding.

"The question then arises: how do they stand before the bar?

"It must be remembered—even," he said, and a certain warning note came into his voice, "by the most partisan—that this is a court of law, and that it is only on matters of law that the Court has authority to act.

"It may well be that one argument or another is valid and superior in an emotional, political, or partisan sense. But it is in the legal sense that the Court must decide.

"The Court," he said, and the tension soared as they realized that he was already into his peroration, "will say frankly that he personally hopes that the National Committee will, when it reconvenes tomorrow—"

("Oh, NO!" Patsy cried in anguish beside her grimly silent brother in the enormous living room in Dumbarton Oaks. "Hot dog!" Hal Knox yelled gleefully in the drawing room at "Vagaries." "Oh, *damn* it, hot DOG!")

"—when it reconvenes tomorrow," Tommy repeated, for there had been an immediate and irrepressible surge of confused sound, mostly angry, in the chamber too, "will proceed in regular order to reconvene the convention.

"That is the personal preference and desire of the Court.

"But the Court is not a Court that decides on the basis of its personal preferences. At least," he said, with a little smile and a certain gentle irony, "we try not to be. And I think for the most part, we succeed.

"Certainly in this instance I am satisfied the Court has succeeded, for I have told you frankly my own feelings. But I put the law above them. As," he said firmly, "it should be.

"The Court," he concluded quietly, "cannot, in all honesty, find precedents or justification for interfering with the normal procedures of the National Committee under its own rules, as is proposed by the temporary injunction from the court below.

"The appeal is upheld.

"These proceedings are now concluded."

And he stood up, and after one last, straight look into the eye of the world, turned with a suddenly great dignity and disappeared through the red velvet curtains.

For several seconds there was a stunned, disbelieving silence, and then a great rush of sound as everyone began talking at once, and everyone began to stand up and leave. Cameramen shouted to cameramen, reporters called to reporters, technical crews began to yank out their long, snaking cables, hood the cameras, trundle out the booms. George Harrison Wattersill and Roger P. Croy, dejected but true to their legal training and the customary courtesies of Washington, shook hands with Bob Leffingwell and Bob Munson, who reciprocated without too much visible triumph. From outside on the lawns there came an ominous, growing roar of angry sound from NAWAC which sent many reporters running through the echoing marble hall to the entrance. But the police were on duty, the barricades were up, and despite the noise, no one broke across the lines: there had not been time for any orders to come through, and violence, it seemed, would be averted long enough for the principals to get safely away.

As Walter Dobius stood between the great white pillars looking across the street at the milling thousands in floodlit Capitol Plaza—already beginning a chant that came clearly through the still-suffocating heat—

> "O Justice Davis!
> "You didn't save us.
> "Your robes can't hide
> "The rat inside!
> "KILL RATS! KILL RATS! KILL RATS!"

the Marshal appeared at his elbow and said quietly,

"The Justice asks that you join him in his chambers, Mr. Dobius, if you'd care to. I'll take you there. . . ."

"What do you want of me?" he demanded angrily when they were alone in the quiet room.

"Just what I said," Tommy told him quietly. "I want

472

you to accompany me on a little visit I'm going to make."

"Where?" Walter demanded suspiciously. "And why should I go anywhere with you, after what you've done?"

"I have upheld the law," Tommy said quietly, "which I am here to do. There is no reason to go with me at all, if you don't want to. But I thought you might."

"Where?" Walter demanded again. The little Justice gave him an odd look, filled with many things that Walter could not interpret, though one of them, he thought with an angry refusal to accept it, might be pity.

"Come along and see," Tommy said. And taking off his robes, he hung them in the closet; folded his yellow note paper carefully and locked it in the drawer of his desk; and turned to the door.

"I'm going to have to go out the back way," he said, "because the crowd may turn violent out front. The President has kindly sent me a military escort."

"He has no right to send Federal troops to this sovereign Court!" Walter said sharply.

"Very true," Justice Davis said calmly. "But tonight I am glad to have them, all the same." He opened the door. "Good night, Walter."

"No, wait," Walter said, although by now, in some sick, foreboding way, he was almost certain he knew where Tommy was going. "Wait, I'll go with you."

But his impulse did not last very long, for as they came presently to Massachusetts Avenue and started around Dupont Circle, toward Sheridan Circle and Oak Hill Cemetery beyond, a strange thing happened.

Abruptly he seemed to shrivel back in his seat, some sort of strange physical contortion appeared to seize him, his whole body set in rigid lines of protest and Tommy could see that he was actually straining back from the door, arms and legs stiff with aversion and a sort of animal horror.

"I don't want"—he broke out incoherently—"I can't— I can't—I can't—"

And with a sudden and quite awful incongruity, he began to cry, in short, choking, agonizing gulps that sounded really dreadful in the closed-off back seat of the big black limousine as it floated gently along behind its Army escort.

"Let—me out!" he managed to articulate at last. "You must—let me out!"

"Driver!" Tommy said sharply through the tube, rapping on the window with his signet ring, "Draw off and let Mr. Dobius out!"

And after he had, and Walter had somehow tumbled out, Tommy looked back as the car drew away and saw him standing under the misty overarching trees of upper Massachusetts Avenue, his arms at his sides, his face straight ahead, his body quivering and shaking with sobs, infinitely pathetic, terribly alone.

But when he had finally mastered himself enough to catch a cab and get back to the office they kept for him at the *Post*, his column came out savage as ever, just the same:

"WASHINGTON—So the nation and the world must face the prospect of a threatened, browbeaten, controlled National Committee, selecting a hand-picked nominee under the massive threat of armed Presidential displeasure.

"Rarely has American democracy witnessed so sad a

spectacle as it seems likely to witness now that Justice Davis has handed down his ruling.

"And rarely, it might be said, has American democracy been so bitterly and tragically betrayed by one it had always thought to be its friend, as it has been betrayed by Justice Davis.

"What will happen now, no one in this fearful capital tonight can accurately predict, but one thing is certain:

"The prospect of new and ever more violent protest is now almost inevitable—against America's futile and tragic foreign policy, against the Secretary of State who created it, against the President who with armed troops stationed in the streets of the capital enforces it, against the National Committee whose deliberations can no longer be considered free and democratic as it shakes and trembles beneath the threat of his bayonet-backed displeasure.

"This is what Mr. Justice Davis has done this night: made inevitable a further tragic tearing-apart of an already tragically torn land. This may make happy his friends the President, the Secretary of State, and the dwindling number of fatally misguided Americans who agree with them.

"But it cannot make happy any American who truly and honestly loves his country; for his country, now, confronts disaster. . . ."

"The Supreme Court of the United States," the President said in a statement issued shortly after midnight through the White House press office, "acting in the person of Mr. Justice Davis, has ruled that the National Committee is free from legal hindrances and may now proceed to do the work for which it has come to Washington.

"Therefore I am issuing a call to Committee members to meet with me again in the Playhouse at the Kennedy Center at ten A.M. today to continue our deliberations.

"Let us get on with the work speedily. The task is imperative."

And in the rather old-fashioned, slightly musty, but very comfortable bachelor quarters at the Westchester that he had occupied for thirty ears, Mr. Justice Davis fixed himself a cup of hot chocolate, poured into it a jigger of Curaçao, and drank it slowly while he watched Frankly Unctuous damn him up and down on some late panel of experts discussing the awful thing he had done. Then he went to bed.

He had not, he realized as he turned off the lamp and snuggled into the sheets, felt so much at ease in his mind for many months; perhaps not since all the dreadful things that had happened as a result of his impulse to pick up the envelope Brigham Anderson had dropped after giving him a ride to work that day. Indirectly, but nonetheless inescapably, Brig had died because of that impulse. For a long time Tommy had not thought about those things, had not permitted himself to, had closed them off from his mind; but now, tonight, he could.

The mood in which he had mailed Helen-Anne's notes returned, strengthened by his visit to her grave, quiet and still on its deserted hillside in the hot, humid night. It was a curiously restful grave for one so full of vigorous life and bounce. Walter's flowers, the President's, the Knoxes' and many others, were drooping now. To them

476

he added the roses he had taken from his secretary's desk as he left the office. They weren't much, but ever since he had read her notes yesterday for the first time, he had intended to bring them to her himself.

In some strange way, it all seemed fitting and peaceful in spite of the terrible, unexplained tragedy of her death. He told her good night quietly, smiling suddenly as he recalled what she had said to him years ago when he had been vigorously denouncing Orrin for some piece of social legislation—he couldn't remember what now, but he was making quite an argument about its Constitutional irregularities. "Constitutional, my hat!" she had said in her raucous way. "You sentimental old coot, Tommy, you can't fool me!"

Well, he was a sentimental old coot: sentimental about a lot of people and a lot of things, sentimental most of all about his poor old bumbling, stumbling, unhappy America, which was probably why he had always felt he must work so hard to help her find decency and justice, even when it meant meddling in things that many people thought weren't fitting for a Justice of the Supreme Court. Even when, once, it had taken him too far and caused the death of a fine young Senator he would give anything to have still alive.

Tommy had seen a lot, in his years on the Court, and imperfect as he knew himself to be, he had still tried to do what he thought was best for America. So he had tonight. He knew his two friends who rested, one in Oak Hill and the other in Salt Lake City, would approve of him, could they know. They, too, had wanted what was best for America. Most people he knew in this strange, fantastic, mixed-up city did, in spite of the wrong turnings they took and the dreadful confusions they got themselves and the country into, sometimes.

The good heart and the good will were still there somewhere—somewhere. He hoped he had helped a little this day to discover them again and make them stronger. Anyway, he had done his best.

He closed his eyes, took a couple of deep breaths, and was instantly asleep.

7.

FAR OFF the sirens sounded and once again within the crowded Playhouse susurrus ceased. "Hail to the Chief who in triumph advances," Anotis Spirotis, National Committeeman from Pennsylvania, murmured to Mary Buttner Baffleburg. Mary Baffleburg said, "Hmph!" But there was no denying he advanced with an extra aura this morning: somehow last night's events seemed to have increased his stature and strengthened his position. It did seem, curiously, that he loomed larger than life, larger than Presidents normally loom, as he passed swiftly once more in his guarded limousine between the long lines of servicemen at ready, through the restless, sullen ranks of NAWAC, to Kennedy Center in the hot, glazed sun.

From his embittered countrymen as he passed, he received the sort of tribute he expected: a slow, growing swell of boos and hisses that came to those inside the Playhouse like a steady, rising wave from some uneasy sea. The wave crested in an angry boom of sound and was succeeded by an intently listening, watching silence. Through it they could hear the sound of motorcycles coming to a halt, an auto engine idling, the slam of a door, the slap of hundreds of hands on rifles as the inner group of guards snapped to attention while he passed from the plaza entrance along the North Gallery to the elevator up to the Playhouse, tucked away in the northwest corner of the second floor. There was a brief period of silence, everything was quiet everywhere; then a stir, a bustle, just outside the door, the crack of more hands on rifles; and there he was, walking down the aisle while they stood, this time not with his eyes lowered or grimly thoughtful but nodding Hellos and smiling as he came.

"Good morning," he said as he reached the podium and turned to face them with a pleasantly relaxed and amiable expression. "Please be seated. I hope everyone rested well after last night's excitement. I did."

There was a murmur of amusement from the room and from outside a revival of the long, slow, savage "Boooooo!" He cocked his head and listened with a quizzical grimace clearly visible in the cameras. The booing increased. His expression became matter-of-fact and businesslike. He picked up the little ivory gavel and brought it down sharply on the lectern.

"This second emergency meeting of the National Committee is now in session. The Chair is pleased to inform the Committee for purposes of the record that the Supreme Court last night upheld the appeal of the Committee against the temporary injunction of the District Court for the District of Columbia. The Committee is now free to proceed at its pleasure to select candidates for President and Vice President of the United States.

"The Chair might say, incidentally, before we proceed, that he would like to raise one point and determine the Committee's will upon it." There was a sudden questioning silence. His tone took on an amused irony. "There has been much talk in the past twenty-four hours about military dictatorship—the ominous presence of the President hovering over the Committee with a threat of armed vengeance—the poor, beleaguered Committee trembling before the possibility of my—I believe the term was 'bayonet-backed displeasure.'

"Well," he said, looking thoughtfully around the room: "Are you?"

There was laughter, but the press was quick to note that several members appeared anxious to speak.

"I didn't really think that you were," the President said, "but I thought we should have it out in the open and have a talk about it, in case anybody is really concerned. Yes, Governor?" he said with an expression that brought much amusement as Roger P. Croy raised his hand and then got slowly to his feet beside his desk. "You rise like the Phoenix, undaunted and renewed. What are you going to tell me this morning?"

"Mr. President," Roger P. Croy said with an easy smile, "we are all renewed and undaunted as we bask in the sun of your amiable good will. I will say—as many of us here who are lawyers by profession know from our own experience—that words and phrases sometimes become somewhat flamboyant in the eager pursuit of what one deems to be a valid argument."

"They sometimes do in the press, too," the President remarked, and there was more laughter as Herman Kappel of North Dakota waved a copy of the *Post*, folded to display Walter's column.

480

"But, Mr. President," Roger Croy continued, and his demeanor became more serious, "there is, it seems to me, a nub of truth here, in that there does seem to be an almost excessive, an almost deliberately frightening display of military power. I don't mean frightening in the sense that it is directed against us, but just frightening in the sense that such displays are always frightening in a free nation, and also because there is the possibility that they may invite the very response and retaliation they are presumably intended to prevent."

"The Chair will say, Governor," the President remarked with a certain asperity, "that there seems to be a rather prevalent tendency on the part of some people to put the cart before the horse. The argument was made yesterday in several places on Capitol Hill, not just before Mr. Justice Davis, but in the House and Senate as well, that violence and threats of violence were being prompted by the presence of the armed forces which I have ordered to protect our deliberations here, and to protect members of the Committee during recess. Now it does seem to me, I will say with all respect to those who make this argument, that they have things slightly topsy-turvy. The violence came first and then my decision to protect us. Now, let's just keep that in mind."

"Very well, Mr. President, if that is the way you see it," Roger Croy said smoothly. "But—but: Is it really necessary to have such an enormous array of troops and firepower to do the job? Is it necessary to have quite such a crushing display of the iron fist? That, it seems to me, is something the Committee may want to consider. Of course I realize, Mr. President, that even if the Committee were to make some formal protest, it would only be advisory. You could continue the overwhelming and possibly somewhat oppressive arrangements if you pleased. You have us at your mercy," he said with a pleasant smile. "You are the Commander in Chief.

'Yes," the President said dryly. "Now I'm overwhelming, oppressive and merciless. What other nice things can you think of to say about me this morning?"

"Mr. President," said Pete Boissevain of Vermont, "will the distinguished National Committeeman from Oregon tell me what he hopes to accomplish by this rigamarole? He knows perfectly well what the situation is out front, we all saw it when we came in. It was bad enough two days ago and it's worse today. The crowd's changed. It's tougher. Some of them are beginning to wear those black uniforms we saw at the convention. Their signs are nastier and dirtier, if that's possible. Their mood is worse. They're spoiling for a fight, Mr. President, and I for one am mighty glad you've taken the precautions you have."

There was a rush of applause which did not daunt Roger P. Croy.

"I can understand," he said calmly, "the agreement of the distinguished National Committeeman from Vermont with the quite possibly excessive military arrangements made by the President, because he is backing the candidate who stands to benefit' most from such inexcus—"

"Mr. President!" Pete Boissevain said angrily. "Now, stop that, I will say to the Committeeman from Oregon! Nobody 'stands to benefit' except maybe you and me, Governor, and our precious necks. Yours may not mean much to you, but I like mine!" Again there was applause, this time mixed with laughter. "Now I think, Mr. President, that the Committeeman from Oregon and everyone who agrees with him had better stop trying to twist everything around into some kind of nasty implication every time he opens his mouth. We had enough of that watching him perform at the Court yesterday, and I for one am sick of it!"

"Mr. President," Roger P. Croy said patiently, "are there no rules of order here? I realize this is a situation without precedents, but even so—"

"The Chair will say," the President applied, "even though under great provocation, Governor, that he agrees there probably should be a few general principles of decorum. But the Chair certainly is not going to reprove anyone who speaks his mind openly and honestly on the wisdom of bringing up things that are somewhat extraneous to our main purpose here. And also, perhaps, are dragged in by the heels to confuse the issue and inflame passions outside."

"Whether they are really extraneous may be a matter of opinion, Mr. President," Roger Croy observed. "To me they seem quite fundamental. Quite fundamental, indeed. Not only are these enormous numbers of troops and this armed-camp aspect inhibitory to a free exercise of discretion and voting by certain members of the Committee dedicated to the cause of one of the candidates—"

"Now, Governor—" the President began with a real annoyance in his tone, but Roger P. Croy sailed on.

"—but they are also designed, apparently, to intimidate and, if you please, drive off, citizens exercising their right of free assembly and democratic protest against policies they feel are wrong and dangerous."

"Governor—"

"However," Roger Croy said, "I gather the Chair is not

going to provide any protection from unbridled personal attacks against those who have the courage to raise these points, so rather than prolong the discussion I shall now move that the Committee request the Commander in Chief to reduce the number of troops to no more than 100, the level commensurate with the actual need for protection under the worst possible circumstances, which I for one do not think are going to occur."

At once half a dozen members were on their feet shouting for recognition as the cameras zoomed in to catch startled expressions, angry expressions, worried and upset expressions. A stir of excitement ran through the press, and in the audience Patsy Labaiya leaned forward and jabbed Bob Leffingwell in the shoulder. "How about THAT?" she demanded. Bob turned with a tired scorn that was not lost upon their neighbors and asked, "Does your brother really need a cheap stunt like this?" "WELL!" she began, but at that moment the President recognized Asa B. Attwood of California and the room abruptly quieted down.

"Mr. President," Asa Attwood said in his rather mousy but determined way, "as you know, California is divided. I happen to be the divisive factor. I am not for California's governor, and this is a very good example why. His lieutenants and outriders here are raising phony issues, Mr. President, in an attempt to engender world headlines and bring pressure to bear upon you in the performance of your duties as chairman, and upon us in the performance of our task of selecting nominees. I despise this sort of thing, Mr. President, but of course it will get them just the headlines and the national and world reaction they want. It will also, I hope, get them the resounding negative vote they deserve on this motion, which is just a delaying and propaganda tactic and has no other purpose in this world."

"Mr. President!" Ewan MacDonald MacDonald cried angrily. "Mr. President, I resent—"

"The Committeeman from Wyoming may speak," the President said tartly. "It isn't necessary to shout."

"I also resent the Chair's tone," Ewan MacDonald snapped in the liquid burr he had brought from Deeside at the age of four. "However: what I most resent is the attempt by friends of Orrin Knox to try to always charge that everything we on our side say in defense of the democratic freedoms of this country is in some way a phony propaganda stunt. Your troops make *me* uneasy, I'll say frankly to you, Mr. President, and I don't think they're necessary and I'd like to see them reduced. And I hope this Committee will so vote."

"Mr. President," Asa Attwood said, "that's exactly what I mean. 'Democratic freedoms,' when it's all the trash from the gutters of America who have come here to try to intimidate this Committee. A fine democratic protest we've got outside now"—faintly but unmistakably, the rolling wave of boos began again—"with its blackshirt bullyboys and its filthy banners. That mob reeks of violence this morning, Mr. President. Who knows what weapons they have concealed among them, or what their leaders, who happen to be friends of the Governor of California—which is another reason I'm not for him, I don't like the company he keeps these days"—the boos grew louder—"who knows what their leaders are going to tell them to do? If we didn't have the troops you've provided for us, they'd be into this Center, I'll say to

Committee members, and we'd be lucky to get out with our lives."

"May be, anyway!" Pete Boissevain shot out, and there was a clash of voices, some earnestly agreeing, others sarcastically derisory. From outside there came, as if on order, what seemed to be a giant laugh, tripartite and distinct: "Ha!—Ha!—Ha!"

"This thing is getting worse," Asa Attwood said. "It isn't getting better. And since I have a Governor who apparently hasn't got the courage or the integrity to break away—"

At this a new, enormous wave of booing could be heard from outside, mingling with that which came from many parts of the Committee and the audience. The President rapped repeatedly for order, and when he got it said quietly,

"Now I do think the distinguished Committeeman from California has gone too far. Tempers are high enough as it is. I think we'd just best not go into personalities of candidates until we reach the point at which, I assume, they will be placed before the Committee in formal nomination. If the Chair could express a purely advisory opinion, I think it would be just as well if we could stop this discussion and have a vote on this motion right now. Does anybody agree?"

"Question, Mr. President!" cried Janette Wilkins Vandervoort of New York. "Mr. President! Mr. President!" shouted Roger P. Croy. "Mr. President, this Committee has not had sufficient time to discuss—"

But Janette Vandervoort was joined by at least fifteen others, some of them friends of Roger Croy, crying, "Second!" and "Question!" and Vote! Vote!" and after a moment he waved his hand gracefully, said, "Very well, Mr. President," and sat down.

"Mrs. Bigelow," the President requested, "if you will do the honors again, please—"

And when she had, it appeared that Roger P. Croy's motion had been defeated 64 to 42, which gave rise to much buzzing and speculation in the press and across the floor. But there was not time for lengthy analysis, because once more Roger Croy was on his feet, and something about his dramatic stance, the little lines of tension around his mouth, his determined expression, brought a sudden silence to the room. "Here it comes," Bob Munson whispered to Lafe Smith; and so it did.

"Mr. President," he said, trying to keep his voice steady but not entirely succeeding, "I move that the National Committee do now recall the convention lately concluded and charge it exclusively with the task of selecting nominees for President and Vice President of the United States."

From outside there came a great roar of cheers and applause, and from within the room a babble of voices in which no particular one was distinguishable. Presently the President's rapping of his gavel, not loud, not excited, just patiently persistent, began to break through the uproar and gradually a reasonable calm returned. Outside sporadic shouts and cheers still came faint but insistent.

"I assume," the President said with a matter-of-fact air, "that the distinguished Committeeman wishes to speak to his own motion."

"Only to say this, Mr. President," Roger Croy said: "that the reasons for reconvening the convention are exactly what my able colleague, Mr. George Harrison

Wattersill, and I said yesterday in presenting them to Mr. Justice Davis. With due respect to the diligence, integrity, patriotism and competence of our colleagues here, we on this side of the issue believe that a much broader democratic base for the selection of nominees will exist in the reconvened convention than exists in this small room.

"Yes," he went on firmly, over the indignant murmurs that came from such as Mayette Stranahan of South Carolina, Lathia Talbott Jennings of North Dakota, Harold Barkley and Diana Smith Watterson of Kentucky, "that is our conviction. And I think Mr. President, that it would be our conviction regardless of any other issues involved here."

"Justice Davis decided that last night!" Renée M. Martensen of Montana remarked loudly, and Roger Croy swung about in a stately, imperturbable way to stare down upon her with a bland, unyielding gaze.

"Indeed, dear lady, he did pass upon it, in his capacity as a Justice of the Supreme Court. But you will recall that he said he was basing his decision strictly upon the law as he conceived it to be, on the issue as it was presented to him. He also said—and I doubt if anyone here has really forgotten—that he personally would like to see the convention reconvened—"

"Did he say it was for the reason you're advocating?" Asa Attwood demanded.

"He said he would prefer that the convention be reconvened—" Roger Croy repeated.

"Oh, stop dodging!" Pete Boissevain interrupted angrily. "He did *not* say he wanted it convened because it would be 'broader and more democratic.' He didn't give any reason at all, and we all know it. He just said he personally would like to see it done. That's the truth of it, if the Committeeman ever bothers with the truth!"

"Mr. President," Roger Croy said patiently. "Now, Mr. President—"

"Yes, the Chair will say," the President agreed, "that it is probably about time to stop these personal attacks. I would remind delegates"—he smiled and there was a fragile moment of relaxation and laughter—"excuse me, Committeemen and women—that we are proceeding here in the full gaze of the nation and the world, thanks to our friends with their cameras and microphones along the sides and back of the room. Now, we as Americans can understand the asperity which sometimes creeps into debate, but I doubt if many of our friends overseas can understand. They can understand something like what we've got outside, of course," he said dryly. "That makes sense to them in their experience. But the habits of democratic debate, allowing as they do for a good deal of release of tension through personal invective, are not known to too many outside the areas where democracy prevails. And also, there's another reason for keeping it down a bit and that is simply that we have to get along here for a while, at least long enough to select our nominees." Faintly came the booing, in the room there was a stirring, but he ignored it. "We are going to have to refrain from too much bitterness, if we can. Governor Croy, do you care to say anything further?"

"Thank you, Mr. President," Roger Croy said. "Only to repeat again that it seems to those of us who will support this motion that it is manifestly more democratic and more in keeping with the very great seriousness of our responsibility here to recall the convention. Obviously,

Mr. President, more than 1000 people are going to furnish a broader base than 106, however perfect the 106 may be. Mr. Justice Davis chose to regard this as not a valid point of *law*, but it is a valid point, period. And it is on that basis that I make my motion and now, Mr. Chairman, request a vote."

"Mr. President!" Asa Attwood said, "I should like to speak to the motion for a moment myself."

("Oh, for God's sake, let's stop all this yakking and have a vote!" CBS exclaimed, not too quietly, to NBC, and Asa Attwood was onto it at once.)

"Yes, Mr. President!" he cried, swinging about and staring with a genuinely hostile expression at the press tables. "That's exactly what's wrong with trying to work in this fishbowl, and it's exactly what's wrong with the convention, and it's exactly why some of us are absolutely determined to block recall of the convention if we can. The press and television have done nothing but meddle, meddle, meddle, since the first day of the first committee meeting in San Francisco. They've been biased, slanted, unfair, one-sided, they've done everything they could to push Governor Jason, they've tried everything they could to blackguard and demean Secretary Knox.

"They tried to do a snow job on the convention, and they're trying to do a snow job here. We've all seen the sort of coverage that preceded this Committee meeting, and we've seen what's come out since our meeting began. It's no secret they want the convention called back so that they can try to pressure it again. And now they even have the gall to make their comments in loud tones so that the whole Committee and the whole world, even, can hear them do it. They're in contempt of this Committee and we ought to send them out!"

"Mr. President," Roger Croy said quickly, "does the Committeeman wish to make that in the form of a motion?"

"Well," Asa Attwood said, slowing down a little. "Well . . . No, of course not! We have a responsibility to the public, these proceedings have got to be public, they've got to be here to report them."

("Bastard," CBS said, relaxing. "Typical of the United Friends of Orrin Knox," NBC remarked.)

"But I will say this to the Committeeman from Oregon," Asa Attwood went on. "Nothing better illustrates the reason why the convention should not be recalled than the sort of smart-aleck comment we heard from the press just now. If there's a better argument, I don't know it! What it does is emphasize very vividly exactly the sort of atmosphere that we can't afford if we're to do the kind of job the country has a right to demand of us."

"Mr. President," Ewan MacDonald MacDonald said, "does the Committeeman from California also argue that the 106 of us are somehow superior and more intelligent and more responsible and more patriotic than the full convention would be? Does he say we're so much better and so much superior to the rest of our countrymen? Are we supposed to be the elite? Is that his concept of democracy?"

"I am saying," Asa Attwood said, "that 106 people, working under difficult conditions but God knows not one-tenth as difficult as in convention, can come up with a more sensible, reasoned, responsible decision than 1000-plus at a convention. Now, if this shocks you, I will say to the Committeeman from Wyoming—"

"And 106 are easier to pressure into voting for Orrin

Knox than 1000 would be, too, aren't they, Asa?" Ewan MacDonald interrupted.

"And 1000 are easier to pressure into voting for Ted Jason than 106 would be!" Asa Attwood shot back.

Faintly came the fetid wind of booing, and in the room a furious gabble.

"On which note," the President remarked with a quick wryness that concealed a purpose, though in the angry rush of the moment no one realized it, "I think if there are no further comments that we had better have the vote. Mrs. Bigelow?"

And for a moment it all hung in the balance, while he held his breath and maintained a bland expression. But with a sort of grumbling return to a minimal good humor, everyone settled down and no one challenged.

"Alabama!" Anna Hooper Bigelow said, and again the split voting began and for a necessary moment engaged attention.

"On this motion, as on the others," Helen M. Rupert said, "I'm afraid, Mr. President, that Alabama remains divided. I vote Aye."

"And I vote Nay," said Henry C. Godwin.

"Alaska!" Anna said.

"No!" said Tobin Janson, and,

"No!" said Mary V. Aluta.

"Arkansas!" said Anna Bigelow, and at that point Roger P. Croy came suddenly to life.

"Mr. President!" he cried, leaping to his feet. "Mr. President!"

"Yes?" the President inquired blandly, and he and Roger Croy knew that Roger Croy was beaten before he began. But he made the attempt anyway.

"Mr. President," he said, his tone an odd combination of anger, dismay, and the reasonableness necessary if he was to have any chance at all of carrying his point, "this vote is irregular, Mr. President, I submit! This is a matter of the utmost importance. This may very well be the most important vote we cast here! It cannot be decided by simple majority, Mr. President. It must be decided on the basis of a weighted vote, on the basis of the votes cast by each state delegation at San Francisco—"

Immediately the room was in pandemonium as at least thirty Committee members jumped to their feet shouting for recognition; as the audience instinctively if irregularly lent its voices to the din; as the television cameras swung frantically here and there to zoom in on contorted, angry faces; as the press clambered onto its tables for a better view and also, instinctively and irregularly, added its excited cries to the uproar.

From outside, harsh and insistent, came shouts, boos, screams, the beginnings of chants, the angry animal wail of a mob on the verge of going amuck.

In the center of it all stood the President, his expression impassive as it had been on so many hectic occasions over the years in the House, his aspect solid, immovable, and, finally, indomitable. When, after some five minutes of wild confusion, it became apparent that he was not going to move, look frightened, act uncertain or show the slightest sign of appeasing anyone, the clamor began to die; and presently, when it had terminated altogether and Committee, audience and press had all resumed their seats, and even outside the chaos had sunk to a distant, ominous groan, he spoke.

"The Chair is sorry, Governor," he said calmly, "but

the Chair sees no way in which you can be accommodated. The Chair raised this point two days ago when our meetings began. I said that it seemed to me that there were certain procedural matters that should logically be decided by simple majority vote, and I asked the Committee's opinion. I gave the Committee a perfectly fair and open chance to discuss it and pass upon it, and even have a vote on it if anyone wanted, and nobody objected, Governor. Not even you.

"And now we have followed a simple majority on two votes so far, the vote day before yesterday on the motion to appeal, and the vote this morning to reduce security precautions. So we have created precedent on these procedural matters. And furthermore, Governor, you know as well as I do that in parliamentary practice a vote once begun cannot be interfered with or recalled, it must be completed. The roll call has begun.

"I'm sorry you are too late to make your points, but you *are* too late. Mrs. Bigelow, please continue the roll call."

"But this is *not* a simple procedural matter!" Roger Croy exclaimed in an anguished tone, his stately white-haired dignity for once considerably shattered. "This is the most important—this is the most vital—"

"I'm sorry," the President said. "Mrs. Bigelow, if you please."

"Yes, sir," Anna Hooper Bigelow agreed with a nervous haste. "California!"

"*Yes!*" cried Esmé Harbellow Stryke with a bitter emphasis, and "No!" triumphantly replied Asa B. Attwood . . .

And presently, as they all knew, and as the nation knew and the world knew, the President announced calmly:

"On this vote the Yeas are fifty, the Nays are fifty-six, and the motion is not agreed to."

But Roger Croy was not down yet.

"Mr. President," he said, trying hard to control his anger and disappointment and succeeding reasonably well, "since you have based your action on an appeal to parliamentary law, I wonder if you are going to permit a little more of it and allow a motion to reconsider the vote, now that it has been completed?"

"If it comes from a supporter of the motion, as is our practice in Congress," the President said, "certainly."

"Mr. President," said Ewan MacDonald, "I move to reconsider the vote just taken."

"Mr. President," Pete Boissevain said promptly, "I move to lay that motion on the table."

"I had forgotten," the President said with a smile, not having forgotten for one moment, "that the distinguished Committeeman from Vermont used to be a distinguished Congressman from Vermont. The gentleman is entirely correct, and the vote now comes on the motion to table the motion to reconsider. If Mr. Boissevain's motion to table is approved, the matter is closed."

"Second!" Lizzie Hanson McWharter said sharply. "Question!" said Lyle Strathmore of Michigan and Luther Redfield of Washington.

"If there is no further discussion—" the President offered slowly, but it was obvious that for the time being, at least, the heart had gone out of Roger P. Croy and his friends. "Mrs. Bigelow, please call the roll."

The lines held.

The vote was fifty-six to table, fifty to reconsider.

And so ended the attempt to reconvene the convention.

"Mr. President," said Perry Amboy of New Hampshire into the exhausted silence that followed, "I think we've had enough for one day. I think we ought to recess until tomorrow."

"What's the Committee's pleasure?" the President asked.

"I move we recess until ten A.M. tomorrow," said Ewan MacDonald, sounding tired.

"Second," said Asa Attwood.

"Question," said Esmé Stryke.

"Question," said Mary Baffleburg.

"All those in favor—" said the President.

"Aye!" shouted the Committee.

"The Committee will stand in recess until ten A.M. tomorrow," the President said; secretly relieved, as were they all, because the situation had reached that psychological point that comes so often in democratic contests, when no one quite knows what will happen and no one quite dares push his luck without a chance to withdraw and regroup and recoup. Out of the votes taken today no really clear-cut pattern had developed. The Jason forces had lost heavily on the motion to reduce security, but there were many individual reasons for that. They had come back up very substantially on the vote to reconvene the convention, and though they had lost, there were many individual reasons for that, too, including Tommy's ruling. It did not necessarily mean that they could not win a vote to make Ted the nominee. Nor did it necessarily mean that the Knox forces were in command. The vote that would show the real relative strength of the two candidates had not come, and nobody wanted to force it just yet.

There was an obvious feeling of relief in the air as they prepared to leave the Playhouse, though millions watching could not understand the subtle but imperative conditions that had made them decide that it was best not to go on immediately to a showdown.

"Look at those bastards," Pete Boissevain said to Asa B. Attwood as the Army convoy started away from Kennedy Center to take them to Fort Myer, moving slowly through the menacing ranks of NAWAC, many now standing silent and ominous in their black uniforms, the rest shouting, chanting, screaming obscenities, flinging filth and ox blood at the cars. "They're spoiling for it. We're in for a rough time, I'm afraid."

"So be it," Asa Attwood said grimly. "If that's the way it's got to be, that's the way it's got to be. If that bastard Croy had had his way, we'd all be murdered now."

"Daddy Croy may have lost himself a Vice Presidency today," Pete Boissevain said with relish. "He just wasn't alert enough when the old fox got to operating."

"He'll never be Vice President because Ted Jason will never be President," Asa Attwood said flatly. He looked out the window with intense contempt. "Even though *they* think they can scare us into taking him."

"They may murder us yet," Pete Boissevain said grimly, "but I'm damned if I'm going to vote any differently than I want to."

"Me either," said Asa B. Attwood.

And so, too, said Roger Croy and his friends, in a different cause but in the same spirit, as the long line of cars passed through the tunnel of hate to the comparative safety of Fort Myer. The events of the day had stiffened determination, strengthened attitude, made position more inflexible; and curiously it was NAWAC that seemed to be putting the final touches to it.

All of the Committee members left the Center determined to vote as they pleased. Even the most timid and worried found themselves hardening into an adamant courage as NAWAC howled and threatened. They suddenly seemed to realize in some way they had not before that this was a matter for *them* to decide. With a stubbornness that was still characteristic of their nation under pressure, they made up their minds that they were going to do it the way they wanted to, regardless of what might happen.

But this was not known to NAWAC or to the clever, sick minds that controlled it, and so well-prepared plans went into effect, not only in Washington, where an ominous, getting-ready sort of quiet descended on the tent towns along the river, but in a number of other cities across the continent. By six P.M. bitter demonstrations for Ted Jason and against Orrin Knox, erupted in the capital, San Francisco, Los Angeles, Denver, Chicago, St. Louis, New Orleans, Miami, Atlanta, Detroit, Philadelphia, Boston, New York. By six-thirty counterdemonstrations had begun, and by seven P.M. at least four persons were dead and the rioting gave no signs of diminishing. Anonymous threatening telephone calls were received by many, including Orrin Knox, Justice Davis, Bob Leffingwell, Bob Munson; the White House received eighteen in half an hour, from widely separated points across the country. Shortly before nine P.M. a terrific thunderstorm hit the District of Columbia and all the demons of hell seemed to have been loosed upon it: a nice touch offered by nature which made the President and many others smile somewhat grimly as they looked out at the roiling clouds and the great shards of lightning that clattered down the sky.

Not even with armed escort did members of the Committee venture out of Fort Myer that night, and in Washington and in the riot-torn major cities, no one who did not have imperative business went upon the streets. In America, as all over the world, the feeling grew that tomorrow would be the day; and what it would bring, not even the desecraters of the night could know for sure, although they were fools enough to think they did, and to congratulate each other that they were somehow helping to bring it about with their insane idiot violence.

8.

NEXT MORNING, with TWENTY-THREE DEAD IN NATION-WIDE POLITICAL RIOTING, with heat and humidity rapidly climbing toward record levels for the summer, the Committee returned to Kennedy Center under a leaden, rain-swollen sky to keep its appointment with history.

It was not an easy passage.

Fifty demonstrators wearing skeleton costumes flung themselves into the road as the President's entourage approached: they were dragged out of it, but their howling hatred accompanied him as he rode swiftly by.

Moments earlier, Lathia Talbott Jennings of North Dakota and Henrietta McEwan of Nevada, arriving in an

Army car together, found themselves the recipients of rotten eggs, putrefying tomatoes and a very dead cat which landed on the hood and exploded all over the windshield so that their driver could hardly see: the car lurched and tottered for several seconds before he righted it and drove on, Lathia and Henrietta crying out in horror and disgust meanwhile.

Helen Rupert and Henry Godwin of Alabama, riding together despite their political differences, narrowly missed being pelted by balloons filled with ox blood as they left their car to hurry into the Center: the balloons burst just behind them and left a great red slick dripping slowly down the marble steps.

Jessie L. Williams and Blair Hannah of Illinois, their car slowing to a near-halt behind that of Roger Croy and Esmé Stryke, found themselves being rocked from side to side and almost overturned: soldiers using rifles as clubs finally drove off their screaming attackers.

Cullee Hamilton, arriving with the Munsons and Lafe Smith, was struck by a large rock in the left shoulder: his left arm suddenly hung limp and useless as he clutched it and ran up the steps after his friends while a triumphant snarl echoed after him.

Seconds later William Everett and Ruth Thompson Jones of Nebraska, impelled by a sudden shout, turned back at the door to see a Molotov cocktail hit the roof of the car they had just left, bounce onto the steps and explode, leaving a huge dirty gouge near the still-dripping smear of blood.

Though none but Cullee suffered actual physical hurt—and his soon proved to be only a temporary paralysis and not a serious wound—the gauntlet they all had to run was wild and foreboding enough so that many arrived inside the comparative safety of the Playhouse in a condition needing only a little more to tip it into hysteria.

"That scum has been smelling blood all over the country all night" Pete Boissevain remarked to Malcolm B. Sherman of Ohio as they found themselves the last to arrive and turned back for a moment to stare at NAWAC's vast sea of ostentatiously silent black-uniformed figures, intermingled with tatterdemalion whites and blacks screaming their hatred and derision. "I hope to hell the President brings in the whole damned Army."

He did not do quite that, but it was apparent the moment he declared the session open that he was going to do something.

"Good morning," he said gravely. "Please be seated. I wish to apologize to the Committee and to the country for the vicious disturbances that have accompanied our arrival here this morning. I wish to state that I called the Secretary of Defense from my car before I entered the Center, and gave him certain orders. These orders will be carried out automatically if there are any further outbreaks. I warn those responsible that is not an idle gesture. The orders have been given and they will be carried out, in strength sufficient to assure their success."

From outside there came a wild booing and screaming, and for the first time he responded to it directly. Looking straight into the cameras he said coldly,

"If you don't believe me, just try something."

Outside the animal cacophony increased until its angry humming seemed to fill the world, coming from nowhere and everywhere. But in the room it was met and drowned out by a fervent and relieved applause in which the friends of Edward Jason and the friends of Orrin Knox joined equally.

"Mr. President," Roger P. Croy said with a gracious air, "I wish to say to you in the presence of these witnesses that I regret the motion I offered yesterday to reduce security arrangements, and I wish to applaud the Commander in Chief for his precautions in defense of this Committee."

There was vigorous if surprised applause inside, a rather puzzled and uncertain booing from without.

"His judgment," Roger Croy acknowledged, "has proved more astute and foresighted than mine—even though," he added in a regretful tone that brought a wry, sardonic turn to the President's lips as he continued "there still remains, I think some reasonable question as to whether, if there had been a less openly provocative show of military force to begin with, there might have been a less hostile response today—"

"Mr. President," Pete Boissevain snapped, "when is the Committeeman going to stop this business of playing all sides? What about the 'hostile response,' as he calls it, across the country last night? Did that have anything to do with the necessary forces stationed here? No, it did not. It was prompted purely and simply by a political motivation and a desire to intimidate the country and the Committee. Your gangs didn't get their way about the convention here yesterday, Governor, so they got mad and rioted, tore up a dozen cities and killed 23 people. Now don't give me that—stuff—again about provocation, and too many troops, and the poor sensitive rioters, and

502

how they're offended by it, and how this makes them twice as irresponsible and twice as bad as they are naturally. Because that, Governor, is—well, you know what it is. And I think this Committee has a right to ask that you spare us any further examples of it."

"Mr. President," Roger Croy said patiently, "the Committeeman from Vermont, like some others on his side of the issue, is not only characteristically offensive but characteristically obtuse. I have just apologized to the President for my motion yesterday, and have just commended him for his thoughtfulness in protecting, these deliberations. Now, I think I have a right, in all fairness to myself and to the many sincerely disturbed and worried citizens who have come to make their patriotic protest here"—there was a faint sound of cheering outside—"to point out what seems to me the ill-advised and provocative nature yesterday of the massive military power displayed around the Center. And to say that if it had not been here, in such large and provocative numbers, there might very likely not have been such hostile response to it as we have seen this morning."

"Mr. *President*," Asa Attwood began in a tone of indignant disgust, but the President banged his gavel sharply and interrupted in the blunt, implacable tone with which Mr. Speaker had so often made the House sit up and think twice.

"The Chair will say to the Committee that there is no point in discussing this matter further. The Chair is not going to debate rights and wrongs when the barn is burning down: that is a matter for the Committee and the country to judge according to each man's conscience and common sense. The Chair will say simply that he regards earlier precautions as necessary; he regards his orders this morning as necessary.

"Those orders *have* been given," he said quietly, "and if necessary they *will* be carried out. Everyone within sound of my voice is on fair notice. I am not fooling. I am not equivocating. I am ready to act. Now, just remember that . . . "

Again there was the angry hum of many boos and shouts, but he ignored it and presently it trailed off, a little uncertainly. He looked slowly and challengingly around the room but this time not even Roger P. Croy ventured to respond.

"Now, ladies and gentlemen," the President said quietly, "we have a job to do and I suggest we get on with it. The business before us, and the only business that logically should occupy our time this morning, is the nomination of candidates for President, followed by the selection of one of them. It would now seem time to accomplish this."

There was a rustle and stir among the Committee, most of whom had been up most of the night arguing, conferring, discussing, debating, in groups that ranged from small to large, all over their quarters at Fort Myer. Milton S. Oppenheimer of New York raised his hand.

"Mr. President, I move that we proceed in regular order."

"Thank you!" the President said with an exaggerated relief that brought some amusement and relaxed the tension a little. "If there is no objection, I shall ask the Secretary to call the roll of states for the purpose of nominating candidates for the office of President of the United States." He waited for a moment, smiled comfortably, and said, "Anna: once more unto the breach, dear friend."

There was genuine laughter as Anna Hooper Bigelow came forward to take her place beside him at the lectern. Abruptly the room, the nation, the world, quieted down.

"Alabama!"

"Mr. President," Henry C. Godwin said, "Alabama agrees at last: Alabama passes." There was good-natured applause.

"Alaska!"

"Alaska," said Mary V. Aluta, "yields to Colorado."

("What the—?" the Seattle *Times* began. The Denver *Post* nudged him excitedly. "So that's his game!" he exclaimed. "No wonder Jessie Clark wouldn't talk to me when I phoned her last night. So that's it!")

But, as the President's oldest and closest friends could have told the Denver *Post*, it wasn't.

"Mr. President," Jessica Edmonds Clark of Colorado said in a voice that trembled with excitement, "Colorado has a nomination."

"It won't get you anywhere," the President said with a smile that no one in the press believed, "but come to the lectern, if you like. Or stay there, whichever you please."

"This floor is good enough for me," Jessie Clark said. "This is an historic floor. I don't have a great deal to say. I will say it from right here."

"Spoken with the true simplicity and directness of our native state," the President said.

("How *cute* the *Post* said in a tired voice to the *New Republic*. "It's sickening," the *New Republic* agreed.)

"Proceed, Mrs. Clark."

"Mr. President," she said, her tall, handsome figure, dressed in a silver-gray suit that matched the silver-gray of her hair, turning slowly as her keen blue eyes looked thoughtfully around the room, "Colorado will not take long to make this nomination.

"Colorado has a son who has proved in forty years in public office in this city that he is honest, courageous, steadfast; devoted beyond all else to the public good; diligent and tireless in his service to his people; eternally and always dedicated, mind, heart and body, to the United States of America, and to her safety and her best interests.

"This we have always known in Colorado, as it has been known here in Washington, and as it is known to all the nation, and to all the world. In these recent days we know something more: that, called as he has been, unexpectedly, with tragic suddenness, to an even higher office, he has measured up completely to the heavy responsibilities thrust upon him. He has earned the permanent gratitude of his country, and he has earned the right to continue to do the magnificent job he has done, and is doing, for us.

"He has already put a successful end to a difficult war. He has offered the proposal of a world statesman to settle another. His integrity, his courage, his honor, are above challenge by decent people"—faintly came the fetid Boooo!—"and in his hands the future will be safe. Mr. President, it is with a deep pride that on behalf of Colorado—"

The President held up his hand.

"Mrs. Clark" he interrupted gently: "dear Jessie, at

whose side I have fought so many political battles over these long, difficult years. If the distinguished Committeewoman will ever forgive me for intervening at this particular moment, I think I have some inkling of the name which was about to come forth."

("I think," the Seattle *Times* observed to the Denver *Post*, "that you were wrong." "Yes," the Denver *Post* agreed. "I underestimated him.")

"I cannot find words," the President said quietly, and his voice, too, betrayed a real emotion, "to express my gratitude for the great honor you were about to give me. I would like to think that if I were agreeable, Colorado might not stand alone in supporting me."

("The old HYPOCRITE!" Patsy whispered to her aunt Valuela Randall. "He knows perfectly well he could get it if he said so!")

There was real applause, and cries of approval, for suddenly it seemed to them that it would be such a simple way out of their troubles, such a good way to dispose of the bitter clash between Orrin Knox and Ted Jason. At that moment, Patsy could have been right. Yet even Roger Croy could join in the applause, for it was clear that it was quite safe.

"But," the President said, "I made up my mind at about—oh, I'd say about one A.M. on the night when I became President of the United States—that I would do my job until a successor was elected and sworn in, and then I would return to my true and only home on Capitol Hill.

"The only office for which I am or will be a candidate is member of the House of Representatives for the Fourth District of Colorado. It is presently empty, I understand. I have some hopes," he remarked with a sudden smile that again brought laughter and applause, "that I may be able to fill it.

"I suppose," he said with a distant, quizzical expression, "that when I leave the White House, I will probably have some sort of profound valedictory to give the country: history shows that a good many of us have, when we have left this office. But for now I don't want to take up the time or the Committee or delay its work, except to say this:

"When I first came in, a couple of weeks ago, the label which was promptly attached to me by a great newspaper, the New York *Times,* was, I recall, 'The Caretaker President.' In my short time in office, and in the time remaining to me, I have tried to take care, and I will continue to try to take care: of the American Government, which is my personal responsibility; of the American people, some of whom"—his expression became ironic—"don't like me, but a lot of whom do—and of something even more precious and vital, because without it there wouldn't be an *American* Government or an *American* people—and that is the essential spirit and tradition of this Republic.

"Now, basically, that's what we're contending for here in this Committee right now. Basically, in their own weird way, I suppose it is what those who are presently desecrating that spirit and that tradition are contending for in their riots and demonstrations across the country.

"The soul of America—that is the prize. Whoever captures that captures the fulcrum with which to move the world. Beset, beleaguered, even somewhat bedraggled as we may have become in the eyes of some—still it is the prize.

508

"I am defending it as best I know how while the burden rests on me," he concluded very quietly, and even outside there was an absolute hush. "Let us pray God that whoever succeeds me will do the same.

"Mrs. Bigelow," he said briskly, before the applause could really get started inside, before they could remember that they were supposed to boo outside, "please continue the roll call for nominations."

But then the applause did begin, and so, dutifully, did the booing. The two contended in a rush of sound that the President allowed to run for a couple of minutes. Then he began rapping patiently with his gavel, and when the Committee finally responded, repeated matter-of-factly, "Mrs. Bigelow!"

"Arizona!" said Anna.

"Arizona passes," said Margaret Bayard Hughes.

"Arkansas!"

"Arkansas," said David M. Johnson, "yields to California."

And the tension shot up as everything returned to normal.

"Mr. President," Esmé Harbellow Stryke declared, her dark little face pinched and strained with excitement, "California wishes to nominate the next President of the United States!"

"I expect California has as much right as Illinois has," the President remarked amicably. "Would the distinguished Committeewoman like to come to the lectern?"

"Yes, I will, Mr. President," Esmé said; and after she had done so—the President and Anna Bigelow stepping back to take seats at the table toward the right of the stage—she adjusted the height of the microphone and began to speak in a voice that was urgent and a little defensive, yet firm.

"Mr. President, California, too, has a native son, and it is now incumbent upon California to give her son to the world—"

("Her only begotten son?" the Chicago *Tribune* whispered to the Miami *Herald*. The Miami *Herald* whispered, "*Shhhh.*")

"—so that the world may at last have peace.

"Mr. President," she said, and the defensiveness became a little more pronounced, "it will not be my purpose this morning to go into matters of foreign policy that are presently dividing this Committee and are very much dividing the nation. I think we all know the basic lines of argument, and we all know, generally, where we stand.

"Certainly, Mr. President, we know where you and the Secretary of State stand"—she looked around at him and he looked back with complete impassivity—"and certainly we know where California's favorite son stands. He, too, I will say to the distinguished Committeewoman from Colorado, is known to us as a man of integrity, courage and honor. He, too, has stood four-square for what he believes in. He, too, cares for America. How could he run for this terrible, difficult office otherwise?

"Mr. President, California believes that the time has come for America to have the leadership of this man. With all respect to you, and to the Secretary of State, we do not believe your policies are best for America. We do not believe that they can achieve a genuine peace as long as they rest solely and exclusively on force of arms. We do not believe that there is any future for America the way we are going. We believe that the policies being followed are old, tired, unimaginative and stale. We believe they lead to disaster instead of redemption. We believe,"

510

she said quietly, "that they are doomed, and we are very much afraid that unless they can be changed, America will be doomed along with them.

"California offers this Committee—as we had hoped to offer the free convention, but that is not to be—a man who can bring us new policies, a new vision, a new approach. California offers you a man who can give us the leadership we desperately need—who can put us back on the high road of American purpose and American idealism—who can save us and save the world—a man who can preserve, protect and defend, if you please, what the President in his very gracious speech described as 'the soul of America.'

"Mr. President, California is proud to offer this Committee, the country and the world, the name of her most favorite, most able, and most distinguished son, Governor Edward M. Jason!"

And she turned and bowed to the President, still impassive, came down the little flight of steps and returned to her seat, as many in the Committee and the audience applauded, and distantly came a long, swelling roar of cheers and shouts, applause and excitement.

("Not as bad as I thought it would be," Senator Munson murmured to Bob Leffingwell, while Patsy strained to hear them from the row behind. "Very reasonable," Bob Leffingwell agreed. "Maybe the President's words have calmed things a little.")

"Members of the Committee," the President said, returning to the lectern, "are there seconds? It seems to the Chair that possibly, since this is not a convention, it might not be necessary to have lengthy seconds—"

"Mr. President," Roger Croy said, "we on our side discussed this last night. We agree that your position is entirely sound. To complete the nominating process for the record, Mr. President, and on behalf of a substantial number of our colleagues—"

("Damn it," AP whispered to UPI. "How can we see how things are shaping up if he isn't going to name them and they aren't going to speak?")

"—Oregon seconds the nomination of the Honorable Edward M. Jason."

"Thank you," the President said. "Mrs. Bigelow—"

"Connecticut!" Anna said.

"Connecticut," said John P. Fanucci, "passes."

"Florida!"

"The great state of Florida," said J. V. Simonson, "yields to the great state of Illinois to nominate the next President of the United States!"

Blair Hannah rose beside his desk.

Tension renewed itself.

Outside an ominous murmuring began.

"Mr. President," Blair Hannah said, looking about in his thoughtful, rather pedantic fashion, speaking in his slow, acid-edged drawl, "we do meet under extraordinary circumstances here, and nothing, I think, illustrates that fact better than the general response and treatment that we on the Committee have received in this city.

"Most of us, Mr. President arrived here a week or so ago to await our meeting in response to your call. Since then, in every edition of every newspaper, and every hour on the hour over television and radio, the opinions of the Committee have been sought.

"When they haven't been found, they have been fabricated."

There was an uneasy stirring at the press tables and all the cameras suddenly zoomed in on Blair Hannah's calm eyes and firm, pugnacious jaw.

"For instance, Mr. President, each day there have appeared, in various newspapers with a national or semi-national circulation that happen to be on sale in this town, such headlines as: MAJORITY OF COMMITTEE SHOWING TREND TO JASON. Or sometimes it's been: KNOX FORCES LOSING GROUND IN PRE-MEETING HUDDLES. And then again it's been: COMMITTEE MEMBERS HINT JASON ON FIRST BALLOT. Or, KNOX WAR POLICIES DRAW COMMITTEE CRITICISM.

"And in the columns and the editorials and the pictures, and on the television and radio programs, the story has been the same. It seems as though there have been sixty dozen dope stories and fifty dozen special broadcasts, all of them adding up to the same thing: Orrin Knox is the villain of the age and he's beaten before we vote.

"Well, Mr. President," he said, and his drawl became increasingly sardonic, "that isn't the way some of us have heard it. In the first place, aside from a few"—he stared thoughtfully into the cameras—"professional leakers, I suppose they might be called—I don't really think too many *responsible* people on this Committee have said much to the press or television. I know that on our side we haven't, because we all reached agreement in the first few hours that we were in town that we weren't going to. So, all these reports and inside-dope stories, Mr. President—these trends and gains and losing grounds—they must have come from somebody else.

"Now, I know, Mr. President, because before I retired

and got into this delightful business of politics, I was in that other delightful business, that this just isn't very good journalism. I mean, I used to run a pretty sizable newspaper in Decatur, you know, and we used to try not to do that sort of thing. Of course now and again it will creep in, but you can guard against it, Mr. President . . . if you're alert and reasonably careful, you can guard against it."

"Mr. President—" Ewan MacDonald MacDonald began, but Asa Attwood snapped, "Regular order!"

"The Committeeman from California is correct," the President said. "This isn't a debate, now, these are nominations. Proceed, Mr. Hannah."

"Thank you, Mr. President," Blair Hannah said. "Wouldn't want to upset anybody too much, but I think it's good to get the background, here."

("As he sees it, the pompous ass," the New York *Post* whispered to the San Francisco *Chronicle*. The *Chronicle* nodded cheerfully. "Never *did* think much of that rag in Decatur!")

"Now, Mr. President," Blair Hannah continued calmly, "ever since we got here, I will admit there has been a powerful lot of stirring around inside the Committee. I remember reading a story a few days ago by Miss Carrew, God rest her soul, whom many of us had gotten to know well and fondly in conventions over the years, and while I don't want to be critical of it or of her, still all that social lollygagging, while it has existed, has only been part of it. As of course she knew, and, I suspect"—he paused and peered slowly around at Ewan MacDonald, who had no choice but to stare impassively back—"knew too well . . .

"Much else has gone on, Mr. President. All of us have

514

been subjected to all sorts of pressures. We've had telephone calls and messages and talks with everybody from you, right on down—or up, as some may wish to look at it—to the distinguished Governor of California, to say nothing of the distinguished Secretary of State. Clear up to three and four o'clock this morning, over there in Fort Myer in that gilt-edged detention home you've provided for us"—there was a ripple of amusement in which the President joined—"people were conferring like mad. And some of them, probably, at this moment don't know exactly which way they're going to jump. In fact, I'd say," he added with a thoughtful expression that brought an intent interest, "that maybe about four or five are still undecided. And four or five," he said quietly, "Can sometimes decide an election. . . ."

("Is it that close?" Hal Knox asked in the library in Spring Valley. "So we're told," Beth said. "Yipes," he said soberly.)

"So, Mr. President, the point I'm making," Blair Hannah resumed, "is that it hasn't been anywhere near as one-sided, right inside the Committee here, as it's been portrayed to the country and to the world. There's been a certain—maybe we should say 'wishful thinking,' that might be the polite way to put it—that has seemed to pretty well color the reporting and the broadcasting that's gone on here. Four or five people here may be undecided, but I doubt there's that many major newspapers, periodicals and networks that are. With them, it's the great Governor, all the way."

"Mr. President"—Ewan MacDonald tried again, but Blair Hannah raised a gently cautioning hand and went serenely on.

"So, Mr. President, I come to the nomination, now that I've paid my tribute to the value of reasonable perspective and objectivity in the press. And the nomination I have to make, as you all know, is that of Illinois' favorite son, the Secretary of State."

("Spiteful old son of a bitch," The Greatest Publication murmured. "What can you expect of a jerkwater-town editor?" the Los Angeles *Times* asked with a shrug.)

"I'm not going to be lengthy about this, because we all know him. We all voted upon him for Vice President scarcely two weeks ago. We know his record, and we know what he stands for. He stands four-square for the only policy that will save America—which to my way of thinking, and that of the people I know," he said dryly, "is possibly even slightly more important than saving the rest of the world. Because without us, there won't be much left of it.

"It is true that the Secretary of State has always counseled, beginning in the very earliest days of a Senate career which even his enemies, I think, concede was very distinguished and outstanding, a firm policy in the world. But it has been a firmness tempered with compassion—"

("Napalm in the jungles of Gorotoland?" the St. Louis *Post-Dispatch* whispered to *The Nation*. "That's known as selective compassion," *The Nation* replied.)

"—and a strength restrained by fairness and justice. He believes that the world is indivisible and that we rise and fall together, and he believes the same thing about the United States. He doesn't think you fragment off your principles and your courage without fragmenting off your chances of survival. He doesn't think the world can survive half-slave and half-free, particularly when the slave side is constantly on the move trying to disrupt and conquer the free side.

"So: he has principles and he stands by them. And because he has, I believe, and many Americans believe, America has been stronger for his presence; and will be even stronger if we here today give him the ultimate office from which he can—and I will use the language of the oath, just as my good friend, Mrs. Stryke, did—preserve, protect and defend the Constitution and the corporate being and future of the United States of America.

"Mr. President, I offer this Committee, in the hope that it will in turn offer the country and the world, the name of the Honorable Orrin Knox of Illinois to be our nominee for President of the United States."

From outside a bawl of boos, harsh, sustained, animal-angry, rose from the rancid ranks of NAWAC. Inside there came applause, vigorous, dedicated, perhaps slightly defensive: not quite as much as had approved Governor Jason's name, the press felt, but still disturbingly substantial.

("That was a longie," Senator Van Ackerman remarked in his office in the New Senate Office Building. "Let the son of a bitch talk," LeGage Shelby said with a shrug. "Knox loses votes the longer his people yak." "Yess," agreed Rufus Kleinfert. "Now ve shall see.")

"Mrs. Bigelow," the President said, "if you will complete the roll of states, please."

And when Anna had, and there were, as expected, no more speakers save for a seconding announcement by Harold Barkley of Kentucky, he brought the gavel down once, sharply, and said gravely,

"These nominations for President of the United States are now closed."

All over the city, the nation, the world, a hush descended, a tense, waiting excitement began.

"We now come," he said quietly, "to the call of the states for the purpose of electing—"

But Roger Croy was on his feet and the tension became so great that it was almost palpable.

"For what purpose," the President inquired, "does the Committeeman from Oregon interrupt the Chair?"

"The Committeeman regrets, Mr. Chairman," Roger Croy said with an edge in his voice, "if the exercise of his prerogative to make a motion is regarded by the Chair as an interruption. The Chair had not completed his instruction to the Secretary, I believe?"

"That is correct," the President agreed calmly. "The Committeeman will make his motion."

"In view of the intense national and world interest in this nomination," Roger Croy began—

("For God's sake," the Chicago *Tribune* hissed impatiently, "what in the hell is it now?" "He has a right to do it," the Baltimore *Sun* snapped. "Shut up!")

"—and to allow time for members of the Committee to ascertain to the fullest degree the opinions of the country—"

("Oh, oh," Hal Knox said softly. "Quiet!" his mother commanded.)

"—I move, Mr. President, that this Committee do now stand in recess until ten A.M. one week from today."

And again tension soared and uproar reigned.

"I further move," Roger Croy said coolly, "that on this vote the votes of the states be weighted to correspond to their votes in the convention in San Francisco."

And uproar increased as eight or ten members jumped

to their feet and began shouting angrily at one another across the little room, while the President resumed his steady, insistent, finally effective, rapping with the gavel.

"The Chair will say to the Committee," he said when an explosive silence had settled, "that it is his opinion that the motion of the Committeeman from Oregon stands on the same bottom with previous motions here, in other words that it is a procedural matter and should be decided by simple majority vote.

"The Chair, in fact, will so rule.

"Now, if the Committeeman from Oregon really wants to prolong this for some strategic advantage he thinks he may see in it, he may appeal the ruling. But an appeal, I warn the Committeeman, is clearly a procedural matter and it *will* be decided by a simple majority.

"The Committeeman evidently feels that he stands a better chance with a weighted vote than he does with a simple majority. Now if the simple majority on his appeal goes against him, the Chair would think," the President said with a certain quizzical wryness, "speaking as an old parliamentarian, that it just might have a psychological effect on the vote on his motion.

"Is the Committeeman really sure he wishes to run that risk?"

"Well, Mr. President," Roger Croy said reasonably, "if the Chair can give me some assurance that when we actually vote on the nominations, we can have a vote that will correspond to the total vote cast by each state in the convention—"

"Now the Committeeman is quibbling," the President interrupted sharply. "I have told the Committee that, repeatedly. Furthermore, it is in the rules. It can't be avoided if anyone wanted to. The Committeeman knows that. The Chair would appreciate it if he would stop these snide implications that the Chair is somehow going to pull some sleight of hand that is plainly and absolutely impossible under the rules. Does the Committeeman," he asked, biting off each word, "wish to appeal my ruling or does he not?"

"As long as I have your assurance, Mr. Chairman," Roger Croy said smoothly, "I shall not appeal. But I should like to speak for a moment to my motion."

"The Committeeman has that right," the President said coldly.

"Thank you," said Roger P. Croy. "Mr. President, it is very obvious from events in the past twenty-four hours, that there is a deep and genuinely dangerous division in the country. There have been outbreaks of violence. There have been tragic deaths. There has been a near-breakdown of law and order in several areas of several major cities. Again, all these things are tied together and related: again they come down basically to a genuine, frustrated, almost hopeless protest against policies whose solution, to many, seems to lie only in the election of Governor Edward M. Jason.

"Mr. President," he said sharply as several voices cried out angrily, "I have the floor! It is time to face up to these realities and stop pretending! It is because a disturbed nation feels instinctively that there is a conspiracy here to deny it the man it wants that these things are happening! Is there anyone here who honestly thinks that if the Committee had approved the recall of the convention, and so paved the way to a free and democratic vote for Governor Jason, that the nation would have seen the turmoil it has seen in the past twenty-four hours? We deny the people what they want and they have no choice but to riot, Mr. President! We deny them the man of peace and so they make war, tragically, upon their own countrymen. How can such things be?"

"Far better, Mr. President," he said as angry voices again protested, "that we should bow gladly and willingly, as we sooner or later must, to the will of the people. Far better that we listen to, and heed, their deeply impassioned desires in this matter.

"They see their future in this man, Mr. President. It is folly to stand in their way, for to do so can lead only to more bitterness, more frustration, more violence. And that way lies final disaster for our beloved land.

"Mr. President, it is because not all members of the Committee are yet fully aware of this that I think they should have time to sample national sentiment, and understand. A week's delay in a matter so vital will not hurt anyone, Mr. President. Rather, it will permit reason to prevail. It will permit truth to be heard. It will give Committee members who may still doubt time to achieve the sure and final conviction that the country does, indeed, want Governor Jason; and that if it is denied him by some conspiracy here, some parliamentary evasion or arrangement, only truly great disaster lies ahead.

"I believe this week may save America. That is why I urge approval of my motion, Mr. President."

And with a graceful little bow to the President, who stared down upon him with a cold and quizzical expression, he sat down, folded his hands before him, and lifted his stately white head with a bland, attentive air. From outside there came a great prolonged roar of approval and excitement.

"Does anyone wish to reply?" the President inquired dryly as some twenty Committeemen and Committee-women stood up and waved vigorously for recognition.

"The distinguished Committeeman," he said, making the choice he thought would furnish the most contrast and be most effective, "from Vermont."

"Mr. President," Pete Boissevain said, so angry that his words came out in a tumbling rush, "I am not a very graceful speaker, as the Chair knows, he had enough trouble with me in the House. I can't pull out a lot of fancy phrases on short notice like the former Governor of Oregon. But I can speak the truth as I see it, Mr. President, and I don't have to do it," he said with a bitter sarcasm, "like Aaron Slick from Punkin Crick, either.

"I've heard plenty of poppycock in my time, but I've never heard anything as twisted and slick and crafty and—and evil—as what we've just finished hearing now. Sure, there's a deep division in the country! Sure, there's been violence and, sure, there's threat of more violence! And why, Mr. President? Because a lot of immature minds, egged on by minds that aren't so immature but know exactly what they want, are trying to overturn the very foundation-principle of democracy, which is that *you accept the will of the majority.*"

Outside there rose again the angry hum.

"The Governor says in so many words that if we'd recalled the convention—and look who's talking about parliamentary conspiracies!—*if we'd given these monstrous babies what they wanted*—they wouldn't have rioted last night. And he says if we don't quit for a week now and then come back and give them what they want, they'll riot some more and maybe destroy the country.

"Good God Almighty, man!" he exclaimed, rounding on Roger P. Croy, who paled but returned him stare for stare, "do you realize what you're saying here? Do you have the slightest concept of what you're really saying? You're saying that if an organized minority—because don't you try to kid us, Governor, we each of us have our own ways of sampling public opinion, and there are just as many who want Orrin Knox, and maybe more—you say that if an organized minority doesn't like something and goes into the streets and breaks the law and raises hell, we've got to appease it and give it what it wants, because if we don't it might do worse. You're saying we've got to crawl to it, instead of putting the law on it and beating it down as it should be beaten down!

"What you're saying, Governor, is that democracy is all wrong. You're saying that if somebody doesn't like something the majority has democratically voted for, he has a right to go out and destroy democracy if he can, just because he's an insane child who has the pouts and isn't mature enough to play by the rules. Men have worked and struggled and died for a long time to make those rules, Governor, and now you want to toss them out the window because the riffraff of America riots for your precious candidate!

"Well, I don't know how others feel," he said, and he glared around the silent room, "but I say, the hell with that! I say it's about time we stopped appeasing these thugs and murderers who are trying to take over the country. I say it's time we stood up to our responsibilities and voted the way we please, and if they don't like it, the hell with them!"

Outside, the angry hum increased until the Kennedy Center seemed to vibrate with it.

"I say it's about time *to make them behave!*

"You can have your motion, Governor," he concluded, more quietly but not much. "I wouldn't be such a betrayer of America as to think like you do and act like you want us to act. I wouldn't be such a coward."

And he turned his back on Roger P. Croy and sat down. Outside, the angry humming grew to a steady, bitter thunder. Inside, about half the Committee and half the audience applauded with an almost hysterical approval, while the other half sat silent, unmoving and grim.

"If there are no further speakers," the President said quietly after a couple of minutes had passed with no signs of anyone else wanting recognition, "I think the Secretary may call the roll on the motion of the Committeeman from Oregon to recess for a week."

"Alabama!" said Anna Hooper Bigelow in a voice that trembled in the hush, and,

"Aye!" said Helen M. Rupert, and,

"Nay!" said Henry C. Godwin.

("If they stay split the way they have on the other votes," the general director of the *Post* remarked to Walter Dobius, "it isn't going to tell us a thing." But the instinct of a longtime political reporter caused Walter to shake his head. "It will," he said, concentrating grimly on the little screen. "It will.")

And so, as the world could see with a steadily rising excitement, it did; for as Anna Bigelow proceeded down the proud roll of names that ring the changes of America, evoking the seas, the plains, the mountains and the forests, three or four delegations that had been split before were split no more; and while this might have been just for the present issue, still there was something about the tone of voice and the manner in which the votes were cast which seemed to indicate that some hitherto undecided were undecided no longer, and that some whom worry and possibly timidity had made uncertain were beginning to find certainty.

"On this vote," the President said into the quivering stillness, "the Yeas are fifty-eight, the Nays are forty-eight, and the motion is not agreed to."

Again there came the great rush of sound, this time, uncertain, puzzled, frustrated, angry, ominous; as though the hordes of NAWAC were not sure what was going on, but whatever it was, knew that they shouldn't like it.

("That's it," Walter said bitterly at the *Post*. "Oh, no," the general director protested, "you're too pessimistic." "That's it," Walter repeated. "Look where the changes came. I'm going to call Ted." But the phone was not being answered in Dumbarton Oaks.)

"The vote now comes," the President said slowly, "on the selection of a candidate for President of the United States. According to the rules of the Committee, selection will be by a majority of the number of votes cast at the convention in San Francisco, each state to have the same number of votes here as it did in San Francisco. Should the two National Committee members of a state disagree, each shall cast one-half of the full vote of the state."

("You see?" the general director said. "It isn't over yet, by any means. You take some of these states that split in San Francisco but didn't split right down the middle, and you divide them equally—"

And as the vote progressed from still-divided Alabama (which stayed five and five, as it had in San Francisco) on through still-divided California (where an equal split favored Orrin Knox), to still-divided New York (which also helped Orrin), to now-unified Ohio (which gave Ted Jason a big boost), and so on to Wisconsin, Wyoming and the end, it became apparent in the tensely silent room and all over the tensely watching globe, that the director was right. The equal division rule was having a decisive effect; aided, though they would probably never realize the irony of it, by the waiting hordes of NAWAC, who yelled eagerly for each Jason gain, groaned bitterly with each advance by Orrin Knox.

Into the deathly hush the President confirmed what they knew already but could not believe in Spring Valley, could not believe in Dumbarton Oaks, could not believe anywhere on earth until his official words in some final, mystical, tribal way made it real:

"On the vote to elect a nominee for President of the United States," he said, in a voice that was steady yet still betrayed something of his own tension, "the vote by states is 635 for Edward M. Jason, 658 for Orrin Knox, and the Presidential nominee of this party is the Honorable Orrin Knox of Illinois."

At once the animal roar screamed up, drowned the world, and came rapidly nearer.

9.

CONCERNING THE EVENT that historians would eventually come to refer to as "the great riot against the National

Committee," or more simply, "the Great Riot," the news stories, the broadcasts, the magazine articles, the books, and the memories were probably as many and varied as the participants. Yet on one thing all agreed: there had never been in the city of Washington, or, in fact in the United States, a scene and mood of quite such fear and terror as that which occurred when NAWAC's ranks, swollen this fateful afternoon to an estimated 200,000, attempted to storm the Kennedy Center following the nomination of Orrin Knox.

What their leaders really hoped to accomplish, what the purpose could be now that their candidate had been defeated, they probably could not have said in any coherent or rational fashion. It was as though some final act of political violence, almost carefree in its own dreadful way, had prompted the unleashing of the enormous mob that now swept screaming toward the ring of troops surrounding the Center.

Perhaps it was a desire for revenge: it could not succeed. Perhaps it was sheer, blind rage at being denied the prize NAWAC wanted, some insane impulse that the verdict could somehow be reversed if those responsible were frightened or killed: reversal was impossible. It may have been simply a desire for martyrdom and propaganda. In that alone it succeeded, but not before half an hour of horror had almost convinced many millions of Americans and many millions overseas that the great Republic was being toppled to the ground at last.

Inside, as the roar increased and seemed to roll over them from all directions (seven motorboats filled with armed men actually did try to get past the Coast Guard launches on the river side, and a small private plane carrying homemade bombs was shot down by one of the Army helicopters as it came in over Theodore Roosevelt Island), the first reaction of the Committee and the audience was one of fright and desperation. But once again the steady, insistent rapping of the gavel finally brought silence even to Anne Rogers of Michigan, Alice Lathrop Smith of Wyoming, Jessie L. Williams of Ohio and other ladies whose screams and outcries were matched by the harsh protests and warning shouts of Pete Boissevain, Luther Redfield of Washington, Cullee Hamilton, Lafe Smith, and many others.

"If the Committee and the audience will keep calm," the President was finally able to call out in a voice loud enough to carry over the tumult inside and the ominous clamor racing ever nearer as the seconds ticked by, "I have given orders, exactly as I told you, and they will now be carried out. I beg of you, be patient—keep calm—keep quiet—and we will get out of this all right. If you will just remain in your seats and don't try to go out the doors, because they are locked and under guard, we have 1000 troops already outside and another three to five thousand, if need be, on their way. They have the latest weapons and they have orders to use them in whatever way may be forced upon them to stop this. We're quite safe here, so just keep calm and it will soon be over.

But for a while it was not at all certain that his final assumptions were correct, because at first there seemed to be no stopping the furious rush that swarmed upon the Center from under the trees and along the boulevards. Some carried high the obscene defiant banners of COMFORT, DEFY and KEEP, others carried rocks and clubs, still others were obviously and formidably armed

528

with pistols, rifles, Molotov cocktails, hand grenades. Members of one well-trained unit of black-uniformed thugs had cannisters of gas strapped to their backs, and even as the soldiers sprayed tear gas and Mace upon them, they sprayed Mace and tear gas upon the soldiers.

Within two minutes gunfire broke out. Within seven it had settled into a steady, vicious, unrelenting exchange of shots. The first death, a soldier, occurred five minutes after the riot began, and in rapid succession seven more soldiers and fifteen civilians were on the ground dying or dead. Overhead the helicopters whirred, spraying more gas upon the mob. A lucky shot from somewhere in the trees brought one down. Pilot, crew and six of the mob perished in its flaming crash.

Nor was all the action in the front lines, for in the rear the sincere democratic protesters of NAWAC also found things to do. "My God!" exclaimed one of the younger reporters of the *Post*, rushed to the scene with many other newspapermen from around town, "do you see what those guys are doing to the flag? They aren't only urinating on it, they're dropping their pants and—" Very soon five Presidents and six Orrin Knoxes were burning merrily in effigy from the trees, and over all, those who were not close enough to do the fighting were keeping up a high, whining, banshee chant that blended in one great howl from the animal recesses of humankind. Its words were at first indistinguishable but soon became distinct as its angry rhythm solidified: "Kill the President! Kill the Committee! Kill the President! Kill the Committee!"

No one present that day ever doubted that these objectives were the real intent and purpose of the riot.

In those first minutes, surprise and desperation carried the mob so close to the Center that five black-uniformed toughs carrying machine guns succeeded in racing up the steps onto the plaza. They were gunned down from inside at the last minute, their blood replenishing the ox blood that had dried to a dull stain, their bodies lying grotesquely unattended on the marble, for no one dared go after them. Nor had anyone time. Encouraged by that first attempt to assail the inner defenses, a solid phalanx of perhaps three thousand formed on the north side and suddenly launched itself with a wild yell at the northeast corner, coming onto the plaza close to the building at an angle that momentarily confused the defenders. In the melee that followed six more of the black-uniformed succeeded in getting through into the North Gallery and machine-gunning the Marines guarding the stairway to the second floor. Two got through to the Playhouse. One died in the middle of the foyer, the other with his hand actually against the door. Two caroming shots splintered through the heavy wood. Even the President turned pale, and women began again to scream and men to shout.

"Get down there and quiet that mob," Orrin snapped from Spring Valley, "if you ever want preferment from this party again!"

"What preferment?"

"The preferment of being an honorable man, if nothing else! But I suppose that isn't enough!"

"I may get killed, you know," Ted said calmly.

"I doubt it."

"You'd like it if I did."

"I'd like it if just once you'd do the honorable thing without thinking of your own advantage!"

"As a matter of fact," Ted replied with an anger of his own, "I had already ordered the car and it's out there now, if you'll get off the line. Incidentally, congratulations. I wouldn't venture out, if I were you."

"God damn it," the Secretary of State said with a savage repugnance, *"get going."*

"Yes, Mr. President," the Governor of California said with an equally savage dislike. "I'm on my way."

And so, after what seemed an interminable time to those inside the Playhouse and to all the horrified millions who watched and feared for them—though it was really no more than fifteen minutes—were the additional troops and helicopters that were destined to put a quick and efficient end to the Great Riot. Force used as force and not as a bargaining point has its own decisive nature, and the President's orders had left no doubt that it was to be used in just that way.

Twenty additional helicopters began methodically saturating the rioters with Mace, and although two were shot down, the remainder completed the job in five minutes. Three thousand additional soldiers and Marines in gas masks then entered the area and began to herd the retching, staggering rioters back toward the boulevards with an implacable, machinelike advance that generated a terror of its own in those who moments before had been so brave in their howling mass. Sporadic gunfire and isolated skirmishes continued for the next five minutes, but for all practical purposes the Great Riot was over.

Just as some semblance of order began to return—just in time so that he could legitimately receive and take some of the credit for it—a great shout went up at the far edge of the now confused and uncertain throng, and into the middle of it, riding in Patsy's Rolls-Royce with two enormous, hastily lettered signs saying TED JASON attached to its sides, came, like some conquering savior, the Governor of California.

Instinctively the nearest Marine officer shouted to his men to form a protective cordon—though from the swelling, joyful shout that accompanied his progress it was obvious that he needed no protection—and in their midst his car rolled slowly forward until it reached the ravaged steps of the plaza. There he ordered it stopped.

He got out, was greeted by another wild explosion of joy; asked two Marines to assist him to the top of the Rolls; pulled a portable stereo loudspeaker from his pocket; and raised his hand.

A great hush fell upon the devastated park, the beautiful desecrated building, the vast concourse of people before him, the few inside the Playhouse, the nation, the world.

"My friends," he said, and his voice boomed out over the silent globe, "I think it would be best, now, if you abandoned this protest and went home."

An enormous groan went up, but again he raised his hand and in a moment, with a reluctant obedience, it died.

"I have no words that can adequately express my gratitude for the loyalty and devotion you have shown me in these past weeks."

("My God," Bob Munson said to Lafe Smith inside the Playhouse. "Does he have no conception of the forces that have been let loose in his name?" "How ironic it is,"

Lafe murmured, "that the new nominee of the party dare not leave his home to come here this afternoon, while Ted rides in like a paladin over the chaos his friends have created.")

"But," Governor Jason went on, "the time for protest is over now—"

There was a long, wailing denial, and he repeated firmly,

"The time for protest is over. At least, the type of protest which so unfortunately has evoked this sort of terrible violence."

"Who's to blame for that?" someone shouted, close at hand.

"It is not my purpose here today to assign blame," Ted said, while an expression of wonder touched the face of a watcher three thousand miles away at "Vistazo."

"Here on this battlefield—and it is a battlefield, of men's hope and men's beliefs—many of those hopes and beliefs have been shattered and defeated today. You came here, most of you, in good faith, because you did not believe in the morass of war in which we find ourselves"— in the Playhouse the President's face set in grim, cold lines—"and you must leave here with that situation unchanged and unresolved in spite of your sincere and democratic protest.

"Some of you, noble martyrs to your deep-held, democratic beliefs, have fallen on this lost battlefield"—in the distance the last ambulance pulled away, siren moaning, to take its dying burden to the nearest hectic hospital— "and the rest must leave disappointed. Yet all is not lost, my friends. You have made your protest before all the world, and there can never be question anywhere again

533

that there is a sincere, genuine, vital and active desire for peace in America which cannot be silenced and cannot be denied. Your honored dead bear witness, as you who live bear witness in this great gathering.

"But beyond that you will bear witness, for you will return to your homes and you will work, now, for victory—"

"Whose victory?" a bitter voice cried out, "Orrin Knox's?" And there was a great boo.

"—for victory in the cause of peace," Ted said. "Whether it will come through Orrin Knox, no man now living, including Orrin Knox, can know. History and fate and the destinies of nations work in strange channels and strange ways; and events may so unfold that the man you have opposed so gallantly on my behalf may yet find himself changing and moving closer to you, as you may find yourselves moving closer to him; especially if those who may be close to him encourage him to change, and to move, as I believe they will.

"Surely we and the nation will not remain static. Indeed, we cannot, for we live in the world, and the world is changing.

"Go now, my friends. I am not angry nor embittered, nor should you be. We have fought the good fight together: the satisfaction is ours. Go now. History will not forget you, nor will America look back with shame upon your democratic protest. Go, and God bless you, for what you have done for the conscience of America today."

And with both arms lifted in a widespread gesture that seemed to embrace the world, he turned slowly north, west, south, east, until he had conferred it upon them all. Then he smiled at his two Marine assistants, who offered their backs for him to step upon to the ground;

re-entered the Rolls and was driven slowly out through the enormous throng, which parted for his passage like the Red Sea for Moses and then turned back with smiles and grins and a euphoric air of released tension to take up its vigil—no longer hostile but, curiously, almost picniclike—outside the Center.

"Well, I'll be God-damned," said Hal Knox in Spring Valley.

"Members of the Committee," the President said quietly, "I shall not comment now on the extraordinary speech we have just heard. The time will come for that, but it is not now. Suffice it to say that we have had a long and difficult day; that we still have ahead of us the selection of a nominee for Vice President; and that in the customary nature of such things, this is usually preceded by conferences between the nominee for President and"—he hesitated for a second—"all elements—in the party.

"I do not know how the Committee feels, but it would seem wise to me that we recess until tomorrow. What is the Committee's pleasure?"

"Mr. President," Roger Croy said, with an equal quietness, "I move that we stand in recess until ten A.M. tomorrow, and that we then reconvene for the purpose of selecting a nominee for Vice President who is able to bind up the party's wounds and the nation's wounds and help us to victory in November."

"The Committeeman from Oregon moves that the Committee stand in recess until ten A.M. tomorrow," the President said without expression. "Is there a second?"

"Second," said Blair Hannah.

"All those in favor—"

"Aye," said the Committee quietly, and it was a sober, shaken affirmation that came almost hesitantly to the watching world.

"It is so ordered," the President said. "I must warn you," he added gravely, "that we will be passing through unpleasant scenes on the way out. But the situation is now under control, and you need not be afraid."

So ended the nomination of Orrin Knox to be a candidate for President of the United States. The media readied their broadcasts, their stories and their head-lines—TROOPS SHOOT DOWN THIRTY-FIVE ANTI-KNOX PROTESTERS AT KENNEDY CENTER. JASON SPEECH CALMS HOLOCAUST AFTER KNOX NOMINATION. The Committee and the audience left the Playhouse past soldiers and Marines with mops and buckets cleaning the blood from the stairways, the plaza and the outer steps, (Lathia Talbot Jennings and Helen Rupert almost fainted, and had to be supported out to the waiting Army cars by Asa Attwood and Ewan MacDonald MacDonald) and returned to Fort Myer. The city, the nation and the world settled back into some uneasy semblance of order and daily living. The still groggy ranks of NAWAC straggled away beneath the trees and along the Potomac, not to go home as their hero had suggested, but to lick their wounds and sing songs about their dead and prepare for tomorrow when they would be back again to attend, though perhaps more peaceably, the selection of Orrin Knox's running-mate. The troops bivouacked around the Center and held their positions, just in case.

And in Spring Valley the first cars began to arrive in

536

the driveway and the first telephone calls began to come in.

III

PRESERVE AND PROTECT

1.

"TONIGHT," said Frankly Unctuous on his evening news roundup, chipmunk face with pursed lips and nubbly teeth earnest and intent, voice heavy and pontifical as always in its rhythmic, emphatic cadence, "Washington waits."

"It does not seem too strong to say that it waits in gloom, depression and uncertainty the next step in the elaborate game of Presidential power politics that has brought Secretary of State Orrin Knox at last to the nomination he has sought so long.

"It waits to see whether any nomination won under such circumstances can bring anything but disappointment to the nominee and disaster to his country.

"It waits to see whether violence will die, now that those who courted violence have used violence to meet the violence their own tactics perhaps made inevitable.

"The view may be exaggerated and unduly emotional, but in the opinion of many in this riot-ravaged capital tonight, only one last, desperate hope for national unity and peace remains. . . ."

"You didn't have to come here," he said. "I'd have come there. All you had to do was pick up the phone—"

539

"I know," the President said, looking back for a moment into the glaring lights, the television cameras, the ring of reporters and still photographers held back by a police cordon three deep around the house in Spring Valley, "but I thought this might emphasize something to people who need it emphasized."

"Mr. President!" the reporters shouted. "Mr. Secretary—will you turn this way, please? Will you shake hands, please? Mr. President? Mr. Secretary?"

"Shall I introduce you as the next President of the United States?" the President murmured as they obliged. Orrin smiled.

"It might be a little premature."

'You don't really think so."

"No, but one never knows. Why don't I introduce you as the next Vice President of the United States?"

The President laughed aloud as the reporters strained closer to try to hear.

"That *would* be keeping it in the family. If only it were that simple."

"Yes," Orrin said grimly. "If only it were."

But of course they knew it was not, and as the minutes went by, and as they decided to call in Senator Munson and Robert A. Leffingwell—KNOX HUDDLES WITH PRESIDENT, CAMPAIGN AIDES. "BIG FOUR" MAY DECIDE V.P. NOMINATION—and as the minutes lengthened into hours, it became even more complicated; until, at nine-forty-five P.M., all the bells on all the news tickers all over town rang merrily to herald a

BULLETIN—KNOX CALLS CROY TO V.P. MEETING

and Frankly Unctuous, holding tightly to his mantle of pseudo-impartiality though it kept slipping and his excitement kept showing, was able to inform a tense and fascinated nation:

"There appears to be a growing possibility at this moment that Secretary Knox may have to accept as his Vice Presidential running mate the man he beat for President this afternoon.

"Former Governor Roger P. Croy of Oregon, who has spearheaded the campaign of Governor Edward M. Jason of California since before the San Francisco convention, is presently arriving at the Knox home in the Washington suburbs. Observers here believe the announcement of Governor Jason's selection could come even before the National Committee reconvenes tomorrow. It is generally felt that—"

"Governor!" they shouted as he left. "Governor! Can you give us a statement, Governor?"

"Why," said Roger P. Croy blandly, "you know of course that any statement will have to come from Secretary Knox himself. I was simply asked to come in and clarify certain things—"

"Such as that Governor Jason *will* accept if the Vice Presidential nomination is offered him?" ABC asked.

"I repeat," Roger Croy said comfortably, "you boys will have to ask the nominee and Governor Jason himself. I'm just a go-between here."

"But a happy go-between," The Greatest Publication suggested with a grin.

"I have known worse days," Roger P. Croy admitted cheerfully.

The President had left, taking Bob Munson and Bob Leffingwell back to the White House; press and television, frustrated by a firm and unshakable refusal to comment had regrouped into disgruntled but ever-vigilant little groups about the lawn; at last there was a moment to think.

It did not last long.

There was a peremptory rap on the study door.

"Who is it?" he asked. A voice he hardly recognized said, "Me."

"Oh," he said, and suddenly felt tense, nervous and sick inside. "Come in."

He glanced up quickly into the haggard, unhappy eyes of his son and glanced quickly away again.

"Sit down."

"I will if you'll look me straight in the eyes," Hal said in a voice so low he could hardly hear it.

"Very well," he said, though it cost him as few things in life had. . . . "Now do you want to sit down, or had you rather stand?"

"*Why?*" Hal demanded, standing. "In the name of God, *why?*"

"Because there are times when politics offers cruel choices," Orrin said slowly, "and sometimes, even with the best will in the world, one gets caught in them."

"Do you realize that that man, or his people, killed my son and your grandson?" Hal asked in a strangled voice.

Orrin sighed.

"Yes."

"And do you realize that his gangs may do anything—destroy the country—put us under dictatorship—anything?"

"I think there is that potential, yes, if they're not controlled."

"Do you think that millionaire lightweight is controlling them? Was he controlling them this afternoon?"

"Sit down, Hal," he said quietly, "and stop being rhetorical. I know just about everything there is to know about the character and motivations and strengths and weaknesses of Edward M. Jason, I believe. I don't think there's much you can tell me. And I don't think there's much to be gained from our fighting about it."

"But I want to know why," Hal said, sitting slowly down on the sofa. "I want to know *why* my father, whom I have always loved and respected and looked up—" his voice began to break but he forced himself on—"looked up to—why he has decided now that this man is worthy to move up one step from the White House. I don't—I don't even know why you think he's worthy to associate with *you* personally, let alone be Vice President. . . . You've got to tell me something" he said, staring at the rug. "I've got to have something left to believe."

For several minutes Orrin did not reply, though his first impulse was to go to his son and put his arms around him as though he were a little boy; but it died, as such things do, because he wasn't a little boy. Instead he tried to piece together something coherent that would make sense. He wasn't sure it would, in Hal's present mood—or in his own, for that matter—but he knew he had to try.

"I think," he said slowly, "that Ted Jason, at heart, is not a bad or an evil man. I think to a large extent he is sincerely convinced that he has a better answer for this country than I do. I think he really believes that if he could be elected President, things would somehow straighten themselves out and he could bring peace to the world at large, and to us domestically. I think he really thinks that."

"Does that give him a license to kill my son?" Hal asked with a withering bitterness. His face suddenly dissolved. "My *son,*" be said in a choking voice. "Like I—like I was for you, when I was born. *My son.*"

Orrin closed his eyes and sat back with his hands over them for a long moment. Then he looked up, though not at his son.

"You make it very difficult."

Again Hal spoke with a devastating bitterness.

"Am I supposed to make it easy?"

"Easier," his father said. "Just a little—easier—that's all. . . . I don't think there's anything you've felt in these past few days that I haven't—well, I'll amend that, because I do remember how it was with you, and I do know you've been feeling things I can only imagine. I don't really *know* because back in those innocent days, this kind of violence didn't stalk America the way it does now. I didn't have to worry about my family then as we all do now. I didn't think I was taking my life and theirs into my hands every time I took a stand on a public issue. But it's getting close to that now. Give us another five years like this, and freedom of opinion will be pretty much gone. Unless"—his expression too for a moment became bitter—"you're on the right side. . . .

"All I'm saying about Ted Jason," he resumed presently, "is that he's in that curious state of mind in which ambition really does dominate all. It dominates so much that everything is related to it. Everything becomes possible to it. Everything seems right to it. Everything can be fitted in . . . and everything that feeds it can be justified."

544

"And that doesn't make him a dangerous man?"

"Of course it does," Orrin said. "Of course it does. And yet not a *bad* man, in the sense that, say, Fred Van Ackerman is a *bad* man."

"How do you separate them?" Hal asked with a skepticism that at least, Orrin was relieved to note, replaced the bitterness a little. "Behind Ted Jason stands Van Ackerman. And all the rest of them. If you take one, you take them all."

"I think they can be separated," Orrin said, "because I think in Ted's mind they *are* separated. I think if he can be shown what they are, and what they're helping to get the United States into, he will break away from them. Because I think, as I say, that at heart he's a decent and well-meaning man."

"But that isn't why you're taking him," Hal said with a sudden shrewd bitterness. "Not just because you think maybe you can reform him someday."

"Sooner than that," Orrin said. "But, no, you're right. That isn't why."

Hal gave him a long look so painful for him that he actually squinted as he did so. His father could barely hear him when he spoke.

"You're taking him because of some deal, then."

"No," Orrin said, and thanked God he could say it truthfully. "No deal." A smile lit his face briefly. "Do you really think if I'd made a deal I wouldn't have made it for more than twenty-three votes, boy? What kind of a dealer do you think I am?"

"Well," Hal said, and briefly he too smiled a little, "Maybe not. But there must be some reason—some reason. There's got to be something that makes sense"—and again his voice dropped very low—"if you are willing to put the murderer of your grandson on the ticket."

Again Orrin sighed and looked away.

"You do have a way of cutting a man up."

Hal laughed, a dry, humorless sound.

"I'm told it's inherited," he said, and at his father's sudden angry look he did not flinch or drop his eyes. "But that doesn't answer my question."

"I'm trying. Give me a chance, will you? In the first place, Ted isn't a murderer—except as I suppose we are all murderers, who let things slide to a point where—things like that—can happen. Maybe I'm equally guilty, Hal. Did you ever think of that?"

Hal made a protesting movement but his father continued inexorably.

"Maybe I should have stepped aside at the convention. Maybe I should have stepped aside now. Maybe I'm driven by power and ambition, too, beyond the point of decency—many think so, here and abroad. If I'd stepped aside, probably nobody would have hurt your wife and your—son. If I'd stepped aside in San Francisco, Harley would have had to take Ted, and maybe Harley would be alive now; who knows? It's a fair assumption, even though Ted of course had nothing to do in any direct way with what happened to Harley. It was the climate, but maybe I'm as responsible as he is for the climate. Maybe if I'd gotten out of the way, Ted's backers wouldn't have felt they had to get desperate and do the things they have done. Maybe Helen-Anne would still be alive. Maybe all of this is my fault as much as his. Maybe all men who don't deny the ambition for power when they catch a glimpse of where it can lead to are guilty. . . . Did you ever think of that?"

"But you couldn't just walk away and let him have it!" Hal protested in a half-whisper.

"No," his father said quietly, "I could not, or I should have betrayed everything I believe in for this country, everything my whole life has stood for. So it isn't so simple. And it isn't for him, either." He sighed. "And that's probably the answer to your question, I suppose. Because he isn't actually a murderer, though some behind him are; and he doesn't consciously mean to do harm, though some behind him do; and he does have good and genuine qualities; and he does, I think, really want to do the best he can to help and save the United States—even though some behind him do not. . . .

"And furthermore, there's another point, which *I* have to take into consideration. The country is badly divided right now. We have enemies everywhere, both inside and outside, who would love to see us brought down, even though the fools will go down with us if we aren't here to protect them. We need unity. He does command an enormous support among a great many sincere citizens who really do see in him the hope for peace that they honestly cannot see in me. This extends overseas as well. I've denied him the top spot by a very narrow margin, and many of those people are not going to be satisfied unless they can see him beside me—unless they can feel that he is offering some moderating influence on my policies, which they think are so horrible."

"But you *can't* accept his views on appeasing and giving in," Hal said in the same dismayed half-whisper.

"No," Orrin agreed again, "I can't. But one thing he said at the Center this afternoon did make sense, and that is that times change and people change." He smiled a

547

wry little smile, almost wistful. "I'm not anywhere near the positive soul I was in the Senate a year and a half ago, you know. I've been close to the center of the machine for a while, and I know it isn't so easy. It isn't all black and white and cut and dried; it's a sort of horrible gray, like fighting your way through a dirty fog where everything is hazy and blurred and you're not even sure that the light ahead *is* a light: it may be just a—just a mirage. . . . No, I've changed, and I like to think for the better. And so can he. So *will* he, if I have anything to say about it. And I think I will. . . . So: he has good qualities—he wants to do what's right for the country, I think—he just needs to be shown. And he does command an enormous popular support—"

"And you want to win the election," Hal interrupted, his tone so bitter again that his father for a few moments was too crushed to reply. "You want the votes he can bring with him. *You want to win.*"

"Yes," Orrin said at last, quietly, "I want to win. Because I think that I can save the country and save the general peace, in the long run, and I want to try."

"And so the death of your grandson doesn't really mean so much to you, after all, does it?" Hal asked, and again his father was too hurt and astounded to speak for a little while. But he managed, presently, and he managed to keep his voice quiet and reasonably steady.

"I won't dignify that with an answer, but I do wonder if you've listened to me at all, these last few minutes. I've been trying to tell you why I've arrived at the decision I have—because you're my son, and you have a right to ask. But I have a right to ask you not to say things like that, don't I? There's a limit to how unfair you should be to your father—I think."

"I'm sorry," Hal said in a desolate tone. "I *am* sorry. But—but"—and again his face crumpled and he spoke in a choked, half-audible voice—"he *is* a bad man and a dangerous man—and I'm afraid—if you make him Vice President that he'll change you, you won't change him, and then—then it will all be pointless: what happened to Crystal and the baby—and what happened to Harley—and Helen-Anne—and all the riots—and what's happening to the country—and everything. It just won't any of it make any sense at all, if you let him do that. And you already have, because the first step—the only step he needs—they need—is to get him in there beside you. They'll be inside, then, and you won't be able to control them, any more than he can."

He stood up.

"I'm sorry," he said with a desolate sadness. "I'm sorry I said the things I did. *But I am so afraid for my father . . .* and for all of us."

"I'm sorry, too," Orrin said in a suddenly firm tone that his son recognized.

"You're losing me," Hal said in his tortured half-whisper.

"I'm sorry," Orrin said again, managing to keep his voice almost steady; and he too stood up, and turned away, and did not look again at his son as he went blindly out. "I hope not."

At the stately glass doors through which so many of the famous quick and the famous dead had passed in their unending cavalcade down the Republic's years of grief and glory, they greeted him with a new respect; escorted him quickly down the long carpeted corridor to the private elevator; stood at attention as he ascended to the study on the second floor; saluted as they left and returned to their posts below.

Four faces, three friendly, one uncommunicative and unfathomable, swung toward him from the chairs and sofa grouped by the windows looking out upon the Washington Monument.

He was the man people turned to now with that special waiting, expectant look.

The knowledge did not make him as happy as he had once imagined it would, in his dreams of this terrible, haunted house.

"Mr. President—" he said, coming forward; the President nodded gravely. "Bob—" Bob Leffingwell gave him an encouraging smile. "Robert—" Senator Munson smiled too, in his eyes the memories of many battles, many understandings, the deeply binding friendship of the Hill.

He hesitated for a second, held out his hand, started to say, "Governor," changed it:

"Ted."

"Good evening, Orrin," Governor Jason said gravely, shaking hands. "Thank you for asking me to come."

There was just enough of Orrin left in this moment of conflicting, unhappy, chaotic emotions, to say wryly,

"I had so many options."

"It needn't have been me."

"Perhaps not," Orrin agreed. "But it would have been even more difficult for the country. And that is what we all have to think about now."

He walked toward the window; instinctively they held back and let him precede them; instinctively he took the chair that dominated the grouping.

550

He sat down. They did the same.

"Have you been waiting for me long?"

"I just got here," Governor Jason said.

"We were discussing," Bob Munson said with a little smile, "the brutal heat of Washington, D.C., in the month of August."

"I'm sorry I was late," Orrin said. "I was having a talk with my son." He paused for a moment, eyes narrowed in thought as he stared at the glowing red carpet. "He does not think," he said in a level voice, raising his eyes and staring straight at the Governor, "that you are capable of controlling the violent forces that have supported your candidacy. He is threatening me with a permanent estrangement if I take you on the ticket. Nonetheless, I am here."

There was a silence during which no one moved or, it seemed, even breathed. The eyes of the Secretary and the eyes of the Governor held each other and did not waver. Finally Ted spoke, with a careful enunciation and a careful choice of words.

"I am sorry he feels that way. I trust he will not be as adamant as he sounds if you take the action of which he disapproves."

"I trust so," Orrin agreed, looking thoughtfully at the President. "Though I cannot be sure. . . . My son," he added quietly, "is not the only one who doubts your abilities in this regard." He looked again at Ted. "You are in a roomful of skeptics, Governor. What can you say to reassure us?"

"What do you want me to say?" Ted asked, and the President stirred restlessly in his chair.

"Something straightforward," he suggested. "If you please."

For a moment Ted flushed. Then he controlled it and replied with an equal quietness,

"Perhaps I deserve that: I wouldn't know. Obviously it expresses what you think of me. I can only say that many others think differently."

"They don't know you like we do," Bob Leffingwell remarked, and this time the Governor made no attempt to conceal his annoyance.

"Oh, don't they! And what do you know of me, really, Bob? What am I to you, but some sort of excuse for your own moral regeneration? If that's what it is. I find it a little difficult to understand, myself."

Bob Leffingwell did not flinch.

"Perhaps *I* deserve that. But the issue isn't my moral regeneration, it's yours. What proof have we got that you are a man responsible enough to be Vice President of the United States in this perilous age?"

For a time Governor Jason did not reply. Then he spoke in a steady, dispassionate voice.

"I came here tonight largely as a matter of courtesy to you, Orrin. I didn't have to come here to take this kind of tongue-lashing from any of you. I could have stayed away and you would still have had to take me for Vice President because there isn't anyone else. I'm so popular you can't avoid it. You couldn't win without me and you know it. Evidently you consider winning important enough so that you are going to take me regardless of what you think of me. What does that say about your moral regeneration, Orrin?"

It was the turn of the Secretary of State to remain silent for a while.

"About what my son says of it, I guess," he responded

at last, "if you look at it on that direct and simple a level. But we all know that when the selection of candidates for President and Vice President reaches this point it isn't that direct and simple any more . . . *Yes!*" he said with a sudden angry impatience. "*Yes*, I want to win! *Yes*, I need you to win! *Yes*, I haven't any choice but to take you if I do want to win! But"—and his voice dropped to a quietly emphatic level—"don't think that means that we aren't going to ask a few questions and expect a few replies, Ted. Because I don't want a running mate I can't trust. I don't want to win and preside over the kind of world some of your supporters want you to help them bring about. I don't want to win and preside over the dissolution of the democracy. I don't intend to administer the graveyard of the Republic."

Governor Jason shook his head with a weary, puzzled, frustrated air.

"How strange a concept you have of the legitimate forces of protest that disapprove of your policies! I have a few things to say, too, on that score. How much longer are you going to continue to regard legitimate protest and dissent as being traitorous and subversive? How much longer are you going to try to maintain that opposition to your policies *must* be subversive, *must* be hostile to democracy, *must* be inspired by a desire to destroy America? Don't you make any allowance for honest dissent? How am *I* supposed to feel, when *I* contemplate running with a man possessed of such—such dangerous egomania—and self-righteousness? What must *I* sacrifice of my integrity and beliefs to accept the Vice Presidency, when you imply you must sacrifice so much of yours to offer it to me?"

Again there was silence, broken finally by Senator Munson in a businesslike tone that effectively shattered the emotional tension and brought the discussion back to a pragmatic political basis.

"I think you'd better tell him what you have, Orrin," he said. "He isn't going to understand anything otherwise."

The Secretary sighed, a long unhappy sound. Then he shrugged.

"Yes, I suppose so."

He took a sheaf of folded copy paper from his pocket and opened it slowly.

"What's that?" the Governor asked skeptically, though a sudden hooded expression in his eyes indicated that he recognized it well enough. "A plan for world revolution?"

"Not quite," Orrin said quietly. "These are notes on a meeting held at the Washington Statler hotel after your sister's reception. They were written by Helen-Anne Carrew—"

"So that's it!" Ted said angrily, turning on Bob Leffing-well.

"—and were sent to me by Mr. Justice Davis."

Ted was silent.

"They tell a tale you ought to know."

Ted held out his hand.

"May I see them?"

"You may."

For perhaps five minutes he studied them carefully, his expression impassive. Then he handed them back and shook his head with a baffled expression.

"They aren't very clear. There seem to be a lot of excisions and abbreviations. I'm not sure I understand—"

"I'm quite sure you do," Orrin said, and his tone was cold and flat. "But if you're in any doubt, let me fill in the gaps for you. It appears, first of all, that you attended a meeting—"

"Which you tried to give me to understand you did not," the President interjected. But the Governor did not look at him or even indicate he had heard him.

—"at which were present Fred Van Ackerman, LeGage Shelby and Rufus Kleinfert. At this meeting, apparently, more or less routine campaign plans were discussed. The assumption on their part evidently was that this would be sufficient to put you off their real purpose, while at the same time giving them the power to hold over you when necessary the fact that you did, indeed, attend a secret meeting."

"Who's trying to hold it over me?" Governor Jason inquired dryly.

"Hold over you," the Secretary repeated calmly, "the fact that you did, indeed, attend such a secret meeting. On that basis they could link you with, and make you responsible for, decisions reached at the further meeting which occurred after you left.

"I understand that you were worried about this possibility yourself, so you later asked these three gentlemen if there had been such a subsequent meeting and they said No. You apparently believed them. This," he observed, "was a mistake, as Helen-Anne presently discovered, through the young busboy who was murdered at the same time she was.

"Shortly after you left, your three friends"—Ted moved angrily—"I'm sorry, your three supporters—were joined by the Ambassador of the Soviet Union, Vasily

Tashikov. Vasily was accompanied by the third consul of the embassy, a young man named Andreiev Susnin. Susnin spends his more informal hours as agricultural attaché, traveling about the United States studying farm experiments and attending county fairs, at which he frequently makes graceful little talks hailing the rosy future of Soviet-American relations under the Agricultural Exchange Agreement.

"In his less informal hours, he is a lieutenant general in the KGB, commanding the Soviet intelligence network for the eastern United States."

Again Governor Jason moved restlessly and remarked in a dry tone, "I told you it was a plan for world revolution."

"Do you think he's lying?" the President asked sharply.

"N—o," Ted said slowly. "But you must admit it's hard to believe."

"Not if you've stayed awake to what's been going on in the world in the past few years," Orrin said with some tartness. "This is the kind of setup, I might point out, that has occurred in many other countries. It has occurred here numerous times in the past, as various arrests by the FBI and various expulsions of Soviet diplomats have revealed. So I advise you not to be too scoffing and too skeptical when I tell you about it. American skepticism has always been the strongest weapon in the Communist arsenal, but it's imperative that you, of all people, not succumb to it. You're in too important a position. Or," he remarked calmly, and the Governor did not change expression, "you may be . . .

"Helen-Anne's notes from here on are not too complete, because her source was only human, and he wasn't in the room all the time, of course. He was in a couple of times, and apparently because he was a Negro, LeGage seems to have assumed that he hated his own country as much as LeGage does. LeGage should have known this was a dangerous generalization for him to make, but LeGage is not the most stable of young men, and so the boy was permitted to come up twice with drinks, and to linger for several minutes each time. LeGage at one point apparently became so drunk with liquor and egotism that he actually said something about, 'We're planning to burn down the whole country if necessary to get our man in the White House.'"

"I suppose I'm 'our man,'" Ted said dryly.

"Evidently. The boy also got the impression that plans were being made for this, and that the Soviet visitors were actively engaged in helping to make them. All of this he told Helen-Anne, who most unfortunately thought she could go it alone with something like this, until finally she got frightened and brought Bob Leffingwell, here, into it. By then she had tipped her hand too much; thinking, as an old Washington operator, that the game could be played by Washington rules, and that with a judicious use of her knowledge she could scare off the fellow Americans who were apparently bent upon destroying the country.

"In this," he said with a sad irony, "she was overly optimistic. . . .

"Everything since has evidently stemmed from that meeting, including the formation of NAWAC—"

"NAWAC was my idea," Ted Jason said coldly. "I conceived of it as an effective means of providing an outlet for emotionalism and tension."

"Are you proud of it?" Senator Munson asked.

"I am not ashamed of it. Properly led and properly used—"

"Has it been?" the President interrupted. His expression became sardonic: "KILL THE PRESIDENT! KILL THE COMMITTEE! KILL THE PRESIDENT! KILL THE COMMITTEE!"

"There are a few unfortunate elements," Ted conceded calmly. "But they can be controlled."

"Do you think you did it?" Bob Leffingwell asked.

"All I know," Ted replied with a rising anger, "is that after I was begged to do so by the Secretary of State—"

Orrin snorted.

"I didn't beg. I believe my exact words were, 'God damn it, get going!'"

"After you sought my aid," Ted said, "because you didn't dare go yourself, and I agree you shouldn't have, it could have been fatal for you at that moment, I went down there this afternoon and brought that mob under control."

"Aided by the armed forces of the United States," the President said.

"But there's the difference! Your troops brought them under control physically, but I brought them under control in the only way that has any lasting effect—mentally and emotionally. Isn't that right? They looked to *me*. And I calmed them. And for that," he said with a sudden bitterness, "I am brought here and subjected to this grateful inquisition. What kind of men are you?"

"What kind of man are you?" the Secretary asked. "That's my worry. What's your reaction to these notes? Do you feel anything about them? Shock? Horror? Dismay? A sense of abhorrence? A sense of satisfaction? Anything at all?"

Once more there was a silence, as once more their glances locked and held. Then the Governor passed a hand over his eyes, squeezed them, and shook his head as though to clear it of some deep oppressive miasma.

"Of course I feel something. I feel as though I were in a madhouse. You take the hysterical notes of an over-imaginative and wildly irresponsible reporter, and from them you fabricate a bugaboo that is apparently supposed to scare me to death. Well: it doesn't. I don't know whether what she has there is true or not, but even if it were true, I am not such a coward or such a disbeliever in the strength of my own country as to think that a drunken conference at the Hilton, even if it were attended by Lenin himself, is going to bring down the Republic. And I must say it throws a strange light on the gullibility and courage of the nominee for President that he should let himself be persuaded that it could."

For a while the Secretary did not reply. Then he leaned forward, eyes again intent upon the Governor.

"You just don't understand what we're talking about at all, do you, Ted? You just don't want to believe that such things can be, and so you aren't going to let yourself believe. You're going to remain skeptical if it kills you. I pray God," he said softly, "that it does not. . . ."

His voice became quiet and uncompromising as they all watched him intently.

"Now, you listen to me, Ted, because I'm going to give you, now, the terms and conditions under which I shall permit you to become the nominee for Vice President of the United States on my ticket. They are these:

"Much as I want to win this election—much as I feel that I can bring my country and the world back to some sort of reasonable sanity if I do win it—I am not going to win it at the price of taking on the ticket a man who either honestly or willfully refuses to recognize the desperate dangers in the violent elements that support him. You can deride Helen-Anne, who isn't here to defend herself, but things like that have happened, and in this case, did. There *is* an element of conspiracy in the country; it isn't all just innocent, democratic, happy-as-a-lark, spontaneous protest; there *are* enemies of America who are trying to use it to bring America down. Good God, man, they'd be fools if they didn't! And one thing they definitely aren't, is fools. . . .

"I don't think they're going to succeed, in the long run. But I think their chances are a lot better if people like you, and some of your friends like Walter Dobius and that crowd, simply refuse to permit yourselves to acknowledge that the possibility does exist. This would be doubly dangerous if something happened to me and you succeeded to the Presidency, with that attitude.

"Therefore if you come on this ticket, Ted, I want from you tomorrow before the National Committee and before the world, a flat-out repudiation, with no equivocations whatsoever, of NAWAC, DEFY, COMFORT, KEEP and any and all other elements of organized violence in the country. I want you to repudiate violence itself, *and I want you to say it and mean it*. Ever since Harley's death you have had repeated opportunities to do this, and you haven't done it. Each time there have been qualifications and a lot of tricky words, until this afternoon, apparently feeling secure again, you virtually endorsed everything the violent have done.

"I'm not going to have it, Ted," he concluded quietly. "I'm simply not going to have it. I'll take Bob Munson or the President, here, on the ticket and we'll go down to defeat together before I run and win with you, if you're still equivocating on this subject. Either you cut those connections altogether or you don't come along with me.

"You decide."

And he sat back and continued to stare at the Governor, who this time, his face shadowed with a sort of weary anger, did not return the look but gazed instead out the window upon the monument to noble George, who had passed through a certain amount of violence himself before arriving at canonization. When he spoke it was not in a tone of anger, however, but in one of sober thoughtfulness that brought at least the beginnings of reassurance to his listeners.

"Of course I am not happy with what has happened to the country. Of course I don't want that element running loose, particularly in my name. Of course I am as concerned as you are about the safety and stability of the Republic. What kind of man do you think I am, that you can contemplate, even for a moment, that I am not?

"But by the same token," he said, and some of the reassurance began to ebb, "I cannot in all good conscience place myself on the side of those who refuse to allow honest democratic dissent its place in the United States of America. There may be conspiracies. There may be subversives. I agree with you, they would be fools if they didn't try it, and they aren't fools. But I cannot agree that the great majority are anything other than perfectly genuine, sincere, loyal, decent Americans who are simply deeply disturbed about what seems to be a drive toward

561

war, and more wars, as a means of settling the world's problems. You can't, it seems to me, discredit that element which I believe—and you probably believe too"—he looked now at Orrin, who nodded—"to be the overwhelming majority.

"Now the question arises, then—how severely can you restrict what may be the few genuinely subversive elements without hurting and undemocratically restraining the genuinely loyal and the sincerely disturbed? At that point we seem to part company, because your way seems to be troops and helicopters, and mine seems to be tolerance and reason."

"How much can you tolerate?" Bob Leffingwell asked in a musing tone. "Where does reason have to take up arms against unreason?"

"Granted, it isn't simple," Ted agreed, while they watched him with the same close attention they had accorded Orrin, "but when were democracy's choices ever simple? I had rather come down, myself, on the side of too much tolerance and too much reason, than on the side of too little."

"Even if it genuinely jeopardizes the stability of the nation," Senator Munson said.

"Who knows where that point comes?" Governor Jason asked. "Who can honestly say—'at this moment'—or 'right here'—democracy is being jeopardized?"

"I said 'stability,'" Bob Munson reminded. Ted smiled pleasantly.

"I prefer 'democracy.'"

The President shifted in his chair.

"I don't," he said bluntly, "because right now, our problem's stability. You can have stability without democracy but you can't have democracy without stability."

"I don't think we can have too much democracy," Governor Jason said quietly. "We can have too much stability."

"And we can also, of course, as we all know perfectly well, have too much democracy," Bob Munson said with an equal bluntness. "We can take liberty to the point of license, which is where you seem to be taking it. And then the country falls apart because there are no sanctions to hold it together." He shrugged and gestured for Ted to continue. "But this isn't a debate. Go ahead."

The Governor nodded gravely.

"In case of doubt, as I say, I prefer to come down on the side of too much tolerance—reason—democracy, rather than too little. So the question then arises—what about DEFY? COMFORT? KEEP? All the organizations affiliated, at my suggestion, in NAWAC? What about violence, which seems at first glance to be the principal unifying feature of this amalgamation that seems to be favorable to me?

"In the first place, how responsible is a man for some of the support he gets? I know in California, and you each know in your states, that there are always freeloaders who climb on a bandwagon and come along, whether you want them or not, or whether you have anything in common with them or not. You can't keep them away. So some of this I'm not responsible for, and can't help. Most of it"—he raised a restraining hand as Senator Munson started to offer some skeptical comment, "I am.

"I'll admit that I have welcomed the support of the responsible elements in these organizations, because I believe the responsible elements predominate. If there are other elements," he said solemnly, "I don't know about them, and that is the truth."

"I know it is," Orrin said. "That's why I'm trying to enlighten you."

"If they exist, of course I shall repudiate them. If there is proof of their subversion, I shall denounce them as vigorously and relentlessly as you. If it is impossible to accept their support without jeopardizing the country, of course I shall cut them off."

"At what point will you admit the danger?" the Secretary inquired softly. "What sort of proof do you have to have?"

"Orrin," Ted said, and something in his tone indicated that he was concluding their discussion, "would you give me a couple of hours to decide that? Would you give me a little while to think about it? After all, you've presented me with some rather startling information. And you've followed it with an ultimatum that may seem reasonable to you, but seems to me to go to the heart of my integrity as an American, as a democrat, and as a public servant.

"That takes a little time to digest. May I have it?"

Once again they exchanged stare for stare.

"How much?"

"Not very long. I'll call you in an hour or two."

"Call me at home," the Secretary said. He frowned.

"I hope you aren't going to consult with them. This is a matter for your conscience and mine, now."

"No," the Governor agreed. "I'm just going to Pat's, and think. All right?"

"All right," Orrin said, and once again they were all on their feet, good nights were said, the elevator arrived.

Ted turned as he stepped in and bowed pleasantly. The door closed, he was gone.

"What do you make of that?" Bob Leffingwell asked.

"I don't know," Orrin said. "I honestly do not know. We'll just have to wait and see."

"I've called you 'Aunt Beth' for so many years that I really still find it difficult to say 'Mother Knox,'" Crystal confessed from the doorway with a smile; but it was a troubled smile, her mother-in-law could see, and so she patted the bed and said,

"'Beth' will do. Why don't you come here and tell me what the trouble is? Is Hal very upset?"

'Yes," Crystal said in a sad little voice, sitting down beside her. "He hates what his father's going to do."

Beth gave her a shrewd glance, closed her book, plumped the pillows and sat up attentively.

"Do you?"

Crystal shook her head slowly.

"I don't know . . . I just don't know. I suppose I've expected it for quite a while . . . ever since the convention, really."

"So have I," Beth said. "But I don't think Orrin knew until this afternoon."

"What made him decide?"

"Basically Ted's popularity, I suppose. The overriding need to restore national unity. And the possibility that the best way to control the mob—"

"—is to put the chief mobster on the ticket," Crystal said with a sudden flash of bitterness.

Beth smiled.

"That sounds like my son talking. The Knoxes have a

gift for the slashing phrase . . . Yes, perhaps so, though I don't really think in fairness to Ted one can quite call him that. He wants all the benefits of the mob without accepting any of the responsibility for it. It's a type that began to come into our politics a few years ago: always wealthy, always willing, always reaching out for anything, no matter how potentially or actually dangerous, that will get them where they want to go. I'm sure he actually believes he can control the mob and the violence. This afternoon must have made him certain of it."

"I think," Crystal said, her eyes shadowed with the memory of her own tragedy at the convention, "that he is a very dangerous man. I hope Orrin knows what he is doing."

"I think he does."

"Why do you think so?"

"I guess," Beth said thoughtfully, "because I believe in my husband."

"I do, too," Crystal agreed. "Yours and mine. But I'm wondering if maybe thinking he can control the man— who thinks he can control the mob—isn't equally unwise."

"It may be," Beth conceded quietly. "It may be. These gambles sometimes have to be taken in politics."

"It's a terrible risk just for the sake of winning."

"Well," Beth said, "suppose he doesn't win, Crys, what then? The country will go along all right I suppose, although the mobs will continue, and they'll grow, and the violence will flourish and increase. And regardless of who sits in the White House—probably Warren Strickland and the other party—things will become steadily more chaotic, until four years from now there won't be anything to stand in the way of the mobs, and violence will take over completely. Ted will make it then, all right, and that will be the end of a free country. At least Orrin is strong enough to turn it back now while there's still time, and at least there's a pretty good hope that Ted will come around to seeing it that way, too, before it's too late.

"And furthermore—what's involved in Orrin's winning? Just ambition? Just to sit in the White House and say, 'I'm President?' You know him better than that, Crystal. He wants it because that's where you can do things—that's where he can try to make real the vision he has of the United States of America."

Her eyes softened with the memory of many things.

"I've lived with that vision a long time, you know. Since way back down the years when I first met him at the University of Illinois and heard how Orrin Knox was going to be President and remake the world. It's a good vision—a decent vision. The world could do worse." She smiled. "I'm in the habit of believing in it. I thought Hal was too."

"He does," Crystal said, "at heart. It's just that my—episode—and now apparently rewarding the man whose supporters did it—have got him pretty well down." She tried to look confident but didn't quite make it. "He'll get over it . . . I think."

"He will if you help him," Beth said. "Will you?"

Crystal sighed.

"I don't have much cause to like Ted Jason, either."

"No," Beth agreed, and didn't argue. "What does Stanley think about it?"

Crystal smiled with a mixture of irony and affection for her father.

"He's a politician. He doesn't like it, but he can understand why it's being done."

"I don't think," Beth said slowly, "that Orrin really has a choice. He couldn't maneuver if he wanted to, really. The need for unity is too great. And that's a hard thing, for a proud man. I hope Hal can come to see that. He will if you help him. It may make him a little more tolerant of his father." She smiled again. "It isn't always easy, being married to a Knox, is it? They're such combinations of idealism and practicality, bull-headedness and sensitivity. They need one's help a lot more than they let on. Hal will accept this, if you help him. Do you think you can?"

Crystal returned the smile, a little hesitantly.

"If you can help Orrin, I guess I can help Hal."

"I hope so," Beth said, "because I'd hate to have anything permanent come between them as a result of this."

"I wonder how Governor Jason feels right now," Crystal said in a quizzical tone. "He must be feeling pretty smart, knowing he's indispensable to Orrin's victory."

"You know," Beth said, "in a way I think I feel sorriest of all for him. Because he actually thinks he's controlling the forces of history . . . and all the time, they're controlling him."

If this were true, he did not know it, as he sat in the glass-enclosed veranda and stared out into the tastefully lighted garden in the still, humid night. Patsy had been up when he came in, but after a couple of attempts to find out what had happened at the White House, she had recognized the fact that he was not going to tell her and had gone to bed.

"Surely there isn't any DOUBT—" she had said in an exasperated yet worried voice, turning at the door.

He had shaken his head impatiently.

"No, I suppose not, but I'm going to think about it for a while."

"Well, just don't take so long he changes his mind!" she urged tartly, and he smiled a tired yet ironic smile at the thought of boxed-in Orrin Knox.

"He won't," he said.

But there was, of course, the possibility, even now; for Orrin Knox, as he well knew, was not as boxed-in as many at this hour wished to think. Orrin Knox could never really be boxed in, because he was still, after three decades in politics, an independent man. He was one of the very few in Washington who still had both the option and the independence to say, "To hell with you," and mean it. Ted was convinced that if he pushed the Secretary far enough, he would do exactly that: he would take Bob Munson or the President on the ticket, he would go down to defeat, rather than make the final compromise. Someone had to yield in this final confrontation of theirs, and the Governor knew that in the last analysis it would not be Orrin Knox.

Therefore the problem came to him, and now as he thought back over all these recent hours and days and weeks and months, there seemed to him no very clear-cut way to approach it. He had deplored violence, but violence had come to his aid. He had criticized violence, but violence had refused to desert his cause. Finally this afternoon he had, in effect, turned on violence and shown it who was master; but still violence marched beneath his banner. How did you get rid of it, once it had made up its savage mind to adopt you?

He had not put much stock originally in the story Helen-Anne had discovered, though he had been the first to think of the possibility of a further meeting, and to try to remove himself from any connection with it. Even now, he could not entirely believe the account of Vasily Tashikov, the agricultural attaché, the dark alliance with NAWAC to disrupt and if possible overturn American society.

There was always something faintly laughable to most Americans about that sort of deep, dark conspiracy: their education, their press, their churches and their literature had conditioned them to laugh at it, and they did. It did not occur to them to reason why they had been conditioned to laugh: they just did, automatically, spontaneously, obediently. It simplified matters greatly.

Now, however, he was being asked to take it seriously, and it had been presented to him in a context in which he must take it seriously or say goodbye to the Vice Presidency now and very probably to any chance of becoming President later. Helen-Anne's scribblings carried an air of conviction, and they were detailed enough to compel belief. As Orrin had said, such things had happened in many other countries; it was quite logical to believe they could happen here. Indeed they had, but somehow in the face of all the facts over all the years, a great many Americans with the power and the position to ridicule had kept the country laughing, and somehow it had all been gradually fuzzed out, chortled away, jokingly forgotten. Meanwhile conspiracy had gone right on, though this, perhaps, was the first time it had moved directly into the campaign of a candidate for President. That it would eventually do so had always been inevitable. Now it had.

So it was up to him to deal with it. And although a

natural pride had prevented him from admitting it at the White House, he had been genuinely appalled and even somewhat frightened by the disclosures in the notes. Not desperately frightened, for he had no doubt that he could control it in the showdown: this afternoon had already proven that. But disturbed enough so that he must acknowledge to himself the existence in his life of a factor he had not anticipated and had not originated—something from outside—something new for a Jason. He had apparently not been a free agent in his own house after all, during recent events. That, perhaps, was what stung and upset him more than anything else.

So what was the problem? Orrin wanted him to make a clean break—the necessity of preserving his own independence made a clean break advisable—the welfare, perhaps the safety, of the country made it imperative—why did he hesitate? Why didn't he stop debating with himself and call Spring Valley right now?

His hand was halfway to the telephone when he paused and slowly withdrew it.

He hesitated because he had too much faith in the country. He hesitated because he really did not believe, as he had said, that a drunken huddle at the Hilton could really shake the innate strength of the Republic. He hesitated because after this afternoon he was confident he could control the violent and presently bring them back to the safer channels of democracy. He hesitated because he felt that Americans had a right to protest policies they did not agree with, and he honestly believed that the great majority who did so were sincere, earnest, loyal.

That was where his real battle came, as he saw it: that was the point at which he had to decide the sort of man Edward Montoya Jason was.

If it were true that alien elements were behind the violence, if it were true that forces hostile to America were active in his campaign—and if it were true that these forces were organized and effective and more helpful to him than any other political element in the country seemed to be at the moment—still he must not lose sight of the fact that protest and dissent were part of the very fabric of America.

He must not be false to the foundations of democracy itself. He must not betray the soul of America to save America, for that would be Pyrrhic victory indeed.

Therefore, how far should he go in repudiating the violent, if to do so would be to repudiate the many perfectly sincere and loyal millions whom the violent temporarily seemed to be leading? They all wanted him: how could he repudiate the leaders and not lose the masses? And if he repudiated the leaders, would he not thereby be robbing the masses—the sincere, democratic, protesting masses—of their right to protest, even as he robbed himself of their support?

He glanced at his watch. It was almost two A.M. The house was very still. His two hours were almost up. He must do something. Weighing everything in the balance—his political future—the fact that he had already begun to prepare his followers this afternoon, in his comment on what "those who may be close to Orrin Knox" might do to change his policies—the possibility of what he could accomplish within the Administration to secure a respected place for honest dissent—it was clear what his choice must be.

Again he reached for the telephone. As he did so it rang under his hand, startling him so that he jumped. He picked up the receiver and the little rushing winds of long-distance came to his ear.

"Yes?" he said, and though he tried to keep the excitement from his voice he could not completely succeed.

"Hi," she said over three thousand miles of troubled continent. "Can you hear that?"

"I hear long-distance," he said, trying to keep his voice steady. "Is there something else?"

"It's the ocean. I'm down at the beach house. Can't you hear the Pacific?"

"Oh, yes," he said, "now I do." And he did, the long crashing roll that pounded in on "Vistazo's" shore. "Isn't it a little late for you to be down there alone?"

"I came down on Trumpet," she said. "Both dogs are with me, and I have your .45. So I'm safe, I guess. Also, I'm about to go back up. I just wanted to call from down here and tell you—"

She hesitated and he said, "Yes?" in an eager, almost desperate tone.

"—to tell you that I've been doing some more thinking." She laughed, a light silvery sound against the slow, withdrawing, returning roar. "*More* thinking! It's all I've been doing for the past ten days. Anyway, I'm coming back in the morning. I think a Vice Presidential candidate needs a wife beside him, not out here."

"I—I do too," he said, his words beginning to tumble over one another in haste and excitement. "What—why—what have I done—?"

"What have you done to deserve this unexpected pleasure?" she asked, and again the silvery laugh came clearly from his native shore. "I don't exactly know, except I just think now is the time I ought to be there."

"Regardless of what I—whether I—"

For the third time she laughed.

"Oh, my dear, I'm not one of the Trojan women. Regardless of what you—whether you—which you. I just happen to think things are going to work out all right and I want to be there when you accept the nomination. You are going to, aren't you?"

He hesitated now.

"Would you come back to me even if I didn't?"

"I told you I've decided that's where I belong. I'm coming in on TWA, noon your time. Shall I come to Kennedy Center or—"

"Pat will send a car to bring you to the house. There's no telling what may be going at the Center."

"Not what went on yesterday, I hope."

"No," he said firmly. "That, I think I can promise."

But how he was going to make good on the promise he did not at that moment know. Nonetheless he knew it had to be. He picked up the phone again, woke Roger P. Croy at Fort Myer, asked him to call George Wattersill, asked them to come to the house as soon as they could make it. "Yes, sir!" Roger Croy said, his voice holding cheerful certainty. At that moment Ted was not so cheerful, nor so certain.

He returned to the veranda, sat motionless, alone, eyes wide, staring into far distances, for perhaps ten minutes; got up abruptly, returned to the study, lifted the receiver, dialed Spring Valley.

So all things in politics finally fell into place, the Secretary thought, if you waited for them long enough. "Time and I," said Mazarin, and so, in some strange way, it had been for him. He had wanted to be President so long, had tried for the nomination unsuccessfully three times—and now at last he had it, in the strange turnings of fate that so often made of men's conscious desires and deliberate intentions an ironic when not pathetic charade.

Had it, and had also the running mate he had wanted—not wanted; sought—not sought; hoped he would have—hoped he would not have. Had it, and had also a situation in the country as grave as any that had ever confronted it. Every resource of good will, good faith, intelligence, integrity, decency, courage, honor, was going to be needed, from him and from all of them; and he had a running mate he could not be sure of in any of these.

What had he gotten himself and the country into? And why?

The cruel choices of politics, he had described them to his son: and so they were. He knew that tonight across the country millions of people who believed in Orrin Knox just as deeply as Ted Jason's supporters believed in him, must be dismayed and appalled by his intention to take on the ticket a man they regarded as so dangerous and so completely opposed to the things Orrin Knox had always stood for.

He regarded him as dangerous, too; nothing had changed his feelings about that. The difference between Orrin Knox and those who held the devil-theory of Edward Jason was that Orrin, as he had also told his son, had a basic faith in Ted's decency as a human being. Given that, he could be brought back from the far paths toward which ambition had taken him.

He knew with a wry certainty that Ted had the same feeling about him. It was not such a bad basis upon which to establish a practical working relationship, though politically there still were major problems.

And politically, of course, was where the bargain would prove itself. Hopefully his own supporters would still have enough faith in him to accept his decision that Ted's nomination was necessary, and submerge or at least suspend their misgivings for the common good. Hopefully Ted's supporters would do the same. Thus together they might be able to re-establish a reasonable unity on which further unity might grow.

This hope was the only basis on which he could justify to himself a decision which even in his own mind was a glaring and almost inexcusable break with a career and philosophy he had always tried, honestly and with a fair success, to keep consistent during his long contentious years in public office.

The hope of restoring unity—the hope of restoring domestic peace and tranquillity—the hope of bringing back to the ever-earnest, ever-muddled Republic some general atmosphere of sanity, kindliness and good will—these were the things that justified in his mind the addition of Ted Jason to his ticket.

If these things came from it, he would have done a great and imperative service for his country. Given the present condition of America, anything else was secondary.

If these things did not come from it, he would have made the greatest mistake of his lifetime.

Too bad the decent and the well-meaning couldn't exist in a vacuum to attempt their little miracles, he thought with an ironic smile in the silent study. Nowadays too many other people had an opportunity to get into the act. Sometimes their intervention proved to be literally fatal, not only to the miracles, but to the decent themselves.

But—one could only hope. One could only do what seemed best for America, challenged though it might be by the dismay of the partisan and the scorn of those who charged betrayal of principles in order to achieve ambition.

Of course he had ambition: no one climbed to the top without it. But he also had a vision, as Beth had said: he wanted to do things for his country. First and inescapable was the task of restoring unity. Without it, no one was going to do anything except preside, as he had told Ted at the White House, over the graveyard of the Republic.

So he guessed he could take a little pounding from the conservatives for a while: he had taken one long enough from the liberals. It would be an ironic and rather amusing switch to be getting it from the other side. When they realized they had a common target, and came to realize what he was attempting, that in itself might be a step toward unity.

Only one thing still bothered him as be prepared to turn out the lights shortly before three A.M. When he reached the upstairs hall, saw light still shining from under the childrens' door and heard a low, argumentative murmur, he decided to tackle it head on.

He stepped along and rapped on the door. Dead silence ensued.

"I thought you'd be interested to know," he said quietly, "that Ted called a few minutes ago. I told him at the White House I wouldn't permit him to be nominated unless he made a complete public break with violence. He says he will. So that about wraps it up, I guess. Good night."

"Did you get it in writing?" Hal asked.

"No. Under the circumstances, I believe him."

"I hope you're right," Hal commented, not yielding much.

"I think I am," his father said. "We'll just have to wait and see. Good night."

"Good night," Hal said, still skeptical. . . .

"He'll come around," Beth predicted. "I gave Crystal a pep talk a while ago, and I'm sure she's giving him one."

"I hope so," Orrin said. "I'm not a great deal more sanguine than he is, actually. It's a gamble."

"But you've decided it has to be," she said.

"Hank," he said, using the old tender nickname, "I've decided it has to be."

2.

THREE TIMES the sirens sounded; three times the sleek black limousines raced swiftly in armored convoy through the 5000 troops at ready, down the somber ranks of NAWAC; three times the shout went up:

"There he comes!" for the President, sitting far back in his seat, looking neither right nor left: the cry today no longer angry, no longer hostile, curiously impersonal, curiously disinterested.

"There he comes!" for Orrin Knox, equally invisible: the animal growl surly, uneasy, yet not violently antagonistic, though the potential was still there.

"THERE HE COMES!" for Ted Jason, leaning forward, arms outstretched, waving out both windows as he sped along: the great exuberant roar happy, excited, welcoming, echoing over the tensely quiet Center, the sleepy meandering river, the almost deserted city, the watching nation, the world.

"My friends," the President said, rapping the gavel quietly once, "this emergency meeting"—he smiled—"hopefully, this final emergency meeting—of the National Committee is now in session. Will the distinguished National Committeeman from Washington once more give the invocation, please?"

After Luther Redfield had done so, with a brief and moving fervor that invoked the blessings of a patient Lord upon these his earnest, unhappy children, the President stood for a moment looking down upon the Committee, all, even Mary Baffleburg and Esmé Stryke, silent and expectant.

"The nominee for President," he said gravely, "has asked that he be permitted to address you. I assume there will be no objections"—again he smiled, comfortable and solid and reassuring—"and so it is my pleasure and my honor to introduce to you the next President of the United States, the Honorable Orrin Knox of Illinois."

From outside there came a surge of sound reflecting the many confusions of NAWAC, whose members did not know exactly how they felt on this confusing day. But from inside, in some instinctive impulse of solidarity, encouragement and hope, there came a genuine standing ovation from Committee, audience and media alike. This was the old, traditional American reaction of good sportsmanship, not yet entirely abandoned though it might be going fast. Obviously inside the Playhouse they hoped it was not, were desperately determined that it should not: as though by shouting extra-loud and applauding extra-hard, they might help to recall it to the hearts and minds of their embittered countrymen, remind them of the great principle of tolerance and good will that held the country together, encourage them to recapture and re-establish it before it was too late.

For several minutes, while Orrin entered from the foyer and walked briskly down the aisle to the stage, NAWAC with its newer traditions was drowned out; though presently, of course, when the tumult inside died down, the grudging uneasiness outside once more became audible, a restless thunder that would not go away.

"Mr. President," Orrin said quietly, and the thunder did at least diminish a little as a listening hush began to fall upon the world, "it is my hope that tomorrow, in front of the monument which symbolizes and pays tribute to the first President of the United States, the nominee for Vice President and I may present ourselves to our countrymen for formal acceptance of the great honor and responsibility placed upon us.

"Suffice it to say at this moment that I accept your nomination"—warm applause inside, the uncertain thunder rising again outside—"and I do so humbly and yet unafraid, for I know that the heart of America is sound and valiant still, and that from it my running mate and I will draw the strength to do what must be done to restore unity and peace to our country and the world.

"We meet in strange times after strange decades in which the law and order vital to the maintenance of a stable democracy and a stable world have been persistently and consistently reduced—persistently by those whose deliberate aim is the destruction of America—consistently by those in authority who, laboring under some strange contortion of thought, have been afraid to preserve law and order because, in their tortured reasoning, to do so might be to 'destroy America's image,' as they have put it—or to 'cause charges of police brutality'—or to 'alienate world opinion'—or to 'jeopardize good relations between the races.'

"So the protections of a stable society have been allowed to collapse, sometimes slowly and sometimes not so slowly, until today no area vital to our national security—no city—no store—no home—no *American anywhere in this land or in this world* is really safe—because if he is attacked, his Government will not protect him.

"The American Government has voluntarily abdicated the first responsibility of government, the preservation of its own security and the protection of its citizens.

"The American Government, in effect, has given up, both domestically and overseas.

"Until, that is, these last few months, when there has been some attempt, both at home and abroad, to reassert and restore the dignity and the strength of the American Government.

"I propose to continue that attempt, and I am inclined to think that whoever leads our friends in the other party as their candidate for President will do the same: so that either way, I think we are reaching a long-needed and long-overdue turning point.

"Pray God," he said soberly, "it may not be too late to reverse the trend toward weakness which has been launched by our enemies and assisted by those we thought we could trust to preserve and protect us.

"As for me," he said, and his voice took on an emphatic edge as his words brought a rising murmur from outside, "if I am elected, I shall have two purposes: to restore order and to restore unity. I do not know which should come first, because to my mind they are indivisible. If you have real unity, order follows more or less automatically. If you have order, unity also follows more or less automatically.

"And lest," he said, his voice rising sharply as the murmur outside swelled again toward its angry humming "—lest any man, any editor, any reporter, any commentator, any writer, any foreigner, any partisan of mine, any opponent of mine, any member of any mob—lest *anyone* try to misinterpret or cynically twist what I say, let me state it very clearly.

"When I say order, I do not mean 'police brutality' or international bullying. I do not mean repressive or harsh or unfair measures. I mean the even-handed administration of justice and the even-handed, impartial *and firm* application of the law, falling equally upon all transgressors, be they rich or poor, liberal or conservative, white or black, big nation or small.

"And that is all I mean.

"There have been disturbances in this city in the past in which the forces of law and order were deliberately held back because someone in authority had convinced himself that it was better to let the mob run amuck than it was to make sure that the law was respected and obeyed. To apply the law might hurt somebody—a few somebodies who deserved it—and so the law was not applied, and everyone had to suffer, because those in authority did not have the courage or the integrity to apply the law fairly and squarely across the board.

"And so the law died some more, and after the event, everyone in America was just a little less safe than he had been before: because somebody didn't have the guts. Somebody didn't have faith in the *rightness* of democracy. Somebody didn't have the courage or the integrity to gamble on the power of law and order, without which there can be no democracy, no society, no nation, no life.

"Government was a coward and afraid. And so government grew less. And anarchy grew great.

"And the same thing happened all over the world wherever America was afraid to do, or allowed herself to be browbeaten out of doing, what she knew to be right.

"That did not happen yesterday, Mr. President," he said quietly, "thanks to your courage and integrity. It will not happen in my Administration, should I be elected, either in this capital or anywhere else in America where the writ of federal authority may run. Or anywhere else in the world, if I can help it."

There was a fervent and heartfelt burst of applause from the Committee and the audience; an uneasy stirring from the media, where clever minds, as always, could see ten thousand qualifications and reasons why it should not be done; and from outside, an angry, sullen mumbling.

"That is what I propose to do about order. Now as to what I propose to do about unity."

He paused deliberately, took a sip of water from the glass Anna Bigelow had placed on the lectern as he began, looked thoughtfully at his few longhand notes. The world began to generate the expectant tension he intended it should.

"I propose," he resumed, "to urge for your consideration as my running mate a man who will be a willing and effective partner in restoring unity and order to America; a man who believes in the law, and in upholding the law; a man who believes in protest within the law and dissent within the bounds both of law and of common decency; a man who repudiates lawlessness as an answer to the domestic and foreign problems of the country; a man who rejects violence, its organizers, its practitioners, its adherents, its sympathizers, and everything about it; a man who believes that lawlessness and violence have no place in America, because if they are given an established place and become a daily part of America, everything that is America will die.

"Such a man," he said, "can surely be found"—there was a great sound of released breath, a long sigh over the world, as they realized suddenly that he was not going to name him—"in the ranks of our party.

"Such a man *must* be found.

"I think, to aid us in our search, it might be well at this time (outside in the foyer, Governor Jason's face was a study in conflicting emotions, so turbulently were they whirling through his mind as he, too, realized that his great antagonist was, in effect, about to put him on trial and force him to make good on his telephoned word) for us to hear from the other major contender for the Presidential nomination, the other leader of our party to whom we look for strength and reassurance in these very tense and difficult times.

"Ladies and gentlemen of the Committee, with your permission, and the permission of the Chair, I should like to introduce to you the Honorable Edward M. Jason, Governor of California, to give us his thoughts on these issues."

"Mr. President!" Roger Croy cried indignantly, jumping to his feet as many angry voices began to rise, in the Playhouse and outside. "Mr. President, that is quite irreg—"

"Mr. President!" Governor Jason shouted from the door in a voice that brought immediate attention as they swung about to stare at him.

"Mr. President," he said more quietly, coming down the aisle to the stage, "I thank my friends, but I am quite prepared to speak. Indeed," he said, as Orrin stepped back to take a seat beside the President at the table to the right of the stage, "I welcome the chance."

He moved forward, bowed to the President and the Secretary with an expression in his eyes that only they could see; stepped to the lectern, placed upon it several typewritten pages; gripped it with both hands; raised his handsome graying head in a challenging, straightforward gesture.

"Mr. President"—he smiled a smile that he managed to make quite cordial and friendly, and they applauded him for it—"Mr. President-to-be—my friends of the National Committee.

"We do, indeed, as the Secretary says, meet in strange times after strange decades. We do indeed confront violence as the central fact of our times, as unity and law and order are the overriding and essential needs.

He folded the typewritten pages and put them back in his pocket. Roger Croy and George Wattersill, who had worked on them until six A.M., squirmed in silent dismay.

"No one," he said quietly, "can deny these things, for they are obvious to all men of good will who wish to serve, and save, America.

"I, ladies and gentlemen of the Committee, so wish. There are some who believe that I have been one who, either deliberately or inadvertently, has encouraged violence and lawlessness in this country."

There was a stirring of protest, a distant denial, but he went firmly on.

"If there is the slightest question in anyone's mind"— he hesitated, and this time it was Orrin's turn to feel concern: was he going to turn the tables and withdraw? But he found he need not worry—"let me make my position clear right now.

"I am absolutely and unequivocally opposed to the use of violence to express dissent or to settle political or social problems in this country.

"Let me too, as did the Secretary, make my position absolutely clear.

"I have always upheld, and shall always uphold, the right of any American citizen to express his disagreement with the policies of his government. I believe, and shall always believe, that the great majority of those Americans who have been involved in protests which in recent years—and months—and days—may have become violent and lawless are sincere and decent people whose basic motivation is within the democratic framework of this Republic.

"I shall always defend their right to organize, to dissent, to protest—"

A happy cheer came on the wind, matched by much vigorous applause in the Playhouse.

"—but I do agree with the nominee of this party"— the cheer and the applause suddenly hesitated—"that the dissent must be within the law, and the protest must be within the bounds both of the law and of common decency.

"Therefore, if, in the organization known as NAWAC" —the sound outside diminished, became uncertain, puzzled, intently listening—"or in any of its member organizations such as COMFORT, DEFY, KEEP, or any of the others—there be any whose purposes are not within the law—who do not wish to keep their dissent within the law and within common decency—then I repudiate them here and now and declare that I wish their support of me to cease forthwith."

From outside there came the beginning of a boo long-drawn yet still hesitant and uncertain.

"Is half a loaf better than none?" the President murmured to Orrin without turning his head or changing his impassive expression. "It's got to be," Orrin replied in the same fashion; "it's a big half-loaf. We'll get him the rest of the way." "Good luck," the President said.

"There is a place for decent and honorable protest and dissent," Ted Jason said firmly. "I shall defend it always. But to those others," he said sternly, "—if others there be—I give notice and fair warning.

"Mr. President"—and he turned to look directly at him and at the Secretary, who returned the look without expression—"I agree again with the nominee: his running mate must be a man who repudiates violence, who works for unity, for law and for order.

"On that basis you should make your choice.

"I await it with the firm conviction that it will be the right one.

"I shall support it loyally with all my heart."

("What does that mean?" The Greatest Publication whispered; "Is he or isn't he?" "Only his doctor knows for sure," the Chicago *Tribune* whispered back; "Damned equivocator. Jesus!" "He's repudiated them," CBS commented angrily; "What more do you want?" "Just—just—Christ, I don't know!" the *Trib* replied with a frustrated disgust.)

To the Committee and the audience, his words were evidently sufficient. As he bowed once more to the President and Orrin, bowed to the room and prepared to step down, a deep and earnest applause commended him: so desperately did they want him to mean what he seemed to mean. Outside, the questioning, uncertain, puzzled murmur of NAWAC's thousands began to take on a deeper, more positive note: clearly they were concluding that he did not mean what he seemed to mean. A ragged cheer began, solidified, grew. A chant took form, the chant of the galleries in San Francisco:

WE WANT JASON! WE WANT JASON! WE WANT JASON!

"If there is no further preliminary business," the President said quietly—paused for a moment, nodded in a businesslike fashion—"the Committee will now proceed to the selection of a nominee for Vice President of the United States. Mrs. Bigelow—for the last time, dear faithful patient Anna—"

There was a relaxing, friendly, communal amusement, and very little tension, as Anna came forward; because there could be, there had to be, only one result.

"Alabama!" Anna said.

"Mr. President," said Helen M. Rupert with a pleased smile, "Alabama agrees! It yields to the great state of Illinois."

"Mr. President," said Blair Hannah, peering about, his drawl if possible even slower than usual, his words chary but sufficient, "Illinois nominates for the office of Vice President the Governor of the great state of California, Edward M. Jason."

Inside applause and ovation, as first one, then another, then all were on their feet. Outside a great roar of excitement and approval, and the chant changing triumphantly to:

WE'VE GOT JASON! WE'VE GOT JASON! WE'VE GOT JASON!

"If there are no further nominations—" the President said.

"NO!" roared the Committee.

"The Secretary will call the roll—"

"ACCLAMATION!" cried the Committee.

"All those in favor of the nomination of Edward M. Jason to be—"

"AYE!" roared the Committee.

The world exploded in hysterical, happy sound.

"Mr. President!" Pete Boissevain shouted after a while. "Mr. President!"

"For what purpose—?"

"To make the motion to adjourn, Mr. President, but first to say just a couple of things—"

"Adjourn! Adjourn!" cried Roger P. Croy. "Second! Second!" screamed Esmé Stryke. "*Regular order*, damn it!" shouted Ewan MacDonald MacDonald.

But Pete Boissevain shook his stubborn Vermont head and plunged right on.

"Now, Mr. President, I have the floor, and in just a minute I'm going to make the motion. But first I'm going to say a couple of things, because I think we'd better keep 'em in mind as we go away from here.

"We've had a tough time of it, and that's a fact. We've met under very tense circumstances, and we've almost literally been killed. We've had a chance to see the terrible divisions there are in this country.

"And the country," he said, and his pugnacious jaw came up and his dark eyes snapped, "has had a chance to see, I hope, that there are some Americans left who aren't afraid to do what they think is right, in spite of everything."

Applause from within, a long, scornful "Booooooo!" from without.

Pete shook his head with an expression of distaste.

"I'm one of those," he said, "who was very much opposed to Governor Jason, so maybe it's fitting for me to express something of what we on our side feel about him now. We hope, Mr. President, and we believe"—he looked straight at Ted, sitting beside Orrin at the table on the stage—"that he means what he says about repudiating violence, and means it all the way. That is the assumption on which we have voted for him, and for America's sake we hope it's the right one. We believe it is, and we commend him for it."

Ted nodded gravely.

"Good," Pete said. "We're mighty glad of it, because things can't go on much longer as they've been going, and have anything left of us. We've got to get back to law and order, Mr. President. We've got to get back to traditional values"—there was an amused stirring at the press tables, and he swung around sharply—"yes, I know all you clever boys think that's very funny. But by God, it won't be funny when you're the ones who suffer for it. When you find your house is the one that's burned down—when you find it's your family that's threatened and maybe killed—when you find that even you aren't allowed to write what you please—then you'll find out. You've all been at one remove from all this, too long, sitting in your ivory towers telling us poor peasants what to do! If this lawlessness keeps up, it's going to get to even you. And then you'll squeal like my pigs at sausagetime, and it will be just too damned bad. You'll know then what all of us old fogies who believe in law and order and decency and fair dealing and good will have been talking about, all this time. But it will just be too late. . . .

"Well, Mr. President," he said, turning back with an impatient disgust, "I didn't set out to fight with the press, and a lot of the press, of course, agree with me anyway. I just wanted to say that if we don't get back to these values I'm talking about, if we don't have a fair, stable, law-abiding society instead of a one-sided, violent, vicious, lawless one, then America's doomed—and I mean doomed right down to my house and your house, and my family and your family. We're right on the edge of nothing being safe, Mr. President. We'd damned well better pull back and think a little.

"Governor Jason says he agrees. I'm glad he does. I

don't think he, or any of us, had better forget the lesson of these sessions and these recent events. We've got to save America, that's the simple fact of it. We've got to save her *now*."

And he sat down, to generally agreeing applause from the room and again a long, sardonic hoot from outside. His little homily rated no more than a line in the late editions, no mention at all in the evening news roundups. But in due time it would find its way into the history books, a minute footnote to the Committee's fateful proceedings. It would be regarded in much the same way as the Great Riot: as a watershed and symbol of something that probably would not happen much again, since soon its purpose would be pointless, and there would be no use for it in America any more.

"If there are no further valedictories—" the President suggested. "Governor Croy?"

"No, thank you, Mr. President," said Roger P. Croy in his most gracious manner. "I think we have had enough. I rise only to second the adjournment motion of my earnest friend from Vermont. We have a campaign to fight and an election to win. I think we had best be about it."

"All those in favor—" the President said.

"AYE!" shouted Committee, audience, media, NAWAC, nation and attentive world, with a great relief.

"This emergency meeting of the National Committee stands adjourned sine die," the President said.

"Now, Mr. Presider, Mr. Temporary, sir!" Jawbone cried in dismay in the packed and silent House. "Why do we-all want to go ahead and pass this vicious little old gag bill *now*? We've got our two candidates down there now, we know what they both said, everything's going to be all right, Mr. Temporary, we just don't *need* this vicious old bill—"

"On this vote," the Acting Speaker announced a few minutes later, "the Yeas are 341, the Nays are 186, and *A Bill to Further Curb Acts Against the Public Order and Welfare* is approved."

"Now, Mr. President," Fred Van Ackerman said, standing in an easy, relaxed posture beside his desk, which was piled high with law books, encyclopedias, bound volumes of the Congressional Record, the Washington *Post* and the New York *Times*, "I think possibly the Senate might just as well settle back and make itself comfortable, because I intend to talk for quite a long time about this vicious, inexcusable, dictatorial gag bill brought in here by this Administration to choke off honest protest and democratic dissent.

"You can always stampede the House, Mr. President, but I'm here to say you can't stampede the Senate. I expect I'll have some assistance in these next few hours and days and weeks, too, Mr. President. Old Freddie isn't alone on this one. . . . "

"I really think the Jason nomination is a most hopeful event," Lord Maudulayne said as he and Raoul Barre met Krishna Khaleel and Vasily Tashikov in the middle of the Delegates' Lounge. "It could mean a whole new approach for American policy."

Raoul nodded.

"This may be the beginning of the return to sanity."

Tashikov shook his head with an air of impatient annoyance.

"It is about time!" he observed sarcastically.

Krishna Khaleel clasped his hands in fervent agreement.

"Gracious, I should say so!" he exclaimed. "Gracious, yes!"

"And so," Walter Dobius wrote at "Salubria," "the long agony of the National Committee and the nation's capital comes to its dramatic end.

"The Battle of Washington, one might say, is over.

"The Battle of America is about to begin.

"By selecting Governor Jason for his running mate, Secretary Knox has bowed not only to the politically inevitable but the nationally imperative. And the Governor, in his brief remarks to the Committee—which will no doubt be amplified tomorrow when he and Mr. Knox deliver their formal acceptance speeches at the Washington Monument—has made quite clear that he sacrifices none of his integrity and none of his beliefs in accepting his rightful and necessary place on the ticket.

"There is, as the Governor said, no place for organized, deliberately destructive violence in America. He took cognizance of the possibility that such elements might be active in the coalition of political forces that support him. But he made amply, and justly, clear that he does not believe that those elements predominate. Nor does he, because of them, repudiate the many millions of decent and loyal Americans who exercise their right of democratic protest against the policies of the present Administration.

"In the remarks of Secretary Knox, a more adamant and unyielding note was present; yet even one so con-

594

vinced of the correctness of his course must have a few misgivings and be prepared to make a few concessions. Certainly the major hope of this—perhaps the only hope—lies in the fact that he should have accepted Governor Jason as his running mate. This was the only kind of recognition that matters in politics: the recognition of fact. Governor Jason was too strong to shunt aside. Those who believe in him were too overwhelmingly numerous to defy.

"This is a ticket of equals, not a ticket of master and subordinate. To it the Governor brings great strength, probably the decisive strength necessary to pull together a divided party and win in November.

"With Governor Jason on the ticket, millions who were uneasy and alienated before must now be reassured. Democratic dissent and the right of protest have a champion in the innermost circles, after all.

"All is not lost, for America: with Edward M. Jason, the new day dawns. . . ."

"In actual practical fact, of course," Frankly Unctuous said in his emphatic rhythm, "this could almost be called the Jason-Knox ticket rather than the Knox-Jason ticket.

"The Governor has repudiated those few elements whose violence has frightened some Americans; he has given new hope to those many millions who look to him to save American democracy from those who would narrow and restrict it. He brings a far greater personal following to the Vice Presidency than most occupants of that office. His voice inevitably will have much more weight.

"It seems fair to state that we can now look for a

greater stress on peace, and at the same time a greater emphasis on the free and untrammeled expression of democratic dissent.

"It is not too much to say that in the minds of many at home and abroad, a new freedom lies ahead for America and the world. . . . "

JASON SELECTION STRENGTHENS U.S. PEACE MOVEMENT, said the *Daily Telegraph* in London. U.S. ADVENTURISM YIELDS TO JASON PEACE STRENGTH, said *Le Monde* in Paris. WARMONGERS LOSE TO PEOPLES' DEMOCRATIC FORCES, said *Pravda* in Moscow. U.S. DEMOCRACY STRENGTHENED BY JASON CHOICE, said the *Times of India* in New Delhi. GREAT ERA LOOMS FOR ALL U.S. TRIBES AS JASON IS STOOLED, said the *Ashanti Observer* in Ghana.

"Thank you for coming," he said cordially. "Did you have any trouble getting through the outer defenses?"

"They're pretty strong," Bob Leffingwell said, returning his handshake with an answering friendliness. "But I managed."

"Good," Orrin said, leading the way into the study. "I think the tension's eased somewhat since this afternoon. We all seemed to get away in fairly good shape from the Center. Even I got a little applause, now that I've put the people's choice on the ticket."

"It could mean an era of better feeling," Bob Leffingwell agreed. "It's an opportunity."

"It is," the Secretary said soberly. "I hope we can both live up to it. I'm going to do what I can, anyway. That's one reason I asked you here: I want you to help me with my acceptance speech for tomorrow. I want to be conciliatory but firm. Or," he said with a smile, "firm but conciliatory, as the case may be. Perhaps you can help me find that magic middle ground."

"Gladly," Bob Leffingwell said, settling into the armchair offered by his host. "But I don't really think Orrin Knox needs all that much help with the speech he's going to give on this occasion. I expect it's pretty well in hand already, isn't it?"

"Are you implying," the Secretary inquired, "that I asked you here under false pretenses?" He chuckled. "Well, you know, I did." He became serious, leaned forward, fixed his visitor with a shrewd if friendly eye. "I wanted to close the books on something, Bob. It may have been a matter of misunderstanding—it may have been a matter of timing—it may have been just one of those things that happen, now and again, in this town. I happen to think it was probably a matter of conviction, for both of us and as such, each of us did what his principles impelled him to do, and neither of us need be ashamed of that. . . . I won't say," he remarked thoughtfully, "that I regret opposing you for Secretary of State a year and a half ago, any more than you regret making the run for it. I just want to say that if any ghosts are still walking from that episode in your mind, I consider them buried in mine. OK?"

Bob Leffingwell looked surprised and genuinely touched.

"I appreciate that," he said after a moment. "I appreciate that very much."

"Good," Orrin said. "So: I'm not going to ask you to

campaign for me, though I would value the support you can bring with you—"

"I'm going to," Bob Leffingwell interrupted. "I want to." He smiled. "Not all the wild horses of NAWAC could drag me from your campaign trail. I've made my decision—I can do it honestly. We aren't very far apart, these days. I've buried a few of *your* ghosts, myself."

It was the Secretary's turn to be touched.

"*I* appreciate that," he said. "Well, that's fine. But what I was going to say was—assuming all goes well and I get elected—I would like to have you in my Administration. Would you be willing?"

Bob Leffingwell nodded gravely.

"Anywhere you can use me."

The Secretary gave him a bland and slightly mischievous glance.

"How about Secretary of State?"

For a moment his visitor looked absolutely stunned; then, quite unabashedly, his eyes filled with tears.

"Why—" he said. "Why, Orrin, I—"

"Blow your nose," the Secretary ordered brusquely. "This is one of the greater unrecorded scenes of American history."

"It is," Bob Leffingwell agreed somewhere between a laugh and a gulp, obediently pulling out his handkerchief and blowing away. "It really is. I tell you what," he suggested, "let me write you a letter. I can't really talk about it right now, except to say—"

But he found he really couldn't talk about it, and stopped abruptly.

"All right," Orrin said. "Write your letter and make it a doozie, and we'll put it in the Archives for release in

598

the year 3002. Meantime, edit my speech for me, OK?" He got up briskly and went to the desk, pulled out some sheets of typescript and handed them to his guest who put away his handkerchief and began to study them with a thoughtful care.

"I have another little kicker up my sleeve," the Secretary remarked, looking for a moment like a small and very engaging boy. "Listen to this." He picked up the telephone and began to dial a number.

"I expect all the rest of the Presidency is going to be sheer hell," he confessed happily, "but right at the moment I'm finding it thoroughly delightful . . . Hello, Tommy? . . .Well, thank you, old friend. I know how much you mean that . . . No, I'm kidding, I *do* know how much you mean that. Or do I?"

He laughed and winked at Bob Leffingwell.

"Say, Tommy, I have a little job for you . . . What? . . . Oh." His expression changed, became momentarily somber. "Yes, I did, thank you very much. It was very good of you—very patriotic. I showed them to him at the White House last night. I think it was the deciding factor in bringing him around. If," he remarked dryly, "he has come around . . . Oh, yes, you're right, he's made some major concessions and I really think he's going all the way on it.

"He told me privately just before we left the Center that in his speech tomorrow he's going to denounce them without any qualifications whatsoever—leave out that 'if violent elements there be' bit, which was sheer sophistry. But he apparently felt that as a matter of pride he couldn't about-face too completely the first time out. Anyway, you'll help me work on him, won't you? He'll still listen to you, I think. We'll get him straightened out." He laughed abruptly. "He no doubt thinks he'll do the same to me, on foreign policy. And who knows? Maybe we'll be good for each other. In fact," he said, sober again, "we've got to be good for each other—we've got to find the middle ground. . . .

"I want this to be the start of an era of reconciliation, Tommy. I want to try to bring the country back to some basis of reasonable unity on which we can all get along. I want another 'Era of Good Feeling.' I won't get it, of course, completely, but I intend to try. You won't find me so arbitrary when I speak tomorrow. Bob Leffingwell is here right now, smoothing out all the sharp edges in my prepared text. He's going to be part of my new era, too, Tommy—you'll be surprised . . . *What?*" He looked quite blank for a moment, then chuckled. "Now, how did you guess that? All right, you have guessed it, and I want your word of honor as a Justice of the Supreme Court that you will tell *no* one, absolutely no one, Tommy, OK? . . . All right, that's your word, now . . . "All right, I trust you.

"But you've got me off the point. The reason I called is that I want you to be part of my era of reconciliation, too. Will you do it? . . . What?" His tone became exaggeratedly heavy and pompous. "Mr. Justice, your President is asking you—very well, then. *If* we can get the party and the country together again, and *if* we can put some good feeling back into this poor old battered Republic, and *if* I can persuade enough unsuspecting citizens to elect me—would you do your bit for democracy by swearing me in at Inauguration? . . . Yes, I know the Chief Justice always does it . . . Yes, I know his wife will be furious with me for letting you do it . . . Yes, I know she won't invite you to dinner any more if you accept. I also know that if all goes well I shall be President-elect and there isn't anybody who can deny me the man I want—except the man I want. So, how about it? The C.J. and his wife may have their noses broken, but I don't think he'll pull your chair out from under you next time the Court convenes. I'll clap him in Fort Knox if he does . . . All right, then, Tommy? . . . You what?" He looked surprised and pleased. "You aren't supposed to make any political speeches . . . Oh, you mean just introduce me tomorrow, as a gesture of national unity? Why, if you—why, I'd be delighted, you know that, Tommy. I'd be absolutely delighted . . . Well, thank you so much. It's very kind indeed . . . OK, Tommy. Bless you. Goodbye."

He put down the receiver and turned back to Bob Leffingwell with a gratified expression.

"You know," he said, I think everybody is really going to try to make this reconciliation idea work. It's marvelous."

And so, with only a few exceptions as the evening moved on, they did.

LeGage Shelby, Fred Van Ackerman, Rufus Kleinfert and nineteen of their fellow members of the executive board of NAWAC issued a statement that congratulated Governor Jason, noted in passing the nomination of Secretary Knox, and expressed the confidence that the nation "now will enter upon a period of sane policy abroad and true democracy at home." NAWAC's multitudes, bivouacked along the river and under the trees awaiting tomorrow's gathering at the Washington Monument, confined themselves for the most part to a series of informal speeches and sing-ins whose general burden seemed to be that the world was on the brink of salvation with Edward M. Jason. The name of Orrin Knox was rarely mentioned. When it was, the FBI was able to report, to the relief of those most interested, it was in a reasonably amicable, not too bitterly hostile fashion. For the time being, NAWAC seemed to be relatively reconciled, now that it had its own man on the ticket. WE CAN STAND KNOX FOR FOUR—WE'LL HAVE JASON FOR MORE, as one banner announced: it seemed to sum up the general reaction of the multitudes whose campfires flickered along the Potomac.

Around the world as the hours wore on, the reaction also settled into a pattern of reasonably calm and sensible appraisal. The world was aware of the status of a Vice President, but as many analysts and commentators pointed out in the dispatches and broadcasts monitored by the State Department, this Vice President was different: personally he was more popular, and politically he was almost as strong as the Presidential nominee. Therefore he could logically be expected to exert a major restraining influence upon policies that most of the world regarded with misgiving and alarm.

In Peking, where he had finally surfaced after several days of being lost to the news, Prince Obifumatta, speaking with a renewed hope, said that the nomination of Governor Jason "will mean a speedy reappraisal of the ill-advised and openly imperialistic U.S. attack against the People's Republic of Gorotoland. In Molobangwe his cousin, Prince Terry, called in the American Ambassador to express worries which the earnest promises of that aging veteran of the Foreign Service did not entirely remove.

602

In Panama, Felix Labaiya also called in ambassadors—in his case, of the Soviet Union, Great Britain and France, and then announced that the nomination of Governor Jason "makes very likely the abandonment of the unilateral attempt by the United States to destroy freedom of the seas with its illegal blockade of the People's Liberation Movement of Panama.

"The P.L.M.," he went on, "with powerful allies at its side, is prepared for any eventuality. We will offer the United States the handclasp of peace or the dagger of war. We expect and we believe that the nomination of Edward M. Jason will play a major part in reestablishing a climate in which our two countries can once more live together as friends."

In Washington, members of the National Committee, released from their difficult duty and their bivouac in Fort Myer, were once again available to the press. Newsprint and airwave were filled with the optimistic predictions of a new day. From both sides the sentiment was virtually unanimous:

"The opportunity for a new rededication to America on the part of *all* her citizens," said Lathia Talbott Jennings of North Dakota, equanimity restored. "A marvelous opportunity for a new, more moderate, more *modern* approach," said Ralph Jansen of Minnesota. "I'm absolutely thrilled at this chance to restore unity and work out a truly national policy," said Janette Wilkins Vandervoort of New York. "Looks to me like we've got a winning combination," remarked Elrod Jones of Kansas, ever practical. "Maybe now we'll bury our differences instead of each other," said Blair Hannah; "Lord knows it's about time." "A great chance for a great tomorrow," averred Ewan MacDonald MacDonald.

Already, as the enormous flood of congratulatory wires, special delivery letters, telephone calls, began to pile up at the houses in Spring Valley and Dumbarton Oaks, the practical effects of the new political alignment were apparent. At the permanent National Committee offices on Connecticut Avenue, Roger Croy and Pete Boissevain, appointed with a certain irony by their respective principles to work as co-chairmen of the joint Strategy Committee, were meeting with twenty of their fellow Committeemen and the Committee staff to plan for the campaign and the prospective new Administration. They were not the only people in Washington who were planning for the campaign and the new Administration, but they at least were working together with a grudging but increasingly friendly cooperation that seemed to promise much for Orrin's "Era of Reconciliation."

At the White House the President, after talking to both Orrin and Ted on the telephone—"I don't mind being a 'Caretaker President,'" he told Orrin with a chuckle that would have put his critics in their place could they have heard it, "as long as I'm taking care for the right man"—issued a statement hailing "the prospects for a new unity and a new approach." Thus he neatly combined the informal slogans of the two candidates in a prediction that reconciliation and an end to domestic political strife would now ensue.

Increasingly, as the clock turned toward midnight, it appeared likely that he might be right. The mood of the country seemed to be swinging rapidly away from bitterness toward renewed courage and renewed hope. However men on each side of the bitter issues that had divided them chose to interpret it, the pairing of Orrin Knox and Edward Jason on their party's ticket was working a certain inescapable magic on their countrymen.

A new day, a new dawn, a new happiness, seemed to be flooding America, so volatile and so basically hopeful were her people still.

"I didn't think," he said, in the quiet, at last, of their bedroom in Dumbarton Oaks, "that I was ever going to get a chance to see you alone again."

"I'm glad you have," she said, smiling.

He looked at her with a humility that was rare for him or any Jason, a hesitant diffidence that she could see was quite genuine.

"I hope," he said uncertainly, "that you think I've done the right thing. I hope I've made you proud of me. I hope you don't still think that I'm—that I'm such a bad man."

"My dear," she said softly, "I've never thought you were a bad man." She smiled with a certain wistful tenderness. "A little confused, maybe, but not a *bad* man."

"Ceil," he said forlornly, "I've missed you so much."

"Well," she said, "I'm here now.

"Don't ever leave me like that again," he said with a sudden consuming anguish. "I don't think I could stand it if you did."

She held out her arms.

"I always find," she said shakily, a while later, "that there's just no point in being arbitrary about you. I try to be, sometimes, but I can't. You're you, and that seems to be all that matters, for me."

"I'm glad," be whispered, like some lost child come home. "I am glad."

"Well!" he said triumphantly, coming out of the kitchen with a glass of milk and a piece of chocolate cake. "Guess who just came in the study and told me that all is forgiven and he thinks I've done the right thing—probably."

"I can't guess," Beth said, closing the book she had been patiently reading in the living room until things quieted down and he was ready to go to bed.

"Everything's all right" he said, again going into an impromptu little music-hall shuffle that threatened to spill the milk. "Everything's all right, all right, all RIGHT! We're going to run a great campaign, and we're going to have national unity, and we're going to have a great Administration and we're going to do such great things for America, and the world. We are, we are, we ARE! I'm going to win, hey, *hey,* and it's going to be GREAT, and everything's going to be *all right!* Do you hear me?" he demanded striking a dramatic pose. "All *right,* I said, woman! All *right!*"

She laughed.

"You're really bubbling, aren't you? Why don't you put down that glass and come along upstairs and we can bubble together?"

He obeyed with alacrity.

"Hank," he said with a cheerful grin, "that's the best offer I've had all evening."

"I'm sitting at my desk in the Senate," Lafe wrote, shortly after midnight, "and you've probably heard on the news who's filibustering. So I won't go into that. Aside from him, though, there seems to be a really great spirit here, and all over town, about what's happened. In fact, it's probably no exaggeration to say it's all over the coun-

606

try. I've been getting all sorts of calls from my people in Iowa, and probably you've been getting the same out there from your friends.

"There are lots of reservations about putting Ted on the ticket, in my mind, and I suppose in the minds of those who like Ted there are lots of reservations about Orrin. But at least having them together on the ticket should bring the party, and above all the country, together again in some reasonable degree of unity. That's the hope, and I think maybe it's a good one. We're lucky—we can still close ranks the way we always have, now that the decision's been made. I think we must, because I think this may very well be the last chance. I know people have felt that way all through our history, but sooner or later there had to come a point when it really *could* be the last chance. I think this may be it.

"There's a mood here tonight—a good mood, in spite of you-know-who. And a good mood in the country, too. I wish my two girls could be here with me at the ceremony tomorrow, but I know you'll be watching. I'll wave for the cameras and maybe you'll see me—we're only expecting 500,000 or so at the Monument Grounds. Then I'll be flying out to join you, early next week, and we'll take that fishing vacation Pidge wants us to take together. I think that little lady is a matchmaker. I hope so.

"Everything is hopeful here tonight. Things look good for America again. It's a nice feeling, after so much sadness.

"Love to my two sweethearts and good night from their

Lafe."

Across three thousand miles of continent, save for the Senate and one or two other places in Washington where men were not reconciled, the lights gradually went out. Over seacoast, mountain, plain and forest, over all their restless inhabitants, darkness deepened into dead of night.

The great Republic slept, in good heart and rising spirit, preparing, after so long a time of hatred, anger and harsh, unhappy things, for the coming of a happier day.

3.

SO THE HOUR of acceptance came, bright and hot and clear, and from all the corners of the two cities, all the corners of the nation, all the corners of the earth, the great throng gathered on the Monument Grounds around the stark white obelisk to fatherly George. Krishna Khaleel, Vasily Tashikov and his agricultural attaché, Lord and Lady Maudulayne, Raoul and Celestine Barre, and almost all their colleagues of the diplomatic corps, were there. Somewhere in the enormous multitude that laughed and yelled and chattered, shoved and pushed and jostled in amiable contest for position, were LeGage Shelby, Rufus Kleinfert, and most of their fellow-members of NAWAC. (Only Senator Van Ackerman was missing. Whispering now, he was in his fourteenth hour of filibuster against the antiriot bill.) The Chief Justice was there, his wife already upset because she could tell from the way Mr. Justice Davis was bustling about near the platform that he must have some preferred assignment she didn't know about. The Munsons, Stanley Danta and more than half the Senate had arrived. From the House, Jawbone Swarthman and Miss Bitty-Bug, rubbing elbows not too comfortably with Cullee Hamilton and Sarah Johnson, led a delegation of more than 200. The National Committee had already taken its seats on the platform.

Television crews were everywhere, and through the crowd there were many television sets in place to bring the ceremonies to the farthest reaches. Police with walkie-talkies were also everywhere, moving constantly, efficiently, yet amicably, their presence giving rise to a few catcalls but otherwise no indication of hostility. At regularly spaced intervals groups of four soldiers stood back-to-back facing their countrymen, guns, bayonets and gas canisters ready. Around the flag-decked platform and the dignitaries' circle at the foot of the Monument, a tight cordon of Marines stood guard. Overhead the ubiquitous helicopters whirred and hovered.

Yet somehow, despite these precautions, there seemed to be something in the air that indicated they would not be needed. Press and police estimated more than 400,000 present on this day that belonged to Orrin Knox and Edward Jason, yet with no visible exceptions they seemed almost to be on picnic, so happy and relaxed did they look and sound. Even NAWAC's banners were good-natured, and this seemed to put the final touches on it:

ORRIN AND TED: THE UNBEATABLES . . . HEY, HEY, GREAT DAY! BAD TIMES, GO AWAY! . . . TED AND ORRIN HAVE GOT US ROARIN . . . WE'LL

HAVE PEACE TOMORROW AND NO MORE SOR-
ROW . . .

Presently from far-off there came again the sound of
sirens, and this time they were hailed with a great roar
of greeting and approval. The sleek black limousine from
Spring Valley came along Constitution Avenue in the center of its police motorcycle escort, turned into the Monument Grounds and proceeded slowly to the foot of the
obelisk. Two minutes later, more sirens, another great
roar; the sleek black limousine from Dumbarton Oaks
in the center of its police motorcycle escort came along
Constitution Avenue, turned into the Monument
Grounds, proceeded slowly to the foot of the obelisk.

Out of their cars stepped the nominee for President
and the nominee for Vice President, and their wives, and
for a moment in the midst of the wave of sound that
seemed to blot out the world, they stared at one another
with a questioning, uncertain, hesitant yet friendly look.
Then Orrin stepped forward and held out his hand, and
as the picture flashed on all the sets, a silence fell.

"Ted," the Secretary said, and his words thundered
over the Monument Grounds, the nation, the world,
"Beth and I are glad to see you."

"Orrin," the Governor replied, "our pleasure."

Impulsively and with a completely natural friendliness,
Ceil stepped forward and kissed Beth and then Orrin.
Beth gave her a warm hug and then turned to embrace
Ted. The television cameras zoomed in, the still photographers pushed and shouted and scrambled. A shout of
happiness and approval went up from all the vast concourse.

Orrin linked his arm informally through Ted's and led

610

the way toward the platform, through the dignitaries' circle where friends and colleagues, opponents and supporters, greeted them with an eagerly smiling, unanimous cordiality.

"It seems to be a happy day," the Secretary said quietly, words no longer overheard as the police held back the press. "I'm glad."

"So am I," Ted said. "I think we have a great responsibility—"

"We do," Orrin agreed. "I'm going to make a conciliatory speech."

"I too," the Governor said. "I had thought of sending it over for your approval this morning, but—"

"Oh, no," Orrin said quickly. He smiled. "I trust you." The smile faded, he looked for a moment profoundly, almost sadly, serious. "We've got to trust each other, from now on."

"Yes," Ted said gravely. "We must. I think we can."

Orrin gave him a shrewd sidelong glance as they reached the steps of the platform.

"I have no doubts," he said quietly.

"They're going to need our help," Beth said to Ceil as they, too, reached the steps and started up after their husbands.

Ceil smiled, a sunny, happy smile.

"I think," she said with a little laugh, "that you and I can manage."

The wild, ecstatic roar broke out again as they appeared together on the platform, standing side by side, arms raised in greeting, framed by the flags against the backdrop of the gleaming white needle soaring against the hot bright sky.

"Mr. Secretary and Mrs. Knox! Governor and Mrs. Jason! Look this way, please! Can you look over here, please? Mr. Secretary—Governor—Mrs. Jason—Mrs. Knox—this way, please! Here, please! Can you smile and wave again, please?"

Finally Orrin called,

"Haven't you got enough?"

And from somewhere in the jostling tumult below them, of heads, hands, flailing arms, contorted bodies and cameras held high, there came a plea of such anguished supplication that they all laughed.

"*Please*, just one more, Mr. President! All together again, *please!*"

"The things we do for our country," Orrin said with a mock despair as they all linked arms and stepped forward once more.

"Yes," Ceil said happily. "It sometimes seems as though—"

But what it sometimes seemed to Ceil at that moment would never be known, for they were interrupted.

No one in the crowd heard anything, no one saw anything. For several moments the full import of the sudden confusion on the platform did not penetrate.

It was so bright and hot and sunny.

It was such a happy day.

They could not quite comprehend, in that bright, hot, sunny, awful instant, the dreadful thing that had occurred so swiftly and so silently before their eyes.

It was not clear then, nor perhaps would it ever be, exactly what those who planned it had intended. But whatever they had intended, by some no doubt inadvertent and unintentional miscalculation, they had accomplished even more.

A husband and wife—but they were not the same husband and wife—stared at one another for a terrible moment suspended in time and history. Then she began to scream and he began to utter a strange animal howl of agony and regret.

Their puny ululations were soon lost in the great rush of sound that engulfed the platform slippery with blood, the Monument Grounds sweltering under the steaming sky, the two cities, the nation, the horrified, watching, avid world.

July 1967–April 1968

CPSIA information can be obtained at www.ICGtesting.com
Printed in the USA
240629LV00004B/55/P

9 781412 812931